———————

THE COMPLEAT
SCHWIEBERT

BOOKS BY ERNEST SCHWIEBERT

Matching the Hatch
Salmon of the World
Remembrances of Rivers Past
Nymphs · Trout
Death of a Riverkeeper
A River for Christmas

THE COMPLEAT
SCHWI

A Treasury of Trout Fishing
from Around the World

Illustrations by
PETER CORBIN

ERNEST SCHWIEBERT

E B E R T

Edited and with an Introduction by
JOHN MERWIN

T·T TRUMAN TALLEY BOOKS/DUTTON/NEW YORK

Dutton
Published by the Penguin Group
Penguin Books USA Inc., 375 Hudson Street,
New York, New York 10014, U.S.A.
Penguin Books Ltd, 27 Wrights Lane,
London W8 5TZ, England
Penguin Books Australia Ltd, Ringwood,
Victoria, Australia
Penguin Books Canada Ltd, 2801 John Street,
Markham, Ontario, Canada L3R 1B4
Penguin Books (N.Z.) Ltd, 182–190 Wairau Road,
Auckland 10, New Zealand

Penguin Books Ltd, Registered Offices:
Harmondsworth, Middlesex, England

First published by Truman Talley Books / Dutton, an imprint of New American Library, a
division of Penguin Books USA Inc.

First printing, September, 1990
10 9 8 7 6 5 4 3 2 1

Library of Congress Cataloging-in-Publication Data

Schwiebert, Ernest George.
The compleat Schwiebert : a treasury of trout fishing from
around the world / Ernest Schwiebert ; edited and with an
introduction by John Merwin.—1st ed.
p.   cm.
"Truman Talley books."
ISBN 0-525-24892-7
1. Trout fishing—United States.   2. Fishing—United States.
3. Fishing stories, American.   I. Merwin, John.   II. Title.
SH688.U6S39   1990
799.1'755—dc20   89-77827
CIP

Printed in the United States of America
Set in Aster
Designed by Earl Tidwell

Grateful acknowledgment is made to the following periodicals, where portions of this book
previously appeared:

Esquire: Chapter 3.   *Field & Stream:* Chapter 7.   *Fishing Yearbook:* Chapter 15.   *The
Flyfisher:* Chapter 25.
Fly Fisherman: Chapters 8, 10, 11, 13, 14, 16, 17, 20, 24, 28.   *Rod & Reel:* Chapter 22.
Sports Afield: Chapters 1, 4, 6, 9, 12.   *Trout:* Chapters 18, 19, 21, 23, 26, 27. Chapter 2 was
originally published by the Theodore Gordon Flyfishers. Chapter 5 originally appeared in
Remembrances of Rivers Past,
published by Macmillan.

Contents

Introduction by John Merwin   ix

Book One: GREAT WATERS

1   Song of the Catskills   4
2   Homage to Henryville   22
3   Legend and the Letort   48
4   A Portrait of the Pere Marquette   65
5   Night Comes to the Namekagon   96
6   The River of Humility   103
7   The Strangest Trout Stream on Earth   119
8   Where Flows the Umpqua   131

Book Two: A HATCH TO MATCH

9   Mixed Palette   162
10   The Longest Hatch   178
11   Understanding the *Pseudocloëons*   193
12   The Time of the Hendricksons   204
13   Something Old, Something New   212
14   The Salmonfly Hatches   219
15   Grasshopper Wind   228

vii

CONTENTS

16 The Anatomy of a Spring Creek   241
17 Secrets of Unfamiliar Streams   252
18 Brown Trout in America   267

Book Three: EDGES AND EDDIES

19 Spring   300
20 Thoughts in Coltsfoot Time   305
21 Summer   311
22 Salmon or Steelhead?   316
23 Fall   330
24 The Ghosts of Treasured Cay   335
25 The Fly Book   347
26 Winter   357
27 Beauty   362
28 The Alchemy of Bamboo   368

Appendix: Matching the *Tricorythodes* and *Pseudocloëon*
Mayflies   382
Index   386

Introduction

In 1978, a Manhattan-based publishing giant called Ziff-Davis bought a small, independent publication in Vermont called *Fly Fisherman* (now owned by Cowles Communications in Minneapolis), where Ernest Schwiebert and I were both employed as editors—I at my desk, and he in the field. I visited often with the Ziff-Davis hierarchy in those days, and recall one of them, who wasn't a fisherman, pausing to define fly fishing as an "aspiration."

And so it is. All fishermen aspire to catch fish. It is a sport for optimists who send their lures into the unknown like an astronomer sending high-frequency signals into space, albeit with more replies. John Buchan, the late novelist, described fishing in similar fashion as ". . . a perpetual series of occasions for hope."

Fly fishing is more than this, however. Aspiration as it relates to fly fishing is an aspiration to a life-style based on angling. Thus the fame of a streamside restaurant may grow with that of the stream, and the wainscoted rooms of an old angling club may become as much a part of a river's tradition as the home pool across the road. No writer in modern times has defined the aspirations of the fly-fishing life more strongly and influentially than Ernest Schwiebert.

If there are Bentleys and Porsches parked around the clubhouse where he happens to be fishing, he's apt to include mention of them in a story or book. If a vintage Château Margaux was served at a streamside lunch, he includes that, too. Or, to pick an example from this book, the superlative food at the Steamboat Inn on Oregon's North Umpqua River (see Chapter 8) is inseparable from the fishing, so it's described at some length. As a reader, I'm made hungry or wistful or both. As a fisherman, I aspire to all of it.

As a magazine editor working with Ernie's material over several years, I was sometimes the lightning rod for the occasional reader who cried, "Snob!" These were, however, relatively rare cries amid the general applause, and my reply was always the same: No one ever aspired to mud and bugs, however much such things might have to be endured on a fishing trip.

This thing we've called aspiration includes angling knowledge, as well. I know of no one, including myself, who wouldn't like to be a better fisherman and thereby catch more fish. Ever since the publication of his landmark *Matching the Hatch* (1955), Schwiebert has made a highly successful career of educating the world's anglers to catch more trout and salmon. You'll see ample evidence of just that in this book, ranging from talk about how better to fish the important hatches on American rivers to a discussion of how the water chemistry of a spring creek affects your fishing. I suppose for a nonangler it may all seem absurdly arcane. But for hundreds of thousands of Schwiebert fans, it's information eagerly awaited and devoured on delivery.

All this has a price, of course, and Schwiebert's work has meant thousands of hours chasing fish not in rivers but in university libraries and private collections around the world. More hours collecting specimens in the field and still more over a microscope for identifications are part of this book too, and for that I'm grateful. When I'm fishing to rising trout, and my flies aren't working, Schwiebert's books are the first ones I check. Because he's done so much of this work, very often I—and others—don't have to bother.

Ernest Schwiebert has probably written more authoritative fly-fishing material than any other author, living or dead. Subsequent books to *Matching the Hatch*, such as *Nymphs* and the remarkable two-volume *Trout*, demonstrated extraordinary depth as a writer and a keen perception of fly fishing's most enjoyable problems. He is a master of instruction by anecdote, and I caution you not to miss the lessons between his lines.

The chapters of this book span more than thirty years of Schwiebert's writing. Some have undergone revision over the years, and the dates at the chapter endings indicate when the chapter was first written. Other chapters describe now-departed friends in the present tense, and I read them with a little regret. Art Flick, Harry and Elsie Darbee, and Arnold Gingrich are among those no longer with us, but their stamp on our favorite waters is a permanent part of our fishing legends.

"Legend and tradition and a passion for bright water are the essence of angling. . . . Many have written of their sport in language as lithe and bright-colored as the fish themselves, and for this we are grateful. Through their books we can . . . relive their experiences, seeking the source of our own fascination in fly fishing with the legendary authors themselves as guides to the best water."

Those lines are by Schwiebert, and although he used them to describe past angling authors, they apply equally well to his own work. So we'll fish these pages with Schwiebert as our guide. We'll listen carefully as he helps with a number of tactical problems. And we'll smile with him at the music of the river.

JOHN MERWIN
Dorset, Vermont
October 1989

Book One

GREAT
WATERS

Here's a unique trout-fishing odyssey across America with Ernest Schwiebert as our consummate guide. We'll fish and learn about some classic rivers in New York and Pennsylvania, and then head west to Michigan and Wisconsin. From the upper Midwest, we'll head for the Rocky Mountains, where we'll learn some new tricks with selective trout. Then our cross-country journey ends in Oregon with steelhead on the famous North Umpqua. There are fishing lessons here too, plus some fascinating glimpses into some of the reasons that Zane Grey was much less popular with his fellow anglers than with his millions of readers.

Many trout fishermen will find one or more of their favorite rivers described in considerable detail in this part, and will find too, that Schwiebert's broad experience brings new tricks and twists to familiar waters.

3

1

Song of
the Catskills

*It had rained all night, and the Beaverkill was in
flood. There would be no Hendrickson hatch this afternoon. The motel parking lot was full of open-
trunked cars as fishermen struggled out of
rain-soaked gear. My green-and-white Vermont license plate stood out among the New York and Connecticut cars, and drew a disgusted question from an
older man nearby: "Why d'ja leave all that good fishing up there for this place?"*

*"Friends," I said. "To see some friends." I didn't
explain that I counted this river as an old friend, as
many do. And I didn't explain that I'd visited with Lee
and Joan Wulff that morning at their home near the
river's headwaters. Or that I'd stopped to get some
exquisite trout flies from Walt and Winnie Dette, who
together with daughter, Mary, still tie flies in a style
world-famous as the Catskill School.*

*I didn't mention the echoes, either. About how I
nodded at an empty house in Livingston Manor along
the Willowemoc where Harry and Elsie Darbee used
to live, or how I'd miss Art Flick's infectious grin*

along Schoharie Creek over the ridge. I kept my own Catskill legacy to myself that rainy day—laughter with some friends, memories of others, and what is likely even now the best public trout water in the Northeast.

More than any other American trout-fishing area, the Catskills are a special blend of fishing and fishing people, those who have in one way or another associated their lives with this sport. So our cross-country angling journey begins here as we join Schwiebert on these most famous of trout streams.

It was a filling station on a high ridge above the Hudson. There were jawbreakers in a glass apothecary jar, a rack of green Lucky Strike packages, and hundreds of colored gum balls filled the penny machine on the counter. The pump circulated gasoline through its tall glass cylinders, bubbles tumbling and churning as it filled the Oldsmobile. We stood in the shade of the station portico, watching a young helper check a patchwork inner tube for leaks.

We searched through floating pieces of ice in the cooler and opened two root beers. It was hot and we drank thirstily. The river wound across its pastoral valley floor. There were locusts in the trees, and the hot wind stirred the acrid smell of gasoline. Beyond the big river and its villages and farms there were mountains.

It's like a picture, I thought.

My father finished his root beer and racked our bottles in their wooden crate. *What are those mountains?*

Catskills, said the helper.

The gasoline spilled over and streaked down the dusty fender. That afternoon was more than thirty years ago, and it was still a time for childhood summers beside lakes of reeds and lily pads, fishing for pumpkinseeds and bluegills and perch. It would be many years before I fished the rivers in those gentle mountains, rivers that have become the classic Catskill shrines of American trout fishing.

Their source lies in a surprisingly small group of ridges west of Catskill and Kingston on the Hudson. It is still a wild

5

and beautiful region behind its façade of roadside diners and elaborate summer colonies and *borscht*-circuit resorts. The high Catskills rise west of the Hudson, rolling ridges covered with forests and smoke-colored in the distance.

The summits are a series of somber outcroppings, wounded with the grinding scars of ancient glaciers. Hawks and eagles soar on the winds that sigh through these hemlock ridges, and bears and wildcats are still killed each season. Sometimes there is even the report of a cougar.

There are still thousands of deer in the dense forests of hardwoods, hemlocks, and pines, deer that wax fat on the apples of Colonial orchards long abandoned and overgrown with trees. Wild turkeys are coming back on the Schoharie ridges. Grouse and woodcock are plentiful enough for hunters who know the coverts. Sometimes there is a horned owl flushed from a hemlock thicket, or a pileated woodpecker threading through the trees.

Catskill rivers are still beautiful, although some of their solitude has been surrendered to diners and automobile graveyards and drive-in movies. The wilderness that existed when the Dutch settlers first named the river and the village of Catskill has retreated into the highest ridges. These settlers lost livestock to the cougars that lived in the foothill valleys that drained toward the Hudson. *Kaaterskill,* the Dutch called the little river that came down from the ridges of Blackhead. *The river where there are big cats.*

The region is a mother of rivers. Catskill Creek is no longer a major trout stream, but its sister river across the Blackhead ridges is the famous Schoharie, winding out toward its junction with the Mohawk. The East Branch of the Delaware has its source on Bearpen Mountain, which turns the tumbling Schoharie north. There are two minor Catskill rivers, the Callicoon and the Mongaup, which rise in the timbered hills of Sullivan County and join the Delaware between Port Jervis and Long Eddy.

But two mountains are the genesis of the most famous Catskill trout streams. Doubletop rises 3,868 feet in the western Catskills, and its maternal springheads are the source of three watersheds—tumbling little Dry Brook, the gentle Willowemoc, and the legendary Beaverkill, perhaps the most famous trout stream in America.

Slide Mountain reaches 4,207 feet west of the Hudson at Kingston. Its forested shoulders are the beginnings of the Rondout, the swift-flowing Esopus, and both branches of another legendary river—the classic Neversink.

This round handful of Catskill rivers is the wellspring of American trout-fishing literature and tactics. Their pools and riffles have been fished by every major American fishing writer since George Washington Bethune, and the Neversink and the Beaverkill have been the home rivers of storied anglers like Theodore Gordon, Reuben Cross, George La-Branche, and Edward Ringwood Hewitt.

Fishing pressure and reservoirs and pollution have decimated the Catskill rivers until the Rondout, the once-famous rainbow water on the Callicoon, and the Mongaup are seldom rated major trout fisheries. Reservoirs on the Schoharie, Esopus, Delaware, Rondout, and Neversink have eradicated some first-rate mileage of river, but in some cases they have created good trout fishing in their impoundments and impressive runs of big spawners in the spring and fall. The cold tailings of some Catskill reservoirs have improved and extended the trout habitat downstream, while others have released insufficient flow to purge their rivers of silt and sustain both spawning and the principal fly hatches.

Some fishing mileage in the Catskills is controlled by private clubs and estates, like the Tuscarora Club and the huge retreat on Dry Brook assembled by tycoon Jay Gould, who was born in the Catskills and forged an empire that included both Western Union and the Erie Railroad. There is extensive private water on the headwaters of the Esopus, Willowemoc, Neversink, and Beaverkill, but there is still excellent public fishing on the principal Catskill rivers.

The beautiful Schoharie is a native brook-trout river in its headwaters on Indianhead Mountain. Its tumbling runs and riffles above Hunter are the classic image of mountain trout water, and in the open valley at Lexington it has changed into a series of sweeping riffles and smooth flats. Its principal tributaries are well-known streams in their own right, particularly the Bataviakill and East Kill that join the river from the north, and the pretty West Kill, which begins high in the grouse coverts on Hunter Mountain.

The watershed has a rich history of famous anglers down the years, and its most famous regular is Art Flick, who once operated the charming West Kill Tavern near the river. His classic little *Streamside Guide to Naturals and Their Imitations* is based on the fly hatches of the Schoharie, with color photographs of its principal mayflies and the exquisite dry flies Flick ties to imitate them.

Other famous anglers often gathered at his inn. Preston Jennings did much of his fieldwork for *A Book of Trout Flies* on the Schoharie and its sister rivers. His pioneer work was the first American attempt to classify and imitate stream insects with the discipline of British fly-fishing writers a century before. Dana Lamb often fished there too, and his feeling for the region is found in little books like *Not Far from the River* and *Woodsmoke and Watercress.* Lamb often came with his sons to the West Kill Tavern, when the April mayflies were hatching or flights of woodcock had settled into the alder thickets above Lexington. Leslie Thompson was another regular on the river in those days, along with Raymond Camp, whose outdoor columns for *The New York Times* were known to a generation of sportsmen. Thompson and Camp badgered Art Flick into writing his book, helped with the streamside work on the Schoharie, and Thompson painted exquisite watercolors of the mayflies they collected.

Their river and its hatches also played a role in my book *Matching the Hatch,* and it included an episode from the first morning I ever saw the river. The night before we had camped in sleeping bags beside the Esopus, and we crossed the mountain from Bushnellsville just after daylight.

Mist hung over the river at Lexington, and we crossed the bridge and turned into the meadows below the town. The flat flowed smooth and dark in the mist, and the sun filtered through weakly as we walked through the wet grass.

The surface of the pool was covered with tiny mayflies, and fish were working everywhere. *Look at them!* I gasped.

What are they taking? my father asked.

8

We collected several specimens and studied their bluish wings and bright olive bodies.

Blue-winged Olives, I said.

The trout were rising steadily now. Several were making impressive swirls and porpoise-size rolls, and we rigged our gear hastily, clumsily stringing our rods.

Nervous? laughed my father.

We shouldered into our wading jackets and edged stealthily into the current. Two heavy fish boiled above me and I knotted a size sixteen Blue-winged Olive to my tippet. The line worked out into the rising mist and settled the fly softly above the fish. The tiny dry fly floated over its feeding position. It rose softly to a mayfly just before my imitation reached its riseform, and it swirled again to a natural just after the fly drifted past. The whole sequence was repeated several times.

They're choosy! I yelled.

My father was working on another fish two hundred feet upstream. *This one won't take either,* he said.

The hatch lasted thirty minutes. We cast over fish after fish until our arms ached. Finally my dry fly was floating badly and a two-pound brown inhaled it. The reel protested, and the hatch was over when it finally stopped splashing and surrendered.

Let's check his stomach, I said.

The autopsy was revealing. The fish had been concentrating on the nymphs before they hatched and fluttered down the current. Its stomach was sausage-tight with dozens and dozens of dark olive-bodied nymphs. The half-drowned imitation must have looked like a hatching nymph, struggling to escape the surface film of the river.

They were nymphing, we shook our heads.

Such choosiness is common on Catskill rivers, and successful fishermen must understand both their annual cycle of fly hatches and the artificial flies that imitate them. The skilled angler must also observe what stage of the hatch the fish are taking. We had seen rises to emerging nymphs and had carelessly assumed they were rises to the adult mayflies we could see riding the current.

There are many memories of the Schoharie, from the

tumbling runs of the Jeanette water several miles above Hunter to the heavy water at the covered bridge below Blenheim and the Gilboa Reservoir. It has been ten years since I last fished the Blue Bell stretch at the schoolhouse above Lexington, where a huge blue-painted bell hangs in the playground, and its April hatches were mixed with snow squalls. There was another blizzardlike morning when we walked down through snow-capped tombstones to the Cemetery water and found a heavy hatch of Hendricksons.

There was also the summer when the river was a lukewarm trickle, seeping through the sun-bleached skeleton of its bottom. The stream thermometer found temperatures better suited to smallmouths, and Art Flick suggested the springhole where the Bataviakill entered the river.

Flick shook his head unhappily. *She's so low and warm,* he said, *that I can't bear to look at her!*

We took several bass in the Schoharie flat below the Bataviakill, working upstream into the heavier run of water where the tributary currents mingled with the river against a series of boulders. My line worked out and dropped the big stonefly nymph against the rocks. There was a heavy swirl in the darkness and I was into a strong fish.

Bass? yelled my father.

It was difficult to tell, and I countered a half-dozen stubborn, bulldogging runs before the fish surrendered, fat and threshing in the meshes.

It's a good fish! I carried it ashore.

Didn't act like a bass, my father joined me.

The fish was slender and heavily spotted. *It's a brown,* I laughed. *It's a good three pounds!*

We worked the nymph free and nursed the fish gently in the cold currents of the Bataviakill. *Shame to kill him,* said my father. *The river needs him to spawn.*

We released the fish in the darkness.

Schoharie fishing has come back since that summer, and in his farmhouse at West Kill, Art Flick still dresses his exquisite dry flies, faithful to the sparse hackles and woodduck wings and slender bodies of the Catskill School. Flick still works his magic on the river each season, but his charming

10

West Kill Tavern is gone. It was lost in a tragic fire that engulfed its rambling clapboard frame, licking at the tiger-maple chairs and antimacassar-covered couches, smoldering in the worn Oriental runners, and melting the glass nineteenth-century cases of woodcock and grouse.

Esopus Creek rises on the north shoulder of Slide Mountain and flows west before winding back in a long question-mark course toward the Hudson. It is still a wild little river at Oliverea, tinkling down ledges and gravelly riffles until it reaches Big Indian. Its main channel begins at Shandaken with a series of strong runs, boulder-strewn rapids, waist-deep flats, and sprawling pools in the shadow of Panther Mountain.

Its flow is quickened with water carried through Bearpen Mountain from the Schoharie, destined for the greedy faucets and fireplugs of Manhattan. This flow is chilled in its subterranean tunnel, maintaining unusually low midsummer temperatures and a fine head of water in the Esopus below its Allaben outlet portal, but it can also mix torrents of pewter-colored silt into the river from its encounter with extensive deposits of marl inside the mountain.

There are sparkling little tributaries like the streams at Stony Clove and Woodland Valley, which are charming and well-known trout fisheries themselves. These little rivers are a refuge from the artificial spates of the portal and often hold big spawners in season.

The New York Board of Water Supply completed its Ashokan Reservoir on the lower Esopus in 1912, forming a sprawling lake that covered a dozen miles of trout water. It also became a tiny freshwater ocean that has fine rainbows and browns in its spring and fall spawning runs.

The river has its share of tradition too. Henrik Hudson anchored off its mouth in 1609, and the Dutch settlers who named the Catskills had already settled the region only five years later, in spite of bloody raids by marauding bands of Esopus Indians. Like its sister rivers, the Esopus has held a circle of famous disciples in its spell. Their headquarters is probably the Folkert general store in Phoenicia, the combi-

11

nation gunshop, tackle store, newspaper stand, ice-cream parlor, and bus stop whose real purpose is a message center for news of woodcock coverts and the fishing.

Paul O'Neill once wrote wry, penetrating articles for *Life* in the halcyon days when its editors would explore any project once it caught their fancy, no matter how outrageous its subject or cost. O'Neill has since retired from its masthead, but his classic article "In Praise of Trout—and Also Me" appeared in the magazine shortly before his departure. Its passages treated the enduring wonder of the sport, focusing on his own experiences with the Esopus, and it firmly established O'Neill as its writer-in-residence.

Other regulars have included fishing experts like Jim Deren, Ray Ovington, Ed Sens, and Al McClane. Deren has run the Angler's Roost in Manhattan for many years. Ovington collated his experience and the original Sens nymph patterns in the book *How to Take Trout on Wet Flies and Nymphs,* the bible of standard wet-fly practice for the Catskill rivers. McClane was frequently seen on the river in his early years as fishing editor of *Field & Stream,* and his work was often punctuated with references to the Esopus, particularly early rainbow water like Seven Arches and the Greeny Deep when the spawners were running in the spring.

The river is a mixture of enigmatic moods. Failure is common on the Esopus, with its uncertainties of temperature and clarity, but its generous days are superb. There was an evening at Phoenicia many years ago, with a heavy hatch of big *Isonychia* flies that triggered a massive rise of trout. We took fish after fish, working up into the heavier currents at the head of the Bridge Pool, until it was getting dark and only the biggest fish were still rising.

One heavy trout was slashing at the fluttering mayflies in a strong rip between the rocks. The line worked out and dropped my big slate-colored variant over his position.

There was an explosive rise. The reel screamed as the fish bored straight into the rapids upstream, jumped wildly in the darkness, and powered back past me. *Look out!* I yelled. *It's a big rainbow and we're coming through!*

My father reeled in. *Good luck!* he said.

The fish was still running, cartwheeled end-over-end, and stripped backing from the reel. *He's still going!* I groaned. *He's got most of my line already!*

The fish turned toward my father and pole-vaulted high in the darkness. *Four or five pounds!* he yelled.

There were three more jumps, and the fish reached the rocky rapids downstream. There was too much line and backing in the current to control. The fish was running again in the rapids, gathering speed until the line raked and caught on the rocks. The fragile nylon tippet parted.

What happened? yelled my father.

It was a big rainbow! I groaned unhappily.

He laughed and waded toward the shallows. *I know it was a big rainbow,* he said, *but what happened? That's what happened!* I said. *Rainbow!*

Neversink fishing has been decimated since completion of its reservoir, but its tradition remains as rich as that of any river in the Catskills. Its fame is secure as the home river of Theodore Gordon, the solitary fly-fishing genius who evolved the Catskill style of fly dressing and adapted British dry-fly theory to American waters. Gordon is considered the father of American trout fishing, and his writing was collected by John McDonald in *The Notes and Letters of Theodore Gordon.* The book verifies his major role in the evolution of American trout-fishing practice. It gives us important insights into the frail, tubercular little man who invented the Gordon Quill and other classic flies. Gordon fished the Neversink faithfully the last years of his life, suffering the harsh winters beside his potbellied stove to dress exquisite flies for wealthy clients, and died in the old Anson Knight farmhouse near the Neversink in 1915.

The river has also been the home water to great anglers of other generations. Edward Ringwood Hewitt had his famous mileage above Bradley before the reservoir was built. Most of his pools are under water now, except for the few cribbing dams that remain above the impoundment on the mileage of the Big Bend Club. Hewitt wrote ten books and pamphlets on fishing, capping his career with *A Trout and*

Salmon Fisherman for Seventy-Five Years in 1950. The old master was a tireless innovator in fisheries management and fly fishing, and carried on a cantankerous, lifelong partnership astream with the equally famous George LaBranche, whose *Dry Fly and Fast Water* is another Catskill classic.

The fly-dressing tradition known as the Catskill School began with Gordon on the Neversink. It continued in the delicate flies dressed by tiers like Herman Christian, William Chandler, and Roy Steenrod. Although it was Gordon who developed the Light Cahill from the older Catskill pattern, Chandler is responsible for the pale modern dressing, and Steenrod was author of the famous Hendrickson.

Two other great anglers were regulars on the Neversink in the last years of their lives. John Atherton often fished with Hewitt, and his experiences on the river are recorded in the pencil drawings and passages of *The Fly and the Fish.* The late Larry Koller lived at Monroe near the river, and fished it regularly from a simple hunting camp at Long Eddy. His books like the *Treasury of Angling* are filled with fishing pictures and experiences gathered on the Neversink.

The river is born in two branches high on opposite shoulders of Slide Mountain. Its clear little West Branch drops down a lovely valley through the Forstmann estate and the beautiful Fairchild and Connell mileage. These upper reaches are all private water, tumbling musically down pale-gravel riffles and sliding through pretty ledgerock pools. There are wild brook trout with darkly mottled backs and bright-spotted flanks and orange fins. The main river also supports them as far downstream as the reservoir, perhaps the largest river south of Maine that still holds wild brookies. These headwaters are all private except for a brief mileage available on the tumbling East Branch above Claryville, where the country church still has a wooden trout for its weathervane.

There is a lot of public water left between the dam at Neversink and the big private estates below Bridgeville, where the late Ray Bergman described a great afternoon of Green Drake hatches in his classic *Trout.* However, the flow released from the reservoir is erratic, often insufficient to purge its boulder-strewn bottom of silt and sustain its once-great hatches. Fishermen can still find first-rate sport around Bridgeville and Fallsburgh when conditions are right, particularly in April and May, during the hatches of Gordon Quills and Hendricksons.

There are many memories from the Neversink. Len Wright shared his mileage with me on the upper river one cold April weekend, catching wild trout on small wet flies in its sweeping riffles and flats. There was a brace of heavy two-pound browns from a deep flat on the Connell water above, while phoebes caught tiny *Trichoptera* flies above the riffles and deer browsed in abandoned orchards.

Still, the most persistent memories of the Neversink are those hours spent with Larry Koller on his hunting-camp water below Bridgeville. There were afternoons with sunlight slanting through the pines, following hen grouse and their broods along paths deep in fiddleback ferns. The last evening I took a big brown fishing the ledges above Long Eddy, with cooking smells of a woodcock cassoulet drifting down to the river. Koller is dead now and no longer fishes the river or stalks whitetails or walks up grouse on the ridges. His friends ended his funeral in that simple hunting camp above Long Eddy and gently scattered his ashes into the river.

The winding East Branch of the Delaware is almost too much river to cover with trout tackle, and most of its best-known trout mileage was inundated with the filling of Pepacton Reservoir. That mileage is permanently lost, although the huge pools that have always wintered Beaverkill fish have been improved and extended downstream, and some really big trout are regularly caught in the reservoir.

Cold discharges from the dam have transformed the East Branch and the main Delaware into trout water as much as a hundred miles downstream. Fishermen can find smallmouths and walleyes sharing their river with big browns and rainbows since the dam was completed. The mileage between Shinhopple and Hancock on the East Branch itself is probably the most productive water for trout-minded fishermen, and like the Esopus with its cold tunnel water

15

from the Gilboa Reservoir, the East Branch stays relatively cold all summer.

Most fishermen find its chest-deep pools and half-mile flats forbidding, but men who know the river catch some huge trout. *It's tough fishing,* argues Harry Darbee, the professional fly tier who lives along the nearby Willowemoc, *but when the hatches are coming it can be great!*

The rise and fall of the river and its temperatures below the Downsville dam make it difficult to predict and locate hatching activity. *It scrambles the hatches,* continues Darbee. *We see all the hatches on the East Branch, but we see the tiny Blue-winged Olives and Orange Cahills nearly all summer.*

Big water like the East Branch requires methods familiar to trout fishermen on western rivers, but unknown to eastern anglers who fish only the relatively small Catskill streams. Most big trout on the East Branch are taken Montana-style on big nymphs and bucktails.

Chuck-and-chance-it, explains Darbee.

Such tactics are a game of percentages, working nymphs and bucktails on a deep bellying swing of a sinking line. Each cast is dropped across the current, fished out with a slow pumping rhythm of the rod, and another cast is made with a half step downstream. The fish are covered thoroughly with a series of concentric teasing circles over the entire pool. It is a deadly method on big trout.

There is a long flat not far below Shinhopple. It has a strong riffle tumbling into its head and turns and deepens into a hundred yards of waist-deep water before it slides into a half-mile pool under high slate ledges.

Jeff Norton and I fished it carefully one evening with little luck. *They're here!* he insisted.

I laughed and made another cast.

You wouldn't believe some of the brutes I've seen working here! He shook his head ruefully.

You're right. I grinned.

The cast looped out and dropped the big Muddler against the ledge where the current gathered deep and smooth. There was a fierce strike and an awesome splash. The fish broached like a marlin and fell heavily and the nylon failed.

Wind knot! I examined it unhappily.
That trout looked mammoth! Norton said weakly.
Looked like a ten-pound brown!
Alligator gar! I laughed.

Roscoe is the village where two of the most famous trout rivers in America meet in its Junction Pool. Both are born high on the hemlock ridges of Doubletop Mountain, tumbling down through abandoned farms and dense stands of hardwoods and conifers. Their headwaters are a thousand riffles whispering into deep pools under ledges dark with lichens and bright with flowers. These are the beginnings of the Willowemoc and the storied Beaverkill.

Their tradition is mixed with a long history of famous anglers. Theodore Gordon often left his farmhouse near the Neversink to fish them, and there he influenced his most famous fly-tying disciple, the late Reuben Cross, who lived many years at Lew Beach on the Beaverkill. Gordon was a secretive man who seldom shared his skills with other fishermen, but he gave Cross several flies during their days along the rivers. Cross worked until he could copy their style faithfully, and he later codified the techniques of the Catskill School in books like *Tying American Trout Lures* and the classic *Fur, Feathers and Steel.* Cross tied some of the most elegant dry flies ever dressed, and his customers still marvel at their delicacy and proportions, wondering how such a powerfully built man could perform such miracles with his huge hands.

Other famous fly tiers were also regulars on these two Catskill rivers. Louis Rhead wrote *American Trout Stream Insects* in farms and boardinghouses along the Beaverkill in the years before 1916. Skilled fishermen like Ray Bergman, Lou Petrie, John Alden Knight, Herb Howard, Preston Jennings, and Roy Steenrod were all regulars forty years ago. Bergman and Knight wrote a cornucopia of first-rate books on fishing, and Steenrod was another Gordon disciple who divided his streamside hours between the Neversink and the Beaverkill watershed. Gordon willed the famous collection of flies sent to him from Hampshire by Frederick Halford in

1890 to Steenrod. Following in the footsteps of Gordon, Steenrod invented an American classic—the Hendrickson pattern.

Willowemoc history begins with Thaddeus Norris, who wrote about its fishing in his *American Angler's Book* in 1860. Other writers who followed included Ladd Plumley, longtime editor of *Field & Stream* in its early years, and expert fishermen like William Schaldach, Samuel Camp, George La-Branche, Edward Ringwood Hewitt, John Taintor Foote, Ray Holland, Emlyn Gill, and John Alden Knight were frequent contributors often found on the Willowemoc and Beaverkill.

Other regulars like John Woodruff, William Bradley, Scott Conover, Charles Campbell, L. Q. Quackenbush, and A. E. Hendrickson all had famous Catskill flies named after them. The tradition of Catskill fly tying still lives in those patterns and the skilled hands of men like Art Flick on the Schoharie, Walter Dette on the Beaverkill, and Harry Darbee on the Willowemoc. Sparse Grey Hackle and Guy Jenkins are living *dramatis personae* telling stories of those years before the fireplace at the Anglers' Club of New York. The fly boxes of Theodore Gordon have a place of honor on its mantelpiece, while Sparse and Jenkins spin their tales of past days on Catskill rivers, smoking and sipping pungent pot-still whisky.

Willowemoc fishing is filled with *pianissimo* moods, particularly when the rhododendron and dogwood are blooming along the river. Its headwaters are small in the private mileage above Livingston Manor, where the holdings of historic little hotels like the Hearthstone and Ward's DeBruce Club are closed to public fishing. Most of the water downstream past Livingston Manor to its junction with the Beaverkill is still open to anglers who ask permission.

Those hotels were our mecca then, sighs Sparse Grey Hackle owlishly behind his steel-rimmed spectacles, *and from Gordon Quill time to the* Potamanthus *hatches in July, they were always full of serious fishermen.*

Harry Darbee is the present Dean of the Willowemoc. Darbee lives in a farmhouse perched above the river, not far from the Covered Bridge Pool that artist John Atherton used in his exquisite pencil drawings of the river. His rooms are filled with fly boxes and feathers and gamecock necks, mixed with stacks of mail from bankers and corporation presidents and stockbrokers ordering flies. There are strutting game-cocks in the backyard, and sometimes Darbee will show visitors his rare Andalusian blue duns.

Beaverkill fishing above its junction with the Willowemoc is mostly limited to private clubs, except for the famous Covered Bridge water painted years ago by Ogden Pleissner. Clubs like the Brooklyn Flyfishers and the venerable Beaverkill Trout Club have become historic shrines, with more than a half century of tradition and mystique.

The cacophony of modern life is muted there. The stream is a charming mixture of riffles and smooth bedrock pools and fast runs along the country-road cribbing. There is a classic tree-sheltered glide at the bottom of the farmhouse meadows that are headquarters for the Beaverkill Trout Club, and its members often close their day on the Home Pool. Sometimes it seems almost open and inviting, but there are somber moods when the river goes sour and its fish are not coming. There was a generous evening years ago when it surrendered a three-pounder to my tiny nymph as the members gathered on the porch for dinner.

That's a good way to finish the day, Bob Abbett laughed as we released it, *but it's a tough act to follow!*

Beaverkill fishing below the Junction Pool is another matter altogether. Its fifteen miles are mostly public water, and its fish see a parade of anglers. The fishing is less idyllic and its character is mixed, ranging from placid flats to churning rips like Hendricksons and Horse Brook Run.

There is a prelude of open riffles, played on strings and woodwinds in a lyric mood, but the dissonance of drums and trumpets lies just downstream, with the counterpoint of whippoorwills and wind music in the trees. Fishing the Beaverkill is a complete symphony.

The first pools are famous water, including the chest-deep slick at Ferdons where the Hendrickson was born. Barnharts is a similar pool below, with a long shallow tail

19

that is fine dry-fly water in the evenings. Hendricksons is a wild blaring of trumpets, tumbling over boulders and ledges, and Horse Brook Run is a churning rip downstream where the current-loving rainbows lie in the cold flow of the tributary.

Cairns is a great flat of productive water where the currents from Horse Brook Run reach down a length of underwater ledges. Its length is often blessed with free-rising trout and Cairns has always been popular.

Wagon Tracks is almost an extension of Cairns, and Schoolhouse lies on a bend away from the old highway. Lockwoods has always been famous for big trout on flies, particularly during hatches of big drakes. Mountain is a theatrical pool with its sheer granite face rising from the river, and Lower Mountain has a perfect dry-fly current down its sheltering ledge. Painter Bend has no connection with brushes and palettes. Like the Catskills themselves, it is named for the panthers that infested the region a century ago.

Hain't seen no painters myself, farmers said on the lower river in past seasons, *but 'spect they still some painters back in them mountains someplace.*

Old legends die slowly among country people, but Painter Bend remains worth the hike from the road. The famous pool in the village of Cook's Falls is two hundred yards of strong boulder-broken water the length of town. Its bridge was the setting for an apocryphal story, involving a city fisherman taking fish on a famous British pattern.

What're they taking? yelled some boys.

Cowdung! the fisherman answered.

There was a long silence from the bridge. *Hey Mister!* they yelled finally. *You ever try horse manure?*

Cemetery and Barrel pools lie downstream from Cook's Falls, although I never fished them enough to know them well. Like the churchyard stretch on the Schoharie, their moods made it difficult to fish under the dressed ranks of headstones above the river. Chiloways is like Mountain Pool, with a wall of granite covered with rhododendron and wildflowers and lichens. Baxters is the last reach of water before

20

the Beaverkill reaches the Delaware at Peaksville, with enough varied water to occupy an angler for weeks.

This is the storied Beaverkill, still the most famous trout stream in America. Its fishing is almost entirely public from Roscoe downstream to Peaksville, and the new fly-fishing-only water offers the best public fishing in the East.

Familiar rivers have a strange charm unlike the challenge of wilderness water. It is a sense of tradition mixed with time, with footpaths worn under the boots of generations, and a patina like the worn barrels of a familiar doublegun. There is also the sense of heritage passed from a parade of famous anglers. Such tradition is typical on the Beaverkill and its sister rivers, and the local Catskill fisherman who watched it all was Richard Robbins. His eyes failed him in his last years along the Beaverkill, and sometimes he hailed another fisherman to change his flies. Robbins lies buried in an unmarked grave in the Riverview Cemetery at Roscoe, above the stream he fished more than half his life, and his enthusiasm for the Beaverkill never waned.

Don't get discouraged! he exclaimed when the midsummer hatches were sparse and the river was low and warm. *It's still early and come a rain to cool her some—you'll see the fishing come back!*

There are still men who fish the river who remember Robbins on the Beaverkill, particularly along the easily waded flats of the lower river. The regulars share whisky and stories in the Home Pool along the cellar bar at the Antrim Lodge. Some nights when the mist is layered over the hills, it is not difficult to imagine Robbins fishing the river and having him hail them for a change of fly in the failing light of age and evening.

[1971]

21

2

Homage to
Henryville

For an activity so widely practiced, fly fishing for trout can be surprisingly parochial. We explored in the last essay the famous Catskill trout rivers that local chambers of commerce proclaim as the "birthplace of American trout fishing," which phrase I once recalled with considerable amusement as I stood in front of a large sign in Cotter, Arkansas, which proclaimed this White River town to be the trout capital of the United States.

The good Arkansas fishing and the Beaverkill's traditions notwithstanding, the region first and most important in American angling history is eastern Pennsylvania. As just one example, The Schuylkill Fishing Company, our first angling club of record, was organized at Philadelphia in 1732—a time when early Catskill settlers were more concerned with warriors and cougars than trout fishing.

In this essay Schwiebert elaborates on the history and tradition surrounding one eastern Pennsylvania stream—the Brodheads. He also refers several times to the old registers from Henryville House, where nineteenth-century angling luminaries from all over the East had recorded their names and fishing notes. I've been privileged to have examined one register, now in the hands of a private angling club, in some detail. As you'll gather from this essay, these are among the most extraordinary documents in our angling history, and cry for proper care and display in a museum or gallery.

The muses of remembrance and history are fickle at best, and the muse of angling tradition is no exception. American fishing tradition has made the Beaverkill and her Catskill sisters the cradle of fly-fishing innovation and the fountainhead of American fly-fishing literature. But in recent years, considerable evidence has emerged that the lesser-known Brodheads in the Poconos of Pennsylvania is probably the true wellspring of American trout-fishing tradition.

There is also considerable evidence that Henryville House on its laurel-sheltered upper reaches is the oldest trout-fishing hotel in America, and its rambling clapboard structure sheltered every major American angler from its establishment in 1835 until the Great Depression of the nineteen thirties.

The Brodheads tradition is old and rich. Its watershed was already famous for trout when Indians camped on its banks to hunt through the pleasant Pocono summers. The Indians never killed more fish than they could eat or cure for the winter or plant with their corn, and trout were still plentiful in the Colonial period. Apprentice indentures throughout the Poconos stipulated the maximum number of brook-trout dinners that frontier laborers would eat, and both Indians and trout were still numerous when the Brodheads was called the Analomink. That poetic Indian name was soon forgotten after the Indian lands were settled.

Captain Daniel Brodhead negotiated for his Pennsylvania lands in 1734, dealing with the sons of William Penn. Brodhead emigrated to the Analomink country in 1737, soon after the infamous Walking Purchase had secured the watershed from the Indians. His wagons passed through the primeval forests that cloaked New Jersey and the Delaware Water Gap. Brodhead carved fifteen hundred acres from the wilderness and sowed his crops and prospered. His original log cabins were replaced with a beautiful fieldstone manor house. The Analomink flowed through Brodhead Manor and emptied into the Delaware, and it was not long before its older Indian name had passed from the speech of its settlers. The little river that empties into the Delaware above the Water Gap had become known as Brodhead's Creek.

The Indians were hostile in those years. Old hatreds still smoldered after the Walking Purchase, which had defrauded the Delaware and Minisink tribes of some twelve hundred square miles that included the Analomink and Brodhead Manor. That festering hatred traveled west with the displaced Indians and erupted later in the Indian wars of 1755.

Painted war parties ravaged isolated farmsteads and settlements above the Kittatinny Mountains, and settled the Walking Purchase score in a series of massacres that drove the settlers south in terror. Brodhead and his five sons refused to join these refugees, barricading themselves into the fortlike manor house, and successfully defended their families and neighbors. Soldiering was an old tradition with them, and went back to an earlier Brodhead who served as an officer with the British grenadiers that took New Amsterdam from the Dutch in 1664. The five Brodhead sons, tempered in these frontier Indian wars and skirmishes, later served as officers under Washington.

There was little fly fishing in this period, and the Pocono angler commonly included his Lancaster long rifle in his fishing tackle. Although there were fly fishermen in the Colonies in these early years—mostly British officers and officials—trout fishing was a matter of food rather than sport. The little Brodheads and its sister rivers did not really become angling meccas until a century after the Walking Purchase.

The genesis of angling tradition on the Brodheads is found in the little Halfway House, which Arthur Henry built on the freight trace between Easton and Scranton in 1836. His primitive log-framed inn prospered with a clientele of mule skinners and occasional sportsmen, and was expanded

24

twelve years later into Henryville House. George Washington Bethune served as editor for the first American edition of *The Compleat Angler* in 1847, and his appendix included fly-pattern and tackle recommendations for the Brodheads and its sister rivers. Bethune undoubtedly visited the Halfway House in his pilgrimages and was probably the first angling writer who paid his homage to Henryville.

The first fly-fishing notable to appear was perhaps Joseph Jefferson, celebrated both as an actor and as a later angling companion of Grover Cleveland on many trout streams and salmon rivers. Jefferson boarded with his family at Henryville House through the summer of 1848, and tells us in his later autobiography about fishing on the Brodheads, and how the little river tumbled through mountain meadows and a forest cathedral-dark with towering pines and hemlocks.

Frank Forester omitted specific mention of the river in his *Fish and Fishing* of 1849, the first American angling book, but like Bethune he recommends the wonderful brook-trout fishing in the Brodheads region, and was probably the second angling writer to explore the river and its tributaries. The third was Robert Barnwell Roosevelt, and the Brodheads was already well known in American angling circles when his famous *Game Fish of the North* called it a great trout stream in 1862. The freight wagons and canalboats were waning, and as the railroad pushed through the Brodheads valley toward the developing coal fields, the Poconos experienced the beginnings of a fly-fishing invasion.

Thaddeus Norris is perhaps the most famous of these early Brodheads regulars. His signature is found in the old registers of Henryville House as early as 1851, and he wrote of the Brodheads in considerable detail in his *American Angler's Book,* which appeared in 1864 and firmly established him as the father of American fly-fishing literature. James Henry was then the proprietor of Henryville House, and his son, Luther, often accompanied Norris on the river. The prose of the legendary Norris has a curious cadence in our ears, patterned on the pastoral fishing dialogues fashionable after Walton, and in one passage he exclaims to his young disciple Luther Henry:

*What pretty bright trout there are in this bold rock creek!
It would be called a river in England, and so it is!*

The hallowed dry-fly method first emerged in England in
1851 with the *Vade-Mecum of Fly-Fishing for Trout,* which
codified tactics worked out by G. P. R. Pulman on the Barle
and the Axe in Devonshire. Norris also experimented with a
dry-fly method in those same years, and his exploratory tactics—described in detail in his *American Angler's Book* fourteen years later—used two flies that settled softly on the
current and floated and were taken by the trout before they
sank. It seems unlikely that his dry flies were more than
well-dubbed heavily hackled wet flies, but however crude,
such primitive dry-fly methods were practiced on the Brodheads almost twenty-five years before the innovations of
Theodore Gordon and the Golden Age of the Catskills.

Norris also played a principal role in the evolution of the
modern split-cane rod. His companion astream on the Brodheads was often Samuel Phillippe, the gunsmith and violin
maker from Easton who invented modern bamboo rod construction. Although British rodmakers had long experimented with various bamboo systems in their rod tips, which
Edward Fitzgibbon described in his *Handbook of Angling*
compiled in 1847, their most successful systems employed
three-strip construction with the power fibers of the cane
inside the finished sections. Phillippe worked with power
fibers outside his finished sections in the present manner,
having independently hit upon this revolutionary theory
with a rod builder at work in England. However, the skilled
hands and inventive mind of Phillippe must be credited with
devising our modern four- and six-strip cane construction.
Phillippe passed his techniques on to Norris, who became
one of the great rod builders of the nineteenth century, and
their buckboard expeditions along the Brodheads played a
considerable role in the refinement of their revolutionary
fly-rod designs.

Norris and Phillippe were joined in those halcyon days
by other American anglers of considerable fame. Perhaps the
best known was Chancellor Levison, whose first visit to Hen-

ryville is recorded in the register more than ten years before the Civil War. Levison was later a founding member of two organizations that have Olympian stature in American trout-fishing history: the Brooklyn Flyfishers and the Anglers' Club of New York.

The Civil War limited his fishing trips to Long Island waters, but Appomattox saw his return with two equally famous cronies—Charles Bryan and Henry Parkhurst Wells. Levison later became a well-known tournament caster who drew sizeable crowds demonstrating his prowess at Prospect Park in Brooklyn and Haarlem Mere in Central Park. He also served as the impeccable bowler-hatted fisherman for the casting plates in *Fly Rods and Fly Tackle,* written by Henry Parkhurst Wells in 1885.

Bryan was another familiar Brodheads pilgrim in later years, with an attendance record of weeks and weekends through the eighteen seventies that remains enviable in terms of modern transportation. These three anglers are remembered on the Brodheads for their impressive catches of brook trout after the Civil War.

Levison and Bryan first joined two other historic founders of the Anglers' Club of New York on the opening weekend of 1885, and their names can still be found in the faded pages of the Henryville register: Edward Baldwin, Chancellor Levison, Edward Rice, and Charles Bryan. The following year they were joined on that April weekend by two British guests, and in 1887 their arrival was cheered with six inches of fresh snow. Bryan and Rice stayed while their less hardy companions returned to New York. Their comments in the register record a river discolored with snowmelt, and include a candid confession that their catch of forty trout was taken on worms.

These men were soon joined by another early member of the Anglers' Club, the late Henry Ingraham, who first visited the Henryville water in 1887. Ingraham later wrote his classic *American Trout Streams,* a collector's item that now brings a hundred dollars in the sporting-book market. His angling poem "On the Heller Branch" was written during a December grouse hunt in 1888, and its happy verses appear

27

in his elegant nineteenth-century hand across two full pages of the Henryville register. Its mood captures an idyllic morning astream with the full-blown romanticism of the nineteenth century and concludes with these lines about another kind of romance:

> *Then when grows the sun more fervent,*
> *And the wary trout, observant,*
> *Says at last, "Your humble servant,*
> *Now we see your treacherous hook!"*
> *Maud, as if by hazard wholly,*
> *Saunters down the pathway slowly,*
> > *There to dangle*
> > *While I angle*
> > *With her book.*

> *Then, somehow, the rod reposes,*
> *And the book no page discloses,*
> *But I read the growing roses*
> *That unfold upon her cheek:*
> *And her small hand, soft and tender,*
> *Rests in mine. Ah! What can send her*
> > *Thus to dangle*
> > *While I angle?*
> > *Cupid, speak!*

The setting for his idyllic verses was the Heller Branch, the small brook-trout feeder also mentioned in the Henryville register as the source of a twenty-fish basket of trout taken by the redoubtable Chancellor Levison.

Another regular on the Brodheads before 1890 was the venerable John Wise, long considered the Dean of Pennsylvania trout fishermen. His threefold renown lies in the disparate worlds of Pennsylvania commerce, politics, and trout fishing. Wise is an engineer whose canny executive skills forged the extensive holdings of the Pennsylvania Power and Light Company. His political conservatism worked in chesslike opposition against another figure of myth-hero stature, the courtly and courageous Gifford Pinchot, the progressive governor of Pennsylvania who had served as a trusted adviser to Theodore Roosevelt. Wise learned fly fishing from his father and his two fishing cronies—George Reeder and Morris Carpenter—who are still considered the first fly fishermen to explore the Brodheads.

Wise caught his first trout on the Henryville water in 1887, using flies tied by his mentors and leaders made of hairs lovingly gathered from the horse that carried them on the final leg of their eighteen-hour trek from Philadelphia. Wise acquired his extensive trout-stream holdings in the Poconos during the First World War, including much of the Tunkhannock and Tobyhanna, and his twenty-odd miles of water have spawned a half-grudging half-admiring limerick among old-time Pocono fishermen:

> *Of all the guys*
> *That fish with flies,*
> *Old Johnnie Wise takes the prize:*
> *And we'll post our bets at ten to seven:*
> *He'll buy a trout stream*
> *Up in heaven.*

Wise still fishes after more than seventy-five years on the Brodheads and its sister rivers, and is usually found studying the current for rising fish each opening day morning from the simple beach above his Sawmill Pool on the Tunkhannock.

William Cowper Prime was another multitalented figure who fished the Brodheads in those same years. His worlds included an extensive legal practice in Manhattan, another career teaching art history at Princeton, and a third career as the author of popular angling books like *I Go A-Fishing*, which first appeared in 1873. Prime was the bellwether for a considerable parade of well-known Princeton fly fishermen whose ranks include men like Henry Van Dyke, Edward Ringwood Hewitt, Otto von Kienbusch, Eugene Connett, Russell MacGregor, Philip Nash, and Dana Lamb. Books like his *I Go A-Fishing* were perhaps the best-known American angling works of the period, and provided fireside reading for an entire generation of gentleman anglers.

Other inns and boardinghouses appeared and also prospered in the closing years of the nineteenth century. Other anglers made regular pilgrimages to the Brodheads from Philadelphia and New York during an epoch of trout-water greatness. The emerging shrines of those storied years—the big ledge pools on the water of the Haase farm, the productive dry-fly flats on the LaBar stretch, the austere little hotel operated by Analomink Charlie Rethoret on the lower river, the little Spruce Cabin Inn, and the old Lighthouse Tavern—have all passed into literature and legend. These places from the old days on the river have fallen victim to fires and floods, or have evolved into private fishing clubs. Henryville House alone survived as a living symbol of those earlier years, a fishing inn as old as American fly fishing, although its historic river mileage has finally become club water too.

James Henry died after the close of the trout season in 1888, and the great brook-trout years on the Brodheads died with him. The Henryville register is filled with yellowed records of phenomenal catches in the twenty years after the Civil War, but then the little river declined. The impressive forty-fish baskets of trout, and the almost carnal lumbering that ravaged the conifers for railroad structures and mine timbers—and left great hemlocks rotting in the woods, their acid-rich bark merely stripped off for the tanneries—had taken their toll. Lumbering and clearing farms had changed the watershed. Its currents had become too warm for its native trout, and the last big stream-spawned brookie recorded in the fishing log at Henryville was a two-pounder taken early in the spring of 1893.

Fly-fishing celebrities began arriving to sample the fishing with these well-known anglers. Henryville House was visited by John L. Sullivan and the storied Lily Langtry and Jake Kilrain, adding the brash glamour of the prizefight world and the music hall. Grover Cleveland and Benjamin Harrison were registered simultaneously for an enigmatic week of fishing before their political campaign in 1880. Fishing and fishing writers were still the nucleus of Brodheads life in spite of such glamorous outsiders, and the Henryville register of that period also includes these lighthearted lines from Henry Van Dyke:

Over the hill to Henryville
'Tis oft' the fisherman's cry,
For I'll catch a fourteen-incher
With an artificial fly!

The celebrated Henry Van Dyke achieved equal fame as a diplomat, a professor of literature and religion at Princeton, and a trout-fishing writer of eloquence and skill. He became a familiar figure along the Brodheads in the eighteen nineties. His angling classics like *Little Rivers* and *Fisherman's Luck* tell us that he often fished the Swiftwater, a tributary to the Brodheads above Henryville. Van Dyke writes of his encounter there with Joseph Jefferson, when the old thespian had made a sentimental fishing pilgrimage back to Henryville, where he had spent the idyllic summer fishing with his family a half century before; but let these lines from *Fisherman's Luck* describe that meeting astream:

> One May evening a couple of years since, I was angling in the Swiftwater, and came upon Joseph Jefferson stretched out on a large rock in midstream, and casting his fly down a long pool. He had passed the three-score years and ten. But he was as eager and happy as a boy in his fishing.
>
> "You here," I cried. "What good fortune brought you to these waters?"
>
> "Ah," he answered, "I fished this brook forty-five years ago. It was in the Paradise Valley that I first thought of Rip Van Winkle. I wanted to come back again for the sake of old times."

Paradise Valley is a local name for the Henryville Branch of the Brodheads. Local legend tells us that the name originated with General Philip Sheridan, who spent a quiet recuperative summer fishing at Henryville after his Civil War cavalry campaigns. Rip Van Winkle was the theatrical role that had made Jefferson famous and led to his fishing comradeship with Grover Cleveland.

Opening weekend in 1895 marked a historic event in the tradition of American trout fishing. The time-stained pages of

31

the Henryville register reveal in intricate nineteenth-century penmanship that fifteen well-known anglers had formed the Flyfishers' Club of Brooklyn. That circle of fishing greats has been immortalized in *Fishless Days,* an American collector's item from the equally famous Sparse Grey Hackle.

These founders of the Brooklyn Flyfishers were a wealthy group of brewers and businessmen, and included Ernest Palmer, Abraham Snedecor, J. J. Sayre, James Rice, Lodie Smith, C. B. Boynton, Chancellor Levison, H. B. Marshall, Charles Bryan, R. M. Coleman, J. L. Snedecor, F. S. Howard, Ralph Burnett, J. E. Bullwinkle, and C. H. Fitzgerald. Their annual ritual of the membership scroll was repeated each season in the Henryville register until 1897, when James Walker and William Oxford were added. Charles Bryan was abroad in England that April. The Brooklyn Flyfishers registered him *in absentia* and fondly wished him good hatches on the hallowed Itchen and Test.

The circle of Brooklyn regulars left Henryville House after that season of 1897, and several members observed with sadness in its fishing log that its storied brook-trout fishing seemed finished. Their clan emigrated north to the Hardenburgh farm on the Beaverkill, and established themselves in a log-framed fishing house on a sunny slope above the river. These earlier Brodheads fishermen played a major role in the growing reputation of the Beaverkill and the other Catskill rivers, and their departure from the Brodheads marked the end of another era.

History tells us they left too soon. Records that survive for the Commonwealth of Pennsylvania in those years reveal that the European brown trout was introduced in 1889. Specific records of such stocking on individual rivers have not survived, but the fishing log at Henryville House records the capture of seven strange-looking trout under the cribbing of the Dam Pool the following summer. These unfamiliar trout averaged fifteen inches, much bigger than the native fish, and the faded notation in the fishing log describes them as dark and curiously colored.

Brodheads fishermen did not realize that the brown trout planted that prior year had survived and multiplied under the conditions that were slowly eradicating their native species, and this seven-fish basket of trout signaled the Renaissance that would rescue a famous river in decline.

The fishing log that covers those first brown-trout years was started just after the Civil War, and in spite of thoughtless vandals who ripped and sliced several famous signatures from its pages, there remains a wealth of historic names and records. Henryville regulars took ten of the European trout better than twenty inches before 1900. Sixteen bigger browns were registered in the decade that followed, including three brutes better than six pounds. The record Henryville trout on flies is a twenty-seven-inch brown caught in 1901. Three twenty-two-inch browns are tied for the dry-fly record, and a thirty-inch ten-pound monster was captured with worms.

Several of these trophies were laid diagonally across the open Henryville register and their outlines were traced for posterity. These tracings are authentic, since the fish slime that penetrated the pages has discolored over the intervening fifty years, and trout scales have adhered to the silhouettes or scattered through the bindings.

The immigrant European trout proved much harder to catch than the native species they displaced, and their challenge soon evolved anglers of greatness. Those skilled anglers who banded together at Henryville to form the Brooklyn Flyfishers later formed the founding nucleus of the Anglers' Club of New York. These patron saints of American angling and fly-fishing literature are registered in the guest books and fishing logs of inns and boardinghouses and fishing clubs the full length of the Brodheads. Their roster includes figures like Albert Rouselle, John La Farge, Henry Ingraham, Alden Weir, Chancellor Levison, Charles Bryan, and the ubiquitous Smith brothers—famous for angling rather than cough drops—James, Milton, and Lodie.

Such pioneers were soon followed by others like John Taintor Foote, Jason Lamison, Edward Ringwood Hewitt, George LaBranche, Henry Van Dyke, Edward Rice, Perry Frazer, Edward Cave, Robert Lawrence, Reuben Held, Harold de Rasloff, Edward Boies, and Charles Stepath. Nine of these regulars were fishing writers of importance, two served as editors on the staff of *Field & Stream,* six were later presidents of the Anglers' Club of New York, and four wrote angling works that have achieved major importance in American fly-fishing literature.

John Taintor Foote authored many books and essays and stories on shooting and trout fishing, and his work is a milestone in the literature of American field sports. Perhaps his masterpiece is *Wedding Gift,* written some years after Foote had passed a similar honeymoon fishing at Henryville House. The later *Pocono Shot* was written there in another summer devoted to both the typewriter and the stream. Foote is well remembered on the Brodheads. The sitting room at Henryville House embraces the original log-cabin inn built in 1835, and was once partitioned off for Foote to serve as his studio.

Foote took his breakfast punctually each morning at six, and then spent the next four hours in the studio, drinking coffee and writing. The children of the Henry family policed the children of the other guests to prevent porch games outside the sitting room when the writer was at his work. Foote finished punctually at ten, just in time for the late-morning rise of fish, and disappeared down the Brodheads with a lunch of cold chicken and thick-sliced bread still warm from the Henryville ovens.

Edward Ringwood Hewitt was a lovable and irascible character who needs no introduction to the fly-fishing fraternity. Hewitt was long considered the dean emeritus of American anglers, and well-known Hewitt books like *Telling on the Trout* and the later *Secrets of the Salmon,* recently incorporated into the autobiographical *A Trout and Salmon Fisherman for Seventy-five Years,* are the high points of a fishing career that contributed ten books to the literature of fly fishing. This master of the American dry-fly technique first used English floating flies at Henryville in 1905, according to his own writings, after his usual methods had failed during a remarkable rise of trout. Hewitt returned the following week, armed with a new Leonard rod and proper flies and the legendary Hewitt determination—and soon captured his first dry-fly trout from the Buttonwood Pool.

Hewitt fished and quarreled and competed with an angling colleague of equal stature in those Olympian summers on the Henryville water. George LaBranche was another giant of angling literature whose early reputation had its beginnings along the Brodheads. Thaddeus Norris and the better-known Theodore Gordon—whose fame in angling circles is more closely linked to the Catskill rivers, although he also fished the Brodheads in his native Pennsylvania—are considered the fathers of American fly fishing, but it was George LaBranche who really taught Americans to fish with dry flies on the swift, boulder-broken currents of our rivers. His little volume titled *The Dry Fly and Fast Water* outlined the emerging American method and had a deserved reputation for both its technical innovations and the qualities of its writing. That slim little masterpiece was published in 1914, when LaBranche was thirty-nine and at the height of his powers, and it remains in print fifty years later. Its passages are rich with references to his experiences along the Brodheads. LaBranche worked his dry-fly sorcery from Henryville House and the Spruce Cabin Inn, and once owned a reach of water now controlled by the Parkside Club of Philadelphia. The sparkling riffles and swift runs of these beats played a major role in the evolution of his theories. George LaBranche loved the little Brodheads, and its quicksilver rhythms have passed into his prose.

The river became a fishing shrine after 1900, and other Brodheads regulars continued their pilgrimages. Forty years after his Henryville fishing poem, Henry Ingraham wrote *American Trout Streams* and was elevated to the president's chair of the Anglers' Club of New York. Edward Cave and Perry Frazer long served with *Field & Stream,* where the first meetings of the Anglers' Club were held. Frazer was one of the great tournament casters in those years, and contributed books like *Amateur Rodmaking,* which remained a standard work for sixty-odd years. Edward Rice and Reuben Held collaborated on the *Angler's and Sportsman's Guide,* which appeared in 1912. Alden Weir was an almost-forgotten landscape painter who was a companion of Whistler, Ryder, Sargent, and Winslow Homer, and was also a diligent and skilled trout fisherman. Weir was the first American painter to embrace Impressionism, and had a principal role in both the Golden Age of American trout fishing and the Gilded Age of American painting.

Still others made pilgrimages to the Brodheads shrine. The last season before his death—after ninety-odd years as a market hunter and poacher of fearsome skills—the legendary Henryville Charlie Ross sprawled with me in the shade below the Upper Twin Pool and talked about the past. His memories of the river were rich and varied. Calvin Coolidge failed with flies he borrowed from an old poacher, but finally caught two Henryville trout on nightcrawlers. Theodore Roosevelt and Gifford Pinchot had also visited Henryville House, traveling by motorcar from Pinchot's estate at Milford, and had excellent luck with flies and their elegant split-cane rods.

Roosevelt and Pinchot could fish! Henryville Charlie had austere standards for politicians. *Coolidge couldn't!*

The old riverkeeper also remembered Buffalo Bill and Annie Oakley, who came to Henryville House both to fish and to demonstrate their marksmanship on the rolling lawns. Henryville Charlie had helped transfer their baggage from the train depot and guided them on the river. He remembered the mountainous pile of baggage he finally assembled on the Henryville porch. There were old leg-of-mutton gun cases and leather rod-luggage and boxes of targets and special ammunition in addition to steamer trunks and suitcases, and a small crowd gathered in awe.

Annie Oakley wasn't no beauty, the old poacher winked and his time-faded eyes twinkled with humor, *but she sure had hell's own pile of trunks for a plain woman!*

Buffalo Bill is still remembered at Henryville for his buckskin suits and elegantly trimmed mustache and beard. Annie Oakley is remembered for her bright blue eyes and soft chamois-skin skirts and gentle disposition. The gallery of guests and local people was amazed with her shooting, especially the market-hunter friends of Henryville Charlie. Their attitude was one of grudging admiration, with some unchivalrous muttering about the difference between breaking thrown targets over an open meadow and shooting ruffed grouse in a hemlock thicket.

Henryville Charlie finished his long career policing the Henryville water against poachers, an irony that would have been fully understood only by his long-dead cronies, since the owners of Henryville House decided that the most accomplished poacher in the entire valley would be the best protection against midnight raids on their trout. Henryville Charlie was still able to fish the river in his ninetieth year, and could mend a skilled wet-fly swing and work a deceitful poacher's retrieve almost to his death.

Henryville had become justly famous and its heritage of famous guests continued to grow. The patriarchal Chancellor Levison, impeccable in his shooting tweeds and regimental tie, rose in those years at a meeting of the Anglers' Club of New York to move that the membership petition the Delaware, Lackawanna and Western about better rail service to Henryville. Presidents and politicians had mingled with great anglers and prizefighters and theatrical celebrities in the fishing inns along the river, but with the guns of the gentle Annie Oakley—and the ominous artillery that rumbled across Europe in the summer of 1914—an epoch of tranquil order ended for both the Brodheads and the world.

Chancellor Levison was the first regular who returned to the river after the Great War, as he had after the Civil War, and the old master is still remembered from those years—not for the flawless casting and impressive catches of his youthful years, but for the seven blankets and hot-water bottle he required for his room. The old angler was accompanied by his nephew-in-waiting, the infamous fortune-hunting Victor Grimwood, who shares the dry-fly record on the Brodheads with a four-pound brown from the Barn Pool below the Haase farm.

Grimwood was a charming anti-hero. He arranged for the seven blankets, hot-water bottles, thick slices of lightly browned toast, special British marmalade, and six-egg omelets specified by his venerable uncle. Grimwood fished beautifully with the most expensive tackle, and like his uncle in earlier years, wore his Burberry shooting coat and regimen-

37

tal mustache with considerable *élan*. His bearing was always ramrod straight, and there are still Henryville ladies who remember his flashing eyes and the dance-floor grace that never faltered, even after long hours astream. These romantic ladies never dreamed that Grimwood would later defraud both friends and relatives of thousands, in a scandal that rocked society in both Philadelphia and New York, and that after an infamous trial his dance-floor manners would be wasted in federal prison.

There was another society scandal in those years, when Broadway glamour and glittering wealth were meshed in the streamside *liaisons dangereuses* of Louise Groody and Jack Harriman. The famous musical-comedy star dominated shows like *No, No, Nanette!* and *Hit the Deck!* Henryville old-timers remember both her skilled casting and her impromptu performances for other guests, especially the lilting "Tea for Two" that she had first performed and taken as her trademark. The old-timers also remember the sleek cream-lacquered Stutz she gave Harriman after a particularly successful Broadway season, and the Henryville ladies still remember the quarrels that ended the affair. The final argument erupted in the tackle-hung Henryville dining room and ended in the New York gossip columns. The regulars remember the beautiful actress and the flawless working of her amber English line in the sun above the Ledge Pool, and the Henryville ladies smile sadly as their thoughts retrace the fickle past.

Brown-trout fishing on the Brodheads was still good in the twenties and thirties, and there were new fishing writers of considerable reputation as well as angling *inamorata* working its storied pools and flats. Eugene Connett fished the Brodheads regularly in those years, and authored such sporting classics as his *Magic Hours* and *Random Casts* and the lovely *Any Luck?* Connett immortalized the difficult stillwater pools on the Brodheads with his essay "In the Tail of the Flat"—included in several angling anthologies and rumored to describe Mary's Flat, a famous reach of water on the Parkside Club. Connett was the energetic president of the New

York Anglers' Club who was instrumental in leasing its first Hanover Street quarters in 1920, near the old Hotel Lucerne. Brodheads acolytes gravitated toward three fishing shrines on the river—the group that fished the lower river from the clapboard Hotel Rapids at Analomink, the group that fished the Brodheads Forest and Stream and the Parkside water and the Haase farm, and the Henryville regulars.

The anglers who fished from Analomink before its hotel burned are a famous group that includes names like James Leisenring, John Alden Knight, Ed Zern, Preston Jennings, John Stauffer, Vernon Hidy, Chip Stauffer, Dick Clark, Sibley Smith, William Thompson, Charles Wetzel, and Don Brooks. Leisenring has achieved legendary stature since the publication of his little *The Art of Tying the Wet Fly* in 1941 and the series of articles about his flies and techniques that appeared a few years after his death in *Sports Illustrated*. Big Jim was the solitary bachelor-master of the Brodheads until his death and was the acknowledged leader of the Twelve Apostles, a circle of dedicated Brodheads fishermen whose ranks included expert fly dressers like Dick Clark and Chip Stauffer. John Alden Knight needs no introduction to American trout fishermen. His distinguished career embraced countless articles and twelve-odd books that range from the *Field Book of Fresh Water Angling* through the *Modern Angler* to the recent *Complete Book of Fly Casting*, done in collaboration with his son shortly before his death.

The first major work on American trout-stream entomology was the beautiful *Book of Trout Flies* written by Preston Jennings in 1935. Its pages are filled with references to both the Brodheads and the Hotel Rapids, and its first edition has become a collector's item. The peripatetic and puckish Ed Zern, whose humorous works range from *To Hell with Fishing* to the hilarious *How to Tell Fish from Fishermen*, was another Analomink regular in those days before the little hotel was destroyed. Sibley Smith was a painter who followed in the tradition of Alden Weir in making regular pilgrimages to the Brodheads valley. Charles Wetzel is now the venerable dean of the Weikert water on Penns Creek in central Pennsylvania, but in the past he was a regular on the

Brodheads. Wetzel is the author of such angling books as *Practical Fly Fishing* and *Trout Flies,* works that continued the entomological beginnings found in the writings of Preston Jennings.

The gentle and venerable Ray Bergman was the best-known fishing writer in America, after a writing career that produced books like *Just Fishing* and the best-selling *Trout,* which counseled an entire generation of fishermen in tackle and tactics. These men and many others came to the Hotel Rapids, and the passages of American angling literature contain many references to Charlie Rethoret and the wonderful French cuisine he prepared at all hours for hungry fishermen, and about a legendary trout named Herman that inhabited the Railroad Pool across from the hotel. Herman was the subject of an epic poem of fishing doggerel called *Herman to His Grandchildren.* Its seemingly endless fifty-four stanzas mention many of the Analomink regulars.

The regulars who fished above Analomink on the club waters at Brodheads Forest and Stream, Parkside, and the Haase farm are equally distinguished, and include fly fishermen like the late Manning Barr, Walter Steel, Robert Kahn, Scotty Scott, Curtin Windsor, Philip Nash, Page Brown, Allen Du Bois, Guy Jenkins, Dana Lamb, and Sparse Grey Hackle. Their founding members included expert anglers like Henry Jenkins, who fished with Theodore Gordon and all of the other great fly fishermen of the Catskill School, and the late Richard Carley Hunt, whose writings include the little masterpiece *Salmon in Low Water.* Fire also destroyed the Spruce Cabin Inn, and other than Henryville House, only the Brodheads Forest and Stream and Haase farm survive from the old days on the upper Brodheads. They have evolved into small private fishing clubs with some of the best water in the east.

During the week, when most of their regulars are occupied with their corporations and brokerage houses and law practices in Philadelphia and New York, the old fishing quarters of the farms fall silent. April rain trickles softly on the windows, and the afternoon duns are coming off the riffles—inside there is still an aura of the Brodheads past in the sitting room memorabilia and the photographs of the famous that watch silently from the walls.

The celebrated Richard Hunt was often accompanied on the Haase beats by anglers like Sparse Grey Hackle and General Theodore Roosevelt and the scholarly Dana Lamb, whose writings included the collections of essays and stories titled *On Trout Streams and Salmon Rivers* and *Bright Salmon and Brown Trout*. Roosevelt and Hunt also fished the Henryville water, and with Robert Barnwell Roosevelt and his father, Roosevelt became the third member of his distinguished family to fish its storied runs and pools. Richard Hunt is perhaps best known for his writings on salmon fishing, but he also wrote the following lines about his beloved Brodheads in 1934:

The lovely stream flows through its friendly valley, and pleasant days await me there. I can feel at one with those who have fished and loved it. I can foregather again with those whose companionship means much to me. I can tell tales of the big ones which got away or would not rise in the biggest of little rivers.

Russell Henry succeeded his father Eugene as the manager of Henryville House in the thirties and became the fifth generation of his family to shelter fly fishermen on the Brodheads. Their rambling white-clapboard hotel had served four fishing presidents and every major fishing writer in America for almost a century. The parade of famous rods that had begun with Thaddeus Norris before the Civil War, and included both Hewitt and LaBranche after 1900, began to decline in the middle thirties. The fishing pressure that came with a reputation for greatness eventually caused some regulars to enlarge the private clubs which controlled the better beats above the Junction Pool. The biggest of little rivers was no longer public water.

Rationed gasoline and tires during the Second World War gave its public reaches some much-needed respite. The brown trout began to thrive again, but the headlong release

41

of peacetime and postwar population explosion soon ended their brief period of euphoria. The once-great river declined rapidly until after 1950, when it offered little more than the popular hoax of put-and-take stocking, and there was little or no decent sport on the public pools. The regulars were in mourning.

Disaster struck in the August hurricane of 1955, and the Brodheads instantly became a maelstrom that tumbled forty feet of dark water toward the Delaware. Bridges were obliterated. Barns and houses were hammered into water-soaked matchwood. Campers were caught and drowned in their bedrolls. Miles of highways were erased and eroded. The Delaware, Lackawanna and Western found much of its roadbed gone, its tracks and ties and rolling stock scrambled into hopeless spaghetti-tangles. The flood churned toward Stroudsburg and the Water Gap in a straight, inexorable line that escaped and ignored the looping tree-lined course of the river. Its force crushed everything in its path. When the flood waters receded, there was a raw linear wound that reached down the valley for miles. Trout were found rotting in the forests and fields, hundreds of feet from the river and as much as fifty feet above normal water. Fly hatches were almost completely eradicated, and the Brodheads regulars shook their heads in despair.

Some still had hope for their river. The several pools held for guests at Henryville House were restored by the Henry family, the sixth generation to shelter anglers. Three deci-sions were then made for the management of their historic water: Henryville House would post its holdings and manage them like a British trout-fishing inn, stocking would be lim-ited to mature brown trout, and the pools would be restricted to fly fishing. Henryville regulars followed these rules and paid a daily rod fee, like fly fishermen have on European rivers for centuries, for the privilege of fishing—in addition to room-and-board costs at the inn.

The restoration under these rules proved remarkable, and although fly hatches were meager the following year, the fishing was surprisingly good. The aquatic hatches have slowly come back in recent years until the sport equals those halcyon days of the brown-trout Renaissance on the Brodheads, when a really accomplished fly fisherman could average twenty good fish in a leisurely day astream. Each new season has brought better fish than the last, and with the demise of a four-pound trout in 1961, there was real optimism again on the Brodheads.

Henryville House still drowses in the trees, but the freight wagons and canal boats and steam-driven railroad trains are gone. Modern anglers drive into the Poconos from Philadelphia and New York, and there is an occasional Porsche or Bentley or Mercedes-Benz parked beside the unpretentious buildings and above the best pools. During lunch and dinner, these cars are draped with tackle vests and waders and split-cane rods and drying socks.

The modern Henryville fishermen have included men like George Kattermann, Stinson Scott, Arnold Gingrich, Richard Wolters, John Randolph, Charles Fox, Samuel Slaymaker, Ted Rogowski, Art Smith, Steve Mills, Ray Ovington, and the late Ken Lockwood.

Kattermann was the acknowledged dean emeritus of the Henryville water, having fished it with his father more than fifty years ago, and is a fly fisherman of the LaBranche School. His fly boxes were limited to two patterns—the delicate Henryville Special first dressed by Hiram Brobst, an old-time Pocono fly maker from Lehighton, and his own high-floating Kattermann. Both are bivisible-like flies that work well during the several *Trichoptera* hatches that emerge on the Brodheads, especially on the pocket-water stretches. When the selective browns refuse these flies, this master angler in the fast-water tradition was simply content to wait until they cooperated again on his terms.

Stinson Scott is another regular whose devotion to Henryville covers many years, having learned his fly fishing from Chancellor Levison in 1928. Scott can easily be recognized astream in the distance, because he still goes hatless and regularly acquires some fierce sunburns through his thinning silver hackles.

Arnold Gingrich is an accomplished angler who doubles

as the peripatetic publisher of *Esquire* magazine. His dedicated angling had its beginning under the enthusiastic tutelage of the late Ernest Hemingway in the early thirties, and Gingrich has become a Henryville regular since 1961. He likes the skater fished on ultralight tackle, and can be found with his Young Midge—the Guarneri of split-cane fly rods—plying that refined art on difficult flats like the tail shallows of the Ledge Pool and the Pine Tree.

Richard Wolters is perhaps better known for books like *Gun Dog* and his prowess on the skeet field, but his trout-fishing hours are sometimes spent at Henryville. Perhaps the best known of the regulars in the years since the flood was the late John Randolph, the familiar outdoors columnist for *The New York Times.* His columns were an admixture of humor working on two levels—the surface that produced chuckles and wry smiles from his newspaper readers, and the undercurrent of inside jokes that produced belly laughs among the *cognoscenti* and cronies he wrote about. One such column filed from Henryville was included in *The World of Wood, Field and Stream,* the posthumous anthology of Randolph's work selected by his friend Richard Wolters. Randolph will be missed at the frenetic midweek lunches of the Midtown Turf, Yachting and Polo Association, an intentionally purposeless gathering of New York friends and disciples who write about shooting and fishing, and he will be missed on the Upper Twin beat at Henryville, the beautiful, rock-filled run that was the last trout pool of his life.

Charles Fox is better known as the leader of a circle of light-tackle experts who frequent the famous Letort Spring Run—and for his recent *This Wonderful World of Trout*—but he has often matched wits with the Henryville browns as well. Fox has continued the tradition of John Taintor Foote, since the final draft of his book was written and polished at Henryville House. Art Smith was outdoor writer for *The New York Herald-Tribune,* and joined the regulars several times in recent years. Steve Mills is a relative newcomer on the Henryville water, but as the youngest member of William Mills & Son—the oldest tackle shop in America—his heritage on American trout water dates back to 1822 with the beginnings of his family as Yankee merchants in Manhattan. His grand-father accompanied Edward Ringwood Hewitt to the International Casting Tournament in London, representing America in the competitions of 1904.

Ken Lockwood was another famous trout-fishing writer who often fished the Brodheads from both Henryville and Analomink. His memorial is the Lockwood Gorge fly-fishing water on the South Raritan, where a monument is inscribed with the following lines:

When mists and shadows rob pool and run of shape and
    substance
When the voice of the wood thrush stills and the
        Dog trout shakes his lethargy
We will remember a stalwart, gentle master of the Angler's
    art,
        Half submerged in the smother,
Unerringly shooting that long line, watchfully
        Mending the drift.
Never more will your skilled hand tempt the
        Patriarchs of the flood.
        Farewell, old timer.

There are still elegiac moods on the Brodheads too. Death has ended the six generations of Henry family tenure, and its famous mileage of water has passed to a private fishing club. The rambling clapboard inn has changed hands for the first time since 1845, although it has been lovingly restored and is still called the Henryville House.

The river remains in good hands. The present Henryville Flyfishers are a skilled circle of anglers from all walks of life. Its roster includes board chairmen, publishers, manufacturers, surgeons, psychiatrists, lawyers, toolmakers, computer programmers, architects, police officers, building contractors, professors, poets, and the dean of a major university. Their tastes vary widely from Ramblers to a regal Bentley, and from beer to a fine Pouilly-Fuissé.

Its current is the single theme that unifies their diversity, and the members are a skilled group of light-tackle fishermen. Henryville fish are particularly choosy, because their water is managed on a no-kill basis through the first month of the season. Their diet ranges from the typical eastern mayfly hatches to a marked taste for minutiae—the tiny little ants and beetles and jassids usually associated with the limestone streams of Pennsylvania.

The fishing mileage assembled by the Henryville Flyfishers has been carefully increased and restored. All of the famous fly hatches have come back fifteen years after the flood. Fast-water mayflies like the March Browns, Gray Foxes, and pale Cahills suffered badly when their clinging nymphs were annihilated in the grinding flood. The bigger drakes were eliminated when high water scoured their burrowing nymphs from the silt beds and flushed them downriver, but the flies have slowly restored themselves. The club has added picturesque little Cranberry Run, which still has wild brook trout, and the Paretta water above Henryville to its holdings. Their pools were once part of the mileage fished from the Henryville House in the classic years of the nineteenth century. This past season I fished the deep-ledge pool above the Paretta meadows and stopped to daydream in the spring sunlight that warmed the ledges above the pool. Its heat felt good, and I was idly sorting flies when I dropped a Wheatley fly box that rattled and clattered along the ledge. It stopped just above the pool and when I scrambled down to retrieve it, I found the names of Charles Bryan and Lodie Smith carved into the rock. The date carved beside their names was 1896, the last summer those founders of the Brooklyn Flyfishers came to Henryville.

The fly-fishing pageant at Henryville continues with its passing years and changing cast. New pilgrims come to sample the Brodheads shrine, and some of the old faces are missing. New tales and traditions are evolving into new legends, and the old history is retold in the firelight. Evenings find the regulars tired after pleasant hours astream, and no one fishes seriously at night. The practical observer will tell you they are simply tired, and have settled into the pleasant lassitude of *après*-fishing, but practical minds are seldom right.

There are nights in the Poconos when the wind is high and strange, and on such nights—and others when storms moan in the hemlock ridges and rain cries on the windows—the river belongs to those shadow anglers who have fished and loved it since aboriginal times. The trout fisherman with a strain of fantasy in his character can imagine them—Thaddeus Norris delivering his Waltonian dialogues to the worshipful Luther Henry, Theodore Roosevelt exclaiming to the solemn Pinchot that the Brodheads is a bully river, Hewitt and LaBranche continuing their rivalry of cantankerous camaraderie, and puckish Henryville Charlie Ross following patiently behind the political entourage, shaking his head in despair as Coolidge makes another awkward cast.

More than a century after Joseph Jefferson and Thaddeus Norris and Chancellor Levison, the new regulars still gather to fish the Brodheads. The biggest of little rivers remains as powerful as any trout-fishing mecca, and Richard Hunt was right when he wrote that it has excellent dry-fly hatches much earlier than its better-known Catskill neighbors. Opening weekends might prove almost subarctic and foul, but bitter or balmy, the regulars will make the pilgrimage and offer their homage to Henryville.

[1965]

3

Legend and the Letort

This is one of Ernest Schwiebert's best-known stories. It originally appeared in a 1961 issue of Esquire *at a time when his friend the late Arnold Gingrich was still active on the magazine that Gingrich had helped to start. This was also eleven years after Vince Marinaro had startled the dry-fly trout-fishing world with* A Modern Dry-Fly Code, *a book based on his own experiences along the southwestern Pennsylvania spring creek called Letort Spring Run.*

Many years later I sat watching the Letort as I often did from a bench behind Charlie Fox's house. I heard a clumping noise along the path and turned to see Marinaro, whom I knew slightly, appear from around a bush. He scowled at me over one of his ever-present Dutch Masters, sat down on the bench, and proceeded to give me a royal chewing-out over an error he'd seen in a fishing magazine I was editing at the time.

I sat red-faced after he'd finished, and we shared silence for a while. I finally asked him why he'd been so vehement. "So you'll remember," he said quietly

48

while unwrapping a fresh cigar. We subsequently be-
came better acquainted and fished together a few
times. And although Vince died a couple of years ago,
the memory is indelible: all the more so as I reread
this wonderful essay.

The remarkable literature and tradition of fishing for trout
is unmatched by that of any other sport. From its treasury we
can draw a single conclusion: anglers are thoughtful men
and angling is a contemplative art, and many anglers have
been the kind of men who have placed their thoughts and
experiences on paper to share them with others. From their
books has come literature, and from the literature of fly fishing have come its legends.

Legend is a nebulous sometime thing, born in the mist-
shrouded half-world between reality and romanticism. Legends are spawned in the spinning of tales and thrive in the
middle ground between things as they are and things as we
would like them, and angling legend is no exception. The
contemplative men who have fished and loved our rivers
have left a rich legacy of their thoughts and experiences, their
triumphs and failures.

Many have written of their sport in language as lithe and
bright-colored as the fish themselves, and for this we are
grateful. Through their books we can return through time
and relive their experiences, seeking the source of our own
fascination in fly fishing with the legendary authors themselves as guides to the best water.

Knowledgeable modern anglers are familiar with the
substance of fly-fishing legend. There is telling and retelling
over campfires on the dark tea-colored rivers of our north
country, over sour-mash whisky after the evening rise at storied Catskill fishing inns, and over leisurely midweek lunches
in Manhattan.

Legend and tradition and a passion for bright water are
the essence of angling. The foundations of angling legend are
mostly European, but not all of the wellsprings are there. The
sparkling rivers of the Catskills and Poconos are the classic
landscapes of our American tradition. Our legend has its

genesis on the big beautiful pools of the Beaverkill and Willowemoc, the legendary water of the Neversink, and the laurel-hung pools of the lovely Brodheads.

There is a legion of legendary names. It begins with Dame Juliana Berners in the fifteenth century, the unknown author of *The Arte of Angling* in 1577, and Walton seventy-six years later. The parade continues through the Cottons and Halfords and Marryats of England, down to the classic Americans like Gordon and Hewitt and LaBranche.

The more knowledgeable know their writings as well as their names, and their accomplishments are part of our American heritage. Angling legend is already more than a century old in America. Few legends are fully formed in such brief time, since most are shaped slowly with stratalike telling and retelling until their origins in fact are all but lost in the embellishments of fancy. Legends are difficult to recognize in embryonic form, and it is rare that we are permitted to participate in their beginnings, rare that we are able to observe their birth and evolution.

There is such a legend forming now, and that new legend might be called the Legend of Letort Spring Run, for it was conceived on the quiet weed-channeled currents of that small limestone stream in Pennsylvania. Hewitt wrote in his *Trout and Salmon Fisherman for Seventy-five Years* that there are no American rivers like the English Test. Hewitt is wrong: there are several from Pennsylvania to the Sierra Nevadas, and the lovely cress-bordered Letort is queen of them all. The Letort is somewhat smaller than the Test, but its trout and its character are much like that of the upper Test on its Longparish or Whitchurch beats.

Anglers are shaped by their rivers, and difficult rivers like the Test and the Letort have evolved accomplished anglers in the past. Their shy trout are the supreme challenge and their skilled practitioners are drawn meccalike to their quiet currents year after year.

The historic challenge of the British chalkstreams caused the classic twelve patterns of Berners and the dry-fly innovations of Halford in the nineteenth century. Selective brown trout are the pleasant enigma of both the Test and the

Letort. The men who fish and love both rivers are an unusual breed, content with a modicum of hard-won success, and willingly accept the challenge.

Letort regulars comprise a veritable round table of great anglers who fish according to a strict code of chivalry. Charles Fox is the author of books like *Rising Trout* and the acknowledged leader of the clan. Vincent Marinaro is a perfectionist best known for the contemporary angling classic, *A Modern Dry-Fly Code,* and is certainly the Merlin of the Letort. Ross Trimmer, the tobacco-chewing retired police officer, is undisputed court jester. There are many others, and the court has no Guinevere except the little river itself. The regulars may be found paying homage each evening in the water meadows above Carlisle.

The love they have for the river is incredible. They scorn the too-easy supermarket scramble for stocked fish that occurs on most waters, because the truck-dazed hatchery trout are robbed of their fear during a pampered hand-fed existence, and their resemblance to wild fish is superficial.

Letort regulars fish solely with flies and kill *none* of the trout they take. The native wariness and selectivity of these fish is honed to perfection with each successive capture and release. Each trout becomes both an old friend and an old adversary, and its holding and feeding lies are familiar as soon as midseason.

These men do not post their water, but permit access restricted to fly fishing and prohibit the killing of trout under fifteen inches. Violation of these rules constitutes trespass. Since these rules went into effect, the regulars have noticed a singular increase in natural spawning and average size of fish, since female brown trout are seldom fully mature until they reach twelve inches.

The character of the river is worth comment. Like other limestone rivers in Pennsylvania, it bubbles out cold and complete from cavern-fed springs of remarkable volume. British chalkstreams are spawned in the cretaceous chalkdowns of southern England, while our eastern limestone streams emerge from the cretaceous caverns of the Appalachians. Each results in lime-rich water capable of supporting unusually heavy populations of fish and fly life. These Appalachian rivers are relatively small, leading brief lives in their pastoral warm-water valleys. Limestone trout are fat with crustacea and are seldom taken on dry flies unless they are already feeding on the surface.

Fishing the water at random, in the classic American fast-water manner, is fruitless unless one knows exactly where the fish lie when not rising. Fishing over known holding lies is possible in grasshopper season, but on the whole, limestone experts have learned to watch the water and fish only to rising trout, like their counterparts on the chalkstreams of Hampshire.

The unique character of the Letort has played a major role in the legendary innovations conceived on its weedy currents. There are no calendar-picture falls or boulder-broken runs or dark pools hung with rhododendron. The little river is born in two large springs that flow strong and full into a gentle landscape of manicured fields and brick-patterned barns and dairy cattle.

The headwaters are cavern-cold and flow smoothly over the pale gravel. Watercress and beds of elodea divide the quiet current tongues. Cress is cultivated on one tributary, and the other has long been defended by a remarkably belligerent bull. Fishing is not feasible on either stretch. Such protection results in undisturbed spawning grounds, blessed with a constant volume and temperature of flow. The trout population is a fine stock of native fish.

Gentle hills protect the Letort from the prevailing winds. Heavy rains are quickly absorbed into the limestone aquifers beneath the valley floor and seldom affect the color or volume of flow except for a slight limesalt milkiness and a barely imperceptible rise in level. It is like the chalkstreams of England or the lava-field rivers of Iceland.

Hewitt described the freshet-free Test in *Telling on the Trout,* and writes of a fine large house near Stockbridge with flat lawn reaching to the river. The house has glass doors opening out to the grass less than twelve inches above the water, yet no freshets ever threaten to enter the house. Hewitt believed this condition was unique to the Hampshire chalkstreams, but on the Letort there was once a small fishing hut on concrete piers less than ten feet from the stream and about ten inches above the water. None of the Letort regulars can recall water rising under the fishing-hut floor.

Constant water temperatures are a major factor in Letort fishing. The midsummer temperatures are extremely cold when compared with other eastern trout streams. Early morning usually finds the water a chilly fifty degrees. During hot weather it warms steadily at about two degrees per hour, until it reaches a midafternoon peak of sixty-five.

The fish begin rising sporadically as the river reaches fifty-six degrees in later morning. Rises increase as the temperature increases, both in the number of fish and in the frequency of rises. Peak feeding begins with peak water temperatures, and the momentum of feeding activity continues until darkness reverses the temperature cycle.

The cold water both limits and benefits the aquatic fly hatches on the Letort. Only those species adapted to low temperatures and slow water are present, and they are limited to a few species that are relatively small in size. The constant volume of flow ensures their survival, while on other streams subject to extremes of temperature and water level, the fly hatches suffer badly. The limited number of aquatic species has a surprising result, too because it has focused the attention of the trout on the minute terrestrial insects found in the Letort meadows.

These two factors, the limited number of aquatic hatches and the importance of the tiny land insects, have had a major role in the Letort story. Letort regulars have been forced to solve the complexities of imitating minute aquatic and terrestrial flies. Like their predecessors on the Test, the Letort fishermen have mastered a difficult river and its selective trout. The importance of such terrestrial hatches throughout the season was relatively unknown, although writers like Ronalds and Halford and Moseley discussed them, until the unusual conditions on the Letort forced an unusually talented group of fishermen to perfect a complete terrestrial theory and technique of imitation for such insects.

Grasshoppers and flying ants have long been observed in

the trout diet, and many fishing writers have discussed their importance. Ronalds was famous for his *Fly-Fisher's Entomology,* which included caterpillars, beetles, ants, and leafhoppers among its imitative fly patterns. However, their importance throughout the season, rather than merely during peak seasons or mating flights, was never emphasized in past angling books. Ants are continuously on the water in great numbers as the season progresses, but their important place in the trout diet has been virtually ignored; and the daily role of the minuscule leafhopper, one of the major foods on meadow streams, was almost unknown.

Here is the source of the Letort legend. The evolution of workable terrestrial imitations is an angling breakthrough that makes the Fox-Marinaro studies on the Letort the modern equal of the Halford-Marryat collaboration that perfected dry-fly theory on the Test.

Modern terrestrial imitations are an angling event of near-legendary stature. The frustration of casting to terrestrial-smutting trout has been ended. Classic patterns for smutting fish were merely tiny conventional dry flies. Anglers mistakenly call them all midges. Yet such adult *Chironomus* midge imitations are consistently refused by selective trout when they are taking terrestrials, since the silhouette of conventional midge flies does not suggest the opaque shapes and light patterns made in the surface film by such insect forms as ants and leafhoppers and beetles.

The day of discovery is eloquently recorded in Marinaro's *Modern Dry-Fly Code,* which describes fishing the meadows with Charles Fox near the little fishing hut. There were no visible insects on the water, but the fish were busily working. Conventional methods had failed miserably in the past and were no better that afternoon. The riseforms were the familiar bulges so frustrating in the Letort meadows. Fox and Marinaro tried fish after fish, resting one and casting to another, exchanging helpless shrugs as they passed.

Marinaro writes that his frustration finally proved too much. He stopped fishing to study the current. Prone in the warm grass, Marinaro watched the slow current-pattern slide

54

hypnotically past. Some time elapsed in pleasant reverie before he was suddenly aware of minute insects on the water. He rubbed his eyes but they were really there: minuscule mayflies struggling with their diaphanous nymphal skins, tiny beetles like minute bubbles, ants awash in the surface film, and countless minutiae pinioned in the smooth current.

His mind stirred with excitement as he hurried toward the fishing hut. There he quickly fashioned a fine-mesh seine with sticks and mosquito netting. Its meshes were not long in the water before his suspicions were confirmed by the thin residue of tiny insects that collected at the waterline. There were mayflies with wings less than an eighth-inch in length and leafhoppers of minute dimensions in astonishing numbers.

It was the moment of discovery. Charlie Fox came downstream and examined the tiny insects. Both men searched their boxes for flies of proper color and size. Several good fish were quickly caught, and autopsies of stomach contents confirmed a diet of minute forms. The frustration of the bulge rises was over.

But modified conventional flies were often rejected in the days that followed. New patterns were clearly needed. Many experiments were tried before a workable fly-dressing formula was perfected. The basic concept was slow in coming, and the early attempts were less than fruitful. Beetle imitations are typical of the problems. Small coffee beans were tried first, filed and mounted on the hooks with cement like tiny bass bugs. They floated too low and landed too hard and the trout wanted none of them. Cork and balsa wood were no better. Clipped and folded deer-hair beetles were too water absorbent. Black sponge rubber worked sometimes, but tended to twist on the hooks and made it difficult to hook the fish. All worked fairly well on other streams, while the Letort fish remained skeptical.

The full shape and thickness of beetles was ultimately forgotten, and a fresh theory of fly dressing evolved. Silhouette and light pattern in the surface film were its essence. Marinaro used large jungle-cock eyes first. Their opacity was good and the fish came well to imitations with wings tied flat, but jungle-cock feathers were fragile and tended to split after a few trout were taken. They are now prohibited from entry into the United States and stocks are dwindling.

Ross Trimmer and I were sitting in the Turnaround Meadow one August afternoon. I was tying flies and noticed some pheasant-skin pieces in a hackle canister. There were a few dark greenish throat feathers on one fragment. We tried them instead of jungle-cock, soaking several feathers together with lacquer to get toughness and opacity. The lacquered feathers were trimmed to proper ovoid shape and tied flat over trimmed hackles. Success was remarkable and immediate. We tried them in the meadows above the trestle and took twenty-one fish. Such a score on the beetle-feeders was unbelievable.

Although the jungle-cock beetles often proved too fragile, the jungle-cock wing proved marvelously successful in another context. It is the key to imitating the ubiquitous leafhoppers with a remarkable series of patterns called Jassids. These diminutive flies are one of the great all-season solutions for difficult, dimpling trout. Much of the surface feeding in the hot low-water months of summer is concentrated on leafhoppers. Alfred Ronalds mentions leafhoppers in his *Fly-Fisher's Entomology,* but his imitations are poor for selective fish. Jassids have proved excellent, and their development will make Marinaro an angling legend wherever big midsummer browns feed quietly in flat water.

Both the ringneck-feathered beetle and the minute Jassid are proof of the same theory: that the fish cannot sense the thickness of small insects drifting above them, and that proper opacity and silhouette and light pattern in the surface film are the critical elements in successful terrestrial imitations.

Their success led the Letort regulars to reappraise their traditional mayfly patterns. Letort trout were refusing dry-fly imitations of the conventional style. Such flies have primarily evolved from the classic Halford formula, with wings and hackles at the hook eye. Body materials occupied the remaining hook shank. Wings were fashioned with fragile wing-quill or duck-breast feathers. Hackles and tail fibers support the fly weight in the surface film.

56

Halford chose his colors in the following manner: hackles suggested mayfly legs, wings imitated natural wing color and configuration, bodies simulated the sternite or belly-segment colors, and tail fibers were chosen to match the color and length of the setae.

Letort observations convinced Marinaro that two basic errors flawed the Halford system of imitation: that leg-color hackles distorted the percentages of overall color distribution and tended to obscure the all-important silhouette and color of the wing, and that the silhouette of the thorax structure ahead of both legs and wings had been forgotten entirely as a component of English fly-dressing configuration.

Experiments on the Letort confirmed that hackles should be chosen to reinforce wing color, ignoring the color of the legs, and that fly configuration should be changed to suggest the mayfly thorax silhouette. Although there were several preludes to such thinking in the writings of Burke and Harding and Dunne, it was the Letort school that perfected a fully workable thorax-fly theory.

The system is revolutionary: hackle-point wings and hackles were placed near the middle of the hook, and body material was used on both sides of the hackle, simulating both the abdomen and the thorax. The bodies were shortened proportionally, since the upward curving posture of mayfly bodies tends to foreshorten length when viewed from below. The thorax style is designed to float the fly on the hackle and body structure, making a light pattern of thorax, abdomen, and legs in the surface film. Tails were cocked upward, just as the mayflies hold their setae high. The thorax-style concept was thoroughly proved on the selective browns of the Letort, and has been adapted into daily practice.

Critics who argue that wings are unnecessary may be right on swift rivers, but they are wrong on smooth water like the Letort. The remarkable experiments that settled this argument among its regulars were conceived and performed. The regulars reasoned that wing-clipped natural mayflies might be floated over a hyper-selective trout that was rising steadily to the hatch. They were particularly interested in watching the reactions of the fish to wingless naturals. The experiment caught their imagination and was quickly tested on the stream.

The test subject was chosen with great care. There was a good brown so legendary for his choosiness that the regulars called him the Trout-without-a-Mouth, because most of them had gotten him to rise without hooking him. The line of drift that carried his food to his feeding position was precise. The little sulfur mayflies were hatching, and the current tongues came together above the fish to concentrate all the naturals in a single, weedy channel. The trout was rising methodically.

Naturals were carefully gathered. Their wings were scissor-clipped, and they were placed back on the water, alive and wriggling. The fully winged mayflies came down and were taken in sipping, confident rises. Thirty-seven wingless naturals were drifted over the trout and each was refused. The trout continued to take the winged naturals without hesitation. Letort regulars have not questioned the importance of wings since that afternoon.

Original experiments in fish culture were also tried. Letort regulars were among the first to use personal fish tags and fin-clipping to study the trout caught and released. These methods were used to keep track of the feeding and migratory behavior and growth characteristics of each fish they caught.

The early data seemed to indicate that three distinct strains were present in the Letort fish population: fish that were easily fooled and seldom survived the fishing pressures of early season, surface-feeding trout that proved difficult and selective, and fish that were never seen except by several skillful old-time bait fishermen who had special permission to frequent the river.

Certain handsomely colored fish of good proportions were taken regularly on dry flies. The regulars thought that such exceptional fish might breed a special strain of trout, with good configuration and a pronounced tendency to seek food at the surface of the stream.

They reasoned that such fish could be artificially isolated to breed together. The theory led to the next project: restoration of an old millrace in the Barnyard meadows for an isolated spawning channel. The millrace was carefully prepared. Sluices were constructed to control current speed over spawning beds. The beds were laid with carefully selected gravel. Cover was placed to provide shelter for the beds, and grilles were constructed to contain the isolated brood stock while letting their progeny escape back into the Letort.

Highway construction ended the millrace experiments before conclusive results could be observed, but all agreed that a noticeable increase in free-rising trout had been achieved. Frequent rises were also recorded earlier in the day than before, and the selective-breeding experiment appeared successful to the regulars on the river.

Consistent Letort water temperatures and volumes of flow and ice-free winters resulted in another experiment: the buildup theory of fish stocking. The regulars believed that fingerlings would have a better rate of survival when planted in the headwaters of a limestone stream than on other waters. Fingerling hatchery trout commonly sustain nearly 100 percent mortality from a combination of birds, high temperature, predator fish, low water, anchor ice, collapsing snowbanks, and other natural causes. Several experiments were tried. One thousand fingerling browns from three to four inches were planted in the springhead meadows. Their ventral fins were clipped to mark them, and the stocking was made in November. The baby trout began to show themselves in April. They were two miles downstream and averaged six inches in length. These fin-clipped fish were present along the entire stream in September. Several were taken on the last evening of the season, and had reached twelve inches in ten months.

The wild trout of the Letort are legendary for their choosiness. The catalogue of their basic riseforms is a mixture of chagrin mixed with humor: the simple rise, which has the fish coming back under the fly to take it quietly; the compound rise, which follows several moments of nervous inspection; and the complex rise, which passes through both simple and compound stages and ends in a rapier-quick rise after several feet of vacillating inspection and refusal. The three-rise catalogue of fish behavior is recorded in *Modern Dry-Fly Code,* and has become a standard part of Letort dialogue and practice. Several years have passed since the three-rise pattern was described and diagrammed. My own experience on the Letort leads me to add another exasperating riseform common to its trout: the compound-complex rise, which proceeds through the entire nerve-shattering sequence and ends in complete rejection.

My Letort odysseys follow the typical pattern of limestone addiction. The fishing intrigued me first because of the writing born on its waters. The first pilgrimage was made to satisfy my curiosity and pay homage to the river and its circle of fishermen.

The sulfur mayflies were hatching on that first trip and my second trip introduced me to the subtle orgy of the Japanese beetles. The third occurred early in the late summer bacchanalia of the grasshoppers. Letort regulars still laugh about that summer: not wanting to purchase a full-season license on the first trip, I took a tourist permit. The pull of the river proved so strong that I finished that summer with a total of seven five-day tourist buttons on my fishing jacket.

The limestone lessons of that summer have helped my strategy and technique on many rivers, and the difficult trout of the Letort have been fascinating tutors for many years. Their lessons have taught me much, and might best be characterized in describing two hot afternoons when I raised my biggest Letort browns.

The first happened in beetle season. Japanese beetles were clustered on the wild grapevines and rosebushes like crawling bronze-colored berries. Beetles droned like bees in the sycamores. They were active at midday, flying across the stream and getting into the water, and the trout were getting many of them.

Below the limestone quarries, the current was divided into two deep channels in the watercress. The larger channel was on the near side of the stream, where the current flowed over gravel and marl. The smaller channel was across the stream, little more than twelve inches wide and bordered by cress and beds of elodea. It was sheltered by wild grapevines. The heat was oppressive and I stopped to rest.

Wetting my face and neck felt good, and sitting in the grass was pleasant. My lassitude was broken by a quiet, sucking rise upstream. The riseform was not visible as I searched the narrow channel for its disturbance. The sound came again. There was no disturbance again, but my eyes were ready as the fish came up a third time along the cress. The rise was gentle. It bulged out imperceptibly against the current and its afterrise was quickly absorbed against the weeds. The rises were small, but the sound spelled a heavy trout, and it was feeding steadily. Beetles were active in the vines above its station and it seemed likely they were getting into its line of drift.

There were plenty of beetle imitations in my fly box and I waded stealthily into position. The thick beds of elodea cushioned the waves of my cautious chest-deep wading. The fish continued to rise. Checking the leader for wind knots, I tied a beetle to the tippet. Then I waited and watched several minutes before trying the fish. The leader was all right, the beetle was oiled with silicone, and I was ready.

The trout came up again, and the cast dropped nicely above his feeding station against the cress. The beetle came down flat and dark on the water. It flirted with the weeds and a shadowlike bulk appeared and evaporated under the fly. The fish had inspected my beetle and rejected it. My leader tippet was reduced a diameter to .0047. The fly dropped softly and drifted back along the cress. It disappeared in a quiet rise. The fish bolted along the watercress channel and wallowed angrily at the surface. Then it jumped twice, stitching the leader neatly through the weeds on both sides of the channel, and was quickly gone.

Four pounds, I estimated unhappily.

This was a typical Letort tragicomedy, since heavy trout on gossamer leaders are difficult to handle in weeds, but the real challenge and accomplishment lay in getting such a trout to rise in the first place. Since that hot afternoon the channel patterns have changed, and no one has seen that particular fish again.

Things went better with the second trout. It was a windy afternoon in August, and the water meadows were filled with ducks from the barnyard. Ross Trimmer had lost a good fish below Otto's Meadow and we went to try it. The trout occupied a deep hole under a brush-pile corner. Ross herded the tame ducks away from the place and we waited. Twenty minutes passed before a quiet rise bulged out from the brush. We waited until the feeding rhythm was finally steady.

Finally, I dropped my grasshopper above the brushy corner and watched it drift over the trout. The rise was splashily audible and I struck gently. The fish jumped and bored deep under the brush. Ross made pungent comments and kept the ducks away and stained the backwater with tobacco while I forced the trout away from deadfalls and weeds. We were lucky. It was a fat nineteen-inch female, and we released the handsome henfish to spawn again that fall.

Letort regulars are philosophical about their little river and seem almost unaware of their own legendary exploits. They gather to celebrate the closing of each fishing season under the buttonwoods. There is always a picnic table heavy with ham and fresh baked bread and beer, and the regulars crouch around the fire telling and retelling the Letort stories that are becoming legends.

There are many such stories. The talk goes on into the darkness, and the river is black beyond the firelight. There is good-natured laughter about the fishless sessions Hewitt experienced on his several Letort visits, and speculation about the sinister monster-fish that engulfed Marinaro's grasshopper and fought him for hours while helpless friends offered fruitless advice. There was the fifteen-pound brown captured in the mill dam that is drained now, and the eight-and-a-half-pounder taken with a dry fly in the upper meadows. The regulars laugh about the free-rising rainbow where newcomers were led for frustration with their Cahills and Coachmen, and the supercilious Trout-without-a-Mouth that once lived in the Barnyard.

There is regret for those who will never fish the little river again, and regret for the wasteful pollution that stains the entire watershed and threatens to erase it forever. The pollution is both an enigma and a tragedy. The once-classic lower mileage has long been polluted in spite of assurances from the factories and a new sewage treatment plant at Carlisle. The river below its final effluent remains unfit for trout. Septic tanks along the entire watershed have polluted the subterranean springs and aquifers with detergents, and the thoughtless use of fertilizers had threatened to choke the stream with weeds. There is tragedy in the dead mileage below the town and its knitting mills, and in the continuing denigration of the richest trout stream in America. Letort fishing could equal the great British chalkstreams if its entire length were rehabilitated and protected in the future, since the brief mileage from its headwater springs to the warmer Conodiguinet has incredible capacity to support large numbers of trout and heavy fly hatches. The continuing loss of such a unique fishery would be a tragedy.

Firelight flickers on the regulars, and they dream of restoring the river. There is speculation about the fame of its past and the sporting potential of its future if proper steps are taken. Carlisle could become a midsummer mecca for light tackle and minute flies.

There is talk of transplanting fly species and the nonmigratory strain of rainbows from Falling Spring Run. Talk always turns to the slow decimation of other limestone waters. There is laughter as someone suggests that rosebushes and grapevines should be planted instead of trout to attract more Japanese beetles. The fire dies slowly, there are only scraps of talk as the men sit looking into the coals, and then finally the talk dies too. Now there is only the soft whisper of the river under its buttonwoods. Water is spilled on the ashes of the fire. The season is finally over and the regulars file up the meadow path to leave. There is always some sadness that last summer evening along the Letort.

See you in the spring! somebody is saying. *See you in the spring when the sulfurs are back!*

The little river is alone for another year. The moon is high and there is mist rising from the current, and the cool September night stirs in the Cumberland Valley. It will not be long until there are yellow leaves sailboating on the surface of the river, and later its black currents will flow through the ice-covered reeds.

Some believe the old-time limestone fishermen are on the river again that last evening, working their ring-and-keeper rods of greenheart and hickory, and complaining about fewer brook trout. The grass is full of ghosts in the meadows. Their spectral lines whisper through the rising mist and fall without disturbing the moon-bright current. Hewitt and LaBranche are still arguing in the Barnyard meadows, while the specter trout of the Letort continue to rise softly and ignore their collective fame.

[1961]

4

A Portrait of
the Pere Marquette

*"PM," the fishermen call it these days. "We're going up
for steelhead in the PM." I've heard those words often
in recent years when visiting Chicago-area fishermen
or those around Cleveland or Detroit. Michigan's Pere
Marquette has become so famous for its steelhead
fishing that it's the only river I know that's recognized
all over America just by its initials.*

*I smile, too, when I hear "PM," thinking of an
absurdly cold winter morning on the Clay Banks
stretch when the line guides on my fly rod kept clog-
ging up with ice as I stood shivering in a riffle. The
broad green back and pink side of an immense steelhead erased all thoughts of cold when the fish chased
a fly almost to my feet. It was a fish I never did catch,
but the memory is so vivid that I can to this day count
the fish's spots.*

*This and succeeding essays may help to dispel the
reputation Schwiebert has in some quarters as only
an Eastern fisherman. As you'll see here, most of his
early fly fishing was done in Michigan (as well as
summers in Colorado); a time when as a young man*

he was meeting and learning from such now-departed greats as rodmaker Paul Young and fly tier Bill Blades.

Owls are often considered birds of ill omen and sorcery, and their cries have fascinated me since boyhood, particularly the soft, almost plaintive trilling of screech owls. Sometimes in our last moments before sleep, burrowed warmly into our sleeping bags and bedrolls, it was soothing to hear them calling in the Michigan woods. Those early memories of campsites along the Pere Marquette are filled with owls and whippoorwills in the jackpine benches beyond Waddell's Riffle and the Clay Banks, melancholy duets in the summer nights, mixed with the river sounds in the cedar deadfalls.

Some people believe that owls can foretell a death in the family, Ralph Noble once told me when we were fishing his water on the upper Pere Marquette, *but I really like hearing them!*

I've never seen one, I said.

Owls are blind during the daytime. Noble repeated the common myths. *Owls hunt at night and hibernate during the day.*

Can they see in the dark? I asked.

Sure can! He grinned.

Like most boys in those summers, I found my first owl high in the trusswork of my grandfather's barn, and I believed the myths and superstitions about owls. We listened to their calling with fascination and delicate shivers of fear.

It was much later that I learned of their acute hearing and the ability to hunt their prey almost entirely by its sounds. Their eyes have remarkable densities of light-sensitive rods and color-receiving cones, their retinal proteins are triggered by minute electrical charges. Sometimes I discovered owls hunting in daylight, too, and flushed them from their thickets of cedars and hemlocks, but it was many years before I learned about the delicate eyelid membranes that shield an owl's sensitive eyes from too much light.

Their comic dish-shaped faces are something more, sculptured like sophisticated parabolic microphones, the feathers adjusting to focus the sounds of a field mouse or vole scuttling in the leaves. Their ears are surprisingly large, with right and left aural passages structured differently in size and shape, sharpening the binaural intensity of their hearing.

Owls swallow their prey whole. Once their digestive fluids have worked, the relatively indigestible bones, feathers, and fur that remain are neatly compacted into egg-size pellets and coughed up. Since a hunting owl retreats with its prey to a single feasting tree and sits there half sleeping while it digests its kill, hundreds of regurgitated leavings are often collected under a favorite limb. There was a dense copse of cedars above the Deer Lick on the Pere Marquette where I once sought shelter from a storm and found a feasting tree.

My God! I thought when I discovered its funeral mound of tiny skeletons and skulls. *It's an owl's feeding thicket, and those are the remains of hundreds of frogs and mice and birds!*

It was an eerie cache that remains stubbornly in the memory, along with the April grouse and red-winged blackbirds and whippoorwills that are similar echoes of the Pere Marquette.

Its character shaped my fishing skills in those boyhood summers, and we made several pilgrimages to Baldwin over the years. Baldwin has changed little from the sleepy Michigan county seat we knew then, except for its supermarkets and bowling alley, and it still has a tackle shop that sells more worms and bow-hunting equipment and minnows than serious fishing gear.

Baldwin had a surprising roster of trout-fishing characters before the Second World War. Some were refugees from its lumber-camp origins, while others found it a backwater that changed little in the bitter years of the Great Depression.

Some of these fishermen would simply disappear into the woods when we encountered them on the stream, rather than risk a conversation. The hard times had made some misanthropic and bitter, while others seemed simply to prefer river things to people. Their sole intercourse with the world of commerce had been reduced to cutting cordwood or trapping in the cedar swamps for cash. There were always stories of whisky stills in the cedar thickets too, although I was too young to sample their wares. The river people fished and hunted deer for food. Filling out a deer permit was sometimes critical in making it through the year, and there are still men in the Michigan jackpine country who survive on fish and game. Jacklighting deer was common in the cutover clearings along the county roads, and although it was illegal, the wardens did little to enforce the law.

These are pretty hard times, my father explained in our camp on the Little South, *and jacklighting a few deer is probably better than standing in the bread lines around Detroit.*

When the river people fished, they often fished at night with huge, crudely dressed bucktails and streamers on heavy tackle, leaving the daylight hours to the wealthy fishermen who were doctors or managed automobile factories around River Rouge or owned furniture plants at Grand Rapids.

Perhaps the best-known character was Harry Duffing, the colorful barber who tied trout flies in his simple shop at Baldwin when haircut customers were scarce. Duffing created the first fly pattern to imitate the big *Hexagenia* mayflies the old-timers stubbornly call the Michigan caddis hatch. His dressing used long-shank hooks and superb furnace hackles from tightly bound bunches strung in Hong Kong, with upright goose-quill sections tied in the elegant double-wing British style. Several slender pheasant fibers imitated the tails of these nocturnal flies, and the old barber baptized them in a solution of cleaning fluid and shaved paraffin. It was several summers of country-style haircuts and fishing talk before Duffing took me behind the curtains to see his workbench and watch him dress one of his famous patterns at a workbench littered with goose quills and hackles and dark gray yarn.

Last season we were sitting in the bar at Government Lake, talking about these nocturnal mayflies, when one of the old-timers on the Pere Marquette lost his patience. *Troublemakers!* the old man exploded. *You newfangled fishermen are troublemakers!*

How's that? I parried his anger.

It's all this mayfly talk about our caddis hatch! He fulminated, and finished his beer. *Caddis is goddamn caddis!*

I'm sorry, I said gently, *but they're mayflies.*

Don't care what you newfangled boys tell us! Old myths about owls and mayflies die hard. *They're goddamn caddisflies!*

No matter what entomology tells us?

Troublemakers! he grumbled.

The first time I fished the Pere Marquette country, it was not on the river itself, but on the brushy little Baldwin that rises in the cedar swamps above the village. Its narrow, willow-hung currents were difficult to fish, and I spent a lot of time retrieving my flies from the foliage in those early years. Its flow was surprisingly strong the first year, when I was fishing in rented waders that accordioned comically along both legs, but the Pere Marquette itself seemed too formidable for my boyhood wading skills.

My first experience on the river was at Bowman's Bridge. It is strange how some things persist in the memory, because I remember little about our fishing that morning, although other things are almost like yesterday in my mind. My most disturbing echo is the mixture of fascination and horror I felt while I watched a fat water snake stalking a trout from the tangled logs below the bridge.

Its strategy was a simple lesson in cunning and stealth. The snake worked patiently over the fallen cedars, sliding down the sun-bleached bark and waiting motionless when the trout seemed nervous. Each time, the trout soon forgot its apprehension and drifted back to lie lazily against the logs. It seemed to like the currents and eddies where the river welled up between two deadfalls downstream.

Suddenly the snake struck with a splash, seizing the trout's entire head with its jaws. The fish seemed helpless in its grasp, but it threshed with such panic that the snake was pulled into the river too. Writhing and rolling awkwardly, the snake and its prey were carried through the swift bend until they were lost in the riffles downstream. It was a grisly episode I have never forgotten.

The Pere Marquette is already a strong little river when it reaches Bowman's Bridge, having received the cold flowages of its three upper tributaries. Its Little South and Middle branches, like the swift little Baldwin, are well-known trout fisheries themselves. The Pere Marquette is deceptively smooth-flowing, but strong enough to have a sobering effect on the inexperienced wader. Several miles downstream, the sluggish Big South adds its swamp-dark currents to make the Pere Marquette itself a little frightening.

Twice in my boyhood I fished the lower river as far downstream as Barothy's and Timber Creek and Walhalla, searching for the first of the early-summer *Hexagenia* flies. The river seemed almost sullen and threatening there, in spite of its smooth bottom, its currents strong and smooth in the darkness. The hatches failed to come on those big-river evenings, and several times I almost lost my footing in the chest-deep water, windmilling my feet precariously along the bottom gravel while the current forced me downstream.

Once I was nearly carried into a deep tea-colored horseshoe near Walhalla Bridge, where the current dropped off swiftly between the tree-lined banks and willows. Fighting the loose sand with churning legs, I finally regained the firm gravel upstream. My legs were shaking when I reached the footpath, and I never fished there again.

The Pere Marquette is a happier place in its headwaters. Its beginnings lie in bogs and cedar thickets and jackpine lakes in the sandy moraines between Baldwin and Big Rapids. Its icy little Middle Branch rises in the grouse ridges that lie near Reed City, flowing toward its junction with the tea-colored Little South. Several times I explored its brushy mileage above the Forks Pool, until its marshy reaches became too deep for wading. Twice I fished its headwaters near Idlewild, taking limits of fat natives with a small wet fly fished patiently like a worm in the holes under the willows.

The Little South Branch of the Pere Marquette is completely different in character. Its bottom mileage above the Forks Pool is still and quiet-flowing under its dense canopy of trees. The Middle Branch is quite swift and clear, while the somber Little South is dark and mysterious, its color leached through the bogs and marshy ponds in its secret headwaters. We often camped along the Little South in those summers after the Second World War, in a time when the only cottages on the lower river were several miles upstream from the Forks Pool, near the county bridge on the Star Lake road. The stream had excellent early hatches in those years, and its

placid currents and sheltering trees made it a difficult class-
room for the neophyte.

Sometimes we traveled upstream to fish the swift mile
above the Powers Bridge with Gerry Queen, a dedicated fisherman from Detroit who often fished the Pere Marquette from
Ivan's Lodge. Queen loved its simple screen-porch cottages
because of their proximity to the Little South, and he knew its
upper reaches better than anyone who fished the river in those
years. Queen had a sense of elegance too, and refused to fish
anything but his straw-colored British silk lines, Hardy silk-
worm-gut leaders, and a remarkable collection of fine Dickerson dry-fly rods. Queen is gone now, and no longer fishes that
water on the Little South, but I remember my feelings of
pride and excitement when he asked me to make his flies,
using nothing but natural Andalusian dun hackles, carefully
dubbed bodies of fur spun between my fingers on British
working silk, and lemon woodduck feathers.

It was downstream from the Forks Pool, under the high
hardwood moraine at Noble's Lodge, that I took my first
fly-caught trout. The Pere Marquette is surprisingly large
there, in its sweeping butter-yellow bends, and I fought its
currents every summer.

My first fly-caught trout took a wet Cahill, with a technique that was perilously close to worm-fishing, since my line
was merely trailing downstream in the current. The fish
barely measured ten inches, but in that boyhood summer it
seemed like a sailfish. It had been lying under the alders,
followed the little Cahill into the sunlight, and had hooked
itself. Such episodes are familiar to any trout fisherman, but
that trout ended several years of fishing worms and grasshoppers, and the praise of my father and his fishing cronies was
a rich climax to countless hours of apprenticeship.

That's a fine trout in your basket, they said.

We celebrated its capture on the Little South, and with
that ten-inch trout in my creel, it seemed that I had finally
been permitted to enter their world. The memorabilia of that
world are familiar still, and I savor them happily after thirty-
odd years.

There were fishing coats with woodcock feathers in their
bellows pockets from bird shooting, pockets stained with

paraffin and citronella, the soft wind in the pines and cedars, the rhythms of summer rain on canvas tenting, their faces in the firelight, silkworm leaders coiled and soaking between glycerin pads, creels lined with mint and freshly picked ferns, jackets bulging with fine English pipes and fishing gadgets and tobacco, bamboo rods bright with varnish and intricate silk wrappings, coffee brewed over a gravel-bar cookfire, and sour-mash whiskey from a stream-washed cup.

Their world of flies and fishing talk and hatches became mine that morning in late August, and we celebrated with my first cup of coffee, while my father and his friends toasted my minor triumph with a stronger catalyst.

The Little South was also the setting for a summer morning when we found some bait fishermen on the water below our campsite. It was our first morning on the river that trip, and there was a man in torn working clothes fishing a nightcrawler just below our tent. His two sons were fishing worms under the willows downstream.

Who's that? my father asked.

Their battered Plymouth was parked near the bridge on the Middle Branch. *Damn!* I said. *They're fishing our water!*

Maybe we can Tom Sawyer them, my father suggested.

You really think so? I grinned and my father laughed softly. *Talk them into fishing someplace else?*

Let's give it a try, my father said.

We walked downstream along the county road to where they were fishing. *Had any luck this morning?* we asked.

Nothing! the man replied.

It's not good worm-fishing water, my father said.

No? The fisherman seemed puzzled.

You have to stand right over the trout to fish bait here, my father explained truthfully. *It spooks the fish.*

That right? He reeled in his nightcrawler.

It's pretty good dry-fly water, my father continued, *but there's better worm fishing over at Baldwin.*

Where over at Baldwin? The fisherman waved to his boys.

Try the fish-hatchery stretch, I suggested. *There's a deep cement channel between the spillways.*

That's right! my father confirmed.

Those trout are used to people there, I continued, *and it's got some really big browns!* Our story was partly true, because we had seen such trout ourselves, and once I hooked a heavy fish in the channel that fought me more than an hour before it shook free.

We're much obliged, the man said.

Their old Plymouth rattled north into Baldwin. *It worked!* We grinned guiltily and waved. *They're going!*

It was a fine dry-fly morning. There was a sporadic hatch of caddisflies, and the trout were rising well. We both took several good fish and were fishing the still, tree-sheltered flats below our tent when a car stopped beside the river. It was the man and his sons in their battered Plymouth.

Hey mister! yelled the boys.

Their father circled back to the trunk. *Sure want to thank you folks!* He grinned. *Can't thank you enough!*

My father looked at me strangely, and we stood there under the county road, with the smooth current sliding past our waders. *What do you think they're doing back?* I asked.

You think they're serious? my father whispered.

The young workman opened his trunk. *Yessir!* He reached inside and dragged out a thirty-inch brown. *Caught this beautiful eight-pounder right under the spillway where you told us!*

Can't thank you enough! his boys shouted.

Such memories are richly engraved in my mind, in a mixture of spring mornings bright with cowslips and pulpit flowers and violets in the sheltered places, and nights that were almost too cold for our summer sleeping bags. Twice in those boyhood years it snowed on our opening weekends, with popcorn-size flakes that shrouded the river, and our tent sites looked like deer camps.

June weather was usually better; the forests were thick with bright young leaves and the spring spates had passed. Thunderstorms could turn the rivers milky, but in early summer their currents usually flowed clear and smooth, winding past the sandy timber-covered hills toward Lake Michigan. Columbines and summer buttercups were blooming, and in

73

the August grasshopper season that followed, the abandoned pastures were filled with gentians and pyeweed. It was a placid time of trout-fishing summers that passed happily.

The Pere Marquette itself is a beautiful stream, cold and serpentine and swift in its hundred-mile journey toward Ludington, and its fishing taught me much in those early years.

The history of the river is surprisingly old. Its beginnings lie during French sovereignty in the old Northwest Territories, with the subsequent arrival of Jacques Marquette in 1666. The young priest left Quebec to spend two years with the mission at Trois Rivières, studying the aboriginal languages of the Great Lakes wilderness. Marquette then traveled inland to the Ottawa mission at Sault Sainte Marie, with the remote wilderness outpost farther west at Chequamegon Bay included in his sprawling parish.

Several clashes with marauding Sioux later forced Marquette and his parishioners from Chequamegon to seek refuge at Fort Michilimackinac, across the windswept straits that separate Michigan, and their mission was relocated to Saint Ignace.

Voyageurs and fur trappers who stopped there told Marquette exciting stories of a gargantuan south-flowing river farther west, and that the plains tribes who had told them about the river called it the Father of Waters. Marquette and his friends subsequently convinced the powerful Comte de Frontenac to dispatch him with the expedition of Louis Joliet, and left to explore the Mississippi.

Joliet had assembled a party of skilled voyageurs, including a trapper who had accompanied Étienne Brule into the Michigan wilderness in 1618. The expedition embarked in three freight canoes along the rocky shoreline on Lake Michigan in the spring of 1673, and followed its high cliffs south until they reached Green Bay and its sheltering peninsula.

The party decided to travel inland there, following the Winnebago deep into its Wisconsin forests. Portaging from the somber Butte des Morts country into the headwaters of the Fox, the expedition worked its way downstream to its junction with the Wisconsin watershed, thirty-odd miles below the Wisconsin Dells. Joliet and Marquette left their echoes in the Wisconsin wilderness, giving beautiful names to both rivers and places, like Fond du Lac and Prairie du Chien.

Joliet led his men down the Wisconsin to its junction with the Mississippi below Prairie du Chien, stopping to make an encampment to rest and gather provisions and hunt before traveling farther. The party left still more French echoes in places like Dubuque and La Grange and Cape Girardeau, following the immense Father of Waters past its union with both the Ohio and the Missouri.

The expedition finally reached the mouth of the Arkansas, more than a hundred miles downstream from the future site of Memphis, and Joliet and Marquette were convinced that their gargantuan discovery was unmistakably the Mississippi, the sluggish giant that reached the Gulf of Mexico near the French outposts at Mobile and Biloxi. Marquette offered a simple mass of thanksgiving in the flood bottoms of the Arkansas there, and Joliet ordered the party back on its difficult journey to Saint Ignace.

Their company pushed hard since it was already late summer, and the nights carried a chill prelude to the coming autumn. Joliet left the river beyond Saint Louis, crossing the rich wheatgrass prairies that bordered the Illinois. Its quiet sloughs and backwaters led them across these frontier heartlands until they reached the relatively short portage to the marshy flowages of the Chicago. Joliet and his voyageurs cheered excitedly when they finally heard the surf pounding the beaches of Lake Michigan.

Joliet and Marquette had successfully traversed two completely unexplored water routes through the American wilderness, linking their colonies at Quebec and the Gulf of Mexico. The untrammeled continent had surrendered its first secrets, and the exhausted Joliet party finally crossed the Straits of Mackinac to their mission at Saint Ignace, just ahead of the first autumn storms.

Marquette remained there, both to recuperate from the arduous expedition and to minister to his neglected parish, while completing the journals started during his travels. His

75

accounts were subsequently published in the famous *Recueil des Voyages,* which Thevenot assembled at Quebec in 1681. It was fortunate that Marquette had meticulously recorded his observations of their journey, since the Joliet logs were lost when his freight canoe capsized in the LaChine rapids, before his party reached Quebec.

The memories of the wilderness odyssey echoed stubbornly in the thoughts of Marquette; such wilderness has its secret melodies once they are heard. The frontier priest brooded about his travels for several months before petitioning his superiors at Quebec, seeking permission to build another mission at Chicago.

Marquette was granted that permission in 1675, and impatiently waited for winter to pass, thinking about the tribes that inhabited the fertile prairies of Illinois. His impatience smoldered through the February storms and the early thawing winds that cleared the ice from the sullen waters of the straits. Marquette could wait no longer and started his party south in the early spring. The weather was still bitter and raw, and the cold lake was only partly ice free. It remained unusually cold that April, and the difficult work of building the mission in its harsh winds would prove tragic.

Marquette soon fell desperately ill, and his party ultimately feared for his life. Lacking medical supplies and skills at their outpost, his voyageurs soon elected to travel back to Saint Ignace, where Marquette might find better help.

The party decided to travel the eastern shore of Lake Michigan, thinking it was the shorter alternative, but it proved a terrible mistake. The eastern beaches of the lake are steep, carved by the constant surf and their massive dunes sculptured by the prevailing winds, and it was a route that would prove a ship's graveyard in later centuries. It soon proved impossible in freight canoes.

The spring weather was still bitter and foul, and its fierce winds often forced the voyageurs to abandon the angry waters of the lake and portage laboriously with their fallen priest along the beaches. Their progress was painfully slow, yet they had traveled more than halfway to Fort Michilimackinac when Marquette's frail health collapsed, and the priest died at the mouth of the Pere Marquette.

The river became my boyhood tutor, and it taught me about selective trout before I was twelve. It was on its headwaters that I first discovered that my father's collection of flies was not enough, that his boxes of elegant Adams spentwings and Corey calftails and Coachmen did not always catch fish. Earlier generations of trout fishermen had been spoiled by their easy sport, and when a fish refused their flies, they simply moved on to find a trout that was less picky. The trout seemed increasingly particular in my boyhood years, but I remember one morning that finally convinced me that selective feeding was a critical factor in trout fishing.

It was a hatch of small *Ephemerella* flies that forced me to stop fishing in defeat, and to collect the last of the emerging duns to discover why the trout had refused my flies. The current had literally been alive with the tiny Blue-winged Olives, and the trout took them greedily for almost an hour.

The fish refused everything in my fly boxes, and when I returned to our campsite with specimens of the hatching flies, their bright olive bodies were a problem. I rummaged through my fly-tying materials in the tent, but the only solution I could find to imitate their body chroma was a frayed green thread on my sleeping bag.

It'll have to do! I thought.

Several flies were tied using the specimen bottle of olive-bodied mayflies as the pattern, with dark-blue dun hackles and wings on sixteen Allcock hooks. It was a morning hatch, and the next day I was waiting after breakfast in the gravelly bend below the Forks Pool. The flies did not appear until almost eleven o'clock, perhaps because the night had been quite cold, and it took longer for the morning sun to warm the river. The dark blue-winged sailboats suddenly appeared on the water, and the quiet current came alive with rising trout. My roughly dressed imitations, with the olive cotton thread scavenged from my frayed sleeping bag, took several good fish while it lasted.

It fooled them! I thought with satisfaction, and it had been an important lesson in subtle variations in color, particularly on trout that see a steady parade of fishermen.

There was another afternoon on the Pere Marquette, in

the swift riffles a half mile above Noble's cottages, that compounded the earlier lessons of selectivity. There was a fine
hatch of pale sulfur-colored mayflies, which the trout took
greedily in the late afternoon, and then stopped when the
activity ebbed. I was wading slowly back to our campsite,
having failed because my flies lacked the proper pale ginger
hackles, and I was discouraged. Some really good trout had
been rising during the peak of the hatch, but they had rejected every pattern I tried. I had covered fifty yards of shallows when the riffles upstream came alive with a mating
swarm of mayflies. Rising and falling rhythmically over the
riffle, these spinners were carrying their butter-yellow egg
sacs, and when their dance was finished, the females started
laying their eggs in the swift current. The fish came upstream
from the deep pool below when the riffle rainbows started
rising, and the trout literally went crazy in an orgy of feeding,
while I frantically searched my fly boxes for imitations.

Lady Beaverkill! I thought suddenly. *It's too dark to imitate the naturals properly—but the chenille egg sac might
work!*

The flies worked well enough, particularly when I
dropped their yellow chenille sacs quickly over a rising trout,
and the fish rose before it took the time to inspect the fly.

It was a ruse that worked almost every evening for a
week, and I easily filled my basket with good fish. Fifteen-
trout limits were still permitted in those years, and my creel
of browns and rainbows often weighed almost ten pounds.
Thirty-odd years later I am ashamed of those trout-filled summers, and the wanton baskets of fish we killed without thinking about the future.

There are memories of big trout too. Our first was a large
brown we discovered working above our campsite when we
returned one night from fishing the lower river. We had
hiked in from the Clay Banks, hoping to find a mating swarm
of big *Hexagenia* flies below the Whirlpool. There was no
activity there that night, but with an irony typical of trout
fishing, we found the echoes of a hatch on our tent when we
came back. Its dark canvas was covered with freshly hatched
*Hexagenia*s that had been attracted to the Coleman lantern

we had left burning. My flashlight pinpointed a mating swarm over the shallows upstream from our campsite bend, but the current was quiet.

There's nothing working! I studied the river with the flashlight. *You'd think the trout would be working!*

They've probably got indigestion, my father said.

You mean they stuffed themselves on the earlier hatch? I grinned in the darkness. *And they won't take those spinners?*

Something like that, he nodded.

We stripped down our tackle and settled into our sleeping bags, but once our camp lantern was extinguished, there was an owl calling softly and the trout had started to rise. Their feeding was tentative at first, and then we were startled by a heavy splash.

What the hell was that? I whispered.

I'm not sure, my father muttered sleepily when another spectacular splash interrupted him. *You think it's a fish?*

Some fish! I unzipped my sleeping bag.

We crawled carefully out through the tent flap, where the faint coals of our campfire still glowed, and listened to the river sounds. The trout rose greedily against the logjam behind our tent. *We were wrong about the fish!* my father whispered softly. *Some of them were still waiting for dessert!*

It was obviously a large brown trout working greedily after the smaller fish had stopped feeding, and the mating spinners had probably started falling into the current after their egg laying was completed. The fish had perhaps been interrupted when we returned to camp, and our headlights disturbed its gluttony. But once we had started to sleep, the fish drifted back out to feed.

You try him! I suggested to my father. *I'm afraid to wade that water in the dark!*

While I crouched in the willows, he crossed the current below our campsite and worked back upstream into casting position. The big trout was still rising. My father started casting, and I could hear his rod working in the darkness. When his casting sounds stopped, there was a wild splash, and his reel protested shrilly.

He's hooked? I shouted.

79

The reel rattled harshly as the strong fish probed angrily under the fallen cedars. *It's more like he's hooked me!* My father laughed in the darkness. *He's like a rhinoceros!*

Hold on! I yelled excitedly.

The trout writhed deep under the logjam, raking the leader along the snags, but the tippet held. Finally my father forced the fish back into open water, worked it downstream to net it in the darkness and waded toward our tent in the flashlight beam. Its spotted bulk looked almost frightening in its shining meshes, with the bushy *Hexagenia* imitation in its hook-billed jaws, and it measured twenty inches.

That's some fish! I whispered in awe.

It was several years before I took a trout that large on the Pere Marquette, although we often saw such big fish in the river. Once I frightened a huge brown from its hiding place under a fallen cedar that completely blocked the river below Noble's cottages, its bright, dime-size spots clearly visible as it bolted past me.

My father discovered a monster fish in the Forks Pool one morning in early summer, and it was large enough to startle him momentarily. Later that season there was a twelve-pound brown taken there at night with a big streamer, and my father is still convinced after forty-five years that he saw the fish that morning.

It looked like Moby Dick! He shook his head in awe.

Another time early in the season, when we were fishing downstream on the Whinnery Riffle, I was working a polar-bear bucktail through a patient series of cross-stream casts. There was suddenly an immense swirl in the current, and a big rainbow rolled up and engulfed the teasing bucktail. It seemed almost frightening, somber and darkly sepulchral after its spawning, with its sides and gill-covers still bright scarlet. The fish was a recently spawned kelt drifting back from its egg laying in the headwaters.

Damn! I thought wildly. *It's really strong!*

The struggle did not last, and my reel simply foundered under the stress, failing to handle the first head-shaking run downstream. Its death rattle was a shattered drag spring, but it probably lacked the spool capacity to fight such a trout. The great fish stopped under a cedar logjam, and the free-spooling reel was a hopeless tangle. The fish did not need another heart-stopping run to end the fight, because it simply forced under the trees and broke off.

It's gone! I groaned.

Such Pere Marquette rainbows come from the first planting of steelhead fingerlings on the river in 1885, although many fishermen seem to think these winter-run fish were part of the fisheries programs that introduced Pacific salmon into the Great Lakes.

The first steelhead were stocked from the old federal hatchery at Northville. Since our pioneers in fish culture had carelessly mixed our original landlocked and sea-run strains of rainbow in their breeding experiments, the first Michigan steelhead were not intentionally planted in the Pere Marquette watershed. Hatchery managers simply called all of these red-striped fish California trout, and the Northville stocking party did not know it was planting sea-run strains.

Steelhead fingerlings were commonly propagated in those years, because the strain was vigorous and displayed rapid growth at smolting size. Our fine landlocked subspecies, like the McCloud strain and the richly spotted Kern rainbows from California, were crossbred with steelhead late in the nineteenth century. Our existing hatchery strains of rainbows are largely such genetic mixtures, and many include obvious fingerprints of cutthroat blood.

The first consignments of fertile eggs to reach the early hatcheries in Michigan and New York included varied mixtures of these parent stocks, and the subsequent behavior of the fish was unpredictable. Some fish seemed to remain where they were stocked, displaying relatively pure landlocked parentage of the McCloud or Kern rainbows, but others soon evaporated into the Great Lakes.

Fisheries experts were completely surprised over the behavior of the first rainbows placed in the Pere Marquette. The plantings seemed quite successful at first, and the small fish stocked below the Forks Pool had reached six to seven inches before the following fall. Biologists had closed that upper mileage to protect them, and their field reports glowed with

81

optimism over the coming trout season. Michigan fishermen waited through the winter with a mixture of anticipation and curiosity. The exotic trout from California were an unknown species in the Pere Marquette, and although many fishermen had read about them in journals like *Forest & Stream,* no one really knew what kind of sport they might provide.

Both biologists and fishermen were disappointed. When the opening weekend arrived in 1886, the heavy winter snows had been purged from the cedar swamps in weeks of high water, and hordes of curious anglers found the Pere Marquette relatively low and clear. The crowds were eager to catch these new California fish, but no one caught anything but the native brook trout, and the biologists were puzzled. The river had been teeming with small rainbows in late October. It would be many years before it was fully understood that these transplanted fish were actually sea-run steelhead, and that their silvery little smolts had migrated to the Great Lakes with the spring snowmelt.

The adult steelhead did not return to spawn until late October, long after the trout season had closed, and some fish arrived sporadically through the winter. There are often large steelhead runs in late February, and some years another sizeable migration occurs in early April. Spawning occurs then in the Pere Marquette, and most of the spawned-out kelts had usually returned to Lake Michigan before opening weekend, except for an occasional big female like the fish I had lost in my boyhood years. But these big rainbows were usually not found in the river during the regular trout-fishing season, and the only people who saw them there were local hunters.

You summer trout-fishing guys! the old-timers liked to chide us around Baldwin. *You summer folks catch them spotted sardines, when we got trout in the Big Pere like alligators— we see them fish during deer season and running our traplines!*

What kind of trout are they? my father asked.

Christ only knows! our tormentors laughed. *Who cares what kind of trout—they're alligator trout!*

And you summer people can't catch them fish! they added wryly.

It would be another thirty years before these steelhead runs in the Great Lakes rivers were fully understood and managed effectively. Techniques for catching them consistently on flies have also been worked out in recent years, but the old-timers who fished them still argue that fresh roe is the only bait a Michigan steelhead will strike.

The big trout we caught were usually browns, which had become established in the Pere Marquette late in the nineteenth century too, and we usually caught them at night. My first really large trout was caught on the middle reaches of the river, fishing with Maurice Houseman of Grand Rapids. We were fishing on the Green Cottage water, anticipating a twilight hatch of big *Hexagenia* drakes. It is difficult wading below its junction with the Baldwin, and I leaned into the darkening current to hold my position.

We should see some drakes soon! Houseman yelled.

The hatch was relatively sparse when it finally came, with the owls and whippoorwills calling in the jackpine thickets beyond the Deer Lick, and only a few trout were working. The fish seemed small, perhaps little better than a pound, when I hooked a surprisingly strong fish along a tangle of logs.

The fish had been working cautiously. Its rise was more a quiet sucking sound than the usual greedy splash of a big brown taking these *Hexagenia* flies, particularly when they are egg-laying spinners or newly hatched duns fluttering down the current. The big trout had simply intercepted the fly with a quiet roll, although its rise was strong enough to suggest a heavy fish among the river sounds.

I've got a good fish! I shouted. *It feels pretty strong!*

Stay with him! Houseman yelled.

The fish held stubbornly in the current the first few minutes, and then it plunged downstream in a wrenching run that stripped into the backing. The trout had hooked itself hard.

It still felt powerful in the heavy flow. It ripped into a bold run that bored angrily upstream, slicing a line in the surface with a shrill violin-string sound. Somewhere in the night upstream, the big fish jumped and fell clumsily, its splash magnified in the silence. Its strength was almost frightening, and I was worried that it might shear my tippet in the stumps and deadfalls under the opposite bank.

God! I thought anxiously. *He's really strong!*

My arms started shaking then, partly with a flush of fresh adrenalin and partly with growing fatigue. The big trout circled stubbornly just beyond my net, until finally it surrendered, threshing in the meshes as I waded ashore.

How big? Houseman shouted in the darkness.

Big enough to wear me out! I said wearily.

Since the hatch was finished, Houseman came wading upstream with his fishing light. *How about some help?* he said.

I could use it, I admitted.

His light found the big trout writhing in the net. It was a hook-jawed cockfish, its bright scarlet spots gleaming in its richly mottled flanks, and it weighed almost six pounds. It was the best fish that I took from the Pere Marquette in those boyhood years.

Those were golden summers on the rivers of Michigan. Great fishermen like George Mason and Ralph Widdicomb and Harold Smedley were along rivers like the Au Sable and Pere Marquette and Manistee. Fly makers like Art Winnie and Len Halliday and Ralph Corey were producing cornucopias of trout flies through the Michigan winters, and craftsmen like Paul Young and Lyle Dickerson were milling superb rods in their Detroit workshops.

The familiar Pere Marquette Rod & Gun Club was a circle of skilled and inventive fishermen in those days. Its members included Widdicomb, who was famous for the elegant badger spentwing that still bears his name. Vic Cramer developed unusual deer-hair flies, including a spent *Hexagenia* imitation and leaf-roller pattern, along with the woven-hair dressing of his Cramer nymphs. William Brush was a well-known automotive engineer who also patented a hook for parachute-hackle flies, which he developed on the Pere Marquette. These men fished often from the club compound, its simple buildings scattered on a tree-sheltered promontory above Waddell's Riffle.

Simmy Nolphe is probably the dean of the Pere Marquette fishermen in our time, and he lives on the fly-only water near Baldwin. Nolphe is a skilled steelhead fisherman who knows every holding-lie between the Highway Bridge and the pools below Danaher Creek. Carl Richards is another Pere Marquette regular, and joined with the equally skilled Doug Swisher to produce the books *Selective Trout* and *Fly Fishing Strategy.* Richards fishes regularly from the old Pere Marquette Rod & Gun compound, and we have shared the river there from Danaher Creek to the swift currents above the Deer Lick. Dave Borgeson is a principal architect of the Pacific salmon program in Michigan, although his secret love is probably fishing the big steelhead with flies in October, particularly in the estuary of the Pere Marquette. Borgeson was among the pioneers who worked out fly-fishing tactics on these big lake-run rainbows, proving wrong the cracker-barrel experts who insisted that these transplanted steelhead would never take flies.

The biologist was my guide the last time I fished these steelhead on the Pere Marquette. *I'll meet you at Barothy's,* Borgeson suggested. *Just bring strong tackle and your alarm clock!*

Alarm clock! I protested.

You're famous for sleeping late! Borgeson laughed. *We like to get on the river early—the first rod through the good water has the best chance of taking these late steelhead.*

You win, I said.

April on the upper Pere Marquette can prove unpredictable, and it was snowing hard when Borgeson stood like Marley's ghost in the five o'clock darkness, pounding on my cottage door with his breath blossoming in the cold. *Reveille!* Borgeson shivered.

You're joking! I stared at the snowflakes in disbelief. *Did you remember the ice spud and tip-up flags?*

Forget the weather! Borgeson stripped his gloves and parka in front of the fireplace. *Steelheading builds character—and steelhead fishermen thrive on a little weather!*

You're nuts! I laughed. *We're going out in that?*

Steelheading builds character! he insisted.

It's crazy! I sighed.

It had stopped snowing after breakfast, but the morning still felt like duck season when we left his station wagon at the Green Cottage. *We could hike upstream and fish the Whinnery stretch,* Borgeson suggested, *but I have a hunch about trying the Deer Lick.*

You're the doctor, I shivered.

It seemed warmer when we had covered a hundred yards through the wintry bottoms along the river. The snowfall had completely covered the winter leaves and deadfalls, and it seemed a little like still-hunting whitetails in a fresh tracking snow. We forded the river at Shapton's Run, in the looping bends below the Whirlpool, and we stopped to watch a wild turkey scuttling ahead through the drifts and trees.

When do these steelhead start coming? I asked.

Our bright fish usually enter the river at Ludington in late October, Borgeson replied, *and those first October runs usually include some of the biggest steelhead of the season.*

Lots of fish in October? I interrupted.

Only a few large bellwether fish, Borgeson continued. *Our biggest runs arrive in late winter and early spring.*

Are they like the winter fish on the Pacific Coast?

They're something like that, Borgeson admitted. *Perhaps more like the late-fall steelhead on the Klamath and Umpqua.*

The big runs come later? I asked.

The river was a dark necklace through the trees, winding back on itself until the high clay benches forced it back toward Lake Michigan, and we walked slowly through the snow-covered branches. *We keep getting fish sporadically all through the winter.* Borgeson held a branch until I passed along the trail. *Our first heavy run comes during the last of February, and our biggest migrations arrive before Easter— but sometimes we get a good run in late April too.*

We've got bright fish now?

You think I'd bring you out in blizzards for nothing? Borgeson grinned menacingly and laughed. *Our biologists are still trapping and tagging some bright steelhead at Ludington—so they're still coming!*

That's great! I felt less cold suddenly.

Borgeson had always believed that these Michigan steelhead could be taken with flies, in spite of the trolling and salmon-egg mythology that argued against such refinements, since he had often caught winter steelhead on the Pacific Coast. Several dedicated fishermen had patiently experimented with standard steelhead patterns and with various combinations of line densities and weighting and other equipment. The secrets were slowly ferreted out in recent years. Their consistent parade of big fly-caught steelhead, including a sixteen-pound fish taken by Simmy Nolphe on the upper Pere Marquette, was irrefutable evidence that finally led to the fly-only mileage on the watershed.

Look familiar? Borgeson asked.

It sure brings back some memories, I admitted. *We fished it every summer from the Forks Pool to Bowman's Bridge—but we never fished it when it looked like winter in the Yukon!*

It's probably fishing better these days, he said.

How's that? I asked.

It's fly-only water these days, Borgeson explained, *from the M-37 Bridge to Danaher Creek—it's got a lot of wild fish!*

No stocking of hatchery sardines?

That's right! Borgeson agreed.

We fished the riffles at Shapton's Run for almost an hour without moving a fish, until the weak April sun filtered through the trees, and we walked downstream toward the Deer Lick. It was still cold and the snow dropped in soft shards from the branches.

You sure we had to start before daylight? I asked.

You feel like we're after pike? Borgeson laughed and threw a loosely packed snowball. *Winter muskellunge?*

Walleyes through the ice, I said ruefully.

Steelhead fishing and suffering are the same thing! Borgeson broke more trail through the crust that had frozen the marshy bottoms. *But getting up early wasn't as crazy as you think, because these fish lie in the deep holes at midday, particularly in bright weather—and move out into the riffles at twilight.*

You mean they spawn in the darkness?

Steelhead spawn on dark days too, Borgeson continued,

87

but usually they hide and work the gravel riffles at daybreak and nightfall—the early morning is probably the best time to fish them, because they won't have been bothered.

Does it hurt to fish spawning steelhead? I asked.

Not really, Borgeson replied. *The entire headwaters are closed to fishing above the M-37 Bridge—and they've got miles and miles of pea-gravel riffles where nobody bothers them.*

Are we fishing spawners? I asked.

Fish that are actually spawning seldom take the fly, Borgeson responded. *Cockfish might attack a big streamer or bucktail to defend their territory, but it's often other fish that are caught.*

Stray males and females? I asked.

Sometimes, he said.

Since the fly-only water on the upper Pere Marquette is unique among the Michigan steelhead rivers, it has proved immensely popular among knowledgeable anglers and can become crowded. Fishing successfully involves some unusual techniques, although many of the flies popular in Michigan are standard western patterns, and would be found from San Francisco to the Shelikof Strait.

Steelhead dressings like the Thor, Umpqua Special, Skunk, Kalama Special, Fall Favorite, Skykomish Sunrise, Brass Hat, Van Luven, Queen Bess, Yellow Comet, and Babine Special are all popular in Michigan. Skilled fishermen like Carl Richards have experimented successfully with Atlantic salmon patterns on Michigan steelhead, and dressings like the Blue Charm, Black Fitchtail, Orange Blossom, Green Butt, Ackroyd, and Orange Charm are finding their proponents. There are also days when bright flies seem to disturb the fish, and Michigan fishermen have started to work out fly dressings intended to imitate some of the major aquatic insects found in their rivers.

Like their winter-run cousins on the Pacific Coast, the Michigan steelhead like their flies on the bottom, and successful flies are typically weighted with several turns of fuse wire under their bodies. High-density lines are sufficient to get the fly on the bottom in the shallow riffles, but some lies are too swift and deep for such tackle. Some anglers have experimented with stainless cable between their lines and leaders, while others have tried short lengths of lead-core trolling lines to sink their flies deep. Such equipment works on large rivers like the Muskegon and Manistee, but there are big steelhead in brushy pockets on the smaller Michigan rivers too. Such holes demand specially rigged tackle, since conventional steelhead methods are often unworkable in small rivers filled with deadfalls and sweepers.

Michigan fishermen have evolved a unique shot-dropper technique on such water. The secret is using a small triangle swivel, with three connections linked to a circular core. The leader itself connects the line to the first swivel, and a short tippet of six- to eight-pound test is attached to the second with the fly. The third swivel trails six inches of nylon with an overhand knot in its free end. Split shot are added to this short nylon to form a shot dropper, and a skilled steelhead fisherman can adjust the amount of lead on his dropper to suit the depth and velocity of the current he is fishing. It is not a pretty method of fishing, but it requires its own combination of subtle skills.

When it's rigged properly, Borgeson explained when we reached the swift run above the Deer Lick, _it's possible to walk the shot dropper along the bottom with the rod held high—you can actually feel the shot ticking from stone to stone._

Skilled manipulation of the shot-dropper technique will ride the fly slightly higher in the current than the weighted nylon dropper itself. Perhaps its most ingenious feature is its ability to foul the bottom without snagging the fly too, and firm pressure will either break the dropper or strip the fouled split shot free.

It's perfect for brushy pockets where you have to sink your fly quickly, Borgeson continued. _You can hear our steelheaders talking about favorite two-shot and three-shot holes!_

Aren't they hard to cast? I asked.

Pretty cumbersome, he admitted, _but good roll casting with a big rod works pretty well._

How large can these steelhead run?

Simmy Nolphe took that sixteen-pounder here last year,

89

Borgeson replied excitedly, *and we've seen fish over twenty!*
That's big enough! I laughed.

Snow started falling again when we walked the brushy
banks along the Deer Lick stretch. The river was swift and
slightly tea-colored from the marshes in its headwaters, and
it flowed with a kind of sullen strength through our waders.

We've often found the fish under those cedars, Borgeson
pointed, *but the light is wrong to see them now.*

The snow doesn't help! I said.

The snow flurries passed, and the weak April sun tried to
warm the swift currents. The dark bottom showed some fingerprints of spawning activity just above the overhanging
cedars, but we could see no steelhead there until the light
changed.

Look there under the trees! Borgeson exclaimed.

The bottom seemed empty at first, but Borgeson pointed
excitedly to the swift run across the river, and suddenly a
smooth current welled up and I saw them. There were three
steelhead lying there, facing into the current, fish that looked
like dark olive ghosts hovering over the bottom of winter
algae.

They're big! Borgeson cautioned.

It started snowing again, and I shivered when I waded
into position in the thigh-deep currents across from the fish,
although not entirely from the cold. The river looped against
the timbered Clay Banks upstream and scoured back swiftly
under the trees. The fresh snow cloaked the cedars, and the
swirling flakes obscured the river until the fish were only
half-seen shadows.

Can you still see them? Borgeson asked anxiously.

Still there! I nodded.

It was snowing much harder when I sharply rolled the
first cast upstream. Its three-shot dropper looped high and
fell clumsily. The weight settled and caught briefly in the
stones, until I lifted the rod and felt it drift free, ticking gently
along the bottom. It took several casts to get it drifting properly, feeling the shot-dropper drag and catch in the crevices
between the rocks.

Borgeson clambered up a small tree to observe the fish.

We've still got three steelhead over there, he yelled excitedly from his perch, *and we've got another fish farther down!*

The first casts worked deep along the bottom, and I took a shuffling half step between fly swings, covering the holding water in a series of concentric drifts. The two steelhead I could still see expressed no interest in my fly, although I covered them patiently.

We've still got others below that pair, Borgeson called. *Just stay with them and fish it through.*

The fly swing feels right! I started another cast.

The shot dropper fell tight against a deadfall, and I stripped a little line into the drift until I felt the lead hopscotching along the stones. It grated momentarily on a gravelly shingle, drifted smoothly under the trees and there was a strong pull.

Fish! I shouted happily.

The big steelhead threshed heavily in the shallows, throwing spray with its angry convulsions, and the reel rasped in protest. The fish held stubbornly in the strongest currents. It shook its head and bulldogged deep along the bottom, and suddenly it cartwheeled under the trees and the reel was running shrilly again.

Good fish! Borgeson shouted.

How deep is that bend downstream? I yelled when the backing started to evaporate from the reel. *Might have to follow him through!*

You can wade it diagonally across the bar!

It might come to that! I said.

The big steelhead sliced past me in the shallows, its spotted back completely above the water, throwing spray into the falling snow. The fish was already thirty yards into my backing, and I picked a careful route along the willows.

The Deer Lick is a little forbidding in its spring flow, particularly in the bend at the Anderson cottage. There is a small logjam on the opposite bank, just where the current shelves back into the bend downstream. It is deep there under the throbbing sweepers, where the strongest currents suck through the tangled roots. When a strong fish decides to leave the Deer Lick, stripping the reel well into its backing,

91

it is a tightrope act to follow it diagonally above the shelving currents between these holes. Crossing there is the only way to follow a troublesome fish, particularly with the April currents running bank-full in the willows.

He's stopped taking line! Borgeson yelled.

But he's still awfully strong! I plunged through the shallows and fought to recover some backing. *Awfully strong!*

I'm coming! Borgeson came sliding down his tree in a shower of bark and fresh snow. *Hold him out of that brush pile!*

I'm trying! I groaned.

The slender rod bucked and lunged heavily, echoing the sullen struggle of the steelhead along the logs. The straining leader hummed in the current. The jackstraw labyrinth of brush and flood debris looked threatening, but the tippet somehow survived.

He's trying it again! Borgeson warned.

Damn! I applied pressure and the rod was a tight half circle. *He's still trying to break me under those logs!*

Still think you can hold him?

My response died in my throat when the fish bored deep under the fallen trees. The rod throbbed angrily under the stress. Its pressure finally turned the fish, until several other brief runs were parried easily and the fight was almost over. The big steelhead worked splashily to avoid the net, but Borgeson captured it expertly and waded triumphantly ashore with the prize.

Good fish! Borgeson said excitedly.

Strong! I agreed. *What do you think he'll weigh?*

Nine or ten pounds! the biologist answered happily. *That's a lot of steelhead on a fly rod in that brushy water!*

Borgeson took a brace of slightly larger steelhead from the Deer Lick before we stopped for lunch. Both fish were carefully released, and we circled happily back through the river bottoms to the station wagon. The fireplace at Barothy's felt good after the icy currents of the Pere Marquette, and we drove back to the river on the Clay Banks county road after lunch. Borgeson suggested that we hike downstream on its timber ridge and then cut down the steep trail to intercept the river at its Waddell's Riffle.

It's beautiful water, Borgeson explained while we walked the Clay Banks with the river winding through the trees, _and we might find a few bright fish there._

Sounds great! I struggled to keep up.

Waddell's Riffle is a beautiful half mile of gravelly shallows, its currents scouring under the cedars and willows that shelter its south banks. The cottages and outbuildings of the Pere Marquette Rod & Gun Club lie concealed in the trees there. Borgeson located a school of silvery fresh-run steelhead toward the bottom of Waddell's Riffle, and we crawled stealthily through the trees until we were perched above them in the shadows. The school of bright fish were pale olive, hovering in the smooth currents under the cedars.

Those are fresh-run fish! Borgeson whispered.

Maybe they'll take, I said.

Steelhead are seldom predictable, and we fished them patiently for almost two hours without observing any interest. We stopped to rest the school of steelhead and sat talking while the shadows lengthened along the riffles.

Finally I tried a bright-tinseled steelhead pattern, and with its first drift through the fish, the river exploded. There was no time to respond to the fierce strike. The rod snapped into a tightly straining circle when the steelhead hooked itself, and it slashed and steeplechased upstream through the shallows. Its strength and speed were startling, and my Hardy surrendered line in a piercing wail. The fish jumped in the afternoon light and stopped.

Bright fish! I shouted.

Better watch it! Borgeson waded swiftly toward me. _There's a pretty bad deadfall under those cedars downstream!_

I'll try! I laughed.

The steelhead came back downstream swiftly. The line ripped through the water, its faint sounds something like tearing linen, and I turned awkwardly to fight its strength. The rod was seated against my waders and my left hand was working high at the stripping guide, tightening into a saltwater lock. The fish shook itself angrily, steeplechasing past the drowned deadfalls, and stopped again.

Crazy fish! Borgeson said.

The steelhead brooded momentarily and erupted again.

Six jumps exploded under the overhanging cedars, and a final wild somersault carried the fish high into the trees. Cedar needles showered into the river as the steelhead tumbled clumsily back through the branches. Its sword-bright length disappeared in its awkward splash, and before I could recover, it was running again.

I told you to fight the fish! Borgeson stood laughing behind me. *Not chase him up that cedar like a 'coon!*

He's chasing me! I protested.

The struggle erupted in the open river, although the big henfish threatened several times to reach the logjams in the bend downstream. It almost reached the drowned cedar twice, its spotted tail sculling weakly now, until I patiently forced it back into midstream. Finally it surrendered, its silvery length fattened on alewives and smelt, and we estimated its weight at twelve pounds.

The steelhead held tentatively in the shallows, tired from its acrobatic fight and no longer fearing us, its scarlet gill covers fluttering until their rhythms settled and grew strong. The fish still held there in the current, until suddenly it was gone.

It's still quite a river! I thought.

It is impossible to capture the Pere Marquette in words, and the memories of its fishing summers crowd the mind. There are too many echoes over too many years, from those first boyhood mornings on the Little South to the recent afternoons fishing for the giant chinook salmon that crowd its headwaters in October.

Watching their spawning rites on the Waddell's stretch was like eavesdropping on the primordial rhythms of the world. The salmon gather in restless coveys, their henfish writhing against the bottom, patiently shaping their redds in the afternoons. The cockfish aggressively defend their mates, quarreling in great gouts of spray and roostertails of wild pursuit in the spawning shallows, and rooting with their backs showing above the water. Finally these fish will die, having completed their restless spawning in riffles filled with October leaves, drifting with the current until their flesh becomes part of the river and its fertility. Such spawning rites suggest that life still pulses in the river, its energies alive in its cold currents and the precious ova hidden in the womb of its bright gravel.

Wild turkeys are coming back along the river in recent years, scuttling though the leaves on the jackpine benches, and the ruffed grouse are drumming in steelhead time. Owls still hunt from its cedar thickets and feasting trees. Although I have learned more about owls since our first boyhood summers on the Pere Marquette, and no longer believe the myths and superstitions, something strange did happen.

During our first summer trip north from Chicago, the automobile we had patiently nursed through the war years broke down at Muskegon, and we finally reached our campsite long after midnight. It was difficult making camp in the headlights of the Oldsmobile, and it was almost getting light when we settled into our sleeping bags. Finally I fell asleep listening to the mournful calling of the owls.

The morning sun was already bright on our tent, tracing its leafy patterns on the canvas, when I finally stirred. The cooking smells of coffee and fried eggs and bacon drifted through our camp. *It's going to get pretty hot,* my father predicted. *Too hot for fishing.*

Maybe I'll go swimming at Nobles', I said.

Makes sense! my father smiled. *They'll know what's been happening on the river this week!*

It was a half-mile hike along the county road, axle-deep in sand beyond the bridge where the Middle Branch comes welling out from its marl-bog beginnings. The road was hot in the morning sun, and coveys of red-legged grasshoppers flushed along its shoulders, settling ahead in the road. I walked slowly through the trees toward the Noble cottages, remembering the screech owls.

Good morning! I called to the college girls who were cleaning the cottages. *Where's the boss today?*

The girls looked startled. *Died last night,* they said.

[1974]

95

5

Night Comes to the Namekagon

We're still headed west, trout fishing as we go. It's been more than twenty years since Schwiebert's northern Wisconsin trip described in this essay, but by all reports the Namekagon River is fishing better than ever. For one thing, the Wisconsin Department of Natural Resources restricted nine miles of the upper river to fishing with artificial lures only starting in 1983 and also introduced more restrictive limits.

There are the usual puzzles of fly hatches and their imitations here, but what's more puzzling to me is that the excellent trout fishing in Wisconsin has gotten so little publicity over the years. I can recall as an editor publishing several articles about little Wisconsin spring creeks over the years that seemed to get less response than anything else I ushered into print. Perhaps Schwiebert is right as he suggests in this essay that "musky fever" answers that question. I think if I were a trout fisherman within shouting distance of this superlative river, I'd do all I could to promote muskellunge fishing, thereby keeping crowds off the trout water. You can find out more about either by writing the Wisconsin Department of Natural Resources, Madison, Wisconsin 53707.

It's musky fever, she said.
The old woman was washing glasses behind the huge mahogany bar. There were worn places in the floor from the boot caulks of lumberjacks, and there were mounted whitetails with a lever-action rifle across one rack of antlers. The place was empty.

Musky fever? I sipped a beer slowly.
You see this town? she asked. *You see any menfolk between twelve and eighty-five?*
No, I laughed.
They've all got the fever, she continued. *They're all crazy for muskies in this town.* She placed the glasses in a careful pyramid behind the bar.
Sounds like a sickness, I said.
Happens every year about this time. She sighed and rinsed the sink. *They're all crazy!*
What about the river above town? I asked.
Namekagon? she asked.
Yes, I said. *Smallmouths?*
Some smallmouths, but mostly trout. She wiped the bar. *Nobody pays much attention to them in musky season.*
Big trout? I asked.
Guess so. She poured herself a beer. *They catch some five or six pounds every spring above the railroad trestle.*
Browns? I finished my beer and paid.
Don't know, she shook her head and frowned. *All they ever talk about 'round here is muskies!*
Musky fever! I laughed.
Some of the best wild-trout fisheries left in America are neglected because they flow through the muskellunge country of northern Wisconsin, and the largest is the Namekagon. Between the once-thriving timber center at Hayward and its junction with the Saint Croix, its sweeping pools are prime smallmouth bass fishing, but above the town and the sawmill impoundment that warms the lower river, it is prime brown-trout water.

Although I spent my boyhood summers on the better-known trout streams of the country above Chicago, the Namekagon was a stranger. My introduction to the river and its almost unknown limestone sister river, the little East Fork of the Iron, was a happy accident.

Several summers ago I was selected to represent Princeton University in a think-tank conference held at Grindstone Lake near Hayward, and three weeks before the conference a letter arrived from a fisherman who had read my book *Matching the Hatch.* The letter thanked me for writing the book and the help it had been in identifying and imitating the fly hatches on the rivers between Ashland and Duluth. It closed with an invitation: whenever travel carried me back to northern Wisconsin, there was a willing guide in Ashland to show me his rivers. "You might be surprised at the fishing," read the teasing sentence at the close, "on our Wisconsin chalkstreams."

Chalkstreams! I thought. *That's something new!*

Chalkstream fishing in the jackpine hills of Wisconsin was a puzzle that nagged me for days after the letter arrived. Finally I telephoned Ashland and announced that I was coming to the conference.

Grindstone Lake? said my host.

Yes, I said, *staying at the Grindstone Lodge.*

I'll call you there, he agreed.

After the opening session of the conference, I wandered down through the trees to the boathouse. Several boats were out and I watched one cover the shoreline below the camp, one man rowing and his partner standing in the bow, heaving a huge lure along the weeds. It hissed out and landed with a horrendous splash.

Musky fever, I thought disparagingly.

Wisconsin hospitality is first-rate and my new friend called during lunch. We agreed to meet at a diner near Ashland. *I'll show you my secret chalkstream,* he laughed.

Art Besse, he introduced himself the next morning.

We drove down the county roads while Besse explained that his real estate business dovetailed neatly with trout fishing and that his tackle was always in the trunk. Besse parked the car along the road with no river in sight. We slipped into our waders and shouldered into our wading vests, and I dutifully followed him into the trees.

We'll cut cross-country, he explained, *and fish the river back almost to where we leave the car.*

It was hot and the forced march through the brush, carrying the rod butt-first to protect it and worrying about snagging its guides in the branches, was getting uncomfortable when we finally reached the river.

East Fork, he announced.

The river flowed smooth and deep between the alders, its current slipping past an occasional deadfall. *It's a little milky,* I said. *You have a rainstorm last night?*

Besse laughed. *That's the chalk,* he said. *The river comes out of a marl swamp and that chalkiness is limestone.*

Like the British chalkstreams, I said.

Exactly, he grinned.

His fly books were filled with juicy-looking wet flies and nymphs, and he selected one carefully. *Try this,* he said.

It was a grublike pattern with a rough muskrat-fur body and a trimmed brown hackle dressed palmer-style on a long-shank hook. *I thought you read my book,* I laughed. *What's this thing?*

Don't laugh until you've tried it, he smiled.

He explained that boyhood fish taken on bait had always been filled with grayish-brown beetle larvae that were thick in the river and that he had worked out the pattern as an imitation. It was clinch-knotted to my tippet, and Besse pointed to a deep run under the alders.

It landed with a plop and I laughed. *That thing has got the glide angle of a brick!*

It's weighted with fuse wire, Besse explained.

The cast worked back deep under the bushes and stopped with a soft pull that spelled trout. The fish bored upstream when I tightened, and it jumped at the head of the run. It finally surrendered to the net, and we admired its color and condition.

It's really fat, I said. *It's only sixteen inches, but it must go at least two pounds.* Its scarlet spots were bright against pale ocher-colored sides.

It's the marl swamp, said Besse.

Alkalinity from the lime-marl deposits, I nodded.

My secret chalkstream, he smiled.

Art Besse was killed in a tragic automobile accident later that summer, and no longer fishes his secret stretches of the Iron and the Namekagon and the Brule, but I will never forget his hospitality and streamside companionship that week. We fished until evening on his secret chalkstream, catching fifty-odd trout on his beetle larva until a hatch of pale *Epeorus* flies made us switch to a small Light Cahill.

The next evening we met at the railroad trestle on the Namekagon above Hayward and rigged our tackle. The river looked shallow, flowing through a hundred weedy channels in the elodea, and there were cottages on both banks. Just above the bridge was a deeper-looking run under a thick clump of flowers.

Those look like irises. It seemed strange to find a flower bed in the middle of the river. *Are they wild?*

No, he laughed. *Probably washed out upriver.*

While we watched, a fish rose tight against the roots.

Try him, Besse suggested.

We waded carefully into position below the fish and I dropped the beetle larva above the flowers. There was a heavy boil and a good three-pound fish hooked itself. The quarter mile upstream produced a half-dozen twelve- to sixteen-inch browns between us.

It's some river, I admitted.

Wait until twilight, smiled Besse. *We've been due for a hatch of big* Isonychia *drakes about now.*

Hate people who read my stuff carefully!

We drove upriver to fish another stretch. *Gooseneck Bend,* said Besse. *The big drakes should be hatching there.*

Sounds good, I said.

The river comes down from a tamarack swamp, flowing strong and deep into Gooseneck Bend. The huge pool eddies and slows against a steep earth bank, gathering its currents again in swift tail shallows past a logjam of deadfalls. The current sucked and slipped along the logs before it broke into a quarter mile of tumbling waist-deep riffles.

We fished the riffles indifferently until the *Isonychia*

hatch began coming off. Big drakes fluttered down the current. Three good fish started working in the fast slick along the logs.

Those are big trout! I whispered.

Besse picked two mayflies off the current and studied them in his palm. *Isonychia sadleri!* he announced.

That's not in Matching the Hatch*!* I grinned

You're right! he said proudly.

The hatch is practically identical to the eastern Leadwing, and I selected a big imitation from my fly boxes. *Works on the Neversink,* I said. *Now for the Namekagon!*

The first fish was rising methodically against the logs. The cast cocked the fly nicely, and it disappeared in a quiet self-satisfied swirl. The trout was well hooked.

How big? yelled Besse.

The fish hung stubbornly for several minutes until I forced it back from the logs. *It's a good fish,* I guessed. *Might go three pounds!*

Suddenly it porpoised and revealed a shark-size dorsal and tail. It shook its head sullenly, turned and bolted into the fast water. It splashed wildly two hundred feet downstream. *Only three?* Besse laughed.

The reel rasped grindingly. *Maybe four!*

We coaxed the trout into the tamarack backwater and finally netted it in the shallows. *That trout could go as much as six pounds!* Besse gasped when he saw its bulk.

The others were still rising steadily. The first was working tight against the jam, and it lunged sideways to engulf the fly. The second fight echoed the first, except for a clumsy jump that ended in a heavy splash. Finally it surrendered, threshing heavily in the meshes.

This one will go four! I laughed.

The third fish splashed for a fluttering drake. *That one would be an anticlimax!* smiled Besse.

These two are fantastic! I agreed.

We walked back through the meadows to the car as the moon rose huge and yellow through the pines. *Let's get them weighed and dressed at the tackle shop,* suggested Besse.

The tackle shop was busy with fishermen buying baitfish

for fishing walleyes, and jointed plugs and huge bucktail spinner-rigs and sucker minnows for muskellunge. The smallest brown measured twenty-one inches and weighed better than three pounds. The second went a fat twenty-four inches and weighed more than five. The largest dropped the store scales solidly to almost seven pounds.

Those are some fish! I said.

The clerk seemed unimpressed. *Those trout were caught on flies!* said Besse. *The big ones took dries!* The tackle-shop clerk looked bored as he dressed the trout for the freezer.

Aren't they something! Besse pressed.

They're okay, said the clerk, *but you should've seen the thirty-pound musky they caught this morning!*

[1972]

6

The River of Humility

For this essay we've moved from Wisconsin to the Rocky Mountains near the junction of the Wyoming, Montana, and Idaho borders. By the time I first fished the Henry's Fork of the Snake River in southeastern Idaho, I'd already heard both Schwiebert and René Harrop describe the fishing as difficult, and I rigged my rod with no little trepidation.

"Watch for the bank feeders!" Dave Engerbretson hollered back as he headed for another spot downstream. He was referring to those often large trout that feed with very quiet riseforms inches from the bank. This occurs on other rivers, including Vermont's Battenkill, but is a famous phenomenon on the Henry's Fork that has produced some notable fish over the years.

So this time my pulse quickened at a quiet bulge in the water near some overhanging grass. This was repeated at odd intervals for about half an hour as I cast and changed flies in vain. Just as I was realizing that I hadn't seen a fin or fish's snout, a muskrat stuck its head above water, grasses hanging comically from

*its mouth. This "River of Humility," I found then, can
be even more humiliating than its considerable reputation implies.*

It was after two o'clock when the bartender closed the pool
tables at the Stagecoach, switching off the lights over their
faded playing surfaces. The waitress collected the empty bottles and cocktail glasses and ashtrays from the tables and
windowsills. The pool cues were carefully racked, and the
young bartender left the yellowing cue ball sitting on the
worn felt. Two fishermen and their bearded guide had been
shooting nine-ball after a long day's float on the spate-swollen
Madison downstream from Varney Bridge.

The young bartender quickly washed and rinsed his
glasses, and stacked them skillfully against the mirrors,
where they caught and echoed the flickering lights of the beer
signs. The local patrons sat nursing their last-call drinks. The
waitress finished clearing her tables and sat with her friends,
other young waitresses who had the night off or had stopped
in for a nightcap after closing earlier. There was an old sheepherder sleeping with his head in his arms, his darkly stained
hat covering his face, and his shabby cowboy boots hooked
in the barstool.

Fishing tomorrow? the bartender asked.

We fished the Firehole today. I grudgingly surrendered a
half-finished drink. *We're on the Henry's Fork tomorrow.*

Those rainbows over there are tough, he said.

The bartender let his local customers out the street door
and carefully closed the blinds. The waitress switched off the
jukebox and pinball machines and beer signs, and the bartender wiped down his bar before trying to wake the old
sheepherder.

André Puyans was already starting a second platter of
fried eggs when we met for breakfast at Huck's Diner. There
were ragged layers of mist hanging in the lodgepoles when
we left West Yellowstone and climbed toward Targhee Pass.
The surface of Henry's Lake was pale and still beyond its
summit, and the bottoms were alive with grazing antelope
and nesting sandhill cranes. We crossed the headwaters of

the Henry's Fork at Mack's Inn, several miles below the gargantuan springs that give birth to the river, and stopped for licenses at Last Chance.

We left the fishing van at the upper fence line of the Harriman Ranch, crossed the irrigation canal on the split rails and walked downstream carrying our waders. Two hundred yards downriver several fishermen were waiting for a mating swarm of tiny *Tricorythodes* flies to finish their egg laying. The morning sunlight was filled with the fluttering of their tiny white-winged swarms.

When their egg laying was completed, and the little mayflies were drifting in the surface film, the trout started to rise. Their riseforms were typical of spinner-fall feeding on those late summer mornings. While the little spentwing flies were still drifting in the surface film, the trout took them with a methodical sipping rhythm, bulging and dimpling steadily while it lasted.

Look at all those fish! I said excitedly.

Such spinner falls last only a few minutes, and the fishermen who had waited for the egg laying to finish were casting frantically to the rising fish. One fisherman was surrounded by working trout, and his casting rhythms grew more and more desperate as the bulging rainbows refused his flies. The minute spentwing flies were almost impossible to see in the current, but the feeding rhythms of the fish grew faster and faster, until suddenly they stopped. The morning rise to the *Tricorythodes* swarms was over.

The fisherman cursed angrily and threw his bamboo rod like a javelin, and its silver fittings flashed in the morning light. It traveled its brief trajectory and splashed into the river. The smooth current flowed quietly again, its tongues undulating in the rich beds of chara and *Potamogeton* and bright-green fountain mosses.

Ever see anything like that? Puyans asked.

We watched the unhappy fisherman cross the river, angrily leaving a wake that scattered trout in all directions. *You mean so many fish rising in one place?* I finished stringing the double taper and added a tippet. *Or a fisherman throw away his rod?*

105

Both! Puyans laughed.

The fisherman reached the grassy bank and stared back grimly at the river. *Remember where it sank?* I asked.

Don't really give a damn! the fisherman growled.

What happened? Puyans asked.

Been fishing over these goddamned fish since breakfast! the fisherman explained bitterly. *I've never seen so many trout rising, and I haven't caught a thing all morning!*

What were you using? Puyans asked.

Everything that usually works! The man shook his head. *Renegades, Humpies, Grasshoppers, Muddlers, and Royal Wulffs!*

Those flies work everywhere but here, I said.

What's so special about this river? the fisherman protested in surprise. *Those are great patterns everywhere!*

These fish don't seem to know that.

You could make a living on the Henry's Fork! Puyans clapped the unhappy fisherman on the shoulder. *Betting people that their favorite fly patterns won't catch these fish!*

· *He's right!* I agreed unhappily.

The Henry's Fork is perhaps the finest trout stream in the United States, its headwaters a marriage of the outlet at Henry's Lake and the remarkable aquifers that rise at Big Springs. Their flowages are virtually constant, measuring almost 90,000 gallons per minute at a uniform fifty-two degrees.

Its drainage basin between Henry's Lake and Ashton includes more than a thousand square miles of forests and bunchgrass flats and sagebrush country. Other springheads and tributaries like the still-flowing Buffalo multiply its volumes of flow to more than 250,000 gallons per minute in the Box Canyon below the Island Park Reservoir. The fertile little Warm River joins the Henry's Fork a few miles below Mesa Falls, and the river discharges more than 500,000 gallons per minute through the reservoir at Ashton.

The watershed of the upper Henry's Fork is largely managed by the Forest Service. Its timber and plant cover and grazing are mostly intact, and its geology is remarkably permeable and stable. The river is relatively shallow, and its profile is surprisingly gentle in its headwaters, measuring less than a thousand feet in its first thirty miles. Its winding flowages are two hundred to three hundred fifty feet wide, except in its braided meadow channels, and its surface drainages are relatively minimal. The ecology of the watershed results in a remarkably stable and fertile aquatic habitat.

Knowledgeable anglers familiar with the river argue that its fertility and fly life make the Henry's Fork of the Snake the finest dry-fly stream in the world. Its prolific hatches emerge steadily throughout the season, sometimes in such profusion that a dozen species might be emerging or egg laying simultaneously.

Such extensive hatches and spinner falls can trigger spectacular rises of fish, although its trout are extremely selective and shy. Its currents are often encrusted with spent and emerging aquatic insects, and there are so many flies on the water that success is less a problem of matching a specific fly hatch, than a more difficult problem of finding which particular species the fish are taking.

These rainbows are really difficult, Puyans explained. *Just when you finally work out what they're taking—everything changes again and they're on something else!*

The river is almost three hundred feet wide at the boundaries of the Harriman Ranch, and its free-rising rainbows are a challenge that attracts skilled anglers from everywhere. During the better fly hatches, it has become a shrine for expert fishermen, and unlike most rivers in our time, the beautiful Henry's Fork is fishing better than it was in my boyhood years. The quality of its sport comes from the happy cornucopia of its character and its natural fertility, and the impact of its recent fly-only regulations.

Its two-hundred-mile valley produces grain and fat potatoes and trout of remarkable quality, and the fertility of the river and its surrounding ranches and farmsteads is rooted in the unique ecology of the entire watershed.

Below the irrigation reservoir at Ashton, the river is multiplied by the flowages of the Fall and the Bechler, which rises in the southwestern highlands of the Yellowstone. The ill-fated Teton is flowing free again, following the tragic collapse of its controversial Teton Reservoir, and it joins the Henry's Fork below Rexburg. Fishing is good throughout its entire river system, but the most productive habitat is found above the Mesa Falls, particularly on the Harriman property—a unique stretch of river willed to the State of Idaho with the stipulations that its ecology be protected and that fishing access be limited to fly-only regulations.

The special fly-only regulations proved so successful that some form of special regulations now applies from Lower Mesa Falls to the Big Springs, and the twenty-eight-mile stretch between the falls and the Island Park Reservoir is managed as a wild-trout fishery without the stocking of hatchery strains.

Between the south boundary of the Harriman Ranch and the Lower Mesa Falls, artificial flies and single-hook-lure regulations apply, but there are no special regulations on the headwaters or the reservoir itself. The brief mileage below Big Springs is closed to fishing. Except for the closed water, and the stretch from Island Park Reservoir to Lower Mesa Falls, the river upstream from Ashton has a limit of six fish daily, with only two trout over sixteen inches. Between the reservoir and the waterfalls, three fish under twelve inches and a single trophy trout above twenty inches are permitted. The Harriman property itself is included in these daily catch limits and is fly-only water.

The philosophy behind these regulations argues that the primary brood stocks should be protected, in terms of both the quantity and the quality of their spawning. Earlier regulations on the Harriman water permitted no fish over fourteen inches in the daily creel limit, and a superb population of big rainbows soon resulted without costly programs of stocking hatchery fish. Some biologists firmly believe that the vitality and configuration and wariness that permit a fish to thrive and grow large are genetically transmitted. Protecting the large brood fish, while culling out the gullible trout below spawning sizes, bore remarkable fruit in recent years, and knowledgeable critics believe the new trophy-fish limit is a mistake.

It was politics again! Jack Hemingway explained recently in Sun Valley. *Some people just can't catch a big fish without wanting to kill it—yet these same people don't manage their cattle by butchering their best bulls and cows each year!*

André Puyans and I met later with René Harrop along the river at Last Chance, and we sat in the warm meadows waiting for another hatch of flies. Harrop is a remarkably skilled fly dresser from Saint Anthony, a small potato-farm community on the lower river, and he understands its moods and fly hatches and fish almost better than anyone in the Henry's Fork country. Harrop has proved those skills many times on the river in recent years.

You know, Puyans studied the current thoughtfully, *that poor guy who threw away his rod had a point about wondering what makes the Henry's Fork so unique.*

You're right, I nodded.

It's really a combination of factors, Harrop agreed. *Starting with the giant springs at its source.*

It's the biggest chalkstream in the world, I suggested.

Don't forget Henry's Lake, Puyans added.

The first trapper to explore the Henry's Fork country was John Colter, the scout who left the Lewis and Clark expedition before it returned to Saint Louis in 1806. Colter helped a second party of fur traders to establish a stockade on the lower Yellowstone and then disappeared south into the Big Horns and Absarokas to explore future trapping grounds. His solitary explorations carried him into Jackson Hole, where he crossed the Tetons to the Henry's Fork in 1807.

The river itself was later christened for Colonel Andrew Henry, who had formed the Rocky Mountain Fur Company with William Henry Ashley in 1822. It was later that Colonel Henry organized the first trapper's rendezvous on the Green River in Wyoming in 1826, but his first party had wintered on the Henry's Fork sixteen years earlier.

Alexander MacDonald described these early years in his charming book *On Becoming a Fly Fisherman,* which was published at Boston in 1959. It was illustrated with a delicate frontispiece of watercolors by the late Leslie Thompson, and his work depicted several important Henry's Fork hatches and their imitations.

Henry Stamp was an early homesteader in the valley, but its angling traditions probably began with Alfred Trude, a wealthy Chicago attorney who acquired a large cattle ranch on the river in 1889. Trude became famous four years later when he successfully prosecuted the man who killed Carter Harrison, the colorful mayor of Chicago who had sponsored the World's Columbian Exposition. Harrison's son subsequently served five terms as mayor, and was a serious angler who often fished the Trude property. The younger Harrison is credited with the first hair-wing trout flies, which were dressed on the Henry's Fork and named for his host after a successful baptism.

Fishermen were also traveling to fish the Stamp property before the close of the nineteenth century, and several wealthy Californians founded the North Fork Club there in 1902. Four years later, another group purchased the remaining acreage from Stamp to build their Flat Rock Club. The famous Coffee Pot Club was founded about 1911, and its members consisted of fishermen and their families who wanted something more comfortable than the spartan quarters and cuisine customary to the North Fork and Flat Rock memberships. The stories of their sport, and the market fishermen who supplied the Union Pacific trains and Yellowstone hotels, are a remarkable testimony to the fertility of the river and its fishery before the First World War.

Some of the mileage they fished lies submerged under the Island Park Reservoir, and both the oral history of the valley and the memoirs of Carter Harrison tell us that they struggled back with catches they found difficult to carry.

However, such reservoirs are not invariably fatal to their watersheds and fisheries. Both Henry's Lake and the Island Park Reservoir function as giant stilling basins in the spring, collecting the spates and spring snowmelt, and settling out the river's murkiness when its sister rivers are high and discolored. The sediments that precipitate out in the depths of the reservoir are a source of fertility too, since the silt beds are composed largely of richly alkaline soils, collected across the past half century. Such silts have apparently magnified the ambient fertility of the river.

The remarkable fertility of the river can pose some unusual trout-fishing problems. Perhaps the most striking are the riddles of multiple and masking fly hatches. Multiple hatches can come in many forms. Sometimes there are several species emerging at once, and a mixture of careful observation and trial-and-error tactics is needed to find which hatch the fish are taking. Trout often concentrate on species that are readily available, or flies more easily captured with a minimal expenditure of energy, but such logic does not always apply.

The masking hatch is another puzzle. It occurs when the trout are working steadily during a major hatch, yet refuse effective imitations of that species. Such selectivity is invariably focused upon less obvious aquatic diet forms, either because they are more easily captured or because the fish have grown accustomed to them. There was a remarkable example of masking-hatch behavior two seasons ago, when I was fishing with Jack Hemingway and Dan Callaghan.

The big drakes are coming, Hemingway observed when we reached the river and rigged our tackle.

We were fishing the Harriman mileage during its early-summer hatch of big lead-winged mayflies, and the first of these large olive-bodied duns were already fluttering down the current when we arrived. Big fish had started working, and it was difficult to rig our tackle because of the steady *blup-blup* of their feeding.

The big mayflies were still hatching sporadically in the early afternoon and were mixed with a regatta of tiny yellow-bodied duns. Since there were more of the mayflies hatching, and the olive-bodied flies were twice the size of the yellowish species on the water, we decided to fish imitations of the larger species. Its flies were everywhere on the smooth current below the ranch and its outbuildings.

We promptly caught several trout. Although the fish were only ten to twelve inches, our success tempted us into staying with the big dry-fly imitations, and I took several more fish before I found a really large rainbow porpoising against the bank. Its leisurely feeding exposed a heavily spotted dorsal and a huge tail that sent waves along the trailing grass. It was working in a steady rhythm, and I dropped my fly cautiously into its line of drift, but the big rainbow simply inspected the float and rejected it.

That's strange, I thought. *The others wanted it.*

The big trout was still working steadily, but it ignored a series of drag-free floats. Several times it took something I failed to see, just before my fly reached its feeding station, and twice it took something just after the fly drifted past.

What's he taking? It was an intriguing puzzle.

Finally I stopped fishing and simply watched the trout. It was obvious that the fish was not taking the big lead-winged duns, although the big flies were still coming down its line of drift. Several times it dropped back under a big fly that was hopscotching down its current tongue and rejected it too, drifting back to its feeding station to inhale something smaller in the film. It was puzzling behavior for a large trout and I was fascinated.

Another big Lead-winged Olive came down tight against the grass, and the fat rainbow drifted back lazily to inspect its passage. The big mayfly struggled clumsily in the current. The fish pushed its spotted nose against the fluttering insect, drifted with it in the current for a heart-stopping moment, and slipped back upstream. The big mayfly finished drying its wings and flew off.

That's amazing! I thought.

The big trout rose again and took something. The fish tipped back again under a fluttering drake, refused it after a brief moment of indecision, and dimpled lazily to take something smaller.

But this time I spotted the pale sailboat-shaped wings of its prey half-pinioned in the surface film. Another pale little dun drifted in its feeding lane and was taken without hesitation.

It's been on the nymphs of those pale flies!

The big rainbow settled into a steady rhythm of surface feeding now that the pale little duns were emerging. Their nymphs had been in the surface film all along, mixed with the somber nymphs and lead-winged drakes that were hatching from them, but the pale-yellowish hatch was the species they wanted. The big drakes had been hatching for only two or three days, but the yellowish *Ephemerella* flies had been a staple diet form for several weeks. The big trout was obviously suspicious of the bigger insects, since they were much darker and larger than the fly hatches of the preceding weeks. Such behavior is typical of large trout that have been caught and released, and I rummaged through my flies for an imitation of the pale-bodied duns.

The fish drifted back under the first drag-free float, intercepted it tight against the trailing grass, and took the tiny fly softly. It shook itself when I tightened, and exploded upstream. *Finally he took it!* I thought happily.

The big rainbow stopped its first wild run and jumped three times in graceful pirouettes that flashed silver in the morning light. Suddenly the reel was protesting again, and the fly line sliced past me in the current. The tippet raked briefly against the fountain moss and elodea, the leader knots throbbed with tufts of pale green vegetation. Finally the trout jumped again and shook it free, stripping the reel deep into its backing. There were other half jumps and wild threshings on the surface downstream, and I was waiting for the fragile tippet to shear against the current drag or the tiny fly to pull free, but the fish was still there.

It's a miracle! I whispered.

The fight had settled into a patient struggle against the straining nylon, with the big fish circling stubbornly and threatening to root into the weeds. It burrowed under a trailing bed of *Potamogeton* late in the fight, but it lacked the strength to break the delicate tippet, and I worked it free.

Almost finished! I thought excitedly.

The big rainbow finally surrendered and measured better than twenty-two inches, and I gently worked the tiny fly from its mouth. It held restlessly in the net meshes, regaining its strength while I waited, and suddenly it was gone. It was a perfect example of masking-hatch behavior, in which selective fish reject an obvious fly hatch to concentrate on some other diet form.

The river sustains a remarkable spectrum of fly hatches, ranging from the huge *Pteronarcys* stoneflies in its swifter currents to the incredible populations of white-winged *Tricorythodes* and *Pseudocloëon* flies in hook sizes as small as twenty-eight. Some of the finest fly hatches on the Henry's Fork occur in the early summer, starting with the salmonflies in its Box Canyon stretch and the big lead-winged *Ephemerella* hatches that follow. There are pale morning hatches in the first weeks of fishing too, and a superb hatch of smaller slate-winged olives comes off at twilight in July. Some knowledgeable big-trout fishermen like the brown-mottled *Ephemera* drakes found in the slow-flowing stretches of the Harriman property. Several other species display heavy mating swarms, and the spinner falls of the *Tricorythodes* and *Callibaetis* and *Pseudocloëon* mayflies can trigger some beautiful rises of fish on the Henry's Fork. Mixed with these hatches throughout the season are swarms of brown- and slate-colored sedges and a rich palette of ants and grasshoppers and beetles. Perhaps the easiest fishing occurs in its grasshopper season.

But it's never really easy! André Puyans argues.

You'll find that its bank-feeders are less picky than the small trout at midstream, René Harrop explained further. *They're always on terrestrials along with their aquatic hatches.*

Those smaller fish out there are usually more selective, Puyans agreed, *because they're almost entirely on mayflies and caddis.*

And our hatches are pretty tiny flies! Harrop added.

Obvious surface feeding to a visible hatch of flies is common on the Henry's Fork, but both men agree that the most spectacular rises of trout usually are found there after a mating swarm of mayflies or sedges, when their spent adults drift flush in the surface film. During those spent sedge spinner falls, the fish lie just under the surface, and porpoise and dimple gently in a steady feeding rhythm. Strong swirls and surging boils usually point to *Trichoptera* feeding, and the fish are either taking the emerging sedges before they can

114

escape into the atmosphere or rising splashily to egg-laying caddisflies. Bold rises at midday are sometimes to grasshoppers and turf beetles.

Sometimes important pieces of the Henry's Fork puzzle are found in a detailed knowledge of the river and its microhabitat. Its watercourse is almost entirely of moderate depth, and its subtle flows echo its relatively gentle profile. Yet it does display some variations on its character, and its fly-hatch activity is directly related to such subtle relationships. Weather can also play a major role in hatch matching on the Henry's Fork.

Microhabitat is an intriguing factor in fly hatches. Major flies like the big lead-wing mayflies, the slate-winged *Ephemerella flavilinea,* and the several pale morning duns are all gravel-loving species that hatch from the flowing channels between the weeds. Mayfly hatches like *Siphlonurus* and the speckle-winged *Callibaetis* and the tiny *Pseudocloëon* flies hatch from the weeds themselves. *Tricorythodes* nymphs are particularly fond of cover along the banks, and the round handful of many-brooded *Baetis* flies that thrive on the Henry's Fork are swimming nymphs that prefer the moderate currents there. The brown-mottled *Ephemera* drakes have silt-burrowing nymphs, and their hatching is concentrated in the slow-flowing stretches. Such knowledge of the relationships between nymph behavior and microhabitat can help determine what the fish are doing in a particular feeding lie.

The egg-laying behavior of mayflies is another intriguing factor in fishing the Henry's Fork. The spinner falls of species with nymphs that prefer flowing currents are invariably found downstream from the riffles and oxygen-rich currents where their eggs are laid. Slow-water flies like *Ephemera* and *Pseudocloëon* and *Tricorythodes* usually mate and oviposit over quieter currents. Since the spent adults of any spinner fall are difficult to see on the water because their wings and bodies are trapped in the surface film, the character of the current immediately upstream from a sudden flurry of spinner-fall feeding is a primary clue in matching those flies.

Weather and wind are often critical factors too. Blustery winds can sailboat the hatching flies off their principal lines of drift, until the trout are forced to concentrate on the hatching nymphs, which are not affected by the wind. Misting drizzles with little wind are particularly good dry-fly weather, because a gentle rain can slow the drying of the freshly hatched wings and keep the flies floating on the current longer. Steady winds can often drive so many hatching flies against a downwind bank that the fish will migrate there to feed, and particularly high winds will sometimes concentrate most feeding activity in the shelter of the upwind shores.

Storms are sometimes a factor in changing the normal patterns controlled by factors of microhabitat. Two seasons ago, during an unusually heavy period of brown *Ephemera* hatches, a twilight squall scattered the emerging duns upstream. So many flies were carried off on the wind that there were strange mating swarms the following nights and a spinner fall of these big brown-mottled drakes on a stretch of the Henry's Fork where they are seldom observed.

What about leader design? I asked.

Some people fish as much as twenty-five feet, Harrop replied. *Hemingway likes his leaders long, and most fishermen use tippets as delicate as 5X and 6X.*

Some fishermen fish still finer tippets?

That's right, Puyans laughed, *but I usually fish about fifteen feet with a thirty-six-inch tippet.*

Three-foot tippets? I said.

Gives you a better drag-free float, Puyans continued, *and we usually fish downstream to these fish.*

They're that tippet shy? I protested.

False casting can scare them too, Harrop nodded in agreement. *Casting upstream usually spooks these trout no matter how well you cast.*

That's really shy! I admitted.

We walked downstream until we reached the islands on the Harriman property, and the fish in their back channels were already rising greedily to a hatch of tiny *Pseudocloëon* flies. I took a dozen rainbows on a little Gray-winged Olive

116

dressed on a twenty-six hook. The pattern has worked wonders during the emergence of these tiny green-bodied duns, but suddenly the fish started to refuse it.

They've switched! I yelled.

René Harrop was fishing a hundred yards upstream, where the still currents riffled down from the islands and shelved off deep against the grassy banks. When I looked upstream to see how he was doing, Harrop was studying the water intently and not fishing. It was obvious that his fish had turned fickle too.

What are they doing? I shouted.

I'm not really sure! Harrop shouted back. *These fish have stopped and I've got a big swarm of tiny spinners here!*

Think it's the spinners?

Might be, Harrop answered. *These little spinners are the green-bodied species that just hatched.*

You think these fish are really that picky?

Sometimes they are! He laughed.

Harrop is perhaps the most knowledgeable fisherman on the Henry's Fork, and his ability to observe subtle changes in selectivity and feeding patterns is widely acknowledged along the river. The minute spinners of these twilight *Pseudocloëon* hatches are almost the same color and size as the freshly hatched duns that emerge an hour before their mating swarms. There is little difference in these two stages of their cycle, except that the duns drift on the current with upright wings and the tiny spinners come down spent, their pale wings pinioned in the surface film. Their imitations are tied on twenty-six and twenty-eight hooks, and it seemed highly unlikely that only the silhouette of their wings lying in the film could prove critical with such tiny flies.

You think a little polywing pattern would work? I yelled upstream. *These fish won't touch the upright anymore!*

Try it and see! Harrop shouted back.

There were several spent polywings in my Wheatley, and I changed flies looking up against the sky. Several large fish were dimpling softly in the smooth currents downstream, where I was looking into the waning light. There was a delicate sucking swirl on my first cast, and a fat sixteen-inch

117

rainbow exploded when it felt the hook. Three more took the little polywing before it refused to float, and I tied a fresh pattern to the tippet in the failing light. The first drift with the fresh pattern hooked an acrobatic four-pound rainbow that stripped the shrill Hardy into its backing.

They seem to like the spinners! Harrop observed.

We found Puyans in the water meadows upstream, muttering to himself about the huge rainbow that he had hooked in the shallows and had lost when it bolted downstream through a submerged fence. *Well,* Puyans grinned happily, *what about these fish?*

They don't make too many mistakes, I admitted.

They're really pretty fair about it too! Puyans laughed. *Henry's Fork rainbows make fools of everybody!*

It really tests you, I agreed.

It's the toughest river anywhere, Harrop smiled. *It's the difference between checkers and playing chess!*

[1975]

7

The Strangest
Trout Stream on Earth

*It's not a long drive from Idaho's Henry's Fork over to
the Firehole in Wyoming's Yellowstone country, but
if the Henry's Fork is demanding, the Firehole is absolutely disconcerting. The fishing is just as challenging,
although the Firehole's hatches are somewhat less
varied. But I've waded the Firehole near the Biscuit
Basin stretch described by Schwiebert in this essay,
and suddenly found myself literally in hot water.
With another step forward, I was back in a cool—
albeit hardly normal—trout stream.*

*Many visitors to Yellowstone come in summer
wanting to fish the Firehole and are disappointed. Its
best fishing is in spring and early summer, when
other Rocky Mountain rivers may be in snowmelt
flood, and in the fall—September and October, long
after most tourists have departed. Visitors are surprised too, to learn that the Firehole above its famous
falls was originally barren of trout and that the
brown and rainbow trout there are the result of turn-
of-the-century stockings. Such stockings have been
long discontinued as the Park Service follows a "nat-*

*ural course" management policy—a policy brought
freshly into question by the savage Yellowstone fires
of 1989.*

Steam rises high on cold September mornings, drifting
across the river. Skeletal trees lie in bleached jackstraw tangles beside the smoking wasteland of geysers and hot springs
downstream. The steam lingers over the river like fog, smelling of sulfur deep in the seams of the earth. It lingers in the
pale windless mornings like an encampment of cookfires.
The river eddies over its ancient ledges, flowing cold and
swimming-pool green into a reach of trailing weeds.

Chutes of boiling water spill into the river across a richly
colored outcropping of lava, hissing steam when they reach
the river. Fish rise softly to the daily hatch of tiny *Baetis* and
Paraleptophlebia flies, rolling and porpoising only inches
from the scalding currents.

The Firehole River in Yellowstone Park is unique among
the famous trout streams of the world. Its smooth weed-
trailing currents are like those of the famous Hampshire
chalkstreams in England, where dry-fly fishing was born a
century ago, slow and rich with insect life and fat surface-
feeding trout. These fish rise freely on most days, dimpling
for minute insects beside weed beds and undercut meadow
banks, but unlike the cold British chalkstreams, the Firehole
is warmed by thousands of boiling springs and geysers like
Old Faithful.

Sulfurous fumes and steam blossom high above its buf-
falo-grass meadows in a weirdly smoking landscape. The
trout sometimes rise inches away from steaming currents
that could literally cook them alive. Geysers rumble ominously beside inviting trout-filled runs, causing the fisherman to watch their smoking vents with a worried frown
while he tries his luck. Other bankside geysers sometimes
erupt, showering the riverbanks with lethal torrents of boiling water. Black volcanic sand bottoms the difficult stillwater
bends of Biscuit Basin, and the swifter reaches are broken
with strange lava ledges. Such fast-water runs sometimes
produce rainbows, but the Firehole is primarily a brown-
trout river.

Its warm currents spawn almost continually year-round hatches of the many-brooded *Baetis* mayflies, and its meadows are alive with terrestrials like ants and leafhoppers. Firehole trout take such minuscule insects with soft little rises that often hide surprisingly large fish; unlike the chalkstream browns of England, these Firehole fish seldom see insects larger than size sixteen flies. Most Firehole hatches are smaller, and such minute insects emerging on mirror-smooth currents cause some of the most difficult trout fishing in the world. The cold mornings of September and October sometimes find trout rising to such minutae in clouds of geyser steam that obscure the river. The wind carries strange fumes long imprisoned in the molten viscera of the earth, and on such mornings the Firehole seems like a river of the netherworld, the strangest trout stream this side of the River Styx.

John Colter discovered the Yellowstone country in 1807, after participating in the earlier Lewis and Clark expedition, but Jim Bridger first explored the Firehole Basin. His outlandish catalogue of exaggerations about Colter's Hell gave the Yellowstone its own Bunyanlike mythology as much as fifty years before President Ulysses Grant signed the law making it into a national park.

Bridger delighted in spinning his Yellowstone tales, and one yarn described a river that was glacier-cold at its source and flowed downhill so fast that friction heated the water and cooked its trout. The Firehole was that mythical river. Bridger exaggerated about its currents, but there are places where its bottom is actually hot. The lava crust which forms the river bottom is so thin in places that it is heated by the boiling springs and geysers underneath. Downstream from Ojo Caliente spring, which spews frightening torrents of scalding water into the Firehole, there are places where the rhyolite bedrock is so thin that the bottom feels hot through the soles of English wading brogues.

Although the Firehole is heavily populated with good trout that rise freely to almost daily hatches, fishing over them can be extremely frustrating. Minute insect forms and quiet currents can pose problems for anglers unfamiliar with such fishing, and trout fished over by thousands of eager Yellowstone visitors are unbelievably sophisticated.

The average fisherman finds them almost impossible, and the experienced fly fisherman who is unprepared to match fly hatches smaller than size sixteen will end most Firehole sessions talking to himself. Selective feeding, which finds the trout refusing anything that does not resemble their natural food, is the rule rather than the exception.

Through some forty-odd years of experience with these Firehole trout, I have found them relatively easy only during a few June mayfly hatches and the late-summer grasshopper fishing. Other times are frustrating.

My first session on the Firehole occurred in the Nez Percé meadows, which border the highway. These meadows have beautiful open water that quickens the pulse of the most knowledgeable angler, although its trout are perhaps too accessible to the tourist hordes. Hundreds of free-rising trout dimple there every day, readily visible from the highway, and this stretch of the river attracts a lot of pressure. Its brown trout are tourist-shy and difficult. The first morning I fished the Nez Percé water was cloudless and bright. Trout were rising everywhere to some minute Blue-winged Olive mayflies, but catching them was another matter. None of my flies was small enough, and the best fish seemed frightened witless by my 4X leaders. There were some sixteen Blue Quills in my fly boxes, but they looked like battleships beside the naturals, and the fish mostly refused them.

The second morning was easier. The hatching mayflies were larger, and the current was riddled with wind and drizzling rain. The looping meadow bends of Biscuit Basin surrendered fifty-odd trout under these less difficult conditions, and I felt my Firehole problems had been solved.

The third morning I returned to the Nez Percé meadows, determined to vindicate my earlier failures. Good trout were rising everywhere in the bright September sunlight. Minute mayflies rode and fluttered down the deep channels between the ledges and undulating weeds. For several hours my 4X leaders and sixteen flies proved worthless. Two days later I left the Firehole, frustrated and fishless and talking to myself, and resolved to return the following year with a lighter rod and smaller flies and finer leader tippets.

That was twenty years ago. Since then our tackle has witnessed a minor revolution: lighter fly rods are commonplace and size twenty-eight flies have become available in the best tackle shops and modern nylons have produced practical 8X leaders. The Firehole has since yielded many of its secrets during subsequent visits, and careful studies of its character and its fly hatches have paid off over the years. Those studies reveal the unique qualities that make the Firehole one of the strangest and best trout streams on earth.

The river rises in Madison Lake above Old Faithful and flows northward through a plateau of rhyolite, looping its placid currents through clustered pines and straw-colored meadows and steaming geyser basins. Since the Firehole drains the principal geyser region in the Yellowstone, considerable temperature and ecological changes occur where the river receives its hydrothermal discharges. Other changes occur below its small cold-water tributaries. These changes and their remarkable effect on both the fish and the fly hatches have been ferreted out in some fifteen years of Firehole observations.

The river is closed to fishing above Old Faithful campground to protect both its qualities as drinking water and the best nursery areas in its headwaters. Such natural spawning is important to the management of the entire watershed. These headwaters are cold from the springs and snowmelt on the Continental Divide, seldom rising above fifty-six degrees in midsummer. Their chemical properties are average for good western trout waters, and both the hatches and the growth rate of the trout are typical. Below the tourist area at Old Faithful, with the influx of its strange pools and geysers and boiling springs, the Firehole changes radically. Even more changes occur below Riverside Geyser, where the winter river temperatures are typical, but the summer temperatures hover at eighty-odd degrees and alkalinity is almost doubled. Such increased alkalinity improves both the fly hatches and the potential trout population. These changes increase progressively until the Firehole reaches Biscuit Basin. The intense hydrothermal flowages there are partly balanced by the waters of the Little Firehole, which enters the main river not far above the Biscuit Basin footbridge. The Firehole is shallow here, flowing over broken strangely patterned ledges, and the average size of its trout has increased. Fly hatches are more numerous, and some big browns are found both in the lava pockets and under the undercut banks of Iron Spring and the Little Firehole itself.

Below this Biscuit Basin water, the alkaline richness of the river is greatly increased and its river temperatures seldom drop below fifty degrees, making for excellent fly hatches and greater growth rate of the trout and better wintering. This stretch is scenic water, with serpentine bends in meadows bordered with spruce and lodgepole pine. There are some swift-flowing side channels and black-lava bottoms, where wise old browns savor minute mayflies along their grassy banks. The river is friendly and shallow here, and its trout are easily frightened by bad casting and a careless approach and heavy leaders.

The experienced Firehole fisherman fishes only to specific rises and spends much time on hands and knees, creeping and crawling to get within casting range without spooking his quarry. The stretch from the mouth of the Little Firehole to the bottom of the Biscuit Basin meadows, where a short loop-road provides parking near the river, is a mile of first-rate water.

The next two miles, between the loop-road and the Iron Bridge just off the highway, is varied water that offers both good browns and an occasional fat rainbow in the faster places. Ledges and deadfalls shelter some selective lunkers. Park rangers warn that grizzlies frequently cross the river in this stretch, and the angler should be watchful there. There are several convenient places for parking. The water above the Iron Bridge is excellent, and was described by Ray Bergman in his familiar classic *Trout,* in the passages about the Firehole and its exceptional dry-fly fishing fifty years ago. Both cold and hot springs add their seepage in this mileage of river, raising its median temperatures while decreasing its alkalinity. The stretch is especially good for caddis hatches and the fishing is excellent.

Between the Iron Bridge and the Midway Geyser Basin,

where the river again parallels the highway, is a mile of broken water with both browns and rainbows. Here the Firehole is a series of fast runs and shallow lava-pocket pools, with occasional hot springs and comical geysers, like the miniature volcano with a *putt-putt* rhythm like a tiny one-lung engine. Temperatures remain relatively warm, although several hot springs raise the alkalinity somewhat. Hatches are good, and there is an occasional lunker brown among the potholes that scar the bottom at Mule Shoe.

The water that lies between the highway and the steep geyser-covered shoreline is often obscured by clouds of sulfurous steam. The geyser waters stain these banks with varicolored deposits where they reach the river. There are several first-rate pools beside the highway, but their trout are hard-fished and shy. Above the Midway footbridge, where torrents of steaming water tumble into the river, the Firehole trout rise steadily to the hatching flies, only inches away from temperatures that could cook them alive. The exaggerations of Jim Bridger about the river were partly true.

Below the Midway footbridge, there is an excellent four-mile stretch of river, accessible from two places off the Fountain Freight Road. About a mile below the Iron Bridge, there is a twin-rut trail that forks down to the river. Temperatures on this water seldom sink below fifty-eight degrees in winter, providing hatches and optimum feeding conditions throughout the year. Its trout grow deep-bellied like Florida bass. The alkalinity is high, creating rich weedy water and heavy fly hatches.

Another half-mile on the Fountain Freight Road is the turnoff to the Goose and Feather Lake picnic grounds. Anglers leave their cars there and hike down to the river bottoms below the trees. There are side channels and undercut banks here, where some really large trout lie hidden, and several excellent pools. One side-channel pocket above the picnic area was the setting for an important Firehole lesson on a September evening long ago. The river looked shallow over an open gravel bottom, and a fish was rising tight against the grass. The rises seemed insignificant. Since the Firehole browns had treated me shabbily that afternoon, even a small fish was a prize, and I worked stealthily into casting position. Kneeling in the shallow current, I watched the rises and selected a tiny Adams to imitate the minute brownish caddisflies on the water. The cast settled right and the float looked good. The little dry fly flirted with the bank-side grasses and disappeared in a sipping dimple. Suddenly the hooked fish exploded from beneath the grass, porpoising and wallowing wildly in the gravel shallows. The leader sheared like a cobweb when the mammoth brown tunneled into the upstream weeds. The lesson was important, and I have never attempted to judge the size of a Firehole brown by its rises again.

Above the Fountain Freight Bridge, there are clearings and meadows where buffalo and elk are often found grazing. The water above the bridge is fast and broken, tumbling over terraced lava ledges and outcroppings. There are good trout in the pockets. Rainbows are often found in these swift well-aerated places.

Below the bridge, violent Ojo Caliente spring spills its steaming waters into the river, raising temperatures and alkalinity to the highest levels in its fifteen-odd miles. Downstream the currents are slow and choked with undulating beds of weeds, over a bottom that varies from rhyolite bedrock to insect-rich layers of marl. Fly hatches here are excellent. Two cold-water tributaries, meandering Fairy and Sentinel creeks, add their flowage to the Firehole below Ojo Caliente.

This reach of the river provides optimal wintering conditions for its trout. When the midsummer temperatures rise too high, which has happened sometimes since the earthquake of 1959 changed the underground hot springs, the fish congregate in the cooler current-tongues below the two feeder creeks. Gene Anderegg and I spent a week on this water once, taking some heavy browns that were selectively feeding in the mouths of these tributaries and the cold runs below them.

The Firehole returns to the highway in the Nez Percé meadows another mile downstream. This is one of the best dry-fly stretches on the river. Large browns populate its deep pools and main weed channels, but it is almost too popular and easily accessible from the highway. The deep stillwater pool just above the mouth of Nez Percé Creek produced an eleven-pound brown in grasshopper season a few years back. The trout free-rise in this mile of water on most days, and because they are so hard-fished through the tourist season, their tippet-shy selectivity is a challenge.

Nez Percé Creek adds its cooling currents and alkalinity to the Firehole near the highway, stabilizing the temperatures and alkaline riches of the six miles below. About a mile below the mouth of the Nez Percé is the famous Rainbow Riffle, which has given up some slab-sided trout with carmine flanks and gill-covers. There are also some heavy browns in this stretch, but with the highway beside the river, they are hard-fished and easily spooked. These educated Firehole lunkers usually lie in the weed channels and runs along the opposite bank, beyond the range of the average fisherman and the rock-throwing children of the tourists. There is some big water here and felt-soled chest waders are needed. Two miles farther downstream, there are some first-rate pools and pockets above the Cascades of the Firehole, but they are adjacent to scenic turnouts and parking areas, and are heavily fished. However, after September there are few visitors in the Yellowstone, and the skilled angler can find them productive.

Two miles below the Cascades, there is a reach of relatively unproductive water above the Firehole Falls. Downstream is some better fishing in the half mile of side channels and pocket water that lies between the falls and the campground at Madison Junction. This stretch is seldom fished, because most anglers become preoccupied with the more accessible meadows of the Madison and Gibbon rivers below the camping area, but in late autumn, when the spawning browns and rainbows from Hebgen Lake are stopped by the Firehole Falls, this bottom half mile of river will regularly produce trophy-size fish.

The river ends in its meadow confluence with the Gibbon, which drains the Norris Geyser Basin to the northeast, and the two rivers join to form the Upper Madison. Some thirteen miles downstream on the Madison is the town of

West Yellowstone, and the western entrance to Yellowstone Park. Regular air service to West Yellowstone is welcome news for Firehole devotees from Los Angeles to Boston, since it is possible to leave either coast in the morning and cover the Biscuit Basin stretch before nightfall.

With few exceptions, the fly patterns needed to fool these ultraselective Firehole browns are small. There is some variation in the distribution of the natural hatches with the fluctuations of alkalinity and temperature. For example, the best hatches of the larger *Ephemerella* mayflies occur in the upper reaches of the river, between Lone Star Geyser and Ojo Caliente. The brief early-season hatches of big drakes are concentrated in the weedy silt-bottomed water that provides the proper environment for the burrowing *Ephemera* nymphs. Caddis hatches are heavily distributed on the entire river, especially below Biscuit Basin. The large *Acroneuria* and dark-colored *Pteronarcys* stonefly nymphs, known erroneously as hellgrammites on western rivers, are numerous in the fast-water stretches, with particularly dense concentrations in Rainbow Riffle and above Riverside Geyser and the Iron Bridge. Minute mayflies like the *Paraleptophlebia* and *Baetis* groups are thick, especially in the quiet weedy stretches, and are numerous enough to form a staple diet for the Firehole surface feeders.

Since most fly hatches on the Firehole are small, the typical flies in the boxes of its regulars are tied on hooks between #14 and #24. Typical patterns are traditionals like the Dark Hendrickson, Light Hendrickson, Red Quill, Blue Quill, Light Cahill, Blue-winged Olive, Iron Blue Dun, Pale Watery Dun, and the Adams. Terrestrial imitations like ants, Jassids, beetles, and grasshoppers are also effective, along with standby wets like the Partridge and Olive, Grouse and Green, Partridge and Brown, and the Gold-ribbed Hare's Ear. Regional patterns like the Muskrat Nymph, Montana Nymph, Whitcraft, and Muddler are also useful, and during the big *Ephemera* hatches, the Dark Donnelly Variant in sizes ten and twelve is needed.

Perhaps the most unusual quality of the Firehole lies in its management regulations. Millions of visitors pass through its valley every season, and the Firehole is possibly the hardest fished trout stream anywhere. Public water everywhere else has degenerated to put-and-take stocking under fishing pressure, with the result that we have trout streams without trout, except on scheduled fish-truck days. Even big western rivers like the Snake and the Yellowstone and the Big Hole, while far from being fished-out, are declining noticeably each year because of excessive kill-limits and thoughtless irrigation methods and rapidly increasing numbers of fishermen. The Firehole lies within a few hours of all these bigger rivers, and although it is fished even harder than the remaining public mileage of eastern streams like the Beaverkill and the Brodheads in the shadow of New York, its fishing has remained pretty much the same in my fifteen years' experience.

Local experts like Bud Lilly and Pat Barnes, who operate famous shops in West Yellowstone and fish the Firehole regularly, point out that the river has not been stocked in the past twenty-odd years.

How can the Firehole remain the same without stocking? asks a typical first-timer.

The answer is surprisingly simple: the river has been restricted to fly fishing for almost thirty years, and its kill-limit is only five trout per day. The result is a watershed in natural balance between its spawning potential and the wild trout harvested each season, even with the extremely heavy fishing pressure.

There has been a slight decline in the number of big trout and the average size in recent years, although a heavy population of fish to sixteen inches is still present. Perhaps the unique qualities of the Firehole should be recognized and its kill-limits even more restricted. Regulations making it a fish-for-fun river with no killing whatsoever, or a trophy-fishing river where one or two trout above fifteen inches are permitted, would probably make its fishing even better. The sulfur content of its water makes most Firehole fish ordinary table fare anyway.

Similar regulations will probably be necessary on all wadable, easily fished streams in the future, if Americans

129

want to enjoy decent trout fishing on their public waters under population pressures, and the Firehole is a graphic example of future management techniques.

The last time I fished above Biscuit Basin, there was a twenty-inch brown rising regularly in a shallow lava pocket. It was a difficult place to approach without frightening the trout, and I spent almost fifteen minutes circling around below his position and working stealthily up the ledgerock riffles on hands and knees. Finally I was in position for a delicate presentation and dragless float, and started false casting when some tourists from Nebraska came down the path to the river. The man was wearing a white shirt and his wife had a bright yellow dress.

Catching anything? they asked innocently.

The big brown had spooked long before they reached me. Their children began running up and down the bank, throwing rocks into the water and splashing in the shallows with sticks. The smaller trout stopped rising in terror. There was no point in fishing after such bedlam, and I reeled-in unhappily to look for a quieter reach of water.

Riverside Geyser erupted as I reached the car, putting on the sporadic show that dwarfs Old Faithful. Tourist cars began stopping everywhere, until crowds of people were milling around me. Cameras were clicking furiously as I put my rod away. The geyser reached its peak and began to subside and torrents of scalding water cascaded down the banks. The morning was filled with the acrid choking odors of sulfur. Clouds of steam towered into the crisp September air and billowed across the landscape until it was impossible to drive or see the river. Such experiences are typical and make the Firehole the strangest trout stream on earth.

[1965]

8

Where Flows
the Umpqua

*Our westward journey ends in Oregon, as we join
Schwiebert in fly fishing for summer steelhead on the
North Umpqua, one of this country's most beautiful
rivers. Steelhead fly fishing has a tradition—albeit a
short one—based on the swing of a sunken wet fly. As
steelhead fly fishing has matured from its early beginnings more than fifty years ago, its wet flies have
become increasingly elegant and now approach the
finest in modern Atlantic salmonflies as an art form.
It's a tradition that emerged in large part on the North
Umpqua.*

*And it's a tradition that the North Umpqua is
helping to alter. For the past several seasons, this river
has had unusually large runs of summer steelhead
and a proportionately large number of fly fishermen
who were willing to experiment. Some found that a
dead-drift nymph and a strike indicator could be
enormously productive. Others found that some se-
ductive black-marabou concoctions drifted deep
would pull fish when regular wet flies failed. And
there was on some nights a clench-jawed, icy silence*

131

*in the Steamboat Inn, as the traditional wet-fly men
glared at some new upstarts who had made such
traditionally difficult fishing seem suddenly simple. It
isn't simple, of course, and traditional wet-fly methods are far from dead, but even now the North Umpqua is playing a pivotal role in the changing face of
steelheading.*

It was getting dark when we finally left Boise, looking into
the dying light behind the Stinkingwater Pass. The mountains rose in layers of stark ridges surrounding Freezeout
Peak and Coyote Wells, their names still bitter echoes of the
frontier trappers who first explored this Oregon country. The
milky currents of the Snake flowed still and deep beyond the
Payette, its brushy islands and shallow bars alive with twilight flocks of geese. Still farther downstream in the darkness
at Farewell Bend, where the travelers on the Oregon Trail left
the river to risk the difficult wagon trace to Deadman's Pass,
the river was purple and mauve. There was a thin moon
rising, and the night seemed full of ghosts.

Still six hours of driving, Jack Hemingway said.

The highway left the river and reached into the darkness,
and I poured us both some coffee when we crossed the Drin-
kingwater Summit. The chill wind moved restlessly in the
sagebrush. We stood in the darkness beside the Peugeot,
watching the headlights of the sixteen-wheel Kenworths and
Peterbilts climbing steadily into the foothills that surround
the arid Malheur Basin.

Beyond the outcroppings of the Stinkingwater Pass, the
lights of the sawmill town of Burns looked toylike and melancholy on the horizon. Its timber comes from the Straw-
berry Mountains and Deschutes Plateau, and the headwaters
of the John Day country.

The saline marshes south of Burns glittered in the cold
moonlight, their waters a surviving echo of the brackish seas
that once shrouded eastern Oregon. Other echoes are found
in half-dry lakes with curious names like Mugwump and
Stone Corral and Bluejoint. The narrow highway reaches
west from Burns like a cartographer's grid, with virtually
nothing for sixty-five miles.

Pretty empty piece of road, I said.

It's empty all right! Hemingway laughed. *Maybe we should stop and take a coffee break in Burns!*

Thermos is getting low, I nodded.

The truckstop was brightly lighted. Its fuel pumps were surprisingly busy at midnight, and the counter stools were crowded too. Some drivers had finished and were drinking beer, while the early crews were starting breakfast to reach their clear-cutting sites at daybreak. The bartender was perspiring heavily, and his bulging waistline betrayed a lifetime of chicken-fried steaks and potatoes and beer. The waitress was feeding coins into the jukebox, and stood listening while Waylon Jennings's hard-driving guitar rose above the kitchen noise and laughter along the bar. She fussed with her lacquered hair while we ordered coffee, and she stopped to add another quarter to the jukebox on her way to the kitchen.

It's not exactly gourmet, Hemingway laughed infectiously. *Things will get better once we get to Steamboat—it's quiet in the cabins along the river and the food is really great!*

I've heard a lot about it, I said.

The moon was still bright beyond Steen's Mountain, its serrated snake-country ridges silhouetted in the darkness. The night was perfectly still and clear. When the waitress had filled our thermos, we started west again, watching the headlights of a solitary truck on the horizon. The desert bottoms at Glass Butte were empty, and once the tractor had passed, the old highway was completely dark for more than forty miles. The moon was getting low and the sagebrush was silvery with frost.

We're still about three hours out, Hemingway said.

Getting cold! I shivered and reached back for the thermos. *We've got plenty of coffee and fresh bread and cheese—we've even got some smoked oysters, but it's too cold for Chablis.*

It's never too cold for Chablis!

Hemingway had chilled a magnum of wine during dinner at Annabel's in Boise, and we carefully wrapped the bottle in a plastic bag filled with crushed ice. The map compartment of the Peugeot bulged with cassettes of Mozart and Beethoven and Bach, and their soaring music filled its multiple speakers.

How about some heat? I suggested.

You haven't heard about our mouse? Hemingway laughed.

Mouse or mousse? I grinned.

Mouse in the heating system. He ignored the question and continued. *It's been rooting around behind the instruments ever since I took delivery on the car.*

The heater's not working? I protested.

It's completely clogged, he grinned. *Smells too!*

What does our visitor eat? I asked.

Beats me! Hemingway laughed. *Some assembly plant worker probably built his leftover lunch into my Peugeot!*

Could we coax it out with some cheese?

It's a genuine French mouse. He shook his head wryly. *It'll never come out of there for a piece of cheddar—it'll probably hold out for Roquefort or Camembert or Brie!*

It's going to get pretty cold, I said.

But how many fishing trips have a French stowaway?

Yours would! I agreed.

We stopped again for coffee at Bend, where the swift Deschutes gathers itself from the lava-field seepages and plateaus, and drops into the white-water canyons between the Warm Springs reservation and its junction with the Columbia. The highway that leads south from Bend climbs steadily into the dense ponderosa forests that rise between Paulina and Packsaddle Mountain. Sawmill towns like Crescent and Gilchrist are virtually the only habitation in the seventy-five miles of plateau country.

There was still fresh snow from the late-summer storms that blanket the high plateau surrounding Crater Lake, and there were fresh drifts in the lodgepoles at Diamond Lake summit. It is country famous for its winter snowpacks, and the highway crews had already placed the reedlike poles to help them plow the right-of-way.

Beyond the timber plateau, the Umpqua highway winds past Cinnamon Butte before it drops steeply toward Toketee and Steamboat. Its headwaters are shrouded in a mixed forest of pine and Douglas fir and cedar. Below the Toketee waterfall, the river tumbles through a steep-walled gorge of ancient lava and the highway winds high above its pools and rapids. It finally reaches the Forest Service station at Steamboat Creek, and the Steamboat Inn downstream.

There were no lights when we finally reached the inn, and found a note telling us where our beds were. Our cabins were behind the inn itself, sheltered in a stand of thick-trunked sugar pines and firs, and the tumbling river lay below in the darkness. Its music was strong, and it was almost daylight when I finally slept.

It was strangely dark the next morning, and I peered outside to check the weather when my watch read ten-thirty. The morning was clear and bright, and the sun was already strong, but the magnificent trees sheltered our cabins so completely that it still seemed early. Hemingway was already fishing the Kitchen Pool.

There are six cabins perched above the river in a gentle half circle in the trees. Their riverfront façades are connected with a curving, fir-slat deck fitted with generous railings and benches, and their split-cedar shingles were dark with moss and pine needles. The Umpqua roared its greetings a hundred feet below the deck, its depths all emerald and spume under the Glory Hole.

It's beautiful! I thought.

I walked lazily up the stonework steps and passed under the grape arbor into the inn itself. Several backpackers and logging-rig drivers were sharing breakfast at the long table with a young professor from Oregon State. Three hunters in a huge pickup with racing tires, and several rifles across the rear window, stopped to fill its tank. There were two deer in its truckbed, and an average trophy head was roped grotesquely across its hood, streaming blood across the brightwork like a pagan sacrifice.

Steamboat Inn leads several lives. It is the principal cigarette and fuel stop in the eighty-odd miles between Crater Lake junction and Idleyld on the North Umpqua, and both travelers and logging crews stop there often. During its daytime hours, it functions as part fly-fishing shrine, tackle shop, short-order kitchen, filling station, and truckstop selling cigarettes and soft drinks and beer.

Its changing cast includes its fishing regulars: a mixture of teachers, attorneys, doctors, stockbrokers and bankers, college professors, writers, book salesmen, editors, photographers, professional fly tiers, artists, fishing guides, manufacturers, architects and builders, engineers, and retired soldiers who constantly return to Steamboat, sharing an ascetic love of fishing its summer-run steelhead, a species perfectly suited to contemplation and self-denial.

The Steamboat Inn is completely transformed at twilight. Its daytime chrysalis is trapped in a cocoon of beer and logging trucks and country music, but its nightly metamorphosis is total. Its doors and windows are shuttered from its daytime universe behind its bamboo blinds, and it creates its own nighttime world.

Its country music is stilled and replaced by Mozart and Beethoven and Bach, mixed with a little Chopin and Brahms. Its gargantuan table becomes a celebration of spotless linen and candlelight, and its beer bottles are eclipsed by Cabernet Sauvignon and Beaujolais and Pinot Noir. The inn is closed except to those with dinner reservations and its steelhead regulars. Its cuisine is a growing legend in the Oregon logging country. Typical fare might include vichyssoise, smoked salmon, mushroom soufflé, beef Wellington, broccoli and cauliflower, and tiny fresh peas served family style, chocolate mousse, and a richly soft California wine in a carafe.

Breakfasts are relatively unusual too. There are several kinds of omelettes, various breads baked on the premises, muffins mixed with bran and dill, perfectly cured bacon and ham, and exquisitely prepared hash-brown potatoes.

I'll try the Steamboat Special, I decided rashly.

The young blue-jeaned waitress disappeared into the kitchen. Dan Callaghan appeared on the back porch, hanging his rod in the grape arbor outside. Callaghan is among the best steelhead fishermen on the North Umpqua as well as a superb photographer.

You're finally alive! Callaghan grinned. *Hemingway told me you were still sleeping—find anything on the menu?*

Steamboat Special, I replied.

Callaghan poured himself a mug of coffee and clattered back across the room to the giant sugar-pine table, his wading calks grating on the concrete-aggregate floor. The young waitress returned with my breakfast, and I stared at a platter heaped with food. There were fried potatoes and several pieces of thick whole wheat toast surrounding a mammoth omelette that barely held its filling of ham and tomatoes and onions, mixed with a few other vegetables.

It's awesome! I protested weakly and faltered. *How many eggs do they crack for that monster?*

Five or six! Callaghan smiled. *Steamboat Special.*

Can't they try a half-egg omelette?

You'll need it! Callaghan insisted. *The river is pretty cold and its currents are strong—and it takes hundreds and hundreds of casts to catch a steelhead.*

You mean I'll burn it off? I asked.

You'll see, he smiled.

We rigged our equipment after breakfast, sorting flies from my duffle and putting up eight-weight rods and organizing other tackle into a vest designed for deep wading.

The North Umpqua is a dangerous river. Its currents are swift and deceptively clear, flowing over a bedrock of river-polished lava that is difficult to read and as treacherous as icy pavement. Even when its bottom is relatively good, in pools like Wright Creek and Kitchen, an angler is forced to wade armpit deep in a smooth current of startling power. There are many places where the river flows swiftly through narrow channels in the ledges, at depths of as much as thirty and forty feet, and other places where a smooth pool gathers itself to plunge into a reach of impassable rapids.

You really think felt-soled brogues are not enough? I asked when I pulled on my waders. *It's really that slippery?*

Callaghan found me an extra pair of wading sandals with a pattern of fresh snow-tire calks mounted in the soles. *You better use these over your wading brogues,* he warned and described their lacing system, *or you'd better tell us where to ship your effects!*

You've got my attention, I admitted.

137

It was starting to rain when we pulled out on the Umpqua highway and started downstream. The logging trucks roared past, heavily loaded with their mammoth trunks of sugar pine and fir chained together and consigned to the sawmills in Roseburg, or racing back upriver loaded with their own rear-wheel dollies and cargo booms. The truck drivers are paid by the trip, which tempts foolhardy drivers to attempt more runs than are wise, and the highway patrol is always fishing their sixteen-wheel rigs from the river.

It helps to be crazy! Callaghan said.

My baptism on the North Umpqua occurred at Wright Creek. Upstream the river stills itself in greeny deeps, its eddies and smooth currents reflecting a stand of towering sugar pines and firs. Huge boulders lie in its depths, their presence betrayed only by the rhythms of flow that disturb its mirrored surfaces. The steep tributary creek across from the highway was almost dry. Toward the swelling tail of the pool, the giant boulders and pumpkin-size cobblestones on the bottom are increasingly visible, all chocolate and bronze with winter algae. There are several boulders across the pool that shelter fish, along with a dozen pockets in the tail shallows that can hold a traveling steelhead that has just ascended the rapids.

Wright Creek has a decent bottom and usually holds a few steelhead in October. Its currents swim the fly smoothly, and its seemingly gentle flow is surprisingly heavy if one wades too deeply or too close to the throat of its rapids downstream, where the flow gathers itself into a steep plunge of river that almost drowns the droning of the logging trucks on the highway.

We can spot fish from the road, Callaghan explained.

We peered stealthily through the willows into the pool, where the dim light penetrated into its secrets. The light rain had stopped, and we could see the bottom clearly in several places.

Suddenly I found a steelhead hovering in the shallows. *Look there!* I pointed excitedly. *Just ahead of those stones!*

There's another beyond that fish, Callaghan said.

Well, I grinned, *they're here!*

138

The best holding-lies are still in shadows. Callaghan pointed. *We've probably got several more.*

Callaghan rummaged through his wading vest and passed me a perfectly dressed Cummings, an elegant steelhead pattern with its roots in the history of the Umpqua. It was misting rain again when we clambered down the steep banks from the highway, studied the holding-lies we had spotted and slipped gently into the shallows.

The river was bone chilling and I shivered slightly, half from its icy currents and half in anticipation. *You'll have to wade deep to cover the first lies.* Callaghan pointed back toward the alders. *Keep your backcast pretty high.*

There was a narrow opening where the steep path came down through the boulders and brush, and the wading-calk graffiti on the bottom cobbles and ledges clearly marked the passage of other fishermen. It was a difficult cast, lifting high through the branches and changing direction in the forward stroke, looping the unrolling line back across the flow and slightly upstream from the rocks.

Mend your line! Callaghan suggested. *Mend it!*

I lifted the rod smoothly, stripping several feet of line free of the sliding current, and looped it back upstream with a counterclockwise rolling of my wrist. The current was deceptively swift and the line quickly bellied again.

Keep mending the swing, Callaghan said, *because even a summer steelhead likes the fly slow and deep.*

I'll try it! I lifted into another cast.

We covered the boulders and pockets carefully, working down into the tail of the pool, and fishing each fly swing out until it hung directly downstream. It held there briefly in the streaming flow, and then I worked the fly back in a steady rhythm of six-inch pulls, before taking a step downstream and repeating the cast. The river flowed secret and still, its smooth surface barely disturbed by the rain.

Perfect steelhead weather! Callaghan frowned when I failed to move a fish. *Change flies and fish through again!*

It was sound advice based on years of steelhead fishing. Callaghan selected his own variation on the Skunk, perhaps the best-known steelhead pattern to evolve on the North

139

Umpqua. His dressing combined the scarlet tail fibers, black chenille and silver ribbing, somber throat hackles, and a polar bear wing with a single turn of fluorescent green chenille at its tail.

Try this Green-butt Skunk, he suggested.

Callaghan clipped the elegant Cummings back in his Wheatley box while I knotted the Skunk to my tippet. We worked slowly back upstream, careful not to telegraph our ripples out across the current, and trying to mute the grating of our calks on the bottom.

There's a big stone out there. Callaghan pointed across the river. _It usually has a fish or two behind it._

I waded into the heavy current, searching out toeholds and firm footing as the river seeped into my wading vest pockets, and I looked back to locate the casting window in the willows. The backcast lifted high and looped the fly across the stream, dropping it behind the submerged stone. I started mending its swing in the spreading flow, and there was a strong pull that telegraphed back toward the surface in a fiercely spreading swirl.

The fish had hooked itself and bolted angrily upstream against the protesting reel. It stopped to brood behind an unseen boulder, perhaps husbanding its strengths and strategies, and then it exploded: full-length from the dark current it came, thrusting itself sword-bright from its watery scabbard and throwing spray in the soft rain.

Excalibur! I thought wildly.

The silvery steelhead spent itself almost mindlessly, jumping six times and holding upstream where it fought both the river and my straining tackle. It settled stubbornly along the bottom, perhaps unwilling to seek its freedom in the wild rapids downstream, remembering a swift maelstrom that had proved difficult to ascend.

Finally it surrendered, sleek and sea-polished and swimming weakly in the shallows. We admired its beauty briefly and unhooked the fly, and the silver henfish splashed free. _They're really something!_ I mumbled happily and watched it holding behind my legs. _They're really something, and your Umpqua is pretty special too!_

We're lucky, Callaghan said. _She's not always generous!_

There are still many steelhead rivers on our Pacific Coast, from the small spate watersheds below San Francisco to the wilderness rivers of Alaska, but most support primarily winter-run fish. It is the summer steelhead that fill our lyric moods.

Many fishermen still cling to the old myths that steelhead seldom take flies. Such myths die hard, and even experienced winter steelhead fishermen believe you must suffer to catch them. Steelhead on most rivers mean snowstorms and cold weather and rivers swollen bank-full with winter rains, and most are still caught with hardware fished along the bottom or with pencil-sinker rigs baited with salmon roe. Winter steelhead fishing is a world of half-frozen fingers. Since the winter-run strains are more widely distributed, entering their parent rivers in late autumn and still arriving the following spring, the steelhead is usually winter's child.

It is also surrounded with a remarkable mystique, rooted in its secret migrations and coin-bright beauty and strength, and there are steelhead stories in truckstops and fishing villages and logging camps from Big Sur to the Aleutians. Claude Kreider caught something of that mystique in his little book *Steelhead,* and in these passages describing his first encounter on the Umpqua:

Another morning we tried Rock Creek Riffle again soon after daylight, and while we raised not even a trout to our flies, we had some glorious excitement.

We learned what can happen when a big steelhead goes over into the wild waters below your pool. A lusty young fellow using a short casting rod and a big spinner followed us through the riffle. Down near the tail, where the water surged through a maze of giant boulders, he hooked a good fish.

"Wow, he's going over!" he yelled.

Leaping from rock to rock, sometimes wading, he followed that plunging steelhead down the river. His thumb was clamped down on his reel spool, for his stiff casting rod was jerking and whipping with each surge of the great fish. He followed it desperately, first like a mountain goat and then like a diver. I saw him wading frantically downstream and fall down, to rise dripping and shouting and still holding on.

And far downstream his great fish, which looked surely a ten-pounder, came out with a mighty leap and was gone!

Although it supports a population of winter-run steelhead, the North Umpqua is perhaps most famous for its summer fish. Unlike the smaller grilse-size steelhead that dominate the runs in sister rivers like the Eel and Klamath and Rogue, the steelhead that return to the Umpqua during the summer are largely mature fish. Other summer steelhead rivers include the Deschutes and Stillaguamish and Washougal, and their fish are the royalty of Pacific watersheds.

Yet these beautiful summer-run fish are rare, and fishing them is seldom measured through success alone. The rivers that boast fine runs of summer steelhead are also celebrated for their moodiness, and among the great summer-run streams that drain into these coastal seas, the storied North Umpqua is perhaps the most ephemeral.

With its handful of sister rivers, the Umpqua is born in the remarkable lava-field aquifers that spread for hundreds and hundreds of square miles around Crater Lake. Its unique depths fill an immense volcanic caldera so large that a secondary volcano formed Wizard Island in its aquamarine waters.

The lake itself reaches more than two thousand feet into the Stygian entrails of its plateau. Its encircling crater is the surviving echo of once-towering Mount Mazama, which erupted and collapsed violently more than six thousand years ago. The immense forest highlands that shroud its lava spillages are famous for their winter snows, which can measure more than thirty to forty feet in depth, and their spring thaws both fill the crater and percolate deep into the sloping lava-field strata that are layered toward the rivers. Its volcanic skeleton and the labyrinth of surrounding lava form the subterranean beginnings of several famous trout streams in Oregon. Starting with the South Umpqua at Fish Mountain, their

142

clockwise roster of flowages born in these Crater Lake aquifers includes the North Umpqua, the swift-flowing Deschutes, the somber Williamson, the spring-fed Wood at Fort Klamath, and the famous white-water of the Rogue.

Clark Van Fleet devotes an entire chapter of his classic *Steelhead to a Fly* to the North Umpqua, and its dramatic genesis in the heart of the Cascade Mountains. His description of the river and its fishing includes the following paragraphs:

The beginnings of the average western river are pretty inconsequential: a trickle through some mountain meadow, a brook purling through a canyon strewn with boulders with an occasional cascade over some precipitous cliff, until finally a full-blown river emerges.

But the North Umpqua comes in roaring: it springs from the living rock as did Minerva from the head of Jove. Presumed to be the outlet by some underground cleavage for part of the overflow of Diamond Lake, it is a river at its very source.

It gathers some volume on its brawling way through the mountains to join the South Umpqua below Winchester, yet it would still be a tremendous stream without the additions brought by its few insignificant tributaries. The roar of its mighty voice fills the canyon of its passage from source to junction as it tumbles down the rough boulder-strewn cleft carved by its journey. A mile of fishing along its banks is a very real test of endurance, as you snake your way over the folds in the bedrock, scramble on jagged reefs, and cross its boulders.

The steelhead to be found there are as wild and untamed as the river they ascend. When you have beached a steelhead of over ten pounds from the waters of this torrent, your pride will be fully justified.

Fly fishing for steelhead clearly had its genesis on the swift summer-run rivers of northern California, and particu-

143

larly in the sweeping bends of the Eel at Eureka. Its fishing pioneers included figures like Jim Hutchens, Henry Soule, Lloyd Silvius, Jim Pray, Sam Wells, Sumner Carson, Josh Van Zandt, and John Benn, the transplanted fly dresser who emigrated from Ireland before the Civil War.

The Rogue soon developed a similar circle of steelhead pilgrims when its summer fish proved receptive to flies, although they averaged half the size typical of the Klamath and Eel. Unlike the California rivers, their banks often crippled with highways and their headwaters stripped of their life-giving timber, the Rogue was a wild river float in the Oregon solitude. Its acolytes were a happy few with a sense of adventure, and their ranks included some half-legendary steelhead pioneers like Rainbow Gibson, John Coleman, Fred Burnham, Sam Wells, Zeke Allen, Captain Laurie Mitchell, Fred Noyes, Major Lawrence Mott, Cappy Black, and the colorful Toggery Bill Isaacs, who later guided President Herbert Hoover on the Rogue.

Zane Grey was perhaps the most celebrated figure among the steelhead pioneers after the First World War. Grey first encountered these exciting sea-run rainbows in 1918, on the Stillaguamish in the mountains north of Seattle. The writer was soon obsessed with these big rainbows, joined the growing ranks on the rivers of southern Oregon, and spent his last twenty years fishing. Steelhead finally killed him, because Zane Grey suffered the stroke that finally led to his death while fishing the North Umpqua in 1939.

Zane Grey was a popular writer, Frank Moore observed recently at his log-framed house high above the Umpqua, *and his fishing books made him a fishing hero to many readers—but there were other fishermen on the Umpqua and Rogue who fished rings around him!*

Grey was clearly not as popular as his books, although he was often held in something approaching awe, even by fellow anglers who did not respect his fishing skills. Grey had been transformed into a celebrity and welcomed the attention of an audience that eagerly devoured the flood of cowboy adventures that followed the publication of his *Riders of the Purple Sage* in 1912.

Other western titles that subsequently became films included *The Maverick Queen, Western Union, West of the Pecos, Robber's Roost, The Lost Wagon Train, Under the Tonto Rim,* and *Wildfire.* Grey wrote almost fifty western stories, and their immense success made him wealthy enough to stop writing popular fiction. His later books were largely devoted to the fishing odysseys of his twilight years. The books that described his angling exploits included titles like *Tales of Virgin Seas, Adventures in Fishing, Tales of the Angler's El Dorado, Tales of Southern Rivers, Tales of Swordfish and Tuna, Tales of Tahitian Waters,* and the immensely popular *Tales of Fresh-Water Fishing,* which ranged from his boyhood smallmouth on the Lackawaxen in eastern Pennsylvania to billfish off the Antipodes.

His popularity soon waned along the Rogue and Umpqua, partially through his obvious vanity and largely through his practice of hiring guards and surrogate fishermen to occupy his favorite pools until he could fish them. Such selfishness earned Grey an army of hostile fishermen and neighbors along both rivers. It is perhaps typical that Grey seldom mentioned the North Umpqua in his writings, although it was his favorite steelhead fishery.

His arrogance and personality ultimately cost Grey the friendship of his best fishing friend, Fred Burnham, whose skills were legend along the Umpqua before the Second World War. There are two beautiful pools on its fly-only water that still bear his name, Upper Burnham and Lower Burnham, and both are still productive today. Grey sought Burnham in his early steelhead years because Burnham was the acknowledged master of the sport, and the writer envied his skills and the admiration of the fishing fraternity.

Trey Combs writes of their ill-fated friendship in *Steelhead Fly Fishing and Flies,* describing its beginnings along the Rogue and Umpqua, and its collapse on a marlin expedition off New Zealand, when Grey deliberately cost his friend a world record:

Early in their relationship, Grey knew so little about steelheading, while Burnham was the acknowledged master of the sport. His skills were respected by

145

Grey, and in some measure, he ultimately learned them.

In the narrow confines of the steelheading hierarchy, there was no better company to keep than Burnham's, and in its limited sense, Burnham was the celebrity. Grey plainly admired Burnham, but behind their mutual respect was Grey's competitive mania. As he learned, he became an angling institution that wrote hyperbolically of his angling fortunes. Grey came to feast on the legend he himself had built, an unfortunate display of ego that would come to end his gifted relationship with Burnham.

Fred Burnham married rich after graduating from the University of California and became a stockbroker, an occupation made to order for already acquired wealth. He was an outstanding athlete, possessing size and strength and coordination. He learned to present a fly with unbelievable skill, casting an entire silk line to a desired spot while wading waist deep. Years after he had patiently taught Grey the intricacies of fly fishing for steelhead, they pursued deep-sea fishing together, and did so in competition.

They ultimately fished New Zealand for its trout, and in separate boats, for its billfish. There came a day when Burnham caught a marlin of record size and signalled Grey to call in the catch. Grey ignored this request.

Had Burnham endangered one of Grey's many records? Whatever the reason, this unique union of angling passion born on the Rogue was permanently dissolved off New Zealand.

Similar echoes are found in the relationship between Grey and his Japanese cook during their years on the Rogue and Umpqua. Grey subjected the diminutive George Takahashi to almost constant ridicule and practical jokes and humiliations.

Grey typically took the best steelhead pools, while his

146

servant was restricted to fishing those places that Grey usually ignored. Takahashi apparently accepted his status in silence, and fished only the pools that Grey designated. Sometimes he caught steelhead when Grey failed on the famous pools, eventually gaining a place in the hearts of the river people along the North Umpqua. Perhaps it is fitting that the river still has pools named for the little Japanese cook, the beautiful Takahashi and Lower Takahashi, while Zane Grey has no similar memorial. These lines from *Tales of Fresh-Water Fishing* offer some telling insights into their relationship:

What a splash when he went down! It was too much for me! I jumped up out of the shade and ran to the water, thrilled beyond measure at the sight of such a wonderful fish! Then I grew horrified that Takahashi was pointing his rod straight in the direction of the fish and winding hard.

"Let him run!" I shouted. "He'll break off!"

George looked across at me with a broad grin, seemingly not in the least surprised.

"Hold your rod up!" I yelled louder. "Let go of your reel! You can't wind him like that! Let him run!"

Despite the efforts to check him, the steelhead took more and more line. He made an angry smash at the surface, and next he leaped magnificently.

Oh, what a wonderful trout!

I saw the silver and pink glow of him, his spotted back, the great broad tail curving on itself, and the great cruel jaws. What I would have given to have had him at the end of my line! I grew increasingly incensed at Takahashi's stupidity, and in stentorian terms I started roaring.

"Hold your rod up . . . let him run!"

Perhaps the sound of my voice rather than the meaning of my words, finally penetrated his cranium. He shouted "All right!" across at me, a little grimly I thought, or perhaps a bit ironically. But I

147

also saw that his failure to stop the steelhead had roused him.

Takahashi cannot bear advice or defeat.

"Fish no come!" he yelled piercingly. "Stick there!"

My exasperation knew no bounds, and if Takahashi had been on my side of the river, I would have committed the unpardonable sin of seizing the rod.

"Let him run then." I choked.

But even as I shouted this last despairing cry, the wild action ceased. His line hung limp in the water. His rod lost its rigidity, and the steelhead had escaped. Without so much as a word or glance in my direction, Takahashi waded out and plunged into the brush.

Grey seemingly had little respect for Takahashi in terms of his steelhead fishing, and resented his angling success, perhaps believing that any fish taken clumsily by his diminutive Japanese cook was a trophy lost to his own skills. Sometimes Grey also expressed a grudging admiration for his stoic servant, and those feelings surfaced in his books. Courage and discipline and skill have many different yardsticks, and these brief observations from *Down the Rogue* are in that vein, although they did not occur on the Umpqua.

Reamy Falls had been the seventeenth rapid we had passed, all in only ten miles of the Rogue, and one boat lost along the way! We sat and lay around Takahashi's campfire, a completely starved, exhausted and silent group wet to the skin, and suffering from bruises and rope burns and aches!

How welcome the fire!

And the wonderful Takahashi was as cheerful and deft, as if he had not partaken of our labors!

"Hoo-ooh! All thing ready! Come get!" Takahashi sang out. "Nice hot soup and all good thing!"

The North Umpqua was already becoming famous in the years that followed the First World War. Its steep-walled canyon in the sixteen miles below Steamboat Creek was still cloaked in primeval forests. Its rocky watercourse was still unblemished except for the fishing trails that plunged steeply down to the best pools from the old highway, winding high above the river in the trees. The beautiful Mott Trail that leads down the south bank from Sawtooth to Wright Creek was only a rough trace in those early years. Fishing the river was a difficult challenge, and even hiking down the steep trails was complicated with ledges and moss-covered dead-falls and boulders. Climbing back to the highway, happily tired from a long day's fishing in strong currents with house-size outcroppings and slippery ledges, could seem like Homeric odysseys into the Himalayas.

It's still tough to wade and fish when you can drive along the river, Jack Hemingway observed after his daily catnap on the porch. *You like it best before you're fifty!*

Make that forty! Dan Callaghan chided us both.

The old river highway wound high along the north shoulder of the canyon, dropping back down to the river at Steamboat, where old Major Lawrence Mott retired after the First World War and started his famous steelhead camp on a beautiful site leased from the Forest Service. His charming North Umpqua Lodge soon became the Valhalla of summer steelhead fishing, and a competitive camp upstream was started by the colorful Umpqua Vic O'Byrne.

There is a photograph of old Major Mott in the Steamboat Inn, showing the portly retired soldier with a huge chinook salmon, taken with fly tackle on the Kitchen Pool in 1930. When Major Mott died at the beginning of the Second World War, his bucolic fishing camp in the sugar pines at Steamboat was taken over by Zeke Allen, who had worked there for many seasons as the cook and chief guide. His tenure at the North Umpqua Lodge was succeeded by the proprietorship of the late Clarence Gordon, who was considered the wizard of the Umpqua through the Depression years. Gordon became as famous as the Umpqua itself.

Other storied steelhead fishermen who regularly fished

149

the Umpqua in those seasons included the ubiquitous Fred Burnham, Don Anderson, Colonel Frank Hayden, Ward Cummings, Roy Donnelley, Don Harger, Charles Stevenson, Cal Bird, and Clark Van Fleet.

Cummings and Stevenson are both credited with the beautiful steelhead patterns that bear their names, and the versatile Harger apparently conceived the original dressing of the Umpqua Special. Jim Pray was the author of the Thor and Golden Demon, and although both patterns evolved on the Eel in northern California, they have since become standard steelhead dressings on the Umpqua.

However, it was Clarence Gordon who developed the Black Gordon, and apparently worked out our modern dressings for the Cummings and Umpqua Special and Skunk. When he decided to sample his first steelhead fishing, the celebrated Ray Bergman sought the tutelage of Clarence Gordon on his beloved North Umpqua. Bergman described his baptism on the Steamboat water in his classic *Trout.*

> The river is wild and beautiful and, at first sight, a little terrifying. You wonder how you are going to be able to wade it without getting into trouble. Despite this, it isn't so bad once you learn to read its bottom. Between the ledges there are often narrow strips of gravel which wander here and there, and criss-cross like downtown city streets.
>
> By walking on these, and stepping only on the reasonably flat, clean rocks or other rocks where you can see signs of previous footsteps, you can wade with fair comfort and safety. The rocks of the routes between most of the good pools are plainly outlined by the tread of many feet, and as long as you know what to look for, you will have no trouble.
>
> But do not try to hurry, and watch each step closely unless you have the surefootedness of a mountain goat or Clarence Gordon. When he gets into a hard place, he simply makes a hop, skip and jump, and lands just where he wants, while you gingerly and sometimes painfully make your way after him, arriving a few minutes later.

He always waits patiently, apparently, but probably in his heart wishing you would get a move on. He finds such wading so easy, it must seem ridiculous to him for other fishermen to be so slow and faltering.

I once thought I was agile, and perhaps I was, from what others tell me. But Clarence Gordon on the North Umpqua—well, just ask those who have fished the river with him!

Bergman found its summer steelhead displayed a strength and moodiness worthy of their reputation. Several of its sea-armored fish were hooked and lost, and there were many hours of fruitless casting on its finest riffles and pools before the Umpqua finally surrendered a fish to his efforts. Bergman returned from the river with a mixture of awe and respect. The steelhead chapter in *Trout* includes the capture of his first fish at Steamboat.

Immediately after lunch I slipped down to the Mott Pool, and about halfway through I hooked a fish. The singing of the reel was music to my ears. Nothing went wrong this time, and I had the satisfaction of looking up toward the end of the fight to find Phil, Grace and Fred watching me. Phil was so anxious that I should save the fish that he took off his shoes and stockings, and with his bare feet, waded that treacherous water just so he could help land it in a difficult spot.

That's sportsmanship for you.

I shall never forget this spontaneous act of his as long as I live. It showed the real soul of the man, his unselfish desire to see that I got my fish. It was all very satisfying. Just one steelhead a day on the North Umpqua makes a fisherman feel like a king!

Clarence Gordon was forced to abandon his beautiful camp on the storied Kitchen Pool when the Forest Service terminated its lease, and there are many regulars still fishing the river who remember the heartbreak he suffered. Its gen-

151

erous dining rooms and fieldstone fireplaces and sheltering porches are gone, along with the magnificent stand of sugar pines and giant firs that surrounded the lodge and its out-buildings. There is a steel trusswork bridge that spans the river above Sawtooth, and anglers and their parties are no longer ferried across Upper Kitchen to the Gordon camp. The Forest Service cut its sheltering trees and razed its log build-ings and replaced them with a new headquarters. Gordon bitterly digested his grief and moved across the river, pur-chasing a smaller site on the highway above the Glory Hole, and starting the Steamboat Inn. The Forest Service head-quarters is a blight, its plywood character between the obvi-ous banality of tract housing and the outright tackiness of a trailer court, but the simple Steamboat Inn and its cabins are worthy heirs of the Umpqua tradition.

Gordon finally found that wading the river was too much, and when he retired in 1957, his operation at the Steamboat Inn passed to the ownership of Frank Moore.

Among the skilled fishermen who still work the Umpqua, it is perhaps Moore who unmistakably echoes the wading and fishing skills of Clarence Gordon. There are some knowl-edgeable anglers who argue that Moore is probably the best steelhead fisherman alive, since he is much younger than the earlier giants of the sport: pioneers like Enos Bradner, Mike Kennedy, Wes Drain, Frank Headrick, Harry Lemire, Karl Mausser, Ken McLeod, Al Knudsen, and photographer Ralph Wahl.

Moore has unquestionably earned his status. His casting is clean and sure, utterly free of surplus effort, and he covers water quickly with a clockwork series of skillful fly-swing mends. His knowledge of the Steamboat mileage on the North Umpqua is remarkably thorough. His strategy in-cludes fishing each pool and taking lie rather quickly, cover-ing its secret places and moving on, eager to fish the next steelhead lie in his private lexicon of the Umpqua.

His ability to clamber goatlike over impossible ledges and labyrinths of boulders, work through seemingly impass-able jumbles of fallen trees, and cover the water without sufficient room to make a conventional cast is already legend.

152

Umpqua lore is filled with stories of Clarence Gordon and his wading skills, but it is difficult to conceive of a stronger, more completely fearless and agile wader than Moore. His river skills are remarkable, lying someplace between raw muscle and the cunning of a log-rolling champion, all mixed with the startling grace of Baryshnikov.

Walton was wrong! Moore insists firmly. *It's not fishing fine and far off—it's wade deep and throw long!*

Moore operated the Steamboat Inn for almost twenty years, and many of its traditions survived intact. It had always been known for its food, from its beginnings under early owners like Mott and Allen, although its cuisine was perhaps best characterized as country-style in the volume usually found in logging camps. Its character changed under the tenure of the Moore family. Although the logging-camp portions keep spilling from the cornucopia of its tiny kitchen, the food gradually became more and more sophisticated, until its candlelight dinners offer some of the finest cuisine in Oregon.

The torch has since passed into fresh hands. The young owners are Jim Van Loan and his wife, Sharon, who skillfully hopscotches between its superb kitchen and her teaching duties at a regional school downstream. The character and atmosphere and cooking at the Steamboat remain virtually unchanged. Its staff still consists of people devoted to steelhead fishing and fine cookery and a sense of place. Van Loan was a book publisher's salesman who tired of his rounds among the schools and bookstores and colleges on the Pacific Coast and settled down to think and fish steelhead and operate his favorite fishing inn on the North Umpqua in 1975.

Its ambiance still holds a circle of fiercely loyal patrons. The immense twenty-foot dining table cut from a single sugar pine was salvaged from the original Gordon camp across the river. Photographs of its dining hall and sitting rooms and sleeping quarters are hung with pictures of its famous anglers. Bottles of wine lie in their shipping crates in the corner, decent vintages of genuine Burgundy and Beaujolais hobnobbing with fine California vineyards like Simi and Stag's

153

Leap and Freemark Abbey. The fieldstone fireplace dominates one corner near the fishing tackle cabinets, and its
hearth often burns with a welcome fire for anglers who have
been wading armpit-deep in the Umpqua. The fly chest is a
treasure of patterns dressed by skilled tiers like Joe Howells
and the colorful Polly Rosborough, and the redwood ceiling
is hung with a collection of old rods. The battle-scarred Winston belonged to Frank Moore, and it is suspended beside an
older Powell and Edwards, both from the collection of the
controversial Zane Grey.

"The people who serve you are dedicated to maintaining
the Steamboat Inn family atmosphere," the dinner menu tells
its guests, "and you are a stranger here but once!"

The Umpqua legends continue to grow, and its fishing regulars have joined together into the Steamboaters, a happy
band of anglers determined to protect their shrine from the
ceaseless threats and subterfuges of the highway men and
timber interests and dam builders. The proposed reservoirs
and the Forest Service network of campgrounds on the primeval south bank of the river have seemingly been defeated,
but the Steamboaters are still watchful.

It's an endless fight, Frank Moore shook his head while
we shared coffee in his kitchen high above the river. *When we
win these fights it's only an armistice—but when those bas-
tards finish a highway or build a reservoir or cut an entire
forest, it's forever!*

There are fresh stories on the river each season. Perhaps
the best concerns the time that Jack Hemingway promised
his wife he would return early for his birthday dinner. The
weather had just changed and a gentle rain drifted upstream
into the mountains. The steelhead changed too and started
taking greedily. Hemingway soon forgot about everything
else: his birthday and the rain and his wife.

There were steelhead everywhere, sea-bright fish freshly
come from the sea, and they had arrived in a taking mood.
Steelhead took his flies in Surveyor and Secret Pool and Sawtooth at the Forest Service bridge. Station and Boat Pool and
Kitchen were generous too, and Hemingway beached and

lost others in the wild chutes of Mott and Lower Mott and the Fighting Hole. Still more came to his flies at the Ledges and Williams Creek and Archie, and a strong fish fought him down through Upper and Lower Burnham before it pulled free.

Takahashi and Wright Creek and Big Cliffs were generous, and Hemingway concluded his exciting day's sport at the Famous and Salmon Racks and the Honey Creek riffles, returning hours late and exhausted and drenched with the steady rain.

Puck Hemingway was furious. *Hemingtrout!* she exploded in tight-lipped anger, *you're four hours late and you're filthy wet—and for two cents I'd break your goddamned rod!* Hemingway stared at his wife in disbelief, still savoring the excitement of a remarkable day's sport on a steelhead river known for its moodiness.

Hemingway angrily stripped off his wading belt and groped through his pockets for the coins, and slapped them on the table. *Well,* he said grimly, *there's your two cents!*

His wife stalked outside, found the Winston in the racks under the grape arbor, and smashed it thoroughly against the paving stones. *Hemingway!* She stood holding the shattered bamboo like a broken flail. *What do you think of that?*

Hemingway started laughing uncontrollably. *Pretty thorough job,* he choked, *except that it's Frank Moore's rod!*

Other stories often involve the subterfuges and strategies that the Umpqua regulars employ to fish through the best pools first each morning. Dan Callaghan likes getting up before daylight and is often the first angler on Wright Creek or Kitchen, but several other fishermen became determined to fish them first one week.

Their dueling soon became serious. Callaghan and his challengers were getting up earlier and earlier to reach the pools first. Alarm clocks were muffled under pillows, starting at five o'clock and reaching back deeper and deeper into the night. Callaghan was clearly winning, with his muffled alarm clock and ascetic discipline, in their competition to reach the casting ledges at Kitchen.

His challengers were getting desperate. *There's only one*

way to get there first! one suggested as they lingered over dinner coffee. *Let's wade out to Kitchen right now!*

The waitress clearing the table was aware of the competition for the Kitchen Pool, laughingly warned Callaghan of their plans, and he gathered his tackle and hurried off into the darkness. Callaghan waded out through the familiar labyrinth of outcroppings and pulled himself out on the ledgerock to wait.

It was so dark I couldn't believe it, he said.

Callaghan sat smiling in the darkness when he heard the others coming down the Mott Trail, laughing and congratulating themselves on their cunning and craftiness. The leaves rustled under their wading brogues, and they switched off their lights when they reached the gravelly shingle that reaches down the length of the pool.

Might spook the fish, they agreed.

The fishermen were not familiar with the river and had trouble crossing its current-polished lava without their flashlights. It is difficult wading in the daylight, and one fisherman slipped enough to partially fill his waders with icy water. The man stood cursing when he recovered his balance in the current.

I didn't make a sound! Callaghan continued.

The other fisherman slipped in the lava channels too, drowning an expensive watch to keep from going down completely, and straining his wrist badly when he caught himself. The night was filled with whispered expletives. Cold and dripping wet, both men finally crossed the waist-deep channels to the outcropping where Callaghan waited silently on the ledge, the current gurgling past his legs.

Well! they chortled smugly. *We finally got here first!*

Callaghan wordlessly lit a cigarette.

There are still many fine steelhead rivers in these Pacific mountains, but such rivers are always moody and changing, and the Umpqua is perhaps the most fickle. Its clarity is deceptive and dangerous, and its moods range from a wild cacophony of trumpets and kettle drums and cymbals to delicate passages of chamber music. But its brief passages of woodwinds and flutes and strings are deceptive too, and its still, aquamarine depths are always lost in the churning chutes and wild rapids that follow each pool.

Its steelhead are often clearly visible from the highway, although there are never many in its pools. Wading is threatening in a strong current that masks its foul bottom, and there is seldom room for a proper backcast. Its sport is perpetually a challenge, and the Umpqua surrenders its fish so grudgingly that its disciples are clearly more in love with its character than its generosity.

The North Umpqua is a quality of spirit that cannot be fully understood or captured. Its shining length is scarred with volcanic outcroppings and ledges, its folded bedrock and igneous serrations polished in centuries of snowmelt and spates. Its gorge is still cloaked in dense forests, their cathedral choirs carpeted in lichens and pine needles and fiddlebacks. The river paths are ankle-deep in leaves when the October fish are running, and other leaves drift in the current or circle lazily in the still backwaters, turning scarlet and gold in their depths.

Steelhead are lying in the silken flow, elusive shadows as brightly polished as a wedding spoon. Its summer-run fish are like rare jewels in its velvet pools, drifting like ghosts in its currents, hovering in shafts of sunlight and spume.

We are precious and we are few. Their restless liturgies are a half-remembered whisper on the wind. *We are coming home, seeking the swift riffles of our birth—catch us if you can!*

[1979]

157

Book Two

A HATCH
TO MATCH

The resounding success of Schwiebert's 1955 book, Matching the Hatch, *and subsequent works gave "matching the hatch" a permanent place in the angler's lexicon. He didn't invent the concept of imitative artificial flies, of course. He often and pointedly credits other authors ranging from Berners and others of the fifteenth century and even earlier to more modern writers such as the late Preston Jennings and contemporary writers such as Doug Swisher, Carl Richards, and Fred Arbona. But Schwiebert's attention to detail in the stream and in print has been remarkably persistent and has built a tremendously loyal following.*

The concept extends far beyond matching insects and has come to mean almost any in-depth examination of the fish's aquatic world. Studies of trout behavior are important too, and follow the sort of thinking equally demanded by aquatic entomology. This part offers some outstanding and helpful examples of just that sort of approach.

9

Mixed
Palette

This essay is an exceptional lesson in hatch-matching tactics for any trout fisherman. The story itself takes place over several days on one of the most fertile trout streams in Ireland, but the problems encountered here with selective trout are ubiquitous, and Schwiebert's solutions to such problems will help any attentive reader and fisherman.

As I mentioned in this book's Introduction, Schwiebert is a master at instruction by anecdote, of which this essay is a wonderful example. Here you'll find new clues to matching egg-laying caddisflies, for example, and a terrific explanation of why different trout in different parts of a stream are sometimes feeding on different insects simultaneously. You'll also find here the quiet beauty of a rural Irish countryside brought to life by a writer whose eye for ambience happily matches his eye for fly hatches and trout.

Mary Colgan stared down from her feather-littered workbench when the horse carriage clattered through Parliament

162

Street. Its fittings and polished-leather coachwork and tack gleamed in the weak spring sunlight, and its high wheels creaked and rattled against the harsh counterpoint of horseshoes on the paving stones. The hansom cab disappeared into the gray steep-walled street, and the startled pigeons rose among the dour chimneypots of Dublin.

The shopgirls were out walking along the Liffey, where the college boys from Trinity were counting salmon from the stonework bridges, but young Mary Colgan was behind in her fly dressing. Her nimble fingers had been working with delicate spentwing drakes for the coming Mayfly season on big Irish lakes like Sheelin and Corrib.

It was almost warm in the cobblestone streets at midday, but the spare fly-making loft high above Garnett's & Keegan's tackle shop still held the chill damp of the Irish winter.

The young girl apprentices at the fly vises were rubbing their cold fingers, and kept their feet on the tin warming boxes filled with coals from the potbellied stove. Their teakettle was kept on the hot plate under bins of gamecock hackles and exotic bird skins, and the girls were heavily bundled against the wintry chill like seamstresses in the stories of Dickens.

What's that sedge pattern you're dressing? I asked.

Welshman's Button. Mary Colgan smiled.

John Hanlon is the proprietor of Garnett's & Keegan's, the finest tackle shop in Ireland, its shelves and glass-topped vitrines filled with exquisite flies and intricately made Wheatley fly boxes and gleaming British reels. Split-cane rods still dominate the racks behind the counters, in a time when most rods are glass or graphite, and another alcove is filled with stag rifles and the graceful straight-stocked doubleguns made famous by British artisans in the eighteenth century. Its principal tackle salesman is perhaps the most famous trout-fishing writer in Ireland. J. R. Harris also monitors the young fly dressers at Garnett's & Keegan's, while his book *An Angler's Entomology* has long been the bible on fly hatches in the British Isles. The richly stocked mahogany fly drawers often surpass the selections available in the tackle stores of London and New York and Paris.

Clare de Bergh is among the finest fly fishers in Europe, and we had first met over lunch in Oslo, after she had spent a highly successful week of salmon fishing. Our paths crossed later on another salmon river in Scandinavia, the swift little Nordurá in western Iceland. We had corresponded about the trout and salmon fishing in her native Ireland, and when the Aer Lingus flight from New York landed at Dublin, I eagerly sought her advice about the fishing at Limerick.

Where can we find some flies? I asked.

Garnett's & Keegan's is the best place, she replied without hesitation. *Dick Harris will be there this morning, and he's fished everywhere in Ireland—and he knows the fly hatches on the Maigue.*

We took an antique, high-ceilinged taxi from the airport into the center of the city and walked across the Liffey into the Parliament Street shop, where Harris was sorting a fresh consignment of flies. Harris was a short, ruddy-faced man in a suit of burlap-colored Irish tweed, and he greeted us with curiosity.

You've taken several days' fishing on the Maigue? Harris asked. *You're really quite fortunate.*

I'm looking forward to fishing it, I said.

It's exceptionally beautiful water, Harris explained, *particularly in the meadows around the castle and the ruined abbey—and it has some of our best fly hatches.*

It's quite a fertile fishery, de Bergh agreed.

What hatches are coming now? I asked.

Harris rummaged through the fly chests, passing their trays of brightly colored salmon patterns. *You'll find quite a mixed palette of flies hatching now.* He selected a drawer filled with delicate little sedges and mayfly duns and spinners. *Sometimes you'll have to observe each fish and its feeding behavior to discover what it's taking—and it might be everything from our little silverhorns to cinnamon sedges or the knotted midge.*

What's a knotted midge? I asked.

Harris brightened with an embarrassed flush. *It's just a name we use to describe our midges,* he stammered awkwardly and laughed, *when the males and females are joined in mating.*

It's two flies dressed on a single hook? I asked.
That's right. Clare de Bergh smiled.
What about the Mayfly season here? I said.
Our best sport when the Mayfly is hatching, Harris continued with a faint smile, *is usually found when the fly is up on loughs like Sheelin and Corrib and Mask—but we have river hatches too.*
What about the Maigue water?
You should find a few coming now, Harris said, *and the fish should be coming to them soon.*
What about your famous Blue-winged Olives?
Too early, Harris replied quickly, *but you might see excellent hatches of our iron blues in rainy weather.*
Let's have what I'll need, I suggested.
Harris selected a beautiful Wheatley box from the cabinet behind his counters and sorted a series of elegant dry-fly imitations into its intricately lidded compartments. We talked briefly about the fishing at Limerick and farther south on the Ring of Kerry and agreed to a tentative fishing date on the Rye water the following week.

We walked back through the narrow streets and stopped for a lunch of perfectly boiled salmon and small potatoes and salad at the charming Buttery in the Royal Hibernian hotel. The taxi carried me through the rainy streets after lunch, and I caught the afternoon train to Limerick. Its polished mahogany and velvet-covered seats and gleaming brass fittings echoed the trains in several Hitchcock films, and the thatchwork villages and whitewashed farms flashed past our carriage in the pastoral Irish countryside.
There was a driver waiting at Limerick, and when I reached the little country hotel at Adare, the young riverkeeper was waiting in its public house. *Roger Foster!* he introduced himself warmly. *We've been expecting you all afternoon!*
I'm really excited about fishing your beats!
We can still fish this evening if you wish, Foster swiftly interjected. *The beat just above the castle is free.*
It's possible to hold your supper, the porter said.
Let's go fishing! I agreed.

165

It was already evening when we reached the Footbridge beats above the castle, swiftly put up our equipment and walked downstream through the water meadows. The river was about seventy-five feet across, flowing deceptively swift and still between undercut banks of waist-deep grass. The surface was like a mirror, its currents undulating in beds of trailing weeds, and the trout were starting to rise.

There were several species of mating Mayflies over the water, in dancing swarms that rose and fell in the lengthening shadows. Foster pointed to several big *Ephemera* drakes, their chalky bodies readily visible in the evening light, and the sedges swarming along the grassy banks. The rises were mostly delicate bulges and swirls, with an occasional wild splash against the banks.

When they come like that, they're usually on the sedges, Foster suggested quietly. *Try that fish along the grass.*

The brown-hackled sedge settled into the current and flirted with the trailing grass. The trout came out from its hiding place and almost took the fly, but it balked and refused in the last moment, half-drowning its hackles with its splashy swirl.

Well, I shook my head, *he looked!*

Seems he found something wrong. Foster nodded. *Let's see if we've got a smaller cinnamon sedge in my boxes.*

The keeper rummaged through his shooting coat and found a sparse little sedge imitation, its dark olive silk and mottled woodcock wings and hackles dressed on a fine sixteen up-eye.

It's beautifully tied, I said.

Our trout are really quite shy, Foster explained. *Sometimes they take an imitation dressed a bit smaller than the naturals.* Foster replaced my larger pattern, and I dropped the fly just above the feeding trout. It took splashily and was gone.

That got him going, I laughed, *but I missed him!*

I'm not certain he took it, Foster said.

The trout were erratic that evening, porpoising steadily in the surface film and showing with occasional splashy rises.

We took two or three fish on dry-fly imitations of the egg-laying sedges, until I watched a bold rise occur where no insect had been fluttering and saw a second splash that almost drowned an escaping sedge that had obviously just hatched. *They're on the hatching flies!* I shouted downstream to the riverkeeper. *They're not on the sedges themselves!*
You're probably right, he responded.

I took a good trout on a sedge fished wet, confirming those observations, before it started to rain and the fish stopped feeding altogether. The soft rain glistened in the meadows when we walked back to the station wagon. We drove back to the Dunraven Arms, and Foster stopped with me in its public house for a glass of Guinness. We talked briefly with a couple who had traveled from São Paulo in southern Brazil to fish the castle beats of the Maigue.

It's just as beautiful as my father told us! Richard Dolan ordered another round. *It's worth the trip from Brazil!*

Where did you fish today? I asked.

Dolan turned to the riverkeeper. *Roger had us fishing the meadows above the castle grounds,* he replied.

They were fishing the upper beats, Foster explained, *and we also took them to try the Camogue water.*

What's its fishing like? I asked.

It's a limestone tributary with excellent fly life, the young riverkeeper explained. *It's the little Camogue that transforms the Maigue into such a fine fishery—the Maigue rises in peat bogs and its waters are quite barren until they mix with the Camogue.*

Where are the principal spawning grounds?

The Camogue is quite fertile and has fine pea-gravel riffles, Foster replied. *Our fish largely spawn there.*

Do you stock any trout? Dolan asked.

We raise pheasants for drive-shoots on the castle grounds, Foster smiled and drained his glass, *but our fish are wild.*

How was your fishing this evening? Dolan asked.

We took a few good fish, I replied.

We're on better water tomorrow, Foster added, and we shook hands. *I'll meet you all in the morning.*

Well, I asked, *what do you think of the river?*

It's really pleasant fishing, Dolan said.

Dolan, his wife chided him drily, *it's simply the most beautiful trout stream in the world!*

We went into the dining room, where the proprietor was holding our dinner, and returned to the public house for cognac later. When it closed its doors and I returned to my quarters in the garden, the gentle Irish rain was drumming on my windows.

The village street is lined with simple thatched-roof cottages, and the following morning it was filled with foxhounds and hunters in scarlet coats. The horses stood and circled restlessly, waiting for the Master of Fox Hounds to start the hunt. It was still raining gently, and the foxhounds shook themselves while the horsemen sat their sleekly groomed hunters, watching the pewter-gray clouds anxiously. Several riders finally disappeared into the hotel for stirrup cups of Irish whisky, while we stood waiting with our fishing gear in the foyer with the old porter.

It's a little early for whisky, I smiled.

Begging your pardon, sir! the old porter laughed when the foxhunters went back outside, *'tis never too early!*

Perhaps you're right, I nodded.

The old man brushed some mud from his uniform. *'Tis a soft morning we're having today.* His lyric brogue richly filled the foyer. *'Tis better for fishing than for chasing after foxes!*

Much softer and we'll need an ark!

The young riverkeeper arrived just as the foxhunters had clattered off toward Limerick, their scarlet coats gathering to cross the stonework bridge that arches the river above the village. Dolan drove off to fish the lower meadows, where the ruins of a twelfth-century Cistercian abbey lie along the river, while we drove in through the castle grounds.

Dunraven Castle is a formidable structure of limestone ramparts and intricately crenelated battlements, but like several famous Irish castles, it was built largely in the last century. Its terraces and sloping lawns and gardens reach down to some of the finest weir-pools on the Maigue. Peacocks and

168

spotted deer and pheasants wander its gardens. Its single Victorian tower dominates the village and castle grounds and meadows, and that morning the roads and roof slates glistened in the rain, although it was steadily clearing.

We crossed the stile above the ruined abbey, where a single masonrywork arch spanned the weirs. The trout were working steadily in the rain. There were several different flies on the water, and merely matching the hatch was unworkable. Some aquatic insects are more common on some types of water than others, and a particular fish can find one species concentrated in its feeding currents. Its response is predictable, and such trout focus their attention on that specific diet form until they will accept nothing else. Such selectivity is the secret of catching trout on difficult waters, and dressing flies to imitate specific insects dates to the *Treatyse of Fysshynge wyth an Angle,* which was written at Sopewell nunnery in the fifteenth century.

The fish were typical that morning on the Maigue. The trout lying under the swift-water weirs were concentrating on the sedges hatching from their currents. Fish in the smooth flats were taking the somber iron blue mayflies that emerge there, particularly on such rainy spring mornings. The trout lying in the deeper pools of the Maigue, like the weedy half-mile lagoon below the castle itself, are often tempted to focus on the *Ephemera vulgata* drakes that hatch from its silty bottom. The sedges along both banks were swarming with caddisflies, and the riverkeeper and his ghillies spend much of their time studying the rising trout to discover what each fish is taking.

Roger Foster is quite knowledgeable about the Maigue and its fly hatches. His early years were spent fishing and working as a ghillie in northern England at Driffield, with its famous trout-fishing club, and this young riverkeeper from Yorkshire is a skilled fly dresser. His knowledge of aquatic hatches throughout the British Isles is formidable, rooted in a tradition that ranges from the early nineteenth-century writings of Alfred Ronalds to the recent books of writers such as Harris and Goddard. During our week's fishing together, I learned to admire his knowledge and skills, both as the gamekeeper for Lord Dunraven and as the manager of his fishery.

The alders and water grasses were alive with somber slate-colored caddisflies, and in the quiet pool above the castle, the little cinnamon sedges were emerging. The trout were starting to work greedily, and the soft rain had almost stopped when we walked upstream from the stile at the old Abbey Bridge.

Loot there! I pointed to the run under the alders. *Look at the iron blues on the water—think they're taking them?*

The rises we could see were splashy and bold. *Perhaps,* Foster studied the water doubtfully, *but I'm not sure.*

Several good trout were rising in the smooth currents above the weir. Tiny iron blues were coming down there, along with a few fluttering sedges. Some large *Ephemera* drakes were also emerging, but the fish drifted back with them cautiously and finally refused to take them. The first cast covered them with an iron blue.

Refused it! I thought in surprise.

The fish rejected several decent floats, although they drifted down its feeding current, riding perfectly and seemingly drag free. The trout finally did not bother to inspect my fly.

They're pretty particular, I sighed. *It's definitely not the iron blue this morning—what are they taking?*

Most of the rises are pretty strong swirls, Foster said. *Perhaps they're still on hatching sedges?*

It's quite possible, the young Yorkshireman nodded, *but I don't believe they're taking anything on the surface.*

Downstream from the stonework bridge there was a splashy swirl in the quiet water, and a sedge escaped clumsily from the rise. The fish tried a second time at the fluttering insect and missed, scattering water in the shallows.

See that fish? I said eagerly. *It tried for a hatching sedge—and it missed the adult too!*

Exactly! Foster agreed.

The young riverkeeper is typical of the British fishermen on the border rivers of Yorkshire, and his leather fly books are filled with soft, partridge-hackled wet flies. *Have you a*

Partridge and Olive in your coat? I asked suddenly. *Or per-haps a sparse Woodcock Spider with a dubbing of dark hare's mask?*
Those are Yorkshire dressings! he frowned.
That's right, I smiled, *but do you have them along?*
I've got both, he said.
Foster searched his fly books for a pair of sparse little Woodcock Spiders, and I quickly knotted one to the tippet. The line darted back and forth in the misting rain that drifted along the river, and I dropped the fly above the fish. It settled and drifted under the surface and started into its swing. I followed the fly swing with the rod, feeling the line bellying the little wet fly past the fish, and I teased it gently with the rod tip. The trout responded with an eager swirl, and I tightened into a strong fifteen-inch fish that telegraphed its struggles back into the throbbing cane.
That's the secret! I thought happily.

The episode is typical of the chess-playing overtones that exist on hard-fished trout waters. The soft-hackled fly was the solution on that particular morning, but as more time passed, the clouds darkened and surrendered a misting series of showers.
The tiny slate-colored *Baetis* flies that had been hatching sporadically were coming steadily now, and the character of the riseforms changed too. The splashy swirls were replaced with confident bulges and dimples in the smooth run above the weir, and the trout picked the iron blues from the surface almost like berries.
They've switched, I suggested.
I believe you're right. Foster nodded and filled his pipe. *Try the iron blue on that trout along the tules.*
The tiny slate-gray pattern worked perfectly. We both took good fish for almost an hour, until the hatch finally passed its apogee and started to wane. Some trout continued to take the little iron blues, but there were some refusals to our flies now. Finally the fish were still working steadily and rejected our imitations altogether.
What's happened out there? I asked.

171

I'm not quite sure, Foster replied. _Let's observe them a while until we discover what they're doing._

Makes more sense than casting!

The rises were coming in a surprisingly steady rhythm now, and the trout hovered just under the surface, pushing their noses into the film when they took something. There were too many rises for the few insects still visible on the currents. The riseforms were clearly to something on the surface, their bulging rings filled with tiny bubbles in the flow. The feeding rhythms increased almost imperceptibly, until the rises were a series of interlocking circles, bulging and drifting downstream in the smooth current.

It looks like they're on spent spinners.

It's quite possible, Foster agreed thoughtfully. _I've observed a few swarms of mating Mayflies—and if their egg laying is finished we might have their spent flies on the water._

It could explain the steady feeding, I said.

That's right. Foster nodded and tapped the ashes from his pipe. _The riseforms rule out gnats and reed smuts._

Perhaps it's the iron blue spinners?

Try one, Foster suggested.

We had worked out the puzzle again, and we both took fish consistently until the brief spinner fall was finished. It was time to leave for our afternoon beat, and we walked back toward the Abbey Bridge. Coming downstream past the weirs, Foster spotted a large fish working boldly under the alders across the river. It was a relatively long cast, perhaps seventy-five feet into the shade of the trees, and the rises were utterly different from the soft spinner feeding.

What the hell is that fish doing? I asked.

It's certain that he's not on the iron blue spinners. Foster cupped his hands to shelter his pipe from the weather. _Not making strong rises like those!_

The rises were both splashy and sporadic. There were still a few large _Ephemera_ drakes coming off, hopscotching and fluttering along the current like diminutive crippled sailboats. The erratic intervals between the rises suggested that the big trout might be taking them. The size of its rises also suggested it might be feeding on something relatively large, and perhaps capable of fluttering or swimming.

You think it might be taking the drakes? I asked.

It's quite possible, Foster replied. *There are good marl deposits in the still water above that trout—but I've been watching him, and he still hasn't taken any of the adults coming over his lie.*

Their nymphs can swim, I suggested.

That's right, Foster agreed excitedly. *They're burrowing nymphs that can swim like minnows when they're hatching—and that fish could be seeing a lot of them in his line of drift!*

You're the chess master, I laughed. *What do you think?*

Foster searched through his leather fly books and passed me two large imitations. *Try one of these nymphs,* he said.

Two large Mayflies came fluttering clumsily over the trout and floated through safely. The fish had ignored them, but just as they were past, there was a dull flash as the fish took something and turned back along the bottom.

He's definitely nymphing! I said.

I believe you're right! Foster nodded. *He's not taken a single one of the drakes coming over him!*

I dropped the nymph well above the trout, let it settle back into its line of drift and fished it teasingly like a minnow when it passed the alders where the fish was lying. There was a bold flash deep in the current as the big trout took it hard, and I left the keeper's nymph in its jaws when my tippet parted.

Rotten piece of luck! Foster shook his head sympathetically. *The fish was at least four pounds!*

Luck nothing! I said sheepishly. *Owe you a fly!*

We had lunch under the huge twisted beeches at the footbridge, and sat in the grass, talking lazily when the weather turned warm and bright. Foster predicted a better fly hatch that evening, but just when the flies began coming and the trout started to rise, a sudden downpour ended our fishing well before twilight.

It was still raining hard when we reached the car. *Well,* Foster laughed as he stowed my wading brogues, *we can *always stop off at the public house for a pint and trade a few lies—more trout are caught in Irish pubs than anywhere else in the world!*

Pub fishing is always good! I agreed.

The following morning I drew the footbridge water with my roll of the dice cup, and the young keeper wandered ahead on the footpath to look for rising fish. Pheasants cackled in the water meadows, and we had seen peacocks in the deer park. Pigeons flew back and forth over the roof slates of the castle, and the rain had stopped, with weak sunlight filtering through.

Foster was hopeful of a hatch of drakes, the classic Mayfly on the rivers and loughs of Ireland, but it was still a little early for such big *Ephemera* flies in large numbers. *The Mayfly is already up on Lough Derg,* the young keeper explained, *and the flies are probably ripe on Sheelin and Corrib too.*

Clare de Bergh has already gone to Oughterard. I nodded. *She takes a cottage there on Corrib.*

She knows her fishing, Foster said.

There's a big drake on the water now! I pointed to the Mayfly under the trees. *But the trout are still refusing them.*

They're not on anything yet!

There were stands of huge conifers along the Maigue, and I stopped to study the rough, reddish bark on the trunks that soared a hundred feet into the afternoon sun. Other species of tall conifers stood deeper in the groves.

These big trees look like sequoias! I shook my head in disbelief. *And those others look like Douglas fir and Engelmann spruce—what are they doing on the grounds of an Irish castle?*

You're right about the trees, Foster grinned. *Lord Dunraven has a collection from all over the world.*

What about monkey puzzles from Patagonia?

His Araucaria *are over there.* Foster pointed downstream toward the castle. *Beyond the deer park.*

It's strange to find them here, I said.

Downstream past the exotic monkey puzzles, the Maigue wound out through its beeches and sycamores and alders to

174

the footbridge meadow. The afternoon was alive with hatching and mating flies.

Thousands of tiny Mayfly spinners were mixed with occasional hatching *Ephemera* flies, and there were clouds of swarming sedges. The bank grasses were crawling with these caddisflies, and I collected them until my specimen bottles were filled with slate-colored silverhorns and mottled *Sericostoma* flies and cinnamon sedges. The river was soon alive, too, with trout rising everywhere.

They're probably on sedges, Foster observed drily.

Clouds of caddisflies rose out over the current as we passed on the footpath. *It's likely with blizzards of caddisflies on both banks,* I almost choked on a fluttering sedge.

Leave a few for the fish! Foster grinned.

We've got five or six species out there. I tried to cough and clear my throat. *How do we tell which flies are hatching?*

Silverhorns hatch mostly at night, Foster explained, *and our season for the Welshman's button is about finished.*

What about the cinnamon sedges? I asked.

Try one, Foster suggested.

The young riverkeeper passed me an elegant sedge imitation, and we walked the footpath, casting to every fish in reach. There were several bulges and swirls of refusing fish under my fly, mixed with one splashy hit that drowned its hackles without actually touching it. Foster was fishing downstream, and I watched him hook and release a fine trout. The young keeper promptly rose and hooked another just above the weir. Two other fish bulged under my fly, and when a third fish refused it splashily, I walked downstream for his advice.

Dry flies aren't working, I complained.

Foster was preening his sedge carefully. *I'm fishing the dry fly,* he explained, *but I'm fishing it with our induced-rise method—sometimes it teases them into taking.*

How does your method work? I asked.

It's not particularly new, Foster explained. *It's been used in England to imitate our Caperer for more than a century— but it really works when the fish are on egg-laying caddisflies.*

What's a Caperer? I asked.

Our Caperer is a little sedge that scuttles and flutters about, the keeper replied. *It really excites the trout!*

Like the other egg-laying caddisflies!

That's right, Foster nodded.

The young Yorkshireman demonstrated his secret over a second rising fish. His gentle false-casting worked out line gracefully, until the fly settled softly over its line of drift, about twenty inches above the trout. The little cinnamon-dark dry fly had scarcely started into its drift when Foster gave it a subtle twitch, let it float freely another six inches and then teased it subtly again.

It was simply too tempting, and the fish took the twitching sedge hard. *So that's the induced-rise method!* I laughed. *You tickled that trout until it went crazy!*

Sometimes it works quite well, Foster admitted.

Breaks the dry-fly rules.

You mean the dry-fly religion of fishing upstream, Foster laughed, *and its dogma of the drag-free float?*

Rules are meant to be broken, I agreed.

His induced-rise method worked miracles that morning. We took almost fifty trout between us, averaging perhaps twelve to thirteen inches, and our best fish was a richly spotted Irish fish of three pounds. Our twitching flies were so effective that we finally stopped fishing, and walked happily back to explore the split-willow lunch basket and its dark bottle of Château Beychevelle.

Later that afternoon, the weather darkened again and a soft rain drifted along the river, triggering a fine hatch of iron blues in the treeless moors of the upper beats. There were a dozen fine trout rising above the meadow weirs, and the currents were covered with a regatta of tiny mayflies.

With trembling fingers, in spite of the trout-filled morning below the footbridge, I selected a tiny slate-hackled Iron Blue from Garnett's & Keegan's.

It's quite strange, Foster laughed. *No matter how many fish we've caught, it's always exciting to see trout start rising to a hatch of flies!*

You're right! I agreed.

We took several fish before the hatch ebbed into late

afternoon and the fickle weather grew stormy and cold. The chill wind blew across the gentle hedgerow country from Ballinskelligs and Killarney, and it was raining hard after our late supper at the Dunraven Arms.

The night lamps flickered in the thatched-roof cottages of Adare, and the dark wind rose in the mountains of Dingle. The cruel seas stormed and seethed against the rocky headlands. Rain rattled down my windows through the entire night, and the storm sighed along the roof slates of the castle. The bad weather did not pass until daylight, with a faint moon showing through the ragged clouds, and after breakfast the Dublin radio promised good fishing weather throughout Ireland.

It was still when I reached the river meadows, cool and still slightly overcast, and the Maigue flowed quietly past the Abbey Bridge. Foster was stringing his old Hardy rod when I reached the stile. *It's a fine morning for fishing,* the riverkeeper smiled, *and we'll find another batch of Iron Blues below the castle.*

Let's fish them! I suggested happily, and we walked upstream as the trout were starting to rise along the beautiful little Maigue, in a soft meadow filled with shamrocks.

[1978]

10

The Longest Hatch

This essay, as do some others in this book, hearkens back to the days when Schwiebert and I shared the masthead at Fly Fisherman. *This particular story came about as many did, in a quiet meeting talking with Ernie about what he might write next. At the time, the only serious magazine article about this mayfly hatch had been written some years previously by Vince Marinaro, who called his piece "The Hidden Hatch," based on the insect's very small size.*

Marinaro was a talented but one-river fisherman (see Chapter 3). Thus his discussion of this nationally important mayfly hatch was generally limited to his Pennsylvania water. I asked Schwiebert if he could use his broad experience for a story that was national in scope, and this essay was the happy result. It's first a superb description of what many consider to be this country's single most important mayfly hatch, and second a ground-breaking work in angling entomology that still serves as a model for other writers. For readability's sake, I have separated Schwiebert's detailed descriptions of naturals and imitations from

178

the main text, and included them as an Appendix starting on page 383.

Rising in the gentle mountains above Manchester, and gathering strength slowly from its cold springheads and tumbling hemlock-thicket tributaries, the Battenkill is born in a Vermont valley of clapboard farmhouses and bright-red barns and outbuildings. The villages are clustered about their greens, with white church spires rising above the trees, and country inns with Grecian pillars and porches.

It winds down its pastoral valley toward Arlington, its seepages cold enough to sustain its wild brook trout, and tumbles west toward the Hudson above Albany. There is a covered bridge on the stretch along which John Atherton lived, and his drawing of the pool there is included in his book *The Fly and the Fish.*

Still farther downstream in New York lies the storied Dutchman's Hole, and the swiftly flowing stretch that Lew Oatman loved and fished for years. His elegant streamer patterns, such as the Gold and Silver Darters, were among the first conscious imitations of baitfish. Lee Wulff lived on the river for many years, fishing the water between Arlington and the famous covered bridge at Shushan. But the river probably belongs to the painter who loved it through the last years of his life; the ashes of John Atherton were ultimately scattered into the Battenkill.

It has been twenty-five years since I first fished the river between Manchester and Arlington, and later I explored the big water that lies a few miles downstream in New York. It was there, on an early morning in July, that I discovered a heavy hatch of *Tricorythodes* at the Dutchman's Hole.

The night had been cool and still, and I wandered upstream before breakfast to try my luck. The fishing was poor after a week of midday doldrums. The river seemed dead, although I covered it carefully that morning, and I took only a single fifteen-inch brown that boiled out from a deadfall to savage the Shushan Postmaster I was fishing.

It was bright and still at the Dutchman's Hole, its depths dark and unfathomable under the trusswork bridge. No rises disturbed its smooth currents. Yet the sunlight upstream from the bridge was alive with thousands and thousands of tiny mayflies in a mating swarm that looked like dancing snowflakes. Several were caught in the spiderwebs on the bridge, and I studied their transparent wings and black bodies with a sense of disbelief.

Impossible, I thought. *They're too small!*

The morning light danced on their tiny wings, and the minute spinners rose and fell above the tumbling throat of the pool. Soon their mating flight was finished, and suddenly the still surface of Dutchman's Hole was alive with tiny rises. I could see some of the fish from the bridge, and several looked larger than twelve to sixteen inches, yet their bulging riseforms barely disturbed the eddying currents. It seemed impossible that the fish were rising so eagerly to such tiny spinners, since their wings and bodies measured less than one-eighth of an inch in length, but I studied the tail shallows of the pool and discovered nothing else on the water.

The smallest flies in my box were simply a few turns of badger hackle dressed on #20 Allcock hooks. The smaller hooks we now use on these minute mayfly patterns were not available then and, lacking a #24 or #26 hook, it was hopeless. My badger-hackle pattern looked like a sailboat among the spent naturals, and I took a few hatchery fish before the feeding stopped.

It was my baptism in fishing the *Tricorythodes* flies, and I have since fished their early-morning hatches and mating swarms throughout most of the country. The classic *Biology of Mayflies* by James Needham listed only eight species a half-century ago; current work lists nineteen species, although only ten are found on trout water. These species are almost universally morning flies, and their spinner falls occur in such immense concentrations that the trout often take them greedily.

There is considerable argument among entomologists and anglers about the *Tricorythodes* flies. Some fly-fishing writers have called them the *Caenis* hatch, mistaking them for the *Caenis* flies that British books have long called Fisherman's Curses. The taxonomy found in the pioneering work of James Needham grouped genera like *Tricorythodes* and *Cae-*

180

nis and *Brachycercus* together in the family Caenidae. His system further compounded the mistaken classification in several fishing books, both in Europe and the United States, although his *Biology of Mayflies* (1935) established a modicum of order in the entomological chaos of our continent.

Such scientific quarrels are puzzling to American anglers, who have matured with the *illusion* that biology is precise, and that our knowledge of our biosystem is fully structured and complete. These same quarrels remind me of the time when I participated in a panel discussion with Doug Swisher, and an obviously knowledgeable member of the audience confronted us with a disturbing question about evident differences in our work on some fly hatches.

When he asked the question, we both laughed. *We've known each other for many years,* I responded puckishly, *and we refuse to accept any responsibility for taxonomic quarrels in entomological circles!*

But such scientific differences do exist. James Needham established the taxonomic structure that included *Tricorythodes* in the Caenidae, and B. D. Burks accepted that system of classification in his *Mayflies of Illinois* (University of Illinois Natural History Survey, 1953), another milestone in American entomology. Six subsequent writers placed *Tricorythodes* in the Caenidae. Justin Leonard also grouped them among the Caenidae in his *Mayflies of Michigan Trout Streams* (1962). However, George Edmunds and Jay Traver proposed that the genus should be placed in a separate family called the Tricorythidae, and have farther pressed their case in Edmunds's recent book *The Mayflies of North and Central America* (1976). Perhaps the Caenidae classification is obsolete, perhaps not; only time and fresh knowledge can resolve such quarrels.

Like the Caenidae, the specimens of the Tricorythidae are quite small, measuring from about one-eighth to five-sixteenths of an inch in body length. The nymphs are easily identified by the triangular gill-covers attached to the second segment of the abdomen. These gill plates protect the sensitive membranes of the gills themselves, which are rooted between the third and sixth body segments, and their triangular configuration is the origin of the Latin name.

181

The configuration found in the nymphs of *Tricorythodes* is quite similar to the general structure of the Caenidae. These subaquatic specimens are easily identified by characteristics other than their operculate (covered) gills. The nymphs typically display an *absence* of tubercles (small, rounded projections) at the posterior margin of the head. Their bodies and thoracic structures are typically short and stout. The femora are moderate to muscular in their proportions and delicately fringed with tiny hairs. Each tarsal claw is relatively long and slightly hooked at its end. The apical margin of the labrum is deeply notched. The canines of the mandibles are apically lobed or toothed and are rather generous in scope. The lacinia are well developed, and the maxillae are conical. The pronotum is somewhat longer than is typical of *Caenis*, and the gill-covers consist of two fully separate plates, completely lacking the thickly fimbriate (fringed) character of either *Caenis* or *Brachycercus*. Nymphal antennae are approximately twice the length of the pronotum and head together. The legs are somewhat longer than *Caenis*, but considerably shorter than the legs of the genus *Brachycercus*. The tails are relatively long, proportionally stout, and are articulated with fine whorls of hairlike setae. Fine hairs cover both the body and the legs, collecting the microscopic silt and detritus in the river until the nymphs often acquire the coloring of their parent streams.

Their habitat consists of fine sand and aggregates in streams of moderate currents. Extensive populations dwell in such aquatic weeds as coontail, elodea, and fountain mosses. Algal growths on bottom stones can shelter many nymphal colonies. Although *Tricorythodes* nymphs seem to require the oxygen saturations associated with perceptible currents, their habitat is typically silty, and their operculate gills are commonly found in species that require such gill plates to protect their delicate respiratory filaments from abrasive sediments. Although the largest hatches occur on sizeable streams providing optimal habitat, significant populations of *Tricorythodes* exist on relatively small tributaries, and in the quiet eddies and backwaters of swift rivers that otherwise lack their typical habitat.

The nymphs are principally herbivorous, and streams

offering sufficient algae and aquatic weeds provide the best hatches. Large colonies often exist in the root structures of aquatic plants, as well as among the exposed underwater roots of terrestrial plants along the stream banks. *Tricorythodes* nymphs are quite clumsy, swimming with awkward undulations of their bodies to emerge, and clambering or crawling as nymphs.

Freshly hatched adults can readily be distinguished from *Caenis* and *Brachycercus* by the several cross-veins in the wings of *Tricorythodes*. The wings are also more slender and less ovoid than the wings of the similar genera. The *Tricorythodes* flies have tubercles on the posterior margins of their heads. Males are typically darker than females, as are most mayfly species. The eyes are rather widely separated. The male forelegs are slender and almost as long as the wings, while the other legs are short and less developed. The subimago flies exhibit three tails, those of the males measuring approximately three times the body length. Female caudal filaments (tails) are equal in length to those of the males in several species of *Tricorythodes*. Generally speaking, the freshly hatched adults have faintly smoky, hyaline (transparent) wings, either black or chocolate bodies, with pale legs and tails.

Although some entomologists disagree, B. D. Burks notes (in his important monograph *The Mayflies of Illinois*) that some species of *Tricorythodes* appear to molt from the dun to the spinner phase while still in flight. Particular conditions of temperature, precipitation, and humidity can play a critical role in the molting time required between hatching and mating. Optimal conditions can result in as little as fifteen minutes between the emergence of the duns and their subsequent gathering as spinners above the point of hatching, although thirty to sixty minutes are more typical. Longer times between the dun and spinner phases are reported by many knowledgeable anglers, particularly in the fall. Burks based his observations on field research with the species *Tricorythodes atratus*, and I have found similar molting behavior with other species such as *Tricorythodes stygiatus* in Michigan and *Tricorythodes minutus* in Idaho.

Mating adults (spinners) lose the smoky cast often found

in the wings of the subimago stage, until their wings are transparent to chalky white, and most specimens display white wings and dark bodies. Hind wings are completely absent in both duns and spinners. Since the mating swarms offer the largest concentrations of flies for both anglers and trout, the imago stage and its subsequent spinner falls are most familiar to skilled fishermen.

Other aspects of the life history of *Tricorythodes* are also intriguing. George Edmunds observes in his recent *Mayflies of North and Central America* that the nymphal populations of *Tricorythodes minutus* are absent from streams in Utah until relatively late each spring. Several species display multiple broods in a single season. Growth and maturity can occupy as little as fifteen to twenty weeks. Field studies of the species *Tricorythodes atratus* indicate that the nymph grows quite rapidly after hatching from its egg. The largest concentrations of nymphs were observed in late spring and early summer, although a second peak in population occurs again in late summer and early fall. Such waxing and waning in a typical *Tricorythodes* population indicates at least two broods per year. R. J. Hall reports that in Minnesota, typical populations of *Tricorythodes atratus* winter in their egg stage, and the nymphs require about five weeks after hatching to reach full growth. Hall observed subaquatic emergence during his studies, with the duns reaching a partly winged state before actually reaching the surface. Males displayed nocturnal hatching behavior that lasted approximately two hours, while the females began emerging at daylight. I have recently observed nocturnal hatching activity on the Big Horn in Montana. The adult life span of the males can reach as much as five to seven hours, while the females expire in less than two to three. The males of *Tricorythodes atratus* shed their subimaginal skins (molted) between daylight and dawn, and the females followed later, according to Hall.

Some species emerge in the surface film, much like other mayflies, and some larger *Tricorythodes* flies apparently molt in streamside vegetation. There is also conjecture that the males alight to molt, while the females shed their

184

subimaginal skins in flight. Justin Leonard tells us in *Mayflies of Michigan* that reared males of *Tricorythodes stygiatus* have survived as much as forty-eight hours in captivity.

Thoughts of past *Tricorythodes* hatches lead to thoughts of many rivers, from the Otter and Battenkill and Lamoille in New England to the prolific spinner falls on the spring creeks of Oregon and northern California. I have even seen these flies on a still brook-trout flowage in Nova Scotia. There are boyhood memories of early-morning hatches on the Whippoorwill water of the Au Sable, and on the still flats of the Upper Pere Marquette. Other Michigan rivers such as the Manistee and Boardman and Rifle provided similar sport, and I remember late-summer mornings in the cottage at Wolf Lake, stealthily making breakfast while the others were still sleeping and the soft mirror of the lake was dark through the trees, waiting for the locust afternoons of August.

Later there were early hatches at Ferdons and Wagon Tracks on the classic Beaverkill, and on the immense Delaware flats below Pepacton and Shinhopple. Sometimes we were baffled by the spinner falls, when we could see nothing on the water and were frustrated by the steady dimpling of the fish in the film. There was a boyhood morning when I stood waist-deep in Cairns Pool, surrounded by so many rising trout that I almost quit fishing in frustration since we lacked the tiny hooks to match such hatches.

What are they taking? my father called.

They're taking those black-bodied mayflies, I shouted back, *but it doesn't matter—we can't tie flies that small!*

Smaller hooks became available in the years that followed, made largely for the circle of anglers that evolved on the limestone streams of central Pennsylvania, and we used them eagerly in imitating both terrestrials and the tiny *Tricorythodes* flies. These first hooks in sizes #22 and #24 were often brittle, but they allowed us to take selective fish that had frustrated us before, and fine hooks as small as #26 and #28 are readily available now from first-rate shops.

It was fishing on the limestone streams of Pennsylvania that finally taught me the secrets of the *Tricorythodes* hatches. Before those summer mornings with Ross Trimmer and

185

Charles Fox, I had fished them through a lot of frustrating mornings. The mind sorts through a kaleidoscope of memories, remembering failures just at daylight on the willow-lined flats of the Upper Ausable in New York. Its fish bulged and dimpled softly in the film, and there were other trials on its sister river, the crystalline little East Branch below Keene Valley.

Heavy spinner falls on the Little Lehigh in eastern Pennsylvania, and beautiful Falling Springs Run at Chambersburg, were the watercress classrooms where I had my first success with these diminutive mayflies. That led me to a Michigan pilgrimage, and our mixture of new fly patterns and cobweb-fine tippets helped to even the score for those boyhood failures in the cool mornings of July and August. Later I found excellent *Tricorythodes* hatches in northern Wisconsin, particularly in the elodea shallows of the Namekagon and on the storied Brule at Cranberry Eddy. Although I seldom fish them, I have also encountered heavy spinner falls on the Pine and Loyalsock and Kettle in northern Pennsylvania, and on the still flats of the Paulinskill and Raritan and Musconetcong. Such eastern rivers provide surprisingly good sport at the threshold of New York and Philadelphia.

But some of the best *Tricorythodes* fishing is unquestionably found on the lime-rich currents of the Fall River in northern California, and on the remarkably fertile Silver Creek and Henry's Fork of the Snake in Idaho. These streams are literally teeming with life, and their gently undulating weeds shelter vast populations of nymphs, crustaceans, and larvae. Rich with dissolved oxygen, generated through photosynthesis by the rich growths of elodea and fountain mosses and chara, these streams are optimal habitat for the tiny *Tricorythodes* nymphs. Such nymphal populations clamber and forage in the root structures and subaquatic foliage of the weeds and are principally herbivorous.

Before the early-morning emergence, the weeds are literally alive with these minute mayfly nymphs, and during the hatch they crawl toward the surface through their watery junglelike habitat. The nymphs struggle clumsily, and a

186

foraging trout can root them from the weeds while they clamber upward to hatch. The fish can gorge themselves on these minute insects, taking hundreds and hundreds of nymphs along a single growth of ranunculus or elodea, until their stomachs bulge like fat sausages.

Some nymphs reach the surface clambering among the weeds themselves, while others drift to the surface after abandoning the shelter of their foliage. Since several species of *Tricorythodes* have been observed emerging from their nymphal skins before actually reaching the atmosphere, partly winged imitations of emerging nymphs are often effective during a hatch, although few anglers fish the nymphal stages.

Such neglect is partly due to the difficulty of fishing the nymph in the weedy habitat of *Tricorythodes* populations, and partly because of the skills needed to fish such tiny nymphs on fine tippets. Since the nymphs are incapable of perceptible swimming, they must be fished upstream with a dead-drift presentation. There are so many naturals available to the fish before and during a hatch that to fish such nymphs blind is usually pointless. Similar problems are involved in fishing the hatching duns or a subsequent fall of spinners; it is better to present a nymph imitation to a specific fish. Such trout can often be found working the borders of the weeds, flashing in the current when their bodies catch the light, or rooting in the weeds themselves. However, a fish taking the emerging nymphs just under the surface, or sipping them in the surface film itself, is much easier to take. The angler can fish to such trout in the same manner as a dry-fly presentation is made, placing his imitation of a hatching nymph just above the trout's feeding station. It is possible to sense the rate of drift of the tiny nymph, watch the fish that is working, and tighten when it rises again. Sometimes the fish is simply taking another natural, but sometimes you tighten and it is hooked. Fishing such minute nymphs in the film demands experience with tiny hooks and delicate tackle, and the development of a gentle touch.

More typical nymph-fishing tactics are possible on some *Tricorythodes* streams, particularly those that are more open with a stable bottom, or in spring-creek shallows where the fish are clearly visible. The tiny nymph is placed above a visibly feeding trout, and its rate of sink and drift is judged while watching the fish. When it moves to intercept something, and its open mouth shows white and closes, it is time to tighten. Such nymphing for fish that are clearly visible is both subtle and exciting.

During a typical *Tricorythodes* hatch, the male subimago flies emerge first. Once the hatches have fully started, the trout actually seem to anticipate their appearance at daylight. Before the first flies start coming, in the mist and dull light of early morning, the rivers seem lifeless. Yet it is possible to find a trout holding here and there in the growing light, almost waiting for the hatch and the spinner fall to follow. Such fish lie poised and obviously excited in their typical feeding lies, and they are easily frightened by a careless angler until the hatch finally begins.

The *Tricorythodes* flies have perhaps the most extensive period of emergence among our mayflies; fishable hatches may occur almost daily for as long as two to three months. Some observers have noted that hatches on our eastern limestone streams usually occur at morning stream temperatures of fifty-two to fifty-six degrees Fahrenheit. Summer hatches may occur earlier than normal so that the emergence is concentrated at optimal water temperatures, while hatching activity in the cooler months of September and October may come in late morning or early afternoon.

Once the tiny duns start coming well, the trout quickly lose their skittish character. Their feeding rhythms become remarkably steady as the numbers of hatching flies increase. Feeding activity may wane slightly as the swarm of mating adults gathers above the river, but then it steadily waxes into gluttony with the spinner fall. Although soft riseforms are usually associated with such tiny insects, the brief character and incredible numbers of *Tricorythodes* flies often cause the fish to lose their typical caution. Their feeding rhythms grow urgent, until their greed makes them unaware of anything except the hatch, and they seemingly hang together in the film to gobble the tiny flies. Sometimes a large fish will hold its mouth open and work upstream with its back clearly visible above the current, greedily inhaling hundreds of the naturals pinioned helplessly in the film.

The most dramatic example of this wanton feeding that I have seen took place on the Henry's Fork of the Snake. It was a bright August morning on the Harriman Ranch, and the early sunlight was alive with a blizzard of *Tricorythodes* flies. The minuscule insects were everywhere, rising and falling for a half mile above the marshy islands, and the sun danced on their delicate wings. It was an unbelievable sight, and the river flowed smooth and still while the mating swarm continued its busy choreography above the shallows.

The tiny spinners rose and fell in glittering swarms that hovered like mist over the Henry's Fork, and then they were gone and the morning sky was empty. *There were millions and millions,* I thought eagerly. *The fish should get started soon!*

Suddenly, the river was alive with rising trout, and my waders were quickly encrusted with tiny spinners. There were several rainbows working against the grassy bank, and I took a half-dozen so easily that I wondered why we considered the Henry's Fork a difficult river. Then I hooked a strong fish that took my entire fly line in a sullen run that fouled my leader in the elodea, and sheared the tippet like a cobweb.

Sure broke the spell, I thought.

While I retrieved the line, and patiently unraveled the leader from the elodea, another huge trout started working in the channel downstream. Its behavior was surprising, and I stopped to watch. The fish porpoised steadily, its dorsal and tail showing lazily while it prowled a backwater eddy. Soon it was taking the flies with a steady rhythm and rises that overlapped, its head projecting from the water and its white mouth showing. The fish ranged steadily along the bank, feeding greedily upstream for almost fifty feet, drifting back with an occasional rise to circle the backwater hungrily, and then turning back against the current for another feeding run. It was a big rainbow, perhaps six or seven pounds, and it ignored me completely.

He's got terrible table manners, I thought as I stood staring at its bulging rises.

The trout repeated its feeding circuit for almost half an hour, vacuuming hundreds and hundreds of tiny spinners that were pinioned in the surface film. Its jaws made a rolling wake, and its porpoising and bulging sent waves against the grass. Its final orgy carried it so close that I could see a heron scar behind its dorsal fin, and suddenly its feeding stopped, and the river flowed still and smooth.

You forgot to fish! I thought suddenly.

Vast swarms of mating spinners are common on the fertile rivers and spring creeks of our western mountains. The entire winged life of these tiny mayflies is expended in the brief hours of a single morning. The subimago is hatched from the nymph, the freshly emerged dun molts and becomes a fully adult spinner, the mating flight and egg laying in the river are completed, and the exhausted imago drops spent to the current in a spinner fall that can number in the millions. Rivers where the *Tricorythodes* flies are common hold enormous populations of nymphs, and a mating swarm that rises as much as thirty to fifty feet above the water can reach for miles along the stream. Looking into the early sun, the angler can see an astonishing sight—millions of wings that catch the light, rising and falling restlessly in clouds that seem like microscopic bits of silvery confetti, and these clouds of spinners will ebb and undulate and flow with any delicate stirring of the wind.

Several factors in the feeding behavior of the fish are important in *Tricorythodes* season. There may be so many insects available that it can be difficult to get the fish to take an artificial, yet there are techniques for inducing such fish to rise.

Arriving well before the morning hatch is important, because a fisherman can observe the beginnings of the rise and pick the best fish to work on. The duns are relatively sparse when compared with the spinner fall to follow, and the fishing is still studied and calm. It seems foolish to waste time on a small fish. Experienced *Tricorythodes* regulars will watch the early stages of a hatch to locate a particularly good trout, and understand that the odds can be better in a secondary line of drift, since fewer insects crowd the currents there. It is profitable to fish out the entire hatching period too, because the best fish are often found feeding in backwaters long after their lesser colleagues have gorged themselves and stopped.

But perhaps the best advice involves understanding that each fish will establish its own feeding rhythm in *Tricorythodes* time, sipping and gobbling steadily with its timing dictated by its feeding position, relative current speed, its sense of security, water temperature, the availability of the hatching flies or spinners, its size and agility and metabolic requirements, and its singular character. It is possible to observe its unique feeding rhythm and introduce an imitation into its line of drift so that the fly arrives at its taking point in sequence, perfectly timed to the rhythm of its riseforms. Such tactics will prove valuable through the full spectrum of the season and are worth remembering on less prolific hatches than the *Tricorythodes* flies.

Early-morning rises to this hatch may occur on streams not usually associated with fishable populations of *Tricorythodes* flies. It should be remembered that all streams have small zones of microhabitat that can sustain these slow-water nymphs, and I have seen them on big western rivers like the Snake and Yellowstone and Green. Their early-morning hatches often come from eddies and backwaters that shelter the *Tricorythodes* nymphs from their swift-flowing currents.

Several options are available in dressing imitations of the important *Tricorythodes* hatches. Male nymphs are active before daylight, and the male subimagoes are often found emerging between twilight and the last hour of the night. Since the duns often start to free their wings from the thoracic skin before reaching the atmosphere, tying imitations of these emerging duns can prove effective with hen-hackle points or a soft wing of smoky-dun filo or marabou fibers.

Freshly hatched subimagoes are often slightly darker and duller in coloring than the spinners that follow, and display a smoky cast in their wings. Spinners are often partly spent when a mating swarm is finished, so both upright and fully spentwing patterns are useful on selective trout. Although there are parallels in the dressings designed to imitate many species of *Tricorythodes* flies, different hook sizes are needed in several cases, since the naturals range from three to seven millimeters in length.

Conventional nymphs might be slightly weighted with a few turns of fine copper wire under the thorax, while emergers might be tied with a tiny tuft of gray marabou or down from the butt of a hackle feather instead of a typical wing case. Some fishermen prefer conventional hackle dressings to the no-hackle style, and others like hackle or hen-hackle spentwings instead of polypropylene. However, both the no-hackle dressing and spent polywing spinner have consistently proved themselves in the past.

Since these tiny glassy-winged insects emerge from mid-summer into late fall and even later on some rivers, their importance outweighs their minute size. There are memories of these hatches on many rivers. Early spinner swarms are still important on the smooth flats of the Schoharie and Battenkill and Delaware. The spring creeks in our eastern mountains still offer fine *Tricorythodes* hatches, particularly on streams like Falling Spring Run. Michigan rivers like the Muskegon and Sturgeon and Au Sable also sustain large populations of these tiny flies. Ozark fishermen enjoy excellent early-morning activity, and there are major western hatches on many waters. The spring creeks of Jackson Hole hold prolific populations, and I have fished excellent spinner falls on several like Flat, Blue Crane, Fish, and Blacktail spring creeks. Big flats on the Lewis and Shoshone Channel and Yellowstone offer fine *Tricorythodes* sport, and Idaho fisheries like the Henry's Fork are among the best. Silver Creek at Sun Valley is famous for its October swarms. Huge swarms are common farther west on the weedy flats of the Williamson and Metolius in Oregon, and on the beautiful Fall River in northern California.

This past season, I have found excellent *Tricorythodes* swarms in Idaho, Wyoming, and Montana. There were thick spinner falls at Silver Creek, and along the Lamar in the Yellowstone country. But the most remarkable hatches took place on the Big Horn, with cock pheasants cackling along the river on those still October mornings.

[1977]

11

Understanding the *Pseudocloëons*

A basic problem in aquatic entomology is simply described: the trout are feeding actively on a hatch, and you're not catching anything. A few anglers are still content to let it go at that, but an increasing number of others—Schwiebert foremost among them—are catching more fish based on the solutions to past puzzles, while constantly confronting new ones. This essay describes one such situation.

It's an ongoing example too, as this hatch is included by most anglers within the catch-all "Blue-winged Olive" group, which is quite misleading. Some Pseudocloëon mayflies are only three to six millimeters long, substantially smaller than many familiar Olives. Imitations are as small as sizes twenty-six and twenty-eight and, together with some experience on the angler's part, can be devastatingly effective from Vermont's Battenkill to Montana's Big Horn in early October, to give just two examples.

The river was particularly beautiful in the fall, its currents flowing smooth over its straw-colored gravel, and its lodgepole meadows already yellowing with the first hard-frost nights. Herons fished patiently in the shallow backwaters just at daylight; the river's mallards had nested and departed. The summer crowds had left the Yellowstone too, and I was almost a week late at college, but the hatches and weather had been good.

That college summer I spent almost two months in the Rockies, fishing like a gypsy from the Cucharas in southern Colorado to the Big Hole in Montana, and sleeping like a folding jackknife in the Oldsmobile. The Lewis Campground was almost empty, except for a retired wheat farmer from Nebraska and its nocturnal bears, perhaps disappointed by the sparsely stocked garbage pits.

It was bitter cold at breakfast, and there was frost in the bunchgrass bottoms. The current flowed smooth and silent, its surface undisturbed by rising trout. Like most trout fishermen, I was too restless to wait for a fly hatch and slipped into the river to fish the water.

It took fifty yards of fishing blind to convince me to wait for rising fish. My random casting accidentally lined two good trout that bolted upstream and under the bank. Another big fish fled when it saw my fly line working in the sun, and my kindergarten lesson was completed when a sporadic _Baetis_ hatch started, and several good fish started rising in the water I had just fished.

Although the flies usually hatch in the morning, the night frosts had delayed their emergence until almost noon. Several good fish began to porpoise steadily along the grassy banks, and I patiently collected several of the dark-olive-bodied mayflies from the current.

Blue-winged Olives, I thought, _but smaller than the hatch we fish back East—and darker too._

The Blue-winged Olives in my fly boxes were a hook size too large, but I fished them with fair success, particularly when the naturals were hatching steadily. During these brief periods, which came when the patchy clouds drifted in to darken the river, the trout became greedily preoccupied with their feeding and I caught several good fish.

But my success proved short-lived. The hatching activity

194

ebbed in the early afternoon, and a light wind broke up a promising swarm of mating *Baetis* flies. The fish worked briefly to another cycle of hatching duns, but suddenly their feeding rhythms changed completely. The soft dimples and sucking rises stopped. The riseforms almost overlapped, and the feeding rhythms became so steady that the trout hovered greedily in the surface film, scarcely sinking back between rises. It was baffling, and the little Blue-winged Olives that had worked through most of the day's fishing no longer worked, although the trout were feeding with greater intensity. Their orgy lasted into early evening, and although I cast to fish after fish, I failed to move another trout.

It was frustrating to fail so completely, particularly after a relatively good day's sport, and finally I simply gave up and waded out into the currents where the last fish were still working. The rise was almost over, and I searched the surface film anxiously for a clue. It seemed curiously barren of life, but in a marshy backwater I found several tiny spent mayflies with pale wings and distinctly green bodies.

Although I doubted that such tiny insects could have triggered such a rise of trout, I picked up more than a dozen and placed them in my small collecting bottle. The flies were half-forgotten in my fishing jacket, but a week later, while describing the puzzle I had encountered along the Lewis to Bud Lilly in West Yellowstone, I remembered my collecting bottle and showed it to him.

Lilly shook his head. *Don't know what they are, but I've seem them before on the Firehole—and when the fish get on them it's always trouble!*

It was my baptism with these minute two-winged mayflies, and my failure with them was a nagging memory. It had been one of the most impressive rises of trout that I could remember. The fish had gorged themselves on the spent green-bodied spinners, rejecting everything I tried after a brief inspection.

Several years later I had a similar experience on the famous spring creek at the Nelson Ranch in Montana. It had been a fine day's sport with a mixed bag of tiny *Ephemerella* and *Baetis* hatches, and the fish had responded well to small ants and beetles fished in the film when the fly hatches ebbed. But in late afternoon, as I successfully fished a brief emergence of *Baetis* duns, the trout suddenly stopped coming. Other trout began feeding and then quit the same way the other trout had quit in my earlier experience on the Lewis.

The fish were working just below the second lagoon, just above the ranch and its corrals, and their riseforms changed. The rhythm of the fish's feeding settled into a steady pattern so consistent that the spreading rings of their riseforms almost overlapped. The rises were soft and unhurried, although the bigger fish held so close to the surface film that its sliding flow was disturbed by every movement they made. Sometimes their rises came so close together that the rings drifted downstream in a rippling figure eight that died against the watercress. Fish after fish rejected the tiny *Baetis* imitation that had worked all day, and when the feeding stopped, I was completely defeated. The backwater downstream still held a flotilla of tiny spentwing flies pinioned in the film, but their bodies were yellowish olive instead of bright green.

It's the same two-winged genus, I thought that night in Livingston, *but it's a different color.*

There were no clues in either British or American writings on fly hatches, but when I finally acquired a worn copy of James Needham's *The Biology of Mayflies*, it contained a partial solution to my puzzle. The specimens in my collection were unmistakably of the *Pseudocloëon* genus, and the slightly smaller flies collected on that Montana spring creek were apparently *Pseudocloëon futile,* but the bright green species remained a mystery. It was surprising to find nothing about my specimens from the Lewis in *The Biology of Mayflies.*

The puzzle seemed more complex when fishing friends in Michigan sent me another vial filled with specimens of still another species of *Pseudocloëon.*

During a September weekend spent with canoes on the Au Sable between Stephan's and McMaster's—without any fishing equipment because the season had already closed—these anglers had witnessed a heavy rise of fish both days.

Their specimens were yellowish brown but slightly larger than the *Pseudocloëon* flies collected in Montana. These Michigan specimens were also strangely missing from the taxonomic keys found in *The Biology of Mayflies.*

Subsequent work in entomology solved the mystery of the two unclassified *Pseudocloëon* flies. The Michigan specimens were described from field research in Minnesota, and the species was designated as *Pseudocloëon anoka.* My puzzle of the bright green specimens, however, was not unraveled until ten years ago, when they were described and classified as *Pseudocloëon edmundsi,* based on taxonomic studies with specimens collected in Idaho. Other undescribed species may still remain.

James Needham identified a dozen species of *Pseudocloëon* flies for his *Biology of Mayflies* in 1935. Since its publication, taxonomists have continued to augment and revise his original generic keys. There are currently nineteen species of *Pseudocloëon* listed by George Edmunds in his *Mayflies of North and Central America,* the most recent work on the distribution and character of our hatches.

Its roster of *Pseudocloëon* populations includes species indigenous to trout streams throughout the United States and Canada. Their nymphs are current-loving types that swim surprisingly well in the gravelly shallows, using their fringed tails and restless body undulations. Nymphal forms are easily identified through their paired tails and a fat vestigial tail half concealed between them. Freshly hatched *Pseudocloëon* flies have no atrophied rear wings typical of other mayflies, and their forewings display tiny marginal wing veins in pairs along the posterior edges.

Any one of the species of *Pseudocloëon* can display local importance in a particular watershed, but six *Pseudocloëon* hatches are clearly major populations in many streams. The nymphs are delicate and relatively slender, except for the nymphal stages of *Pseudocloëon carolina* and *Pseudocloëon anoka,* which are rather corpulent.

Perhaps the most familiar species is *Pseudocloëon carolina,* although few fishermen know that its relatively heavy hatches are actually *Pseudocloëon* flies. Even knowledgeable anglers assume that these little Blue-winged Olives are *Baetis* flies, although such two-tailed species are slightly larger. Both genera seemingly have only two wings, but *Baetis* actually display small pairs of hind wings. The *Baetis* hatches are sporadic, usually starting in the morning and lingering well into the afternoon, while the olive-bodied *Pseudocloëon* duns usually emerge in early evening. Cloudy days can change these patterns, mixing both species sporadically through the afternoon. Since there is a significant size difference between these *Baetis* and *Pseudocloëon* hatches, in spite of their similar coloration, a single imitation will not work for both. Eastern fishermen from South Carolina to Maine are familiar with both hatches, and they have often experienced problems much like mine on that September afternoon in the Lewis meadows thirty years ago. The *Baetis* hatches often trigger successful fishing through most of the morning and afternoon, only to have an imperceptible transition to the smaller *Pseudocloëon* species lead to failure during the evening rise. Such problems are typical of early summer fishing on many eastern rivers, such as the Beaverkill.

Pseudocloëon dubium is the most widely distributed of our eastern species. Its populations are reported from Canada to the Carolinas, and inland to our middle western states. Its rusty-brownish body is often confused with other species like *Baetis cingulatus* and *Baetis brunneicolor*. Another species often confused with these smaller *Baetis* flies is the *Pseudocloëon cingulatum*, with its dun-colored wings and sepia body. It is common from Pennsylvania to Quebec.

Pseudocloëon anoka is widely important to trout fishermen from Ontario to Minnesota and hatches sporadically from late June through early September in Michigan and Wisconsin. It emerges in late morning, and heavy activity can last well into the afternoon. The best hatching concentrations are found in July and September, and good daytime activity is triggered on overcast days. Spinner falls occur in late evening, with heavy feeding in the gravelly shallows just at nightfall. Last year I experienced several puzzling evenings on the Au Sable in Michigan, where I often fished in boyhood.

We had fished in the mornings on its north branch near Lovells, finding good early hatches of tiny *Tricorythodes* flies. The smaller fish took them well, particularly when their mating swarms ended in dense spinner falls. Sometimes a sporadic hatch of *Ephemerella lata,* a particularly dark little Blue-winged Olive, was mixed with these *Tricorythodes* flies. The hatching olives often lasted well past lunch, until finally the river flowed silently through the hot afternoon and the hatches stopped.

I was fishing from Thunderbird, which sits on a sandy bench in the birches a half mile below Priest's Bend, with my old friend Arthur Neumann. We had explored farther afield during the daylight hours, fishing the Upper Manistee and the Lovells and Wakeley stretches, and returned to supper at Thunderbird in late afternoon. Later we traveled upstream to fish the Whippoorwill water with Don Philips, expecting to find a typically decent spinner fall.

Since the mating swarms of *Ephemerella lata* occur in the evenings, fishing the spinner falls with dark-olive-bodied spentwings seemed logical. We had encountered good daytime hatches of these dark olives on other beats, although we did not fish Whippoorwill until twilight.

On our last evening I waded upstream through the weedy shallows to a riffle above the Philips cottage. Swifts had been working their choreography high above the river, and we knew they had found a mating swarm of mayflies. It seemed likely that a spinner fall would start the fish working too, once the spent flies were on the water. The dark-olive spentwings had worked each evening, and I knotted a fresh pattern to my tippet and waited.

Several minutes later a dozen fish started to work softly and steadily along the weeds upstream. Sure that my Olive Spinner would work again, I cast it gently over the rising fish. It drifted back awash in the film, and when a trout rose I tightened, only to frighten it badly. It had refused my fly and taken something else. My failure was quickly repeated on the other rising trout, and I stopped fishing to let them forget and resume their feeding. My fly pattern was obviously wrong.

What are they doing? Don Philips called.

199

I'm not sure, I called downstream, *but they're doing something else tonight!*

They're not taking the Olives?

Not my fish. Crouching low to conceal my light, I studied the surface film well below the trout. *It's* Pseudocloëon *spinners—they're everywhere!*

There was barely time to change flies before the spinner fall ended, but my first cast over a softly feeding fish worked. It dimpled and I tightened expectantly and it was hooked and bolting across the shallows. It was not a big fish, perhaps eleven or twelve inches, but it was a wild brown trout and it had salvaged our night. The fish had stopped feeding before I netted the trout, and as I finally disengaged the fish from the meshes and released it, the Au Sable flowed silently again.

Pseudocloëon *spinners,* I thought. *Since we haven't seen them on the water we've been fishing, and we didn't fish this stretch when* Pseudocloëon *duns were hatching in late morning, it just didn't figure that it might be* Pseudocloëon *spinners.*

How did you figure it out? Philips asked.

I didn't figure it, I explained sheepishly. *Guessed wrong until it was almost over!*

There are two western species that offer remarkably heavy hatches: the green-bodied *Pseudocloëon edmundsi* and the *Pseudocloëon futile,* which is smaller and more yellowish. Both species emerge in two separate broods each season. The early brood hatches on streams like the Henry's Fork in July, and the autumn broods come in September and October. Over the past thirty years, these autumn broods have sometimes proved more important than the hatches of early summer. Emergence usually takes place in the evening, although the fall activity can occur in early afternoon, particularly when the preceding nights are cold.

Jack Hemingway and I learned about this on Silver Creek near Sun Valley a few years ago. It was early October, but there were still good main swarms of *Tricorythodes* mixed with tiny yellow *Ephemerella* flies. We fished that morning at the Point-of-Rocks stretch and took trout steadily until we met upstream for lunch. Hemingway produced

200

some fine cheese and cold chicken from the hamper, and we sat in the coarse grass, trailing our waders.

We ate hungrily, watching a late brood of mallards across the creek, until the trout began to work again. Their rises began tentatively, slowly increased their rhythm, until they settled into a steady pattern of heavy feeding. *They're still hungry,* I said, *but what are they finding to eat?*

Hemingway waded out several feet. Pseudocloëon. He seemed puzzled and then surprised. Pseudocloëon!

During lunch? I asked.

It's been pretty cold at night, he explained. *Sometimes they hatch when they feel like it.*

You have any imitations that green?

Sure, he laughed, *but let the fish enjoy themselves—we both took enough trout this morning, and we've got something they don't!*

Hemingway rooted back under the bank and lifted a chilled bottle of Sancerre from a springhole. We sat in the warm October grass, drinking the wine and watching the trout until they stopped rising.

But the most pervasive memory of these green-bodied *Pseudocloëon* flies took place in the Yellowstone. It was almost wintry that October afternoon on the Firehole, and steam billowed high from its hot springs and geysers. Several elk were grazing in the Nez Percé bottoms. Two herons were stalking voles in the hawkbill and wheatgrass across the river when I stopped just below Sentinel Creek.

Squalls drifted in somber layers of cloud along Pitchstone Ridge, and the chill wind already smelled of winter. Sleet rattled across the grassy bottoms and died. The flickering sun reflected weakly in a current that looked like polished silver. It did not seem like an evening for fishing, but the Firehole is moody and unpredictable. The wind had dropped and a fine mist rose from the river. Tight against the dry-grass bank, there was a bulging rise.

It seemed impossible, and I stared at the smooth current until the fish showed again. Its rise bulged out from the trailing grass, and its echoing ring slipped into the riffle down-

201

stream and was gone. The trout came again, sipping twice in a pair of interlocking rises. It was feeding steadily now, but it was merely a prelude.

Another fish started working against the bank upstream, and soon a dozen were showing. The cold made it difficult to rig my tackle, since I had been fishing a big muddler on the Madison that morning, and I fumbled clumsily with the fine tippets. Stringing a smaller rod went shakily too, but finally I circled down through the meadows, well behind the rising fish in the bend.

The afternoon darkened as another squall cloaked the entire Pitchstone Ridge until its serrations were lost completely, but there was still no wind along the river. Tattered clouds drifted in the lodgepoles. Dozens of fish were feeding greedily now, rising all along the fifty-yard bend below the road.

No other fish showed. It seemed the only activity was in the Lodgepole Bend itself, and I watched briefly from the shallows to verify that observation.

The first fish still worked lazily, and the smooth current was literally covered with tiny *Pseudocloëon* flies. It was much too late in the season for their hatching, according to most literature on the species, yet the river was alive with the tiny green-bodied flies. There were several imitations in my fly book, and I selected one and quickly dressed its wings with silicone. Faint sunlight glittered on the still current, and the trout rose again.

He's still feeding! I thought.

The tiny polywing settled just above the grassy outcropping where the fish lay, and I tightened hopefully when the fish rose again. The big trout shook itself angrily as it sensed my gentle pressure, held its station for several seconds, and exploded upstream along the bottom. It stripped line greedily from the reel while I clambered out to follow.

Strong fish! I thought.

The fight was comically brief. The trout bored deep in the channels among the weeds until I felt the leader catching among their leafy stems. It caught and sheared off, and the fish was gone.

Snow started falling again while I attempted to repair my tackle, and a fierce squall scattered tiny pebbles against the Jeep. The mountains beyond the river were completely lost in ragged, ink-colored clouds. It was suddenly bitter cold, and a thick snow filled the valley while I broke down my tackle. The storm ended as quickly as it began and the raw wind dropped down. Its huge flakes had whitened the Firehole meadows, clinging to the hawkbill and coarse grass, and I shivered.

Summer's over, I thought sadly.

Beyond the still bend in the river, coming like a skirmish line of dark ghosts in the fresh snow, were several buffalo. The herd was led by a giant bull, its shaggy coat flopping almost comically as it came.

The buffalo stopped in the meadows upstream, tested the wind briefly and plunged into the shallows. The others followed the big male, their plodding silhouettes black against the silvery flow. The file moved slowly like a winter's dream, until finally they were across, steam rising from their woolly flanks like hot springs in the bitter cold.

[1979]

12

The Time of
the Hendricksons

*This essay is a distinctively detailed lesson in fishing
the most important early-season hatch on many rivers from Michigan and Wisconsin east to New York
and Maine. These flies emerge when water temperatures have risen sufficiently to allow aggressive surface feeding by larger brown trout, and on such
streams as the West Branch of the Ausable in the New
York Adirondacks it may be the best time for big trout
on a dry fly.*

*By the early 1960s, Schwiebert was experiment-
ing in another facet of Hendrickson fishing with patterns designed to match the emerging insect partway
between the nymphal and dun stages. Such work by
Schwiebert, René Harrop, Doug Swisher, Carl Richards, and others on so-called rolled nylon stocking
emerger patterns has been most important. I've often
seen large brown trout feeding on emerging nymphs
exclusively, which can make fishing a standard dry-
fly imitation totally futile.*

It is still winter outside the farmhouse. There were several
whitetail does foraging in the snow along the woodlot this

morning. Their coats are almost as gray as the winter woods, and it has been a lean year. My fly-tying table is littered with lemon woodduck feathers and a pair of fine Andalusian gamecock necks. There is a delicate Hendrickson half-finished in the vise, and a flock of crows just settled in the oaks outside, showering a dust of snow through their rattling limbs. It is a time for winter daydreams.

Each angler has a favorite hatch of flies on his home river, and each favorite echoes his experience with its timeless cycle of the seasons. Each river is unique too, with its singular fingerprint of fly hatches.

Some fishermen like the early *Paraleptophlebia* hatches. Others prefer the larger Gordon Quills that emerge on April afternoons, perhaps because they are the unmistakable harbingers of another season astream. Others prefer the later *Stenonema* flies, and fly fishermen on the classic limestone streams anxiously await the Pale Sulphur hatches. Some anglers still give their allegiance to the Green Drakes, although these big *Ephemera* flies are sadly in decline on most rivers. Fishermen who live on the larger eastern rivers happily await the slate-winged *Isonychias*, perhaps because they are large enough to coax big trout to the surface in early summer. There are still others on the storied eastern rivers who like the pale hatches of late spring and summer—the straw-colored duns best imitated by their delicate Gray Foxes and Cahills.

There are many hatches worth the notice of the serious fly fisherman. Men who frequent the Beaverkill and Fishing Creek and Musconetcong have learned to love the Blue-winged Olives common on their waters. Skilled fishermen are becoming aware of ants and leafhoppers and beetles in the cycle of the season, particularly since we have mishandled and damaged our familiar aquatic hatches in past years, with the careless lumbering and tanneries and highway construction and pesticides typical of our technological myopia. The decline of the Green Drake has been partly compensated for by the ultimate heresy of the summer leafrollers—the apple-green tree worms that emerge a few weeks later to perform their acrobatics suspended above the river on silken threads, tempting the bigger trout.

Each fisherman has his favorites, and those favorites may change with his rivers and the layers of experience he accumulates across the years. Mine follow a similar pattern of experiment and continual change. The early summers were spent in Michigan, where I learned to like the egg-laden *Ephemerella* spinners that swarmed over favorite boyhood riffles on the Pere Marquette. There were giant *Hexagenia* drakes in the midsummer darkness on big Michigan rivers like the Boardman and the Manistee. Other favorites have followed in later years, and each of these hatches triggers memories of many rivers; but on this winter evening I would probably choose the hardy *Ephemerella* hatches of late April—the ubiquitous Hendricksons familiar to most eastern fishermen from Minnesota to Maine.

There are many memories of Hendricksons from these past few seasons. Such memories include an April float on the familiar Au Sable in Michigan, with weak sunlight and fresh snow in the swamp birches along the river, and the wonderful hatch of *Ephemerella* flies that came off the river in the sweeping bends below Grayling.

Hendrickson memories tumble down the years, like a reach of broken water between favorite pools. There was a heavy hatch one afternoon on the Yellow Breeches, when the warm winds of the Shenandoah country eddied north and transformed winter into spring, and the dark ridges above the Cumberland valley became faintly touched with green overnight. Memory returns to the excellent hatch that emerged one April on the classic Ferdon's Pool, that shrine on the Beaverkill where Albert Everett Hendrickson himself first tried the Steenrod dry flies that would later carry his name. There have been Hendricksons on many rivers over the years, and sometimes they have rescued me from the misfortunes of April, like the hatch that triggered an impressive rise of trout on a bitter day of snow squalls along the Schoharie.

There are many memories and reasons for loving the time of the Hendricksons. The trout are already conscious of dry flies and have been conditioned to surface food by the smaller stoneflies and mayflies that usher in the season. Hendricksons appear when the first brave leaves are budding in

206

the trees, touching the branches with yellow and rose. The first real warmth is found in the midday sun, and there are violets in the sheltered places. Bloodroot is often blooming when the Hendricksons are hatching on the Raritan and Nissequogue, and there are dogwoods in blossom when the hatch reaches the Neversink and Battenkill farther north.

Some signals are found elsewhere, like the barometer of forsythias and magnolias. Commuters on my morning train pass the richly flowering magnolias along Blair Walk, which leads down from the Princeton campus to the railroad station, without realizing the significance behind the blossoms—the anglers among us try to forget them, hiding our disappointment in the *Journal* and the *Times* because we are deskbound on a day that promises Hendricksons.

These familiar hatches are typically composed of three closely related species. Perhaps the best known is *Ephemerella invaria*, first described for anglers by Preston Jennings in his classic *Book of Trout Flies*, and perfectly imitated by a properly dressed Hendrickson. Almost as familiar is *Ephemerella subvaria*, its darker abdominal segments flushed with the rusty pinkish markings described by Art Flick in his little *Streamside Guide*. His book has helped a generation of Catskill fishermen to know their fly hatches, and his version of the Hendrickson is tied with the pinkish belly fur of a red fox vixen to suggest the pinkish abdominal cast of the *subvaria* hatches on the Schoharie. Sometimes I tie Hendricksons with dun hacklepoint wings, and bodies with rusty pink dubbing ribbed over a base of cream fox when the browns are particularly choosy. *Ephemerella rotunda* is the third insect of the Hendrickson group, and has its distinctly yellowish abdomen ringed with faint brown tergite and sternite markings. It is smaller than its sister hatches. Its nymphs are fast-water dwellers, perhaps requiring more oxygen than its *invaria* and *subvaria* cousins, and its activity is concentrated in the more broken reaches of river. The familiar Red Quill developed by Art Flick is also an excellent imitation on rivers which have good hatches of *Ephemerella subvaria*.

Some mayflies are quite temperamental, emerging

sporadically throughout the day, and often failing to appear when conditions seem absolutely perfect. Hendricksons are unusually punctual and predictable. There is nothing timid about them once their hatching is started, and they often last from mid-April until the third week in May. Hendrickson hatches are still relatively heavy, perhaps because these hardy *Ephemerella*s have survived the damage we have inflicted on the ecology of our eastern rivers. Perhaps because of their hardiness, the Hendrickson will probably continue as a major hatch, and eastern anglers can enjoy them in the future—as much as our fathers have loved and fished them in seasons past.

There is something civilized and particularly charming about Hendricksons. City anglers can rise late when they are hatching, spend a leisurely breakfast, dress flies, fuss with their equipment, and lazily reach the river after eleven o'clock—secure in the knowledge that an angler with little interest in flogging the water with heavily weighted nymphs and early-morning bucktails has missed nothing of importance.

The nymphs of these *Ephemerella*s clamber about the bottom in all types of water, although most specimens are found in moderate riffles and currents. The nymphs of the *invaria* species are medium to dark brownish, with darker mottlings and light markings of buff and olive. The nymphal forms of *subvaria* are generally dark brown, with several pale tergite markings and a rather olive-colored cast. The thorax and wing cases are almost black before emergence. The back segments of the abdomen are dark brown near the thorax and the tails, with the gills and gill segments a somewhat paler brown. The belly segments are brown, darkening toward the tail filaments. The legs are olive with dark brown mottlings. The tails are light olive and banded with brown. The nymphs of the *rotunda* species are yellowish brown mottled with darker markings on the thorax, wing cases, and tergites. Both legs and tails are tan mottled with brown. These three species are remarkably abundant in the richer streams and thrive in all types of water from tumbling runs to gravel-bottomed riffles and the silt of quiet backwaters and

208

eddies. Particularly fertile rivers support as many as a thousand *Ephemerella* nymphs in a square yard of bottom.

The spinner stage is also important, but few anglers are familiar with it except to imitate the egg-filled females during the evening mating swarms. These spinner flights occur after the duns have hatched from the river and molted, and the mating swarms in good seasons can resemble a winged blizzard. Male spinners are also important trout foods.

The spinners of these Hendrickson flies are surprisingly different in color. The *invaria* species is perhaps the most familiar to anglers, since it was described in Jennings's *Book of Trout Flies* more than fifty years ago. It has clear wings, a reddish-brown thorax, yellowish legs, light brown tergite mottlings on a pale brownish-yellow body, and three pale tails ringed with brown. The spinners of the *subvaria* flies are somewhat darker in coloring, having clear wings, a dark reddish-brown thorax, olive legs flushed with brown, a dark reddish-brown abdomen ringed with pale amber markings, and olive tails ringed with brown. The mating swarms of *rotunda* flies have clear wings, a yellowish-brown thorax, pale yellow legs, amber-yellow bodies ringed with yellowish brown, and pale tails marked with brown. Each of these spinner species has bright yellow egg sacs extruding from the mating females. Pale versions of the Female Beaverkill have long been a favorite with fishermen during these spinner flights, although better imitations are likely in the future.

These spinners are usually as punctual as the Hendrickson duns, and appear over the river between five and six o'clock in the late afternoon. The swarms rise and fall high over the river, moving gradually upstream until the females drop lower to oviposit over the riffles. Once the eggs are extruded, the females fall exhausted to the surface with their wings askew. Later their wings lie spent in the surface film, and both spentwing males and females are sometimes still available the following morning. During the mating swarms, the trout often rise eagerly to the egg-laying spinners, since the heaviest insect activity lasts little more than an hour. The feeding activity is rather splashy. The riseforms encountered with spent spinners the following mornings are soft and deliberate. Fishing during these *Ephemerella* spinner flights is rather more at the mercy of the weather than it is for the Hendricksons, and relatively warm spring evenings with little wind are typically best.

But enough stream entomology, because the memory is filled with Hendrickson fishing, and a typical April day on a familiar reach of the Brodheads is taking shape in the mind. The morning was dark and squally before breakfast, but the rain had stopped at daybreak. There was nothing to entice me outside, and I spent two hours dressing fresh Hendricksons and Red Quills before wandering upstream to look for rises. There were no rises in either pool where sporadic morning hatches are often good. I wandered upstream toward a deep run under slate ledges, its current tongue spilling from a heavy riffle where I have often collected nymphs. The riffle typically holds hundreds of *subvaria* and *rotunda* specimens, and it seemed a good place for nymphal activity.

There were no rises, but I was sure the nymphs were restlessly anticipating their afternoon hatch. The morning seemed less cold when I changed reels and strung a sinking line through the guides. The first cast reached out and dropped the weighted imitation above the ledge, and I mended line where the riffling currents slowed in deeper water. The nymph drifted deep and tightened against the sinking line, swimming over the bottom gravel where it was stopped by an unseen trout. It was a twelve-inch brown, its gills dark with unswallowed Hendrickson nymphs, and I released it gently. Several more were taken on the deep nymph, fished tight against the bottom of the ledge. There were still no rises when I left the river for lunch.

Lunch was leisurely and pleasurable, and filled with anticipation as the weather steadily improved. Patchy clouds and half-warm sunlight were welcome when I reached the river at one o'clock. The improving weather was still blustery, and a chill wind gusted downstream. There were already a few fluttering duns coming off, and twice I saw trout chase freshly hatched mayflies that were sailboating with the wind.

There was still an hour before the regular afternoon hatching period, and I did not want to disturb the long pool I had chosen for the main hatch. I ignored occasional splashy rises and fished the nymph instead, casting to both the rise-forms and the known holding-lies where I had taken fish before. Several more trout were taken in the hour that followed, and I killed a fifteen-inch brown to check its stomach contents—there were three adult mayflies and twenty-six *Ephemerella* nymphs in his gullet.

Two o'clock arrived, and I walked back to the pool I had chosen for the afternoon. The wind had dropped, and I waited in a sheltered pocket of sunlight until there were mayflies coming off everywhere. I watched patiently until the trout had settled into good feeding rhythms, determined that the insects were *subvaria,* and moved stealthily into position with a workable imitation. Fifteen trout were working, including one heavy fish at the head of the pool. Sometimes there are days when everything goes predictably and well. This was one of those rare days when the main hatch came at precisely two o'clock, the imitation worked perfectly, and each decent float over a rising fish equaled a rise. The trout were so busy with the naturals that bad casts and poor floats did not disturb them. The final count was thirty-seven browns, including the fat two-pounder working at the head of the pool, and I released these fish gently.

Fly hatches are seldom that predictable. Some mysteries and moods of the river are impossible to explain. Sometimes the hatches simply fail to appear, and sometimes the fish puzzlingly ignore a current covered with flies. April and its hatches share moodiness and many pleasant enigmas, and I often think of both when late-winter snow is sifting through the trees.

[1968]

13

Something Old, Something New

George Grant of Butte, Montana, is the elder states-
man of Rocky Mountain trout fishermen and justly
famous for his stonefly-nymph imitations on which
this essay is partly based. Stoneflies are important in
many trout streams, but especially so in the tumbling
streams of the West. Grant-style nymphs have under-
bodies made flat by the addition of a brass pin along
each side of the hook. The bodies are then colored to
match various stonefly nymphs before being over-
wrapped with flat monofilament, which gives a seg-
mented effect and also a wonderful diffusion of the
underlying pigments. Wing cases and hackle are then
added.

There are many other stonefly-nymph tying
styles, and most commercial versions are large,
shaggy, and impressionistic. Work by Grant and others has been more realistic and sometimes ridiculed
by those who feel such imitation isn't necessary.
Grant himself responded to this once by writing: "For
many decades I have tied and fished my own woven-
body rough hair nymphs, which possess to an even
greater degree all of the favorable qualities of dub-

212

bing bodies. I have fished them on the same water, with equal intensity and skill (or lack of it) as I have fished hard-bodied nymphs, and I have consistently had greater success with the latter."

This won't, of course, still the old arguments of impressionism versus realism, but at least it's a voice from the modern minority. Grant's flies are sufficiently complex that you won't find them in most commercial fly bins. Any good fly tier, however, could certainly make you some on special order. They are worth the effort.

The old cabin stands in the pines and hardwoods, its full-length porch surrounded with dense thickets of tree-size rhododendron. Pine needles carpet the forest floor. The main room is two stories high, with a massive pine-slab table and a towering fieldstone fireplace anchoring its ends. The log staircase rises into a gallery under the roof timbers and connects the sleeping rooms upstairs. Cane River Camp has the quality of a museum, with its *art sauvage* furniture and sporting prints and photographs of long-ago summers in the Great Smokies, and I fished it happily one weekend with Nathaniel Pryor Reed and our host, Borden Hanes.

Below the camp, Sugar Mill Creek comes down through its tangled thickets of laurel and hemlocks on Mount Mitchell, and the swiftly flowing Cane itself lies just beyond its sheltering copse of trees. After breakfast, Millie Hanes disappeared into the camp kitchen.

You're not fishing this morning? I asked.

I'll be along, Millie called. *I've got to fix these ramps the boys just brought in from the mountain.*

What are ramps? I asked.

Something like wild leeks with the bite of garlic, she laughed. *We make them into a soup when we're here.*

Like a French onion soup? I said. *With a thick beef broth?*

Exactly, Millie nodded.

Borden Hanes and I had drawn the lower water, where the Cane finally escapes its water-polished gorge and tumbles through the trees that cover its long-abandoned hardscrabble farms. It is pleasant fishing, its pools and flats connected by

A HATCH TO MATCH

shallow, boulder-strewn runs and swift riffles. The fish are not stocked, and although they are relatively small on the lower pools, these wild strains are some of the most colorful fish in the world. Even the brown trout are spectacular, their adipose and caudal fins edged in shockingly bright scarlet.

We fished a mile of water without moving a fish over ten inches, fishing dry flies and small nymphs, although the small trout cooperated greedily. It was beautiful water that seemingly held great promise, and finally we stopped below a strong run of chest-deep current.

Can't understand where the big fish went.

They're here, I said. *And if the big fish are anywhere, they're in a deep run like that one.*

But how can we get them? Borden asked.

My fly book held several weighted stonefly nymphs dressed on long-shank #8 hooks. The flies were tied after the George Grant technique, using flat monofilament bodies wrapped over a yellow base, with dark lateral margins and mottlings showing through the coils. The tails and hackles were beautifully marked ringneck saddle feathers, and the wing cases were formed of ringneck saddle too, reinforced with Flexament and scissored to suggest the wing cases of a big stonefly nymph.

Working carefully up the run, I cast well ahead and let the nymph sink deep along the bottom stones. The nymph came back deep, drifting dead in the swift current while I watched the floating point of the line for the sign of a taking fish. Several casts worked back along the run before the drifting line paused sharply in its float, and I tightened into a fine sixteen-inch rainbow. The trout tail-walked back downstream without disturbing the throat of the pool, and I took two more good fish.

That's more like it! I thought.

Borden Hanes came over as I netted the last fish. *Why did you pick that particular nymph?* he asked.

It's not complicated, I explained. *That current over a rubble bottom is perfect stonefly water—and since these nymphs spend three years under water, they're almost always available to the fish.*

And juicy enough to interest them, he nodded.

214

Big stonefly nymphs are perfect for fishing the water, prospecting an unfamiliar river, or covering a stream when nothing obvious is hatching. Since they require considerable amounts of oxygen, the best populations are usually concentrated in fast-water stretches with the rocky bottoms that provide a sheltering habitat. Unlike most aquatic insects, with a yearlong life cycle that provides the fish with mature nymphs only a few weeks each season, these big stoneflies are readily available in several year-class stages of growth throughout the year.

There was a similar experience last spring on the Au Sable in Michigan, fishing the beautiful flats above Black Bend. We were staying in the Averill camp there, with its beautiful green lawn reaching down to the canoe dock along the water.

It is a remarkable stretch of river, lying about halfway between the famous Stephan and Wakeley bridges. Its unique fertility comes from miles of watercress springheads that trickle in through the cedar sweepers and logjams that line both banks, subtly doubling its volume of flow without a single major tributary. The gravelly bottom and smoothly flowing flats are optimal mayfly habitat, and this water is almost legendary for its early hatches of big *Ephemerella* flies. Walter Averill and I enjoyed some remarkable dry-fly sport on these flats for several days, particularly on some blustery afternoons with a softly misting rain.

Finally we had a fine morning, warm and without a trace of wind. It seemed like a perfect day for hatches, and I decided to dress some flies for the afternoon's fishing instead of fishing the water blind before lunch.

Walter Averill and I walked downstream to fish up from the shallows below Black Bend, expecting a heavy hatch of *Ephemerella* subimagoes, but the hatch never came. There were a few duns coming off, and the small brook trout took them halfheartedly. The big browns at Black Bend never started to work.

That's strange, Averill shook his head. *You'd think the flies and fish would be everywhere.*

The weather's too nice, I smiled.

215

It's already three o'clock, Averill said, anxiously checking his watch. *It's not going to happen.*

Looks like no hatch today, I agreed ruefully. *Looks like we should try something else—maybe just work a big nymph.*

Sounds good. Averill waved.

The shallow flats of the Whippoorwill stretch narrow into a gathering current below the Averill boathouse. The river gathers itself, sliding into a neck-deep current that scours deep among the deadfalls along the south bank. Black Bend is a hundred yards of big trout water, flowing deep and strong under the trees.

Downstream its tail shallows spread smoothly over the pale gravel and sweep back into a sliding, fan-shaped flat. These shallows swing north past a sprawling logjam, gather into a swift chute against the sweepers, and spill into a heavy three hundred yards of water. The swift currents drop down, working against the fallen cedars that line the channel, until the river stills its music in Priest's Bend.

Looks like good stonefly water, I thought.

It was a solution for that hatchless afternoon on the Au Sable. Fishing the same nylon-bodied nymph carefully, working and mending its fly swing deep on a sinking line, I took and released a dozen brown trout between twelve and sixteen inches. Although the smooth-flowing river is not optimal stonefly water, it does have swift stretches that shelter good populations, and in such places an imitation is often effective.

Since stoneflies demand swift water, relatively pollution-free volumes of flow, and a sheltering habitat of coarse bottom-rubble, perhaps the best stonefly populations are found in our western rivers.

Many knowledgeable anglers believe the Madison, which rises in the Yellowstone country and flows northward to form the Missouri in Montana, is perhaps the finest stonefly habitat in the world. Certainly the hatches of big *Claasenia* and *Pteronarcys* stoneflies that emerge on the Madison in late spring and summer are the heaviest hatches anywhere. These species have three- and four-year life cycles, making them continually available as trout forage, and the same dressings that suggest the smaller *Phasganophora* nymphs on eastern and midwestern streams are workable imitations of the western *Claasenia* flies.

It is fitting that the basic theories for these nymphs were first worked out by George Grant, the master flydresser who is widely acknowledged the dean of the Big Hole country. His innovations provide remarkable lifelike nymphs to imitate the hard-bodied stonefly naturals.

But my favorite experience with these Grant-style nymphs came on a wintry spring afternoon on the Madison. Dan Callaghan and I were fishing on the Henry's Fork in Idaho when a spring storm dropped a surprising three-inch snowfall on the western slopes of Targhee Pass. The Henry's Fork rainbows sensibly stopped feeding, and we stopped too.

What now? Callaghan shivered.

Best hatch I've ever seen. We stood looking at the popcorn-size size snowflakes. *Let's drive over and try the Madison across the pass. With all the hot springs in its headwaters, it might still be fishable today.*

Let's go, Callaghan agreed.

We found less snow across Targhee Pass, had lunch at Huck's Diner in West Yellowstone, and drove into the park. The stretch of the Madison around the Nine-Mile Hole has always been a favorite of mine, and we rigged our gear beside the river hopefully. It was cold after the snow stopped, but the river was still almost sixty degrees in spite of the changing weather.

My favorite run lies more than fifty yards from the road, where a boulder-strewn riffle shelves off into a chest-deep reach of water that lies deep in the shadow of the trees. Nothing was hatching and no fish rose. The trout were apparently feeding deep along the bottom, because I took a dozen fish from sixteen to twenty-two inches, working the big nymph with a carefully mended fly swing. Two hours later, the wind turned so wintry that the line started freezing in the guides.

Callaghan came downstream slowly. *It's too cold,* he shivered wildly. *I've had enough for today.*

Me too! My reel was freezing up.

You did pretty well. Callaghan struggled to start the car. *You must have caught a dozen—what were you using?*

Big stonefly nymph, I said.

Those Grant-style nymphs with the monofilament? The wipers struggled against another squall. *Like the old rhyme?*

What old rhyme? I was puzzled.

You know the rhyme I mean, Callaghan laughed. *The wedding rhyme about something old, something new . . .*

I don't get it, I confessed.

There's something old in these soft pheasant hackles, he explained puckishly, *and something new in that mono body.*

Something borrowed in the Grant techniques, I agreed laughingly, *but what's blue?*

My fingers! Callaghan grinned.

You're right, I laughed. *Let's get back into West Yellowstone and get thawed out—I've still got some old pot-still whisky.*

Almost worth getting frozen, he said.

[1976]

14

The Salmonfly Hatches

The term salmonfly *confuses many new anglers, who think immediately and wrongly of salmon. The term started as a local name for large stoneflies of the* Pteronarcys *genus common in many Rocky Mountain trout streams, perhaps because some adults show tinges of salmon- or reddish-orange coloring. In any case, both the nymphs and the adults of this genus can produce exceptional fishing, especially since they are both large and numerous enough to tempt trout measured in pounds rather than inches.*

During a hatch, the big adults can be found in incredible numbers throughout the streamside willows and flying over the river. These adult flies can be more than two inches long and quite disconcerting, as I discovered when one found its way inside my shirt. They are harmless, however, and my squirming and flapping was soon forgotten as we had a field day with browns and rainbows along Montana's Big Hole River.

My first encounter with salmonflies came when I was young and fishing the Gunnison River in Colorado. It was early summer, there were hundreds of flight ducks in the flood bottoms at Tomichi Creek, and there were pale leaves on the cottonwoods and willows. The foliage along the river was crawling with freshly hatched stoneflies, and when their egg laying started in late morning, the trout went crazy. The river was swift and silt-colored at the McCave Bridge.

I was startled suddenly by the rises of several big rainbows working along some willows. Nothing that I had witnessed before, including the nocturnal *Hexagenia* hatches in Michigan, had prepared me for these greedy rainbows. The fluttering salmonflies came down the current along the willows, their dark-veined wings and bodies struggling to escape its flow, until the trout took them explosively. Their rises were not just splashes, but wild gouts of water that erupted in the swift currents.

Look at those pigs! I recall thinking.

There was another fisherman working the water upstream. *Don't wade too deep!* he shouted in mock warning. *Those big trout look hungry enough to eat fishermen!*

Right! I waved in response.

The swift flow tumbled past our waders, making it difficult to wade in spite of the pea-gravel bottom. The other fisherman struggled with a wading staff to hold his position under the bridge. It was difficult to reach the willows while leaning into the heavy flow, the backcurrents sweeping the gravel from under my feet, and several big trout held beyond my casting.

Although their wild rises scattered spray in the wind, the fish were still selective and stubbornly refused our flies. We tried pattern after pattern while the trout foraged along the willows. The egg laying lasted until late afternoon, until the smaller trout had stuffed themselves like sausages, and only two big rainbows were still working. Both fish were holding in surprisingly strong currents, high in the swift throat of the pool. When the other fisherman abandoned his beat, I returned to the shallows and struggled out where fish were still feeding.

Nothing in my fly boxes worked until I tried a big, brown-winged bucktail, its chenille body rust-colored with hook stains. It was not really a dry fly, but I greased it heavily with line dressing and tried it with a sense of desperation. It was engulfed in a wild splash.

He's hooked! I shouted to the swift-flowing river. *He's hooked, and he's huge!*

The struggle was over as quickly as it started. The big rainbow shook itself angrily and showered the willows with spray when it turned downstream. It did not spend its strength in mindless cartwheeling. It bolted through the primary current tongues, gathering momentum as it passed me and telegraphing its sullen strength back into the rod. It stripped the full double taper as it gathered speed, until the reel sounded the death rattle of its broken drag spring, free-spooling and spilling loops of backing, and the reel jammed.

I'm beaten! I groaned.

The leader hummed like a guitar string and snapped, and the big rainbow made one final jump downstream. It was the biggest fish I had ever hooked, but twenty years later the thing I remember best is the wild explosion of its feeding. Since that baptism on the Gunnison, I have seen these big salmonflies emerging many times.

Although there are other important fly hatches on our western rivers and several species that emerge for longer periods of time, these big stoneflies offer perhaps the most spectacular surface feeding of the year on such famous streams as the Deschutes, Henry's Fork, Big Hole, Madison, and Yellowstone. During particularly good years, the nymphs and egg-laying adults of these aquatic insects are so numerous that even the largest fish gorge themselves. Sometimes fish from ten to fifteen pounds work on the surface, and only too much snowmelt can spoil the fishing in salmonfly season.

The principal stoneflies involved in these hatches are of the *Pteronarcys* genus, and it is the nymphs that are the so-called black hellgrammites popular among bait fishermen from the Chama in northern New Mexico to the swift rivers of British Columbia. These big nymphs display three- to four-year aquatic cycles, concealing themselves among the detritus and coarse rubble and stones of the bottom. Mature

221

nymphs hatch to mate and lay their eggs in late spring and early summer. Fully grown *Pteronarcys* nymphs can measure as long as two inches when they finally migrate to the streamside alders and willows and hatch into adult stoneflies with slightly longer wings. The coloration of both nymphs and mature flies varies subtly from river to river, depending on temperatures and water chemistry and clarity, and the color and character of the bottom.

Nymphal coloring is typically black or bitter chocolate, with dull orange to dirty, orangish-yellow on the thoracic segments and sternites. Both specific habitat and separate species are involved.

There are two principal species involved, although some field studies suggest that isolated colonies of a third *Pteronarcys* species are also involved in the salmonfly hatches. Such relict populations are also reported from the watersheds of the Platte and Missouri. The common species in these stonefly populations is perhaps the familiar *Pteronarcys californica*, which is extensively distributed throughout the western mountains. Populations are described from British Columbia to California, and from the Pacific watersheds to the rivers of Wyoming and Montana. The lesser-known *Pteronarcys princeps* is widely distributed from California to British Columbia, with its zoogeography largely confined to the Pacific drainages, although colonies are also reported in Utah and western Colorado.

Although some entomologists who work with stoneflies discount the field studies of knowledgeable fishermen, there is considerable evidence that the eastern *Pteronarcys dorsata* is also found in surprisingly large colonies in some rivers draining the eastern Rockies.

The Colorado sometimes has both *Pteronarcys* flies and populations of the similar *Pteronarcella badia,* with colonies reported from Colorado to northern California, and from drainages northward into Montana, Alberta, and British Columbia. The related species *Pteronarcella regularis* is primarily a Pacific hatch, distributed from California to Alaska. My boyhood collection of nymphs suggests that both *Pteronarcys princeps* and *Pteronarcella badia* were involved in the famous salmonfly hatches on the Gunnison thirty-five years ago, and recent field studies on the headwaters of the Colorado at Hot Sulphur Springs suggest that the willowflies there are primarily *Pteronarcella* populations. Both the slim-bodied *Pteronarcella badia,* with its sharply rectilinear wing cases and thoracic covers, and the better-known *Pteronarcys californica* are important populations during the salmonfly hatches on the Big Hole in Montana.

Since the rivers are typically in spate with snowmelt, these big stoneflies seldom emerge like their closely related populations on our eastern rivers, which clamber out on half-submerged stones to split their nymphal skins and become winged insects. The western species have evolved in alpine drainages that tumble wildly in spring flooding, and populations that merely migrated to emerge on stones in the shallows often failed to survive and reproduce. The sustaining populations of *Pteronarcys* and *Pteronarcella* flies have largely evolved from progenitors that climbed high into willows to hatch and learned to escape the punishing spring floods that scour the mountain rivers each season.

Their adults have dark-veined wings with a dark brownish-gray cast, dark chocolate-colored legs and bodies and tails, and dull-orangish sternum and belly sections. The forewings of the female can measure forty-five millimeters, and the male wings are as much as thirty-eight millimeters. Mating typically occurs in streamside foliage and vegetation. Both males and females are lethargic in the cool mornings of early summer, and egg laying does not commence until the temperatures rise at midday. Particularly cold nights can postpone ovipositing swarms until afternoon, and such egg laying is usually limited to females flying over the current to jettison their ova. Their fertile eggs are extruded in a dark, tea-colored cluster, which is dropped from heights of three to ten feet above the current. The clustered eggs are so dense that an egg-laying female can suddenly rise in flight when its ova are dropped. Windy weather can force the egg-laying females into the river, and high winds can even blow the males from the foliage along the banks, but their clumsy ovipositing flight can also commit large numbers of flies to the current.

Comparative analysis of several famous salmonfly rivers

reveals a number of intriguing parallel factors. Each watershed has a relatively steep profile and a swift current free of pollution. Typical bottom consists of coarse aggregates and rubble. Rich colonies of algae and aquatic vegetation are typical. The headwaters are still free of development, particularly on the Madison and Yellowstone, which both rise in Yellowstone Park. These nymph populations also display relatively high oxygen requirements, although specimens can display remarkable ability to survive when oxygen is limited, and the best salmonfly streams exhibit high concentrations of dissolved oxygen. Alkalinity contributes to their nymphal exoskeletons. Streamside foliage and vegetation are important too. Since mature nymphs climb into the alders and willows to escape spring flooding and emerge and find shelter there from late blizzards and storms, the banks of the better salmonfly drainages are densely bordered with alders and coyote willows.

Microclimate also plays a subtle role in the ecology of our famous salmonfly rivers. The best salmonfly hatches are almost invariably found in watersheds having a north-south axis, receiving optimal solar exposure in early summer. Obvious examples are the Deschutes, Henry's Fork, Madison, and Yellowstone. Although the Gunnison is primarily a west-flowing river, its best salmonfly hatches historically occurred in its open-flowing stretches between Gunnison and Sapinero. The Big Hole in western Montana is a sickle-shaped river and rises in the Bitterroots. Its cold, grayling-filled headwaters flow northward, circling east toward the sheltered basin at Wise River, finally dropping swiftly into the canyon below Watercress Spring. Although it holds sustaining populations of *Pteronarcys* and *Pteronarcella* flies as far upstream as Dickie Bridge, the best mating swarms are found in its mileage between Melrose and Divide, where the Big Hole turns southeast through Maidenrock Canyon.

Sometimes these big *Pteronarcys* and *Pteronarcella* hatches are combined with other important species. Particularly common are the smaller *Hesperoperla pacifica,* the dark willowfly species once included in the better-known *Acroneuria* genus. The darkly veined female wings measure thirty millimeters, while the male forewings are slightly smaller. Bodies are dark orangish-chocolate, with a bright orange chroma to the belly segments. The smaller blue-winged stoneflies that also play a considerable role in these hatches are the dull yellowish *Claasenia sabulosa,* another swift-water species, with forewings that measure twenty-seven millimeters. The males display atrophied wing structures and are seldom a factor in the trout diet, except in their nymphal stages and in windy weather, when clambering adults are often scattered from the streamside foliage into the current.

Oecetis avara is a coarse-veined caddisfly that is classified among the case-building Leptoceridae. These sedges are typically found in both lakes and streams. The larvae are distinguished by their slim, scissorlike mandibles, echoing a diet primarily composed of immature aquatic organisms and zooplankton. Their larval cases are constructed of sand and fine aggregates, mixed with tiny pieces of bark and vegetable matter, and sculptured into a delicately curving conical shelter. The adults have brown, smottled wings measuring thirteen millimeters, and the male forewings are slightly smaller. Both the *Oecetis* males and females have dark, sepia-colored bodies, and a large Blue-winged Adams dressed with a moleskin dubbing is a fine imitation of this important caddisfly species. Knowledgeable guides and fishermen understand its subtle role in the better-known salmonfly hatches.

Peak hatching on the better salmonfly rivers can vary with climate, topography, and latitude. Deschutes hatches typically start in late May, and there are heavy hatches on the Henry's Fork during the week that follows. The Box Canyon stretch below the Island Park Reservoir is prime water on the Henry's Fork. The famous willowflies on the Gunnison emerge in this same period, and the peak emergence on the Big Hole occurs in June. Its hatches start in the lower reaches at Glen, progressing upstream toward Melrose and Maidenrock Canyon, and finishing at Dickie Bridge later in the month. The salmonflies on the beautiful Madison start coming in its Beartrap Canyon, before the hatching stops on the Big Hole, and the hatch progresses steadily upstream until the first days of July. The Yellowstone is often too discolored with snowmelt for good fly fishing over the big *Pteronarcys* flies that are hatching below Livingston in early July, but the river is usually more fishable when the big stoneflies start emerging at Yankee Jim Canyon a week later. Its salmonflies are still coming in late July, when their hatching finally reaches the magnificent gorges in Yellowstone Park.

Local information is available about these hatches from several tackle shops and outfitters. Knowledgeable fishermen can follow these salmonfly hatches from river to river, finding peak mating swarms for almost two months in some years. The salmonflies can offer superb fishing.

Most fishermen assume that the fishing is always simple and superb during the salmonfly hatch, and sometimes it *is* remarkably simple when conditions are right. But sometimes it can become a frustrating puzzle.

During one memorable afternoon while float fishing the Madison, perhaps the river most famous for salmonfly hatches, the foliage was alive with mating stoneflies. Although it was still early in their hatching cycle, some of the fish were unmistakably rising to all three *Pteronarcys, Hesperoperla,* and *Claasenia* genera. Others were selecting the smaller stoneflies. Mixed with these mating Plecoptera were caddisflies that filled the willows, and mating swarms of these sedges were increasingly obvious toward evening. During windy afternoons, large numbers of these dark-bodied *Oecetis* flies are blown into the currents from the willows, and although they are relatively large insects, they are difficult to see in the swift current.

Fishermen have observed these *Oecetis* sedges for years, noting that salmonfly egg laying wanes in the cooling temperatures of the afternoon and that caddisflies begin to gather in mating swarms as soon as the shadows start to reach across the waters. Before most day floats are finished, from the wild Deschutes in Oregon to the cottonwood bottoms along the Yellowstone, selective fish can demonstrate a surprising preference for these smaller caddisflies. Since these *Oecetis* flies are often emerging well before the first salmonflies appear, the trout have already long accepted them with confidence. The large orange- and yellow-bodied stoneflies, however, are often greeted with suspicion and distrust by wild fish.

It is a dramatic example of the masking-hatch principle, in which the most selective fish reject a larger diet form when it first begins to emerge and continue to focus on a smaller species of the size and silhouette and coloration they have already come to trust. Such patterned feeding reflexes are widespread on difficult trout waters, but such behavior is also more common during the brief explosion of the legendary salmonflies than many skilled anglers suspect.

[1980]

15

Grasshopper Wind

Like careful gourmet, trout love grasshoppers, but only in season at the right time of day and in the right spot. I once shared a number of grasshopper trout with Montana guide Bob Jacklin along that state's Madison River as he guided the drift boat while I cast assorted grasshopper patterns to waiting brown trout along the bank.

The trout were cautious on that day, perhaps because of the drift-boat parade of anglers that had preceded us downstream. I could often see trout as they followed the floating fly in the current, nose to the feathers, and turned away without taking. My answer that day was a Letort Hopper, that now-standard pattern that Schwiebert developed, in a smaller than normal size that the brown trout accepted with surprisingly gentle rises in the turbulent current.

Many trout-water summers ago, my fishing apprenticeship began with live grasshoppers in Michigan. Getting bait was sport in itself, and we gathered the grasshoppers in the mornings when they were cold and clambered stiff-legged in mead-

228

ows still delicately beaded with dew. The grass was still wet against our boots, and the large insects held almost motionless as we picked them like berries.

My first trout was caught below a timber-sluice culvert above the farmhouse. Its pool was sheltered under a huge elm, with the trout lying tight in the run along its roots. Our rods were stiff in three pieces of pale split-cane popular in those days. They were well-suited to dapping the live, wriggling grasshoppers over the trout. The first trout came on a windy afternoon in August. Our stalk was made on hands and knees through the alfalfa until we sprawled belly-flat under the elm, its roots pressing up into our rib cages. My father crawled close and outlined tactics with whispers and gestures.

The grasshopper dangled five feet below the agate tip of the rod, and I lowered it slowly between the tree and the fence that crossed below the culvert. The action was eager and immediate. There was a splash and the stiff rod dipped down and I reacted. The trout was derricked violently up into the elm and it hung there, struggling feebly in the breeze. Somehow we extricated it from the branches and sat in the meadow admiring its beauty. Wild twelve-inch brook trout are still treasured in the world of adults, but to my boyhood eyes that fish seemed bigger and more beautiful than any other I have ever caught.

The next summer saw my introduction to the dry fly. June was a good month and the mayfly hatches were heavy, and I caught my first dry-fly trout with a spentwing Adams in the Little Manistee. But that first dry-fly trout was only nine inches long, and in August there was grasshopper feeding in the meadows. My father gave me several Michigan Hoppers and told me to try them when it got hot in the middle of the day. They worked, and along a sweeping bend in the river where the coarse grasses trailed in the current, I caught my first big trout.

My casts with the grasshopper imitations came down along the undercut bank or ticked into the grass until I coaxed them loose. One cast came free and dropped nicely along the bank, and the fly floated past the trailing grass.

229

After three feet of float, the fly was suddenly intercepted by a shadowlike trout, and its rise was vicious, and I was into a fat seventeen-inch brown.

This meadow water was open and undercut along the deep grassy side, and I fought the fish down over a pale rippled-sand bottom. There were no visible snags or deadfalls, and I was able to handle such a trout in spite of my tremble-fingered excitement and the errors of inexperience. After this grasshopper triumph came a week of doldrums. The trout became sluggish and fed little. One could see them lying on the pale bottom against the sand and gill-panting weakly as they waited for cooler weather.

We gathered in the local tackle store and talked of fishing with local fishermen. *You be nice to your boy,* they teased my father, still twinkle-eyed about the big grasshopper trout. *You be nice to your boy,* they laughed, *and maybe he'll tell you how he did it.*

My father always smiled.

Maybe he will! He was pleased and generous about the big trout. *I've never caught one any larger,* he said, *even during the caddis hatch!*

Talk always returned to the late August doldrums.

No decent rise of fish for two weeks, observed the town doctor and the others nodded in agreement.

What we need is a mackerel sky, said the ice-cream proprietor, *mackerel sky with some good windstorms and rain to clear the weather.*

We sure do, agreed the old logger who fished at night in the marl swamps, *rain and a grasshopper wind.*

The season ended in doldrums that lasted until after Labor Day, and I did not see the grasshopper wind that summer. The winter was spent learning to tie flies. My father bought some Michigan Hoppers tied by the late Art Kade at Sheboygan, and I used them as prototypes. My copies were less than elegant, but the originals were exquisite: scarlet hackle tailfibers cocked down under a tufted yellow-floss body palmered with brown multicolor hackle. Brown turkey-feather wings tip-lacquered with feather glaze held the body hackles flat along the sides. Stiff multicolor hackles completed the flies. The hooks were elegant long-shank English up-eyes. These Kade patterns were so classic in proportions that they still influence the style of my flies.

Several summers later I saw my first grasshopper wind. The incident occurred on the upper meadows of the Arkansas in Colorado during the late-August haying. Rock Creek was low and clear, and the trout had not been rising well for several days. The haying started and the irrigation ditches were closed off to dry the fields before mowing. The irrigation water was diverted back into the stream. It came up several inches and the water was measurably colder. The trout became active again, and the men began working in the fields. Grasshoppers rose up in front of the mowing machines and the hay rakes, and the warm wind moved up the valley and carried them in shaky, precarious flight patterns over the water.

The lower reaches of the creek were once dammed by beavers, and their leavings consist of two long chest-deep flats divided by a shallow gravelly riffle. Both flats are deeply undercut along the banks and their bottoms are soft and pincushion thick with old beaver sticks. Approach from the hay meadow side was easy, and that bank was well worn with the boots of fishermen. Everyone fished from there. But this approach was in plain view of the trout, and I never saw anything from there except small fish.

On the morning of the grasshopper wind, I came down through the willows and brush on the other side, keeping some distance below the stream. The evening before I had been reading my fishing bible of those years, Ray Bergman's now-mellow classic *Trout,* and had covered several passages about fishing difficult pools from their less-traveled sides. I was absorbed with this idea, and the ranch was quiet when I put the book down and turned out the lights in the bunkhouse.

It worked on the beaver-dam flats. The brush was thick where the smaller creek riffled out into the wide Lake Creek shallows, and I was sweating heavily when I finally stumbled

231

out and sat down on the bank. I checked my clothes for cattle ticks and washed my face and wetted my hat while I watched the mowing machine pass in the meadow. Grasshoppers rose up ahead of the sickle bar, and the warm wind carried them over the creek. Several faltered and came down like mallards in the lower flat. Wakes appeared in the smooth water, and the unfortunate grasshoppers were collected swiftly in a series of calm rises that spelled size.

I was utterly spellbound. The trout were large, larger than any I had seen before except for hatchery breeders or mounted fish on tackle-shop walls, and I watched them cruise the flat like hungry alley cats. There were no more grasshoppers on the water, and the big trout vanished. Finally the mowing machine chattered back toward the creek and I hastily got ready. The fragile 4X gut tippet was clipped off, and I searched frantically for a grasshopper in my fly boxes. One battered split-winged hopper crouched forlorn and neglected in a compartment full of Hendricksons. Hooking it out of the box with my index finger, I clinch-knotted it firmly to the tippet. I tested the leader and crawled up the riffle to wait for the mowing machine and the grasshopper wind.

Three grasshoppers settled into the quiet current and started kicking toward shore. There was a heavy boil and the fish were feeding again, and my artificial flicked over the pool to drop near the undercut bank. Two big browns came cruising down the flat and each took a grasshopper as he came. I held my breath. One came toward my floating grasshopper and then detoured swiftly to take a kicking natural. I twitched the slowly drifting artificial, and the trout turned like a shark and came ten feet with his dorsal fin showing.

The fish wallowed clumsily when I struck, and bulldogged deep into the beaver sticks under the bank. I felt the leader pluck and catch as it slipped over the sunken branches, but it did not foul and the trout turned out into the open water of the channel. Then the fish made a mistake. It bolted down over the shallows where I crouched, its spotted back showing as it came, and I followed the trout with much splashing into the open water below.

The rest was surprisingly easy. The fish finally recognized its danger and tried to get back into the pool again, but I splashed and kicked and frightened it back. It was tired now when it circled close, but pumped out again when it saw me waiting with the net in the shallows. It measured an even twenty-six inches, heavy and hook-jawed with maturity, and I ran back up through the meadows to the house with its strong-muscled bulk threshing convulsively in the net.

That was my biggest dry-fly trout for several years, and it held the title until my second encounter with a grasshopper wind. It occurred in the Cooper Meadows of the Gunnison in Colorado. There are high-water side channels of the big river in these meadows, and there are big trout under the brush piles, trapped in the side channels by the receding water of summer.

On this afternoon I hooked and lost two dry-fly fish, both dark heavily spotted brutes, and returned talking to myself. The first was grasshopper feeding under a high bank. I changed to a big wool-bodied hopper and clinch-knotted it hastily. The trout saw the fly land and came upstream and splashed water wildly as it felt the hook. It bored up the pool, rolled deep along the bottom, and turned. It came back strong, and I stripped line clumsily, and it wallowed in the shallows, smashing the leader at my feet.

Five pounds, I whispered.

The second fish was slashing at grasshoppers above a log tangle that bridges the narrow channel. It took my imitation on the first float and spurted upstream in a series of bucking rolls. Then it hung high in the current above the logs and reconsidered. It turned and bored brazenly through the log tangle. The fish was below me now, below the jumbled logs and brush, rolling feebly on the leader in the quiet water downstream. Several seconds passed. It was simply too big to force back through the brush.

I remembered the brush-pile trout Charlie Fox once hooked on Cedar Run in Pennsylvania and passed the rod carefully through the logs to continue the fight below. The trout shifted gears as I tightened and it turned back through the brush. This time it broke off and hung in the current

233

above the jam, shaking his head at the annoying fly and leader before drifting back into the logs trailing five feet of nylon.

There had been only two grasshoppers in my jacket and both were lost in trout, and I went downstream toward the ranch and the fly vise. Just above the junction of the side channel with the main river was a deep log-lined pocket, and Frank Klune crouched beside the water. He was studying the water and not casting. I yelled and he waved me away and continued to watch the water. I circled through the meadow well away from the stream, and I could not see the water, but Frank was casting again. Then he yelled and stood up to handle his flailing rod. The fish was running and I was running, too, and the reel was going. The trout was high and rolling in the deadfalls before Frank finally turned it. Then the fish writhed and turned and flashed silver deep at our feet, boring back upstream. It seemed confused and I watched its big rose-colored gills working.

What did he take? I asked.

Grasshopper, said Klune. *The one you tied yesterday.* He gained some line and had the big rainbow back on the reel.

Took right there in the brush!

Can't see the fly, I said. *He must have taken it deep.*

Then the fish exploded wildly. *He's got it deep all right,* he yelled and we were running again.

The trout porpoised down the side channel toward the big-water Gunnison. The reel was going again and we were still steeple-chasing down the high meadow bank. Thirty yards downstream was a narrow gully. I was running ahead with the net and broad-jumped the gully, but Frank was too busy playing the fish and missed. The fish was still on, and Frank was trying to scramble out of the gully and handle the rod. It was bucking dangerously and suddenly the fish was gone.

Good one! he yelled sadly. *You ever get a look?*

Yes! I said. *Six pounds!*

The artificial grasshoppers I was dressing then were still similar to the Kade patterns I had used for prototypes as a boy.

The yellow-silk floss had been abandoned. Floss turned olive when it was wet, and such bodies were too delicate and slim for bulky grasshopper bodies. Dubbed yellow wool was the best we could do, achieving a fat hopperlike body silhouette that did not change color when wet. Between the turkey wings was an underwing of fox squirrel to achieve more buoyancy and counteract the absorption of the wool.

This version seemed workable for several years, particularly on the less-selective trout of our big western rivers. But the unusually selective brown trout of the small Pennsylvania limestone streams were another matter. Old patterns worked much of the time, but there were also many refusals, particularly from the larger fish. Anglers on limestone water had long experimented with grasshopper patterns: many used the traditional Michigan and Joe's Hopper types, and some even tried the more radical fore-and-aft dressings. Charlie Fox had used fore-and-aft grasshoppers for years on the difficult fish of his Letort Spring Run, and these flies had actually been tied for him by the late Ray Bergman. But the selective Letort trout seem more difficult every year, and they were refusing these old-time imitations with nose-thumbing frequency. New variations were obviously necessary.

Our first attempt was created in the Turnaround Meadow on Charlie Fox's Letort water. Western experiments with deer hair had worked well on the big Jackson Hole cutthroats, and many anglers had reported good luck with the Muddler Minnow fished dry during wild sessions of grasshopper feeding. Using this information as a beginning, we conceived some lightly dressed wingless hoppers with deer hair and yellow nylon wool. They seemed to work better than the earlier patterns, but it was July and the grasshoppers were still small, and not many fish were looking for them.

Subsequent refusals and successes caused us to restore the old-time turkey wings to the new hoppers and alter the deer-hair dressing. The silhouette of the wings and the trailing deer hair proved important. The absence of hackle permitted the bulk of the fly and its yellow-dubbed body to float flush in the surface film. The light pattern created by the dressing in the surface film looked hopperlike and promising.

Looks pretty good, observed Ross Trimmer. *Maybe we should call it the Letort Hopper.*

The trout liked it fine. We used it with good success on the Letort and pulled up trout that were not feeding on many occasions. But there were some refusal rises, too, and that was still disconcerting. We experimented further, and the final improvement came near the end of the season when the grasshoppers were at full growth. Tying bigger imitations resulted in the change: when the deer hair was looped and pulled tight, it flared out like thick stubby hackles tightly bunched, and these butts were scissor-trimmed in the blocky configuration of a grasshopper's head and thorax. The earlier versions had these deer-hair butts trimmed close and covered with the head silk. The bulky version proved better. We tried the following pattern the next morning on the Letort, and it worked wonders on demanding fish:

Tails—none
Body—yellow nylon wool dubbed on yellow silk
Wings—brown-mottled turkey glazed with lacquer
Legs—brown deer-body hair
Head—trimmed deer-body hair butts
Silk—6/0 yellow
Hook—sizes six through sixteen 2x long down-eye

We later found another proving ground on a small privately owned limestone stream in central Pennsylvania. The browns were big and stream-spawned, and they were trout that had been caught and released many times during the season. Charlie Fox and our host walked down through the meadows with me to the stream in the early afternoon. Five hundred yards below the deep sapphire-colored spring, where the stream wells up full-blown from limestone caverns, is a long marl-bottomed flat. The flat is smooth-flowing and clear, and colder than sixty degrees through the worst heat of August. One side is bordered by limestone ledges and sheltered with trees. The shallow side is bordered by a marl shelf and a sizeable hay meadow. Charlie Fox decided to try the water above the flat where he had spotted a big brown that morning. Our host walked with me where the meadow was alive with grasshoppers.

We reached the flat and moved cautiously down the path toward the water. The sun was high and the hot wind moved down across the valley and its hay meadows. We stopped short when we saw the water: big wild browns were schooled and cruising the flat in twos and threes.

We crouched low and studied the riseforms to see what they were taking. The rises were quiet, and we decided the jassid was the probable answer, since it had produced several fine trout that morning. The little jassid was already on my leader when we felt the hot wind and saw the grasshoppers. They rose up as the hot wind crossed the meadow and were parachuted out over the flat. The water was quiet, too wide for them to cross once they were committed to the wind, and they came down hard. Their shallow, faltering trajectories were futile, and the big trout stalked them when they fell. The trout had learned that the grasshoppers were helpless, and their rises were quiet and calm, completely lacking the splashy eagerness characteristic of most grasshopper feeding. We watched the quick demise of several big insects.

It's the wind, I said. *It's a grasshopper wind!*

Five of the new grasshopper imitations were in my fly box, tied the night before at my inn on the Letort. I changed to a grasshopper pattern, but neglected to change the fragile jassid-size tippet to something heavier. It was a mistake. Two big fish came up above us over the marl shelf, and I placed the imitation between them. One turned and took the grasshopper without hesitation and bolted thirty yards into a brush pile. The delicate leader sheared like wet tissue paper.

I replaced the grasshopper after cutting the leader back to a heavier calibration. Under the trees a big muskie-size trout took another natural. The roll cast dropped the fly in the sun, but the trout had disappeared somewhere in the shadows along the bank. The float was good, and it flirted with the bank shadows, and I was already picking up the cast when he slashed at the fly. The big mouth closed and I tried to set the hook, but the fly came back in a loose leader tangle at my feet. The heavy trout rolled in panic and bolted up the length of the flat, brush-pile black and leaving a frightened wake.

My shout of disappointment died. *My fault,* I groaned.

Five pounds, consoled our host.

The other fish were still feeding, and the first cast with the fresh grasshopper produced a fat reddish-bronze two-pounder. The fish was released after a strong fight. The fish were so intent on their grasshopper prey that they ignored the heavier nylon tippet. The new grasshopper patterns worked beautifully, and none of these big selective browns refused the imitation after a brief inspection.

Three casts later I was into another. *Should have brought my rod!* said our host. *I'm going back.*

The fish went eighteen inches and had the reddish tail and adipose coloring of wild limestone-stream browns. It was released and I promptly hooked and lost another.

You have an extra 'hopper? asked my host.

Sure, I laughed. He disappeared to get his rod.

The fishing was fast and Charlie Fox appeared at the head of the flat fifteen minutes later. The best fish of the afternoon was recovering its strength on the marl shelf at my feet, hook-jawed and heavy at twenty-three inches.

Grasshoppers! I yelled.

He was already casting over a good brown. His rod doubled over and there was a heavy splash under the trees at the head of the flat. We took twelve browns between us from fifteen to twenty-three inches, releasing them all.

Our host returned late in the rise and promptly left our last grasshopper in a heavy fish. Light rain misted down the valley and the wind suddenly turned cool. The grasshopper activity was over. There were no rises when the rain finally stopped, and five big suckers were the only fish in sight.

Good score for the new 'hopper, said Fox. *These big wild browns were a really perfect test.*

No refusals mean something, I agreed.

Our host was amazed at the grasshopper feeding. *They haven't come that fast all year,* he said.

We stopped to feed a fat brook trout from the suspension bridge over the big spring. *Had refusals on the fore-and-aft 'hoppers,* said Charlie. *It was a good test.*

How do you tie its legs and head? Our host was examining the new pattern.

Like bass bugs, I said. *Bunched and clipped.*

Charlie and I drove back down to the Letort that night, and we had a final day with the grasshoppers before the end of the season. Ross Trimmer met us in the Turnaround Meadow early that afternoon and went upstream with me above the Barnyard. We were in high spirits and Ross periodically stained the stream with tobacco. We were paying an end-of-season visit to the logjam farther upstream.

We ought to try the Bolter, Ross had suggested at the Buttonwood corner. *It likes 'hoppers.*

The Bolter was a heavy brown trout several of us had hooked and lost when it bolted upstream and broke off. The fish was an estimated twenty-two inches. It was already feeding quietly along a cress-bed cover when we approached under the trees. The rises were methodical and gentle, but several ugly white ducks squatted on the logs just below the trout. The ducks were notorious for swimming ahead and spooking the fish.

Trimmer crouched and moved above the ducks. *I'll drive 'em downstream away from the fish,* he said.

The ducks waddled along the logs and dropped clumsily into the current. The trout happily continued to feed. The ducks drifted downstream, protesting Trimmer's efforts noisily. When they were twenty yards below the fish, I slipped into the stream and edged slowly into casting position. Trimmer sat on the logs and we waited. Five minutes later the trout came up again.

There he is! said Ross. *How's that for ghillying?*

You make a good ghillie, I grinned.

Well, my part's done and I'm waiting. The heavy trout came up noisily again and its rise was impressive. *Catch him!*

Okay, I said.

The cast was difficult and the first two attempts failed, but finally the grasshopper fell right. I could not see its entire line of drift down the face of the watercress, but I heard the soft rise and saw the rings push gently across the current as

I tightened. There was a heavy splash instead of the usual rapier-quick bolt and the trout wallowed under the cress. It probed deep up the channel and I turned it just short of the tree. The fish was under the cress bed again and I forced it out into the open water with my rod bent deep in the current. It was getting tired now and I kept the fish high in the water and free of the elodea. The light was wrong and we still could not see the fish. Then it rolled head down and its broad tail fanned weakly at the surface. I turned the light rod over for the final strain of the infighting, and it turned slowly into the net.

Looks better than twenty, said Ross.

I worked the hook free carefully. *Henfish,* I said. *She's perfectly shaped and colored.*

Well, Ross said, *let her go!*

We crossed the current and walked back along the railroad. That evening we gathered under the buttonwoods and celebrated the end of the season. The old stories were recounted about Hewitt and LaBranche going fishless on the Letort, and the heavy sulfur hatches on Cedar Run in the old days, and the record fifteen-pound brown once taken on a fly from the Upper Mill Pond on Big Spring.

For big trout I'll take the shadflies anytime. Somebody was talking about Penns Creek in early summer.

They only last a week, said Charlie Fox, *but the grasshopper season lasts over a month.*

Right, said Trimmer. *I'll take the 'hoppers.*

I'll take the 'hoppers, too, I agreed happily. *'Hoppers and meadow water and a grasshopper wind.*

The others murmured in agreement. We fell silent, and the little Letort whispered past the bench in the moonlight. The year was over again. Somewhere above the buttonwoods a trout came up in the darkness, and we turned to listen.

[1961]

16

The Anatomy of
a Spring Creek

*American spring creeks are found from Maine to
California, but are perhaps most common in the
central Rocky Mountain region. They are collectively
the crown jewels of our fly fishing—typically small
and clear-flowing with abundant fly hatches and unusually large stocks of trout. Many of the fly-fishing
methods associated with small fly patterns and gossamer leaders evolved on these streams and are
spreading now to other hard-fished rivers as anglers
increasingly discover the need to hone their flat-water
tactics.*

*Silver Creek in Idaho is a strange oasis, bringing
fly fishermen from all over the world to the middle of
a near desert. Its gentle green meanders are a remarkable contrast in color to the uniform tan in the surrounding hills of bone-dry dust and rock. It had also
been sadly abused by overfishing and poor soils management. Happily, much of this has been corrected
after the Nature Conservancy acquired a large tract
on Silver's upper portions. This was made possible
through a nationwide campaign in the 1970s, on*

*which Schwiebert worked with Jack Hemingway and
which this essay was originally written to support.
Schwiebert subsequently chaired the preserve's early
management committee and helped to improve grazing and tillage practices at Silver Creek.*

During the late afternoon, the smooth wind-polished hills
below Sun Valley look soft and straw-colored in the waning
light. The cottonwoods in the river bottoms are touched with
the first hint of bright autumn color, echoing the first cold
nights in August. The valley is steadily more arid below Hailey, with the patchwork fields of a few irrigated ranches on
the high benches above the Big Wood.

Beyond the tree-lined streets of Bellevue, a solitary eagle
circled lazily in the last thermals of the afternoon, watching
the foothills for careless jackrabbits. Cattle and sheep forage
among the sagebrush slopes. The cottonwoods are already
sparse along the Picabo road, and except for irrigation from
the river and several spring creeks in this arid Idaho country,
the valley enclosing Silver Creek is virtually a desert between
its pale sheltering hills.

Although I had fished Silver Creek many years before,
during a boyhood summer spent traveling in the Rockies,
that early experience was both brief and myopic. It takes the
perspective of time to savor and understand a spring creek,
just as it takes time to see that the act of fishing itself is
perhaps the least important part of fishing.

My second baptism on the marshy reaches of Silver occurred with André Puyans and David Inks, two well-known
fishermen from San Francisco. Their camper was filled with
a cornucopia of tackle, wading gear, clothing, rod cases,
sleeping bags, bottles in varied stages of emptiness, and fly-
tying equipment from their richly stocked shop in Walnut
Creek. Inks was driving while Puyans passed me incredible
slices of cheese and cups of Cabernet Sauvignon, spicing the
trip with anecdotes about the fly hatches and free-rising rainbows on Silver Creek.

Silver is pretty special, Puyans concluded.

The valley widens steadily below Hailey, where the
chalk-colored bluffs rise beyond the river and its yellow cot-

tonwoods. There are potatoes and grain fields and hay meadows across the valley, watered with intricately rigged irrigation sprinklers that move like giant water spiders in their changing rainbows of misting spray.

Late summer is perhaps the best time to fish Silver Creek, except for the prolific Indian summer hatches in October. After the summer dies, the stream has a brief season of cold nights and glittering stars, followed by shirtsleeve weather when the current is covered with tiny mayflies. The mornings are cool and still under cloudless skies, and the wind gathers lazily at midday, stirring the stubble fields and scattering its bright confetti of leaves from the cottonwoods.

The smooth sagebrush hills are almost pewter-colored beyond their potato-field bottoms, where the county road reaches out for miles across the valley. Gannett lies ahead in the trees. Except for the scattered ranches and their weathered outbuildings, lying against the pale foothills, the basin is completely arid outside the irrigation ditches that lie straight as surveyors' lines across the fields. When we left the Picabo road, the pasture dust billowed out behind the camper, thick and chokingly bitter with its alkalinity in our nostrils.

Doesn't look like trout country, I said.

Not like most trout country, Puyans agreed, *but it's trout country all right—wait until you see its fly hatches!*

Sounds good! I said happily.

Silver is virtually unique among our western trout streams. Although there are many similar spring creeks in the Rockies, and in the Sierras and Cascades farther west, none of these little rivers equals its character and remarkable volume of flow or its curious isolation in a half-arid basin. Unlike most trout streams, which are born in the snowmelt of alpine meadows or the seepages of their headwater tributaries, spring creeks rise almost full blown from the earth. Such creeks are not always fertile. Some bubble from pale-bottom lagoons so empty of life-giving oxygen that they are virtually sterile except for their headwater growths of stoneworts and fountain moss and elodea. Others abound with free acids or metallic constituents that make their icy springheads actually hostile to life. But still others are rich with oxygen and alkalinity, tumbling from the earth to shelter an aquatic world absolutely teeming with fish and fly hatches.

Several factors are typically found in the birth of a spring creek. Some are simply the subterranean flowages of adjacent rivers, leaching though their primordial beds of gravel to emerge again downstream in the side channel incised during some Pleistocene spate. The famous spring creeks above Livingston, in the fertile valley of the Yellowstone, are typical of that type. Similar spring creeks are found in the sprawling alluvial bottoms of the Snake at Jackson Hole.

Some spring creeks are born in immense outcroppings of fractured lava, which collect both rainfall and snowmelt in their spongelike aquifers and eventually surrender their secret flowages miles away. Typical rivers of this type are found in the volcanic regions of Oregon and California. Spring-fed tributaries of the Deschutes, like the Crooked and Warm Springs and Metolius, are archetypes of volcanic spring creeks. Others are found draining the volcanic barrens of Lassen National Park, or the immense lava plateau that surrounds Crater Lake in Oregon. Several excellent streams are triggered in the sudden rebirth of the Crater Lake aquifers, particularly the spring creeks at Fort Klamath and in the headwaters of the Williamson. The extensive lava aquifers formed over thousands of years above Mount Lassen have also spawned a network of unique fisheries in the fertile Hat Creek and Rising River drainages—and in the surprisingly large flowages and fertility of Fall River in northern California.

Our counterparts of the famous chalkstreams of Europe are found in limestone country. The chalkstreams are spring creeks that tumble out from the unique cretaceous aquifers that border the English Channel. These chalk outcroppings produce not only the famous White Cliffs of Dover, but also chalkstreams like the Risle and Andelle in Normandy, and classic British dry-fly rivers like the Itchen and its pastoral sister, the Test.

The rivers in the United States that have their origins in immense limestone springs are not confined to trout fisheries. Ozark smallmouth streams like the Buffalo and Mammoth Springs and Current are well-known exceptions. Other limestone streams are perhaps more famous because they have played a role in the history of American trout fishing. Such waters include the famous Castalia Club in northern Ohio, and the Spring Creek at Caledonia in upstate New York, where the half-legendary Seth Green worked out the rudimentary philosophy of fish culture that led to trout and salmon hatcheries around the world. Huge limestone springs give birth to several western rivers too, particularly the famous Spring Creek at Lewiston in the Montana foothill country, and perhaps the largest spring creek in the world—the incomparable Henry's Fork of the Snake in Idaho.

Still other spring creeks are spawned in strange hydrothermal basins such as the geyser country of the Yellowstone. Hot springs bubbling from deep in the molten fissures of the earth are in some cases toxic and in others richly fertile. Hot Creek in the eastern Sierra of California is typical of a hydrothermal spring creek. But perhaps the best known of such streams are the serpentine Gibbon and its sister river, the remarkable little Firehole in the Yellowstone. Both are born in the snowmelt of the high country, and both have icy little tributaries, but their ecology is radically modified in a series of unique geyser basins that mingle their rich hot-spring alkalinity with the rivers themselves.

Silver is less dramatic than the Firehole, with its smoking hot springs and spectacular geysers, but its character is equally intriguing. It is remarkable in less obvious terms, in the sense that its ecology parallels the storied chalkstreams in Hampshire and Wiltshire where fly fishing had its genesis five centuries ago, and its springheads rise without warning from a table-flat valley floor. The principal springs that give birth to Silver are found on headwater tributaries like Stocker, Grove, and Loving. These three cress-bordered creeks are surprisingly large and swift, with exceptional volumes of flow at their sources. Each almost explodes from the arid earth, spilling thousands of gallons per minute from their Stygian labyrinths underground.

Hydrologists believe that these giant springs are fed with water from the Big Wood, which drains the entire Sun Valley country from Galena Summit in the Sawtooths farther north. The valley floor is a remarkable aquifer that combines immense alluvial deposits of coarse stones and boulders and fine aggregates with a bedrock structure of permeable limestone and fissured lava. Pleistocene lava fields spread across the valley, completely burying the original channel of the Big Wood and forcing its surface drainages toward the Camas Valley. Its earlier flowages continue in the opposite direction under the volcanic strata that filled its valley, welling up again in a series of fertile spring creeks. These tributary springheads and their remarkably stable volumes of flow are a unique treasure. It is the chemistry of its soils and subsurface geology of the entire basin that structure Silver Creek and its unique ecosystem.

Soils in its headwaters are often so alkaline that, in largely agricultural terms, they lie at the threshold of toxicity. Well-meaning anglers have continually tried to introduce trees along its grassy banks, and expand its sparse stands of aspen along Grove Creek and the Sullivan Slough. These men were always mystified when the soil chemistry killed their trees, while the ambient strains of willows and cottonwoods and aspens thrive. Freshly tilled acreages are typically permitted to lie fallow for one or two seasons, simply working the soil without planting, while precipitation and sunlight and exposure to the atmosphere leach out their excessive chemical properties.

The subsurface geology is equally fertile. The hydrology of the valley is filtered through sedimentary limestones and phosphates, mixed with porous beds of lava and immense deposits of river-polished aggregates. Concealed sources of alkalinity are also possible, like hydrothermal caverns and subterranean deposits of marl, hidden deep in the secrets of the earth. Hot springs also exist in the drainage of the Big Wood. Each of these factors ultimately combines to affect the water chemistry of Silver Creek, leaching both water and fertility from twenty-odd miles of varied subterranean geology. The character that rises from such latent life-giving chemistry and stable volumes of year-round flow is unique. Its echoes are obvious in the rich communities of elodea, watercress, chara, ranunculus, tules, bulrushes, stoneworts, and water lilies that distinguish Silver Creek from the typical western trout stream. Such alpine fisheries, tumbling steeply

246

from their barren high-country origins, are usually less fertile in their headwaters. The fertility of Silver Creek is completely unlike its sister rivers throughout our western mountains, and that fertility is also obvious in its remarkably heavy populations of fish life, both healthy free-rising rainbows and the abundance of coarse species too.

Since the springheads are relatively constant in both temperature and volume, the stream is also a sanctuary for wading birds and waterfowl during both late-summer drought and winter freezes. Its fish enjoy relatively stable rates of growth, because its temperatures remain fairly close to their optimal metabolic requirements and are sheltered from the 60 percent factors of winter kill that typically decimate an average mountain fishery.

Both birds and trout are sustained by the exceptionally abundant food chain in the watershed of Silver Creek. The fish-eating birds and rainbows alike thrive on a surprising population of frogs and baitfish, and virtually all of its aquatic species sustain themselves on its incredible numbers of terrestrials and tiny stream insects and crustaceans. Flycatchers and swifts and other birds gather along the stream, competing with predatory swarms of dragonflies and damselflies for the clouds of mayflies and sedges that hatch daily. These exceptionally heavy aquatic hatches are sustained and sheltered in the fertile growth of weeds that undulates in the current. Yet their fertility is only another symptom of its rich water chemistry, and the nutrients in the sediments that support their roots.

Some fishermen find the stream sluggish and strange, and its selective trout are a puzzle for a fisherman accustomed to the easier fish of our alpine streams. Anglers who complain about Silver and its difficult rainbows remind me of a lecture at Princeton, in which a sophomore blurted the opinion that he had disliked *War and Peace.*

The professor struggled to conceal his amusement. *That's an interesting opinion,* he remarked as he carefully filled his pipe, *but I think it tells us rather more about you than it tells us about Tolstoy.*

Silver is particularly alive in the spring. There are redwinged blackbirds calling in the marshes, geese clamoring

247

for nesting sites, cattle and sheep in the pastures, bees gathering pollen in the wildflower meadows—all mixed with the subtle music of its big rainbows working to its midday fly hatches.

Since it remains open and relatively ice-free in winter, at least above the irrigation gates in its middle reaches, Silver Creek is a haven for extensive populations of ducks and geese and wading birds.

The Idaho summers provide optimal nesting conditions for ducks and geese, which love its marshy banks and sloughs. Plovers and sandhill cranes and curlews are common, mixed with solitary birds of prey. There are red-tailed hawks working the foothill thermals, and surprising numbers of golden eagles. Ospreys and kingfishers abound too, foraging with marsh hawks and kestrels and prairie falcons. Burrowing owls and goshawks are numerous. Sandpipers and yellowlegs and killdeers are migratory visitors, mixed with substantial numbers of snipe, and Wilson's phalarope seeks the headwater marshes before its autumn odyssey carries it toward the Argentine pampas.

But perhaps the most remarkable example of its thriving birdlife lies in a stand of aspens which shelters a thirty-nest heron rookery beside the Sullivan Slough. Although the herons eat some trout, their graceful flight is so beautiful against a twilight sky that even the hardcase trout fishermen must accept the fish they kill. Coarse fish and frogs are much easier to capture, and most biologists would probably agree that any trout they harvest are foolish specimens that deserved the fate of Darwinian selection.

Silver has received extensive plantings of hatchery rainbows over the past century. Our hatchery stocks are hybrid mixtures of our original landlocked and steelhead strains, which exhibit the disconcerting habit of migrating downstream like their anadromous ancestors. However, these hatchery trout are somewhat isolated in the cold headwaters of Silver Creek by the desert heat that lies downstream. The unfavorable water temperatures in the lower reaches of its watershed tend to inhibit the downstream migration typical of hatchery rainbows.

Yet the resident population of rainbows, particularly on the private ranches that are not stocked with hatchery fish, still bears strong traces of its origins in the McCloud River of northern California. The nonmigratory strain of rainbows originally found in the McCloud was perhaps our most valuable American subspecies, although it was quickly lost through hybrid mixing with migratory steelhead strains in our first hatcheries. However, the first planting of rainbows in Silver Creek occurred late in the nineteenth century, before the complete hybridization of our hatchery stocks, and the echoes of these relatively pure strains of the beautiful McCloud fish still persist in Silver Creek.

During the past year I have been working with Jack Hemingway and the Nature Conservancy to raise sufficient money to purchase the Sun Valley Ranch, keeping its prime fishing mileage open to the public. Hemingway is the son of the late Ernest Hemingway, still lives in Sun Valley, and serves on the Idaho Fish and Game Commission. When the Sun Valley Ranch was first offered for sale, threatening public access to its remarkable fly-only water, Hemingway worked out a strategy with its present owners and the Conservancy both to protect its fishery and keep it public. The Nature Conservancy performed a remarkable job in seeking out corporate grants and a series of challenge donations from both private donors and foundations, raising more than $500,000 to acquire the property and establish an endowment for its management in the future. Extensive amounts were also raised in a public campaign for the preservation of the fly water on Silver Creek, and although a few thousand dollars remain to be raised this year, the campaign has largely succeeded. The Nature Conservancy now holds the property, and the remarkable fly-only mileage in the headwaters of Silver Creek will remain in public hands in perpetuity.

The Conservancy has already appointed a resident biologist, and a distinguished management committee has already held a number of planning sessions. Several graduate students at neighboring universities have started research programs in various aspects of Silver and its ecology. The

committee includes experts in herpetology, fisheries management, ecology, ichthyology, siltation, entomology, experi-
mental agriculture, hydrology, botany and avifauna. Some
preliminary studies on the soils chemistry, plant cover, fly
hatches, reptiles, and the heron population have already been
completed.

The management committee intends to explore in depth
the ecology of Silver Creek and its equilibrium with the agricultural and pastoral land-use in its watershed. Silver Creek
will help us learn more about the intricate fabric of life found
in our western spring creeks, and the fragile relationship
between its ranches and its ecology. There are proposals for
reducing livestock densities, fencing cattle away from stream
margins, modifying existing techniques of agriculture and
tillage, and even rebuilding the marshes in its headwaters.
Perhaps we can discover a world of fresh knowledge that
may help both ranchers and fishermen protect spring creeks
throughout our western mountains in the future, with an
optimal mixture of agricultural techniques and enlightened
fisheries management.

Still, it has been the character of Silver and its fishing
that has brought me to Sun Valley over the years, and its
selective rainbows are always a challenging puzzle. Our afternoon on the Purdey water was typical of Silver Creek in late
summer, and we fished a sparse hatch of sedges and pros-
pected for grasshopper fish until evening.

We should get a pretty good evening rise, André Puyans
said. *We've got lots of mayflies and sedges coming.*

Pretty heavy feeding then? I asked excitedly.

Heavy enough, David Inks nodded.

Our afternoon was leisurely, fishing a partridge-hackled
wet above the ranch and its outbuildings, and Puyans took
several fish with a grasshopper pattern below the irrigation
gate. But we spent most of our time sitting in the warm grass
with fresh bread and cheese and a fine bottle of claret.

But later we crossed the stream, anticipating a rise of fish
in the still flat above the irrigation hatch. The smaller fish
were already working, and we took several on tiny *Baetis* and
Pseudocloëon imitations in the mirrorlike surface. Finally
there was a heavy spinner fall, and several good rainbows

started sipping busily in the film. Puyans produced a few pale-bodied spinners dressed on #26 hooks that worked well, and we took trout steadily in the gathering twilight.

Look at the trout! Dave Inks sighed.

The still flat reflected the evening sky, and fish were dimpling in the weedy channels as far as we could see. Beyond a dense growth of elodea, a really large trout porpoised in a narrow channel, sending bow waves down along the weeds.

That was some fish! I gasped.

The big fish know how to survive, Inks laughed. *They're not dumb enough to come up over here!*

I'm going to try him anyway, I muttered.

It was too deep to wade close, and it meant making a long cast with the line lying across the weeds. Since the leader and line could not drift with the current, my dry-fly float would be painfully brief. The channel flowed still and smooth beyond the weeds, and for a moment I wavered. The big fish came up again, its dorsal and powerful back silhouetted in the dying light, and I started the cast.

The line worked swiftly, delivering the tiny fly beyond the weeds, and settling it above the fish. It floated spent in the film, impossible to see in the darkness, but I tightened when the fish rose.

There was an explosion. Spray showered across the weeds, and an immense rainbow jumped several times in a drum-fire rhythm, stitching my leader through the elodea. Finally it was hopelessly woven into the weeds and the fish was gone, still jumping to free itself from the annoying bite of the tiny hook. The leader was so tightly knitted though the weeds that I hand-lined it back, uprooting huge growths of fountain moss and elodea, and started to untangle it with shaking fingers.

That was some fish, Inks shouted.

Bigger than I thought, I yelled back in the gathering darkness. *I should have known better—that'll teach me!*

Probably not! Puyans said wryly.

[1977]

251

17

Secrets of
Unfamiliar Streams

The premise was simple enough: Let's get Schwiebert
to do a nuts-and-bolts story about what he does when
faced with an unfamiliar river. I smiled a little at the
nuts-and-bolts part and stood as a mostly innocent
bystander almost fifteen years ago while another
magazine editor badgered the author for what
amounted to a formula fishing story.

To Schwiebert's undying credit, I don't believe
he's ever written a lockstep instructional piece with
the inherent appeal of old Saltines. This essay ap-
peared as a result of that badgering, and is a chroni-
cle of trout and salmon adventures worldwide. The
lessons are here, though, woven through the anec-
dotes and easily extracted by any attentive reader.

It was a rainy morning in April, nearly forty-five years ago,
when we opened the trout season on the Pegnitz north of
Nürnberg. Mist hung in the forests along the half-finished
Autobahn. Several roe deer crossed the highway where we
turned off toward Hersbruck and Bayreuth. The rain stopped
mercifully when we parked the mud-spattered Opel *Kapitän*

in a hops field below Pegnitz, rigged our tackle, and walked upstream to the footbridge trestle.

It was my first exposure to a European river, and the Pegnitz is utterly unlike the waters I had fished in boyhood. My early summers on the Beaverkill, the gravelly shallows of the Au Sable and the Pere Marquette, and the tumbling little rivers in the Colorado high country had not prepared me for the Pegnitz and its sister rivers in Franconia.

The trout are not found everywhere, the old riverkeeper explained. *Most of the rising fish are grayling.*

Where are the trout? my father asked.

Trout like the flowing places, the old man replied. *There are many* Bachforellen *in the bend above the bridge, lying along the weeds—and there are many in the flowing currents below the weed racks.*

It sounded baffling and I studied the river. *What about the narrow channels between the weeds?* I asked.

There are trout there, the old man assured me, raising his walking stick. *Petri heil!*

Petri dank! my father replied properly.

The Pegnitz was completely alien, its currents filled with undulating weeds as it flowed deep under the footbridge trestle. The river was mysterious and slightly murky, its olive channels working lazily among the ranunculus and stonewort. The Franconian plateau is a surprisingly large limestone formation, and the Pegnitz itself is a fertile limestone stream. It would be another six to eight years before I would fish the classic limestone spring creeks in Pennsylvania, streams like the Letort and Falling Spring Run and Big Spring, and my first exposure to such fertile water was a Chinese puzzle.

The weak sunlight warmed our spirits, but the cool April wind eddied down the valley and chilled our fingers. It was late morning before I found a few rising fish. They were working in a quiet bend in the sunlight, and I tried a half-dozen patterns before the old riverkeeper came downstream to check each angler.

Grayling, he called and pointed.

When I continued to work on the rising fish, the old man

crossed the footbridge, thinking I had not heard him. *I understand that those rising fish are grayling,* I said, *but I still want to catch one.*

The riverkeeper smiled and fumbled inside his loden cloak for a fly box. *Try this,* he suggested.

The old man explained that he often found late-morning hatches of *Paraleptophlebia* flies on the Pegnitz, particularly on rainy spring mornings above Hersbruck. Glancing upstream to make sure the grayling were still rising, I knotted his delicate little Iron Blue Dun to my tippet. It looped out and settled above the biggest fish and it cocked perfectly on the smooth current. It disappeared in the plucking surface rise typical of grayling, and I tightened.

Grayling, the keeper grumbled stubbornly.

It had been an impressive example of fishing knowledge, and I waved in grudging admiration as the old man crossed the bridge and disappeared into the hops field. There were a lot of flies hatching now, and I walked slowly upstream, studying the quiet water for rises.

With the right fly pattern, and a growing respect for the keeper's skills, I started to read the unfamiliar river for its trout lies. The bend produced a fine sixteen-inch brown in a sheltering current that had scoured under the weeds. The fish burrowed upstream along the ranunculus, frightening two others that had been working there. Several other fish were rising together in a quiet run, and I remembered the advice of the riverkeeper about the tendency of grayling to feed together gregariously. I tested his wisdom with a short cast and briefly hooked a fish just long enough to identify it.

Farther upstream I ignored another school of grayling, and walked stealthily along the path until I located a good fish porpoising in a swift channel in the weeds where the current had scoured the bottom gravel. *Trout!* I thought. *That fish has to be a trout!*

The second cast produced a fat eighteen-inch brown, and I netted it gratefully after a brief struggle. There were several more trout in the tumbling currents below the weed racks, and we happily stopped for a lunch of potato soup, sauerkraut, fresh sausages, and a dark beer that was served in a huge bottle with a spring-loaded porcelain stopper. It had been a morning filled with lessons. It had reinforced a growing conviction that matching the hatch was increasingly important, and it was a remarkable example of learning to read the character of a river that was utterly foreign to my experience. Since that April morning in Germany, I have applied those same lessons on similar rivers and spring creeks everywhere, and have come to believe that problem solving on trout water closely parallels medical diagnosis. Successful fishermen combine acute powers of observation with a mixture of knowledge and past experience to reach a series of possible solutions. Testing those options on a rising trout will quickly sort out those tentative solutions that will not work, and hopefully can isolate the correct solution to such riddles.

The problem of confronting an unfamiliar river with unique problems in its character and fly hatches is typical. Without a guide or riverkeeper to help, solving its mysteries will demand a synthesis of our knowledge and past experience on other rivers with the disciplines of observation and fishing hard. My thoughts are filled with examples on both trout and salmon fisheries, particularly with the fine-spotted cutthroats of Jackson Hole.

Bob Carmichael was the lovable, cantankerous character who operated a little tackle shop at Moose Crossing in those days. It was a simple place not far from the log-framed Chapel of the Transfiguration, but it was the principal meeting place for good fishing talk in western Wyoming. Carmichael was the central figure in a whole cast of colorful fishing characters that populated the Jackson Hole country thirty-five years ago. His reputation was fierce, stemming in part from irascible good-natured dialogues so formidable that I never really dared to engage him in conversation until after my college years.

My first conversation was obviously a mistake. Carmichael was sitting like some puckish bulldog beside a mahogany chest of beautifully tied flies. When I finally expressed my disappointment over the lack of brown trout in the Teton country and ventured a vaguely lukewarm opinion about cutthroat fishing, the old man glowered fiercely and cleared his throat.

Young man! he grumbled with swiftly failing patience, *when you know enough about our Teton country to have an opinion about its fishing, you'll know there's cutthroats and there's cutthroats!*

Carmichael was unmistakably right. His strategy for my education started on the Gros Ventre, describing two pools along the county road to Kelly, and carefully diagramming their chalky ledges and emerald-colored throats on the back of an envelope. Carmichael warned me that I would see many rises in the smooth middle currents of both pools, and in their spreading tail shallows.

Whitefish, Carmichael snorted contemptuously. *You'll find our cutthroats lying right in the strongest currents, tight along the flow in the throats of the pools.*

That's strange, I said. *That's not like cutthroats.*

These fish ain't pantywaist cutthroats! Carmichael exploded into a gravelly laugh. *They're Jackson Hole cutthroats!*

They sure sound tough, I admitted.

His description of the pool along the county road was accurate, even to the huge sandwich-bite break in its ledges. Late-afternoon sun penetrated deep into the pool, highlighting its jade green throats, and there was a hatch of flies starting when I reached the tail shallows. The smooth reach of the pool was quickly covered with rises, just as Carmichael had predicted, and I foolishly made the mistake of wasting time there.

The fish worked steadily throughout the lower current tongues, and when I finally hooked one, it was a whitefish. *Forget your matching the hatch,* Carmichael ragged unmercifully. *Fish these big variants right in the heavy rips—and you'll learn something about cutthroats.*

The tumbling chute upstream shelved off deep against the chalky bluffs and ledges across the river. Swallows were working among the hatching flies, and in the gathering twilight I thought I saw the splash of a feeding trout in the heaviest currents. It was impossible to get a decent dry-fly float over the trough where the fish seemed to be feeding. The primary current tongue caught each cast and dragged the fly clumsily downstream. The only possible presentation was a cast from directly below the trout's position, with the line and leader and fly all lying in the same current, and I crossed the tail shallows to fish the ledge from directly downstream. The current was deceptively strong, and I crossed it warily, leaning hard into its flow.

There he is again! I thought happily. *Rising with a quick splash when the current roils up smooth!*

The river tumbled around my knees, and I shot a short cast into the twilight upstream. The Donnelly Variant had scarcely settled before it disappeared.

He's hooked! I thought.

The big cutthroat was surprisingly strong, boring straight into the heavy throat of the pool. It gave a stubborn fight, hard and muscular in the swift water, until finally the trout surrendered and circled wearily. It slipped into the net, threshing heavily in the meshes.

Twenty inches, I whispered to myself. *Biggest cutthroat you've ever caught!*

Six casts later with a fresh variant, I hooked another big cutthroat, but its fight had a different character. I was crouched on the ledge itself now, since the pool was too deep for wading. The fish bulldogged past me so angrily that the line sliced audibly through the water, and it actually wrenched the rod tip into the current. It was a fish I never saw. The fight lasted five minutes, stripping ninety feet of line from the reel in seconds. The trout hung momentarily in the tail shallows, and accelerated past me again, hugging the bottom into the heaviest chute in the throat of the pool. The bellying line ripped harshly upstream until its dragging weight sheared the tippet, and the cutthroat settled back in the current with my fly.

Broke me like nothing, I explained later.

Thought you said our cutthroats were pantywaists, Carmichael taunted. *Weak sisters!*

You were right, I admitted ruefully.

What size tippet were you using? Carmichael asked.

Three-pound test, I shook my head.

Cobweb! The old shopkeeper laughed. *You got to*

come with more muscle to fish our Jackson Hole cutthroats!
   You're right, I said.

The lessons of those Jackson Hole rivers, and major tributaries of the Snake like the Hoback and Salt Fork, were quickly learned that summer. The trout were always along the swift current tongues and gathering tail shallows, while the whitefish dominated the holding places that most trout fishermen would cover. Our careless stocking of the Snake itself with less vigorous Yellowstone cutthroats has changed things today, and the hybrids in the river now are less challenging. Such trout often lie together with whitefish. Years later I finally understood the parallels between reading the differences in prime trout and whitefish water, and the currents preferred by trout and grayling in Europe.

   Sometimes a strange river is difficult to read, particularly if an angler knows little of its fly hatches. Perhaps the best example that comes to mind occurred on a small brown-trout river in Ontario. It was late summer, and I was fishing with Peter Hurst and Don Moore of Toronto. Their favorite river is the placid Saugeen, a smooth-flowing stream that drains a plateau of scrub-country farms and cedar thickets teeming with grouse.

   The Saugeen is a series of still flats in late summer, so crystalline that every pebble and stone is clearly visible. Its flats are connected with swift rubble-bottom chutes, and there are tangled logjams in its bends. The morning sun was already high, and every feature of the bottom was starkly highlighted.

   No trout were visibly working. Three grouse flushed noisily from a jackstraw pile of fallen trees, exploded into a twisting flight that threaded into the cedars, and were gone as quickly as they had appeared. The river was a beautiful puzzle, and I stood on the logs and studied its still currents for clues. Among the fallen limbs, there was a huge spiderweb still glittering with breakfast dew.

   Suddenly I discovered a half-dozen *Isonychia* spinners trapped in the cobwebs among the logs. The swift chutes between the flats were a perfect habitat for their current-loving nymphs, and since some *Isonychia* species have a two-year life cycle, good populations in varying sizes are available throughout the year.

Give it a try! I thought.

There were several nymph imitations in my fly book, and I selected one tied with purplish dubbing and a pale feather quill laid along its back to suggest the pale dorsal stripe typical of the naturals. It was a solution compounded of luck and some knowledge, and on the second fly swing in a heavy chute I hooked a fine sixteen-inch fish. Covering each swift run carefully, I took a dozen good fish during the afternoon and released them gently. The *Isonychia* imitation worked until late afternoon when a hatch of the big slate-colored duns broke out in the fast-water stretches and the trout started surface feeding. It had been a fine day's sport.

You get those fish on nymphs? Peter Hurst asked.

That's right, I said. *Without a hatch coming down, I decided to cover the chutes with an* Isonychia *nymph.*

How did you hit on that? Don Moore interrupted.

Our biologists tell us that the Isonychia *flies are easily our most numerous aquatic insects,* Hurst added.

Lucky guess, I said. *It looked like* Isonychia *water.*

Not entirely luck, Moore smiled.

Another example of prospecting an unfamiliar river without help of a knowledgeable guide occurred on the sprawling Rio Grande in Tierra del Fuego. We were fishing from Estancia Maria Behety, a vast sheep ranch owned by Fernando Menendez-Behety. The river winds in braided channels across a hundred-mile plateau pampa, with the Darwin Range and the Straits of Magellan in the distance. There had been several days of high winds and rain, typical weather less than a hundred miles above Cape Horn, and the river had cut the sandbar barriers at its mouth, spreading its pampas scents through the coastal seas. Its sea-run brown trout had ascended the river on the last high tide in February, their coin-bright sides reflecting the sun as they rolled in its murky currents.

We fished the pools hard. *It's strange,* I thought finally. *We can see fish, but we can't catch them.*

We had been fishing trout for several weeks, searching

them out in feeding lies that offered shelter. Yet fishing these places proved unproductive. Finally it occurred to me that these were sea-run fish not interested in foraging, and like migrating salmon, they were instinctively searching out spawning lies and currents. Remembering the seatrout on the Laerdal in Norway, which like the edges of primary currents and gathering tail shallows, I changed my tactics completely.

Below the spreading Dos Palos water, named for two wind-seared cypresses in its treeless bottoms, I found a current that shelved off against a deeply scoured bank. It reminded me of a fine seatrout lie on the Laerdal, and I started to work the upstream eddy with a big Mylar-bodied bucktail. Five casts later, there was a savage splash and I was into a twelve-pound brown that jumped several times and ran me deep into the backing. The puzzle was solved, and I beached a half-dozen between six and twelve pounds that day.

Such experiences have convinced me that success in fishing an unfamiliar river is based on powers of observation and skill in reading its currents for the taking and feeding lies. *Fishing ain't just luck,* Bob Carmichael had argued persuasively in his shop at Jackson Hole. *It's mostly knowledge and experience—but a little luck don't hurt!*

Atlantic salmon are good teachers too, and their classrooms are among the most beautiful rivers on earth. Their names alone have the quality of magic, flowing swiftly toward the sea through rolling hills and coastal mountains covered with fir and hemlock and pine. The Miramichi is known for its half-mile flats and shelving riffles, like the dark-flowing Matapedia farther north. Famous salmon camps lie on timber-covered moraines above the canoe-drop pools on the Restigouche and the Grand Cascapedia, which surrendered the Canadian salmon record of fifty-three pounds. The Upsalquitch has its ghosts, haunted by dry-fly pioneers such as Colonel Ambrose Monell, Edward Ringwood Hewitt, and the elegant George Michel Lucien LaBranche. Farther north is the swift little Matane, and beyond the pewter-colored Gulf of Saint Lawrence lie the gargantuan pools of the Moisie, perhaps the finest salmon river left in Canada.

These are classic rivers filled with classic pools and holding-lies, and even a moderately skilled salmon fisherman can often read their secrets, quickly finding those quickening currents and sheltering boulders that always hold fish. But there are rivers in the salmon angler's world whose secrets are less obvious and whose pools and tumbling runs are shrouded in a series of sphinxlike enigmas.

After the sprawling pools and shingles of the Matapedia and Miramichi, fishing the wildly flowing George in northern Labrador proved difficult. There were no spreading shallows that demanded coverage with hundreds of concentric fly swings and no obvious tail shallows where a migrating salmon might stop to rest.

The George is a vast flowage of boulders and shattered ledges, sometimes measuring as much as a half mile in width, and sometimes trapped in a roaring labyrinth of chutes and rapids like Helen Falls.

Its size and broken currents were confusing. We camped on the jackpine bench where the rapids spilled into a lakesize lagoon and moored the floatplane on the beach, rooting its shovel-type anchor into the gravel. It was a summer when the first salmon camp on the George was just starting, and the upper camps beyond Helen Falls were still years in the future. There were no guides to tell us where the salmon were holding or point out their taking currents, and it was simply a matter of prospecting a wild subarctic river ourselves.

We walked the boulder fields and ledges along the river, studying the currents for the gathering shallows above an outcropping of bedrock, the bulge of a current tongue against a ledge, or the silky flow welling up along a tumbling chute that can spell salmon.

The most likely place seemed a fifty-yard reach of smooth current between the plunging edge of the rapids and a shelf of granite that rose a few inches above the river. I studied it for several minutes, wondering if the fish were concentrated toward the bottom, when a good salmon jumped restlessly at the top. Although a jumping salmon is seldom in a taking mood, it can reveal a holding current where others might be lying. I decided to start just above the jumping fish, and since the smooth run was only chest-deep,

261

I rigged a floating line and knotted a small Minktail to the eight-pound tippet.

Fish through with the greased line, I thought.

Greased-line fishing takes its name from the heavily dressed silk lines used by Arthur H. E. Wood, who developed his method of shallow-water salmon fishing on the Scottish Dee at Banchory. It is both simple and sophisticated. Its basic technique involved a floating line and small sparsely dressed flies on the waist-deep flats of his Cairnton beats. The cast is delivered directly across stream in slow currents and quartering downstream in a faster flow. During the swing, while the fly is working back across the current, the line is mended to modify and sustain its speed. Upstream mends are used to dampen the fly swing, slowing the fly with a teasing arc in a swift run. Downstream mends are effective in slightly accelerating fly speed, multiplying its desirability in a sluggish current tongue. The small flies used in the greased-line method swim just under the surface, and the bulge of a taking salmon is often readily visible.

My fly worked out and dropped tight against the tumbling currents in midstream, and I mended upstream to sustain its fly speed, and in a few swift places it took a continuous series of mends, rolling the fly line upstream steadily as the fly came teasingly around. Mending line requires concentration, and after a dozen casts I was taken by surprise when a good salmon porpoised and intercepted the fly. Threshing wildly upstream, the fish cartwheeled tight against the ledge and showered me with water.

He thinks salmon fishing is a contact sport! Bob Bryan shouted. *That was a check against the boards!*

Bryan played hockey at Yale, and he hopscotched skillfully among the boulders to help with the fight. The salmon jumped a half-dozen times and made two long runs that threatened to carry into the wild rapids at midstream. Finally I worked it back into quiet water, coaxed it close along the ledge, and seated my thumb and forefinger around the wrist of its tail. The salmon struggled briefly until its weight hung head-down, and I carried it ashore to deliver the *coup de grace.* Its sea-muscled length weighed sixteen pounds.

Prospecting slowly downstream, we found fish in a number of places, both obvious and obscure. The run where I hooked the first salmon proved so productive that week that we christened it the Aquarium. We found other fish in the sliding currents that eddied smoothly against a shelving ledge, and a room-size eddy among three giant boulders held fish where a primary current escaped between the rocks. There was a channel in a bedrock ledge that usually sheltered a dozen fish, and I discovered it totally by accident, flushing its salmon like quail in the shallows. We gave the salmon an hour to forget and discovered that the narrow channel was perfectly suited to the riffling hitch, which swims a wet fly teasingly in the surface film.

Farther downstream, the river spills wildly down a ten-foot outcropping in a series of churning chutes. The giant pool under these chutes looked exciting, but it was filled with wild crosscurrents and proved unproductive in our first days. Later I was fishing it with little luck when I saw a big salmon porpoise lazily in the eddy below the principal chute. It was holding in the strong reverse currents that flowed back toward the falls. The fish rolled again, and I saw that those upstream currents were so swift that it was lying in their flow, facing back downstream. The George is such a turbulent, sprawling river that these reverse currents often are strong enough to provide consistent taking lies. The big fish that had revealed the secret of this turbulent pool was surprisingly cooperative, and it took my delicate Blue Charm on the first swing. We tailed it among the boulders a hundred yards below, a sea-bright henfish of eighteen pounds.

Although we explored the last quarter-mile of rapids carefully, casting across the current and fishing out each fly swing, it failed to surrender a fish that week. We fished it several times, casting and taking a step and casting again. Our prospecting covered this reach of water with a precise series of concentric quarter circles, making sure each fish saw our flies work through several times.

It sure looks like salmon water, I thought unhappily, *but it seems barren—at least at this level of flow.*

But the last outcropping, which divided the flow just

before the rapids reached the lake-size lagoon downstream, was a happy surprise. Salmon did lie along this granite ledge, which bulged above the current like a beached whale, and I took several there with a riffling hitch.

The swelling currents upstream were a complete surprise, since they looked too slack to hold fish and we ignored them. But one morning I saw a fish roll there twice. The outcropping itself had proved unproductive, so I decided to try fishing the slack water. Casting directly across stream failed to work, since the fly swing was much too slow, so I broke the rules of basic salmon fishing with a quartering cast upstream. When the bellying line started to work the fly back, a ten-pound salmon stopped its swing and exploded wildly into the sun.

Sometimes the fish tell you where they are and sometimes you guess! Bob Bryan laughed. *But sometimes you just have to fish everything!*

The Laxá in Pingeyjarsýsla, which drains the Mývatn plateau in the north of Iceland, is even more difficult to diagnose. Its source is the shallow Mývatn Lake and its famous geothermal basin, bubbling with geysers and hot springs. The bottom of the lake consists of a twelve-foot layer of phosphates and marl. The result is a river so fertile that it is like an English chalkstream displaced to the Arctic Circle.

Its taking lies are often found in immense slow-flowing flats with no clues transmitted into the surface currents to betray their presence. Graustraumar is more obvious, its currents funneling through an hourglass waist of lava ledges and its salmon lying tight along an underwater ledge. But its tail shallows are less readable. Their currents spread and dwindle quickly into the lake-size Mori lagoon, with its noisy regattas of young eiders and swans. Yet the currents shelter salmon and have enough flow to work a fly swing properly, long after their eddies have seemingly died.

You must believe me, the old riverkeeper Steingrimur Baldvinsson insisted gently, *even if everything you have learned about salmon on other rivers tells you otherwise—the fish are there!*

Downstream the river bends into a boat pool called Vitadsgnafi, where it flows like a mirror over the black-sand bottom. Its holding-lie is formed over a current-polished ledge that barely projects above the bottom. The ledge is betrayed only by the imperceptible swelling of the still surface, and the salmon lie there.

Presthylur is a classic chalkstream beat. Its taking channels are formed in a changing jigsaw puzzle of channels in the weeds, and it is the weeds that focus the smooth holding currents at Thvottastrengur too. Downstream its salmon lie above a hidden outcropping on the bottom, and the gathering tail shallows are formed over a shelving ledge. Its serrations form a two-hundred-foot barricade that blocks the current, except for a swift chute along either bank. The fish lie between the bulging, half-seen outcropping and the smooth ledges below, yet there is virtually nothing in the still current to suggest their presence.

Kirkjuholmakvisl is perhaps the most famous pool on the Laxá in Pingeyjarsýsla. Its reputation is based partly on its role in the poetry of Steingrimur Baldvinsson, and its fishing character is defined by a narrowing of grassy banks. Yet its upper shallows can conceal a salmon anywhere in a series of bathtub-shaped depressions scoured from the lava. The primary holding-lies are easily located, since the grass is worn bare at the best casting places, and a long cast across the current drops a fly tight against the trailing grass.

Still lower pools like the gentle Skriduflud and Sandeyrapollur and Oddahylur are easier to decipher, with their primary lies in the gathering flow above the ledges at their tails. But each of these pools has its hidden secrets too, and an angler must simply fish carefully to discover them.

Knowing a river is a little like a marriage, Roderick Haig-Brown observed one day last winter in his library at Campbell River. *Both are things that seem to mellow.*

There is a pool on the Grimsá that seems unlikely at best, and I fished it first without the help of the riverkeeper. According to the fishing logs, Strengir is the single most productive pool of the entire Grimsá watershed. It consistently surrendered five hundred to seven hundred fly-caught salmon per year, more than all eight salmon rivers in Maine put together. Yet the first time I drew the Strengir, it looked like a fishless shallow filled with broken ledges.

Except for a gentle, half-plucking take, my first encounter with the Strengir beat led me to dismiss its quarter-mile of water as a fishless fraud. *Never saw a fish all morning,* I explained later at Hvitabakki farmstead. *You sure it's really a salmon pool?*

It's our best pool, Kristjan Fjelstad smiled.

Later I discovered that its secret was a narrow cooling-fault crevasse running the length of its shallow ledges. The ragged slot in the bottom lava varied between six and twelve feet in depth. It was as narrow as five feet in some places, and its maximum width was a cast of about seventy-five feet. The salmon lay everywhere at varying levels of flow.

Strengir was a complete surprise. It had five pools in its full length, from the steeply tumbling throat at its beginning to the relatively shallow bedrock flat at its bottom. The throat is a narrowing funnel in the ledges, and I had fished Strengir several times before I discovered that it held fish.

The second holding-place is the canal-lock gut through a massive lava outcropping. It was thirty yards long and thirty feet wide. The first time I fished the beat, this surprisingly symmetrical fault in the bottom was a virtual torrent. Later I found it welling up smooth and almost glassy toward its tail currents, and it held fish everywhere. The cooling fault opens into a more conventional pool downstream, its throat split around a thumblike formation in the lava. Both currents hold fish, but the tumbling tail shallows are more productive at most levels of water. The river slides over a sawtoothed ledge downstream and then narrows into a stomach-shaped lie in the bedrock. Its exit channel divides around a single boulder and plunges through a narrow crevice in another ledge. Here the cooling fault in the bottom ends, fanning out into a rocky shallow that is fine riffling-hitch water.

It took three seasons to understand the Strengir, and then some imperceptibly subtle changes deep in its secret depths seemed to have transformed its generous character. The last two summers it has suddenly been less productive. Yet I can clearly remember its past riches, and on a nineteen-fish day I once had on the Grimsá, the inscrutable Strengir surrendered fifteen salmon.

[1976]

18

Brown Trout
in America

This essay was commissioned in 1983 for the centennial of the introduction of brown trout to the United States. As you'll see, if you don't already know, this species drastically altered American fly fishing by virtue of its shyness and selectivity. By the late nineteenth century, many of our native brook-trout fisheries were in sad decline, the victims of wanton habitat destruction. The brown trout thus filled a growing void in American angling and brought with it a discerning eye for faulty flies that to this day sends thousands of anglers back to their fly-tying equipment in search of better imitations.

Schwiebert offers here a survey of this species' history and introduction, coupled with some remarkable observations on the trout's selectivity in feeding that have a direct bearing on your fishing. As ever, his acute insights into the nature of things—in this case brown-trout behavior—can pay dividends on your own particular water.

It was a bitter February morning.
The Atlantic crossing had been troublesome, and the

wintry seas still rolled in awesome swells. The trawlers work-ing the Georges Bank had pitched and shuddered helplessly. The sea writhed with a sullen power, leaden waves rising almost angrily above its troughs, until the wind stripped a sickly green spray from their crests. The storm was ebbing slightly off Montauk. The ship still pitched and rolled, but it no longer rose shuddering, its stern lifting and twin screws throbbing free of the water. Its passengers and crew felt bet-ter, and the ship struggled patiently toward New York.

It was the German steamship *Werra,* and it sailed grate-fully past Fort Hamilton into the Narrows. Its masts and deck-fittings and railings were still partly sheathed in ice. The ship was riding low in the water, straining under the weight of its chill shroud, and trailing dark scraps of smoke from its tall stacks.

It was late winter in 1883.

Because of the winter storms, the *Werra* was behind schedule, and it met the harbor pilot off Governor's Island. The pilot scrambled up its Jacob's ladder, bundled against the wind. The ship steamed quickly up the Hudson, meeting a tugboat off the Battery. Steering expertly against a mixing tide, the *Werra* edged cautiously into its berth, screws churn-ing in the brackish winter-green river. Anchor cables and mooring lines were quickly secured, and a queasy line of passengers gathered gratefully to watch the gangways low-ered to the pier.

Virtually ignored in the bustle of cargo and passengers and baggage were eighty thousand fertile trout eggs, tiny pearls and moonstones and opals gleaming dully in their chilled moss-lined trays.

The brown trout had come to America.

Its delicate ova had been patiently stripped from ripe henfish and their roe was mixed with rich, milky sperm at the Black Forest estate of the Baron Friedrich von Behr. The German nobleman had been experimenting for several years at his private rearing station and had consigned this ship-ment to the hatchery at Cold Spring Harbor.

Fred Mather waited anxiously in the poorly heated cus-toms shed. Officials sorted through stacks of customs declara-tions and bills of lading and forms. Mather operated the new rearing station at Cold Spring Harbor, and he spent several impatient hours before the fragile consignment of eggs was finally admitted into the country. Mather accepted the tiny shipment with a mixture of relief and growing excitement. The ova were still alive. Lamplighters were already working in the February streets when Mather crossed the wintry city, bound for Long Island and the train that would take him to Cold Spring Harbor. The Brooklyn Ferry carried Mather and his tiny cargo past the spidery cable-hung sculpture and brickwork towers of the Brooklyn Bridge, which was nearing completion and would open to traffic that spring.

Mather did not reach his hatchery on Long Island until well after midnight, and he worked several more hours before his precious trout eggs were safely at home. Bone-tired and happy, Mather finished in the grimy daylight.

Like most Americans, the brown trout is an immigrant from Europe. Its natural range reaches eastward from Iceland to the Ural Mountains beyond Moscow, and still farther east into the north-flowing drainages of the Kirghiz, above Tashkent in the Asian provinces of the Soviet Union. Its longitudinal range lies between the Finnmarksvidda, deep in Arctic Norway, and curious relict alpine populations found in Turkey, Iran, Lebanon, and Morocco.

The ova shipped on the *Werra* were not the first brown trout eggs to reach the United States. That honor goes to a tiny consignment of four thousand eggs sent from England to a farsighted amateur ichthyologist W. L. Gilbert of Plymouth, Massachusetts.

His shipment had arrived in 1882, a year before Mather received his eighty thousand fertile ova from the Black Forest, but most of the British eggs had perished at sea. The tiny eggs had shriveled like rotting fruit in their moss-lined trays, and Gilbert succeeded in hatching only twenty-five fry.

These survivors were patiently coddled to fingerling size, but only three of the British trout reached maturity. Their offspring played no role in the American distribution of the species. The fish simply remained in Gilbert's private collection at Plymouth, and eventually his tiny brood of British trout atrophied and died.

Fred Mather had other dreams.

Unlike his colleagues, Mather had actually fished for brown trout before introducing them into our waters. His love for the Eurasian species began in the tumbling little rivers of the Black Forest, swift tributaries of the Upper Rhine that wind past villages of steep-roofed German farmhouses. Hemingway later fished those rivers in his early Paris years, hiking the country roads beyond Freiburg-im-Breisgau. His short story *"The Snows of Kilimanjaro"* described those experiences in the fever-ridden passages of its hero's delirium:

> In the Black Forest, after the war, we rented a trout stream and there were two ways to walk to it. One was down the valley from Triberg and around the valley road in the shade of the trees that bordered the white road, and then up a side road that went through the hills past many small farms, with the big Schwarzwald houses.

Hemingway explored the Black Forest streams just after the Treaty of Versailles, after his serious wounding at Fossalta di Piave, and the Argonne guns were finally stilled. Their sport obviously played a role in the writer's painful recovery from the First World War.

But Mather had fished them almost forty years earlier. His fascination with brown trout began with a trip to Berlin in 1880, which he made as the United States delegate to the International Fisheries Exposition. It was a remarkable accident of history. Mather had eagerly sought out the European pioneers in fish culture. He found a common spirit in the Baron Friedrich von Behr, a German nobleman who was president of the German Fisheries Society.

Von Behr invited Mather to fish his private beats in the Black Forest. Mather enjoyed their sport, but he was more impressed with the shyness and selectivity of the red-spotted Eurasian species. He was intrigued with its obvious ability to tolerate warmer waters than our native brook trout, whose habitat was dwindling rapidly as our eastern forests were stripped.

Mather quickly discovered that brown trout were more difficult to catch than the speckled natives he enjoyed on the Nissequogue and Conetquot, his favorite trout waters on eastern Long Island.

Their wariness convinced him that brown trout might withstand the fishing pressure from growing cities like Boston and New York and Philadelphia. Timber companies were stripping our Appalachian forests and were greedily acquiring the rights to clear-cut the primeval stands of Michigan and Wisconsin. Brook trout cannot survive temperatures past seventy-five degrees. The Appalachian acid factories and sawmills were a harsh dirge sounding the death of their spring-fed habitat. The farsighted Mather thought that brown trout offered hope for rivers that were being crippled, stripped of the conifers that had cooled their primeval springheads.

Mather hatched his eggs without fanfare at Cold Spring Harbor. His precious fry were stocked in several famous eastern rivers, but their introduction was almost secretive and surprisingly few records remain. Both Pennsylvania and New York seldom bothered with official records of these first plantings. Few people took them seriously. Other historic shipments of brown trout ova took place during the winter of 1884, coming from Sir Ramsey Gibson Maitland at his famous hatchery on Loch Leven, and from rearing facilities on the chalkstreams of southern England.

Although our records of the first brown-trout plantings are sparse, there is considerable evidence that the species was soon thriving. The century-old logs of fishing clubs like Wyandanche on the Nissequogue and South Side on the Conetquot suggest that such Long Island streams were among our first brown-trout fisheries.

The species quickly became established in the Catskill drainages of the Beaverkill and Willowemoc, and their sister rivers soon followed. The Musconetcong in northern New Jersey was stocked with brown trout fry from its Hacketts-town Hatchery, and the gentle Brodheads received considerable plantings of the species in 1888. Other fertile ova were shipped to the Northville Hatchery in Michigan, and fingerlings were first introduced to the Pere Marquette.

The guest book from Henryville House records the capture of several large brown trout in 1890, telling us how quickly the species established itself on the Brodheads in Pennsylvania. The fish were taken under the cribbing at the Dam Pool, and averaged fifteen inches. Such trout were much bigger than the native brook trout on the Brodheads. The log describes the unfamiliar trout as dark and curiously colored, and among its wealth of historic signatures is a record of the Eurasian species in eastern Pennsylvania. It thrived with such vigor that the Henryville regulars took ten browns better than twenty inches before 1900, and a twenty-seven-inch trophy was caught the following season.

The remarkable success of the species on the Brodheads was typical, yet its early history is missing from the records of the Commonwealth of Pennsylvania. It is found only in the guest register at Henryville. Several trophy browns were laid diagonally across its open pages and traced for posterity. The tracings are authentic. The fish-slime that penetrated the paper has discolored over the past century, and brown-trout scales have adhered to these silhouettes or scattered through the bindings. The species was soon planted in other rivers and, in its migrations to winter and spawn, it spread quickly in suitable habitat. It seemingly thrived in streams where the speckled trout was dwindling rapidly.

But its odyssey is a classic American parable, with a bitterly misunderstood hero, and a century of controversy and struggle before its final curtain. The story of the brown trout in America is still unfinished, and in many parts of the country the polls remain unclosed. Some old-timers still fervently dislike browns. Since Mather had been right, they proved harder to catch than our native species, and they were harder to raise in a hatchery too. The wind music in the hemlock ridges and whippoorwill bottoms along our rivers was drowned in a threnody of cracker-barrel opinion.

The brook-trout fishermen were angry and quickly invented a roster of sins that surrounded the alien species. *Them German browns just ain't worth a damn!* the brook-trout crowd used to argue along the Black and Pine in Michigan. *Them fish just lie there looking at you, but they don't never take—and they're dull-colored and ugly, too!*

The old-timers were right about some things. Brown trout did not feed as greedily or often as our native species. Tactics that worked on pretty little brookies seldom fooled browns. Coarse-gut tippets and three-snell rigs triggered suspicion, and no brown trout took readily once it had spotted the fisherman.

And the old-timers were right when they argued that brown trout ignored their flies. But the problem lay with our fly patterns, and not with the newly arrived species. Except for the glacier-scour lakes of Lapland, where the brown trout are as gullible as Labrador brookies, the European strains have been heavily fished since before the flowering of Greece and Rome.

Aelianus recorded fishing them in Macedonia in the third century, and modern biology suggests that so many centuries of fishing pressure and culling can alter the genetic character of a species, in a Darwinian selection accelerated by man. Foolish strains have simply not survived our centuries of harvesting, leaving only the skittish and shy.

Our eastern native species have been exposed to less than three centuries of fishing, and our indigenous western trout were relatively unknown until the railroad survey parties that preceded the Civil War. Our native species are more easily caught in most waters, and it was the brook trout that first shaped our theories and tactics. The European strains of brown trout posed other problems, and flies that had been brook-trout favorites often failed to solve them. Our fly books were as brightly colored as a kindergarten child's paintbox, with gaudily feathered patterns like the Red Ibis and Parmachene Belle and Tomah-Jo.

Taxi dancers! observed a teaching colleague of my father's one opening day in Michigan. *Painted ladies for foolish brookies and hatchery trout!*

Some fishermen stubbornly cling to these beginnings and argue that trout are not selective feeders. There are even some biologists who insist that trout are predators and will always take advantage of big, juicy insects and other gullible prey. But cracker-barrel wisdom always has its footnotes of truth. Selectivity is more common with brown trout than our native species, although there are exceptions to that too, like the brookies at Big Spring in Pennsylvania or the Henry's Fork rainbows in Idaho. There are even cutthroats, like the unique fine-spotted strains in the spring creeks of Jackson Hole, that are remarkably selective.

Selective feeding only occurs when a diet form is available in sufficient numbers to trigger such behavior. It is most obvious on fertile waters of rich alkalinity, and our awareness of selectivity was awakened by the European browns.

Biologists still argue that trout merely respond to the largest diet forms available in reasonable numbers. Such behavior is quite common, particularly in less fertile habitat and on high-altitude streams where the feeding season is brief. But fishermen who are widely experienced on more fertile waters, from the Rising River in northern California to the better-known Letort Spring Run in Pennsylvania, have commonly witnessed more complex feeding behavior. Such fish often display a puzzling quality that contradicts the least-effort theories of most wildlife biology. They often reject large insects, particularly large insects of a color unlike the species they have just been seeing, to concentrate on fly hatches of smaller insects they trust.

The memory is filled with examples.

The Henryville water on the Brodheads holds a fine population of brown trout that are fished hard and seldom killed. Each season they display a curious pattern of feeding behavior. Our hatches there begin with dark winter stoneflies of the *Capnia* and *Taeniopteryx* species. The first mayflies our fish see are also dark slate-winged species, ranging from tiny *Baetis* flies to the better known *Epeorus* and *Ephemerella* hatches. The trout are conditioned across several weeks to a variety of fly sizes; but the species are all relatively dour-looking until late spring, when our sulfurs start hatching—the yellowish *Ephemerella* flies that old-timers called Pale Evening Duns.

Our trout seldom take them, although they work greedily during their hatching. The fish are seemingly suspicious of

274

these straw-colored flies after weeks of feeding on dark slate-winged insects. Trout can be observed when the sulfurs are emerging, drifting back warily under a freshly hatched dun and rejecting it. But the same trout will rise greedily, taking the hatching nymphs as they drift just under the surface and wriggle in its film. The secret is simple: The emerging sulfur nymphs are dark brown, like the nymphs of the earlier hatches.

There are several instances of such behavior on widespread rivers, and there are many western examples too. Perhaps the most striking occurs during the first days of the salmonfly hatch, when many of the best fish react suspiciously to its large stoneflies, but continue to take smaller *Oecetis* and *Hydropsyche* sedges, caddisflies they have obviously learned to trust in earlier weeks.

Another important example occurs on the famous Henry's Fork of the Snake. The big Lead-winged Olives and *Ephemera* drakes of early summer are among the best hatches of the year. Small trout and whitefish take both species greedily, almost the first day they start emerging, but the big trout often eye them warily. The big *Ephemerella* flies, with their yellow-ringed olive bodies and mottled legs, start hatching in late morning. Brown Drakes are twilight hatches, when their burrowing *Ephemera* nymphs escape the silty weeds and wriggle toward the surface. Such hatches are often mixed with spinner swarms of these big mottle-winged flies.

Many times I have watched large trout reject the big olive-bodied flies to take the tiny Pale Morning Duns they have seen for weeks. Both species fall spent at twilight, when the Brown Drakes are also hatching, but the fish often take the little rust-colored spinners instead. Other times, the best trout ignore the fluttering *Ephemera* drakes to focus on small Slate-winged Olives or tiny soot-colored sedges. It seems to take a few days before the best fish trust the bigger flies, in the classic brown-trout fashion.

Anglers who frequent less fertile waters find such feeding behavior puzzling. Many refuse to accept either matching the hatch or such complex behavior as masking-hatch feed-

275

ing, in which a bigger diet form is rejected in favor of a smaller species. Selective feeding and hatch matching are not mere theories subject to opinion, but are important factors in trout biology and behavior.

Selectivity? André Puyans once observed at Steamboat Springs. *Some guys seem to think we invented bugs and biology—we're only guilty of trying to understand them.*

Brown trout were the fulcrum. Our awareness of selectivity, and its interlocking disciplines of aquatic entomology, has its genesis in British fishing books and the introduction of brown trout into American waters.

Brook-trout fishing was relatively easy, and our wilderness trout were so guileless that American anglers were almost completely unschooled in the riddles of selective feeding. Its chesslike problems are seldom simple. Many fishermen choose to ignore its obvious disciplines, since consistently unlocking its secrets is impossible without serious effort and study.

Obviously, selective feeding is not always a factor. Sometimes fish concentrate on a single diet form or stage of a hatch. Sometimes they forage indiscriminately, particularly when nothing is hatching in significant numbers. There are doldrums between hatches too. When trout are foraging widely, the fish will take both general patterns, like the Adams and Muddler and Humpy, and patterns that imitate specific nymphs and fly hatches they have been seeing.

Most everyone catches some fish when things are easy, but only a few take trout consistently when things are hard, and selective browns fall into that category. Specific imitations will take fish when a colorful Royal Wulff is working too, but the converse is seldom true. During specific hatches and spinner falls, only workable imitations score consistently, and the secret is knowledge rather than mere hunt-and-pick fly selection.

Many skilled anglers carry a sparse selection of flies, and the spentwing Adams with its salt-and-pepper hackles is a familiar choice. *Why do guys who talk about fishing only one pattern always pick the Adams?* André Puyans laughed. *It*

276

only looks like hundreds and hundreds of caddis species—why don't these turkeys fish a Parmachene Belle or Red Ibis all year, and then tell us hatch-matching doesn't matter?

No knowledge of matching the hatch is needed to catch fish some of the time; but such knowledge is critical in catching fish most of the time. And it is the selective brown trout that really taught us that axiom.

Brook-trout fishermen quickly discovered that brown trout were more difficult to catch. Victorian fly books filled with bright silks and barred woodduck and jungle cock, snelled with silkworm gut and brightly hackled with a spectrum of orange and canary yellow and scarlet, no longer worked. Brown trout stripped an entire generation of American anglers of its illusions, quickly teaching us that our fishing skills were relatively primitive.

Cracker-barrel opinion fought back with a chorus of criticism, and several fish and game commissions pronounced the brown trout an unfortunate mistake. Michigan actually attempted to eradicate the species, particularly in the watershed of the Pere Marquette, and happily failed. The failure of that program tells us something important about the tenacity of brown trout, and its survival in a future of armpit-to-armpit fishing.

But popular criticism dies stubbornly.

Several fish and game commissions still refuse to introduce brown trout. Biologists often insist that brown trout are a poor choice for catch-and-release fisheries, because they are not gullible enough to satisfy the public. Biopoliticians argue that freshly planted browns are not caught quickly enough, since fish-stocking programs have political motives and echoes too. There are even zealots who believe that brown trout and other alien species should be eradicated from our national parks in favor of the native species originally found there. It is tragic to think that such a philosophy would eradicate both browns and rainbows from the Firehole, and that Yellowstone waters that were fishless in frontier times would be poisoned out, yet such proposals have been voiced.

Fish culturists joined the chorus too. Rainbows had

proved the perfect species for hatchery programs. Brown trout were less malleable, resisting the hybridization that has led to more pounds of poultry rainbows for less money in less time. American logic can seldom resist such bottom-line equations. But hatchery rainbows are foolish, have enough steelhead in their ancestry to search fruitlessly for salt water, and have made the Faustian bargain of economically quick growth for a short life span. The brown trout has resisted such hatchery manipulation, and the species has suffered less genetic tinkering. Hatchery rainbows have largely become like cocker spaniels, wriggling belly-up in your lap and tail-wagging, but the hatchery brown trout is still a furtive coyote in a cage.

Brook-trout fishermen also argued that brown trout were ugly. The species clearly lacks the gaudy mating colors of our native char, and it disdains the carmine stripes and rose gill-covers of the rainbow, but it is hardly ugly. It has richly spotted sides and dorsal surfaces, with bright accents of orange and scarlet. Wild strains often display deep, reddish tints on their dorsal, adipose, and caudal fins. Their lower fins are often edged in white, although such coloring is less sharply defined than the lower fins of the brook trout. Brown trout that subsist on tiny shrimp and sowbugs are brightly colored and often have a sheen of silvery turquoise on their flanks and gill plates. Females in spawning time display butter-yellow bellies, and the cockfish are even more colorful, with bellies like a pumpkin-colored moon.

Brown trout have the beauty of woodcock and grouse, completely lacking the gaudy plumage of the ring-necked pheasant. Alive in a riffling current, their subtle palette quietly echoes the bottom stones, dancing with leafy shadows and sun. Lying in a creel lined with ferns, and laid gently in a meadow of harebells and buttercups, brown trout have a quiet beauty that is unique.

But they don't fight! rainbow fishermen still argue fervently. *They never jump!*

It is correct that brown trout seldom fight with the wild, cartwheeling abandon of rainbows, or the stubborn bulldogging fight of big Labrador brook trout. But their fight is shrewd and strong, trying to reach a fallen tree or boulder to foul the leader. But wild browns often jump when hooked, particularly on big, western rivers like the Deschutes and Big Horn and Green.

Look at that fish jump! I had hooked a big dry-fly brown in salmonfly time on the Beaverhead. *He's not supposed to jump like that!*

He doesn't read books! Phil Wright said wryly.

Brook-trout fishermen still believe that brown trout drive out our native species. Such arguments are more rooted in myth than fact. Decimation of wildlife habitat is still the most serious threat to our fisheries. It was our unthinking rapacity that lumbered off our eastern forests, and mindlessly stripped the hemlocks of their bark for the tanneries, to cure the flood of pelts and hides shipped east by the trappers and buffalo hunters.

The first hatcheries sought to compensate for such dwindling habitat with brook-trout strains bred by Seth Green in northern New York. His theory involved a strain of fish bred to spawn sooner, and at smaller sizes. Green and his colleagues reasoned that prolific spawning and restored populations would follow. But their legacy was short-lived brookies spawning at juvenile sizes, and streams filled with small char. These hatchery strains gradually mixed with the bigger wild trout, until the long-lived hardiness of our native populations was diluted in a kind of genetic pollution.

It is a too-familiar tragedy. The conifers had been stripped from the Adirondacks to the Carolinas, and from Maine to eastern Minnesota. Once the pines and hemlocks and cedars were cut, every springhead ran warmer or dried up altogether. The deciduous forests that replaced the conifers lacked their permanent shade and root systems and a thick pine-needle carpet that held rainfall and snowmelt like a sponge. The ecology of our brook-trout fisheries was changed forever. Except for fall spawning competition, it was loss of habitat and its icy springheads that favored the brown trout and forced our native brookies into the cold tributaries. The tillage that followed the tree cutting accelerated the erosion begun by the lumberjacks, and the rivers grew silty too. The rivers had become too warm, and the immigrant species readily filled the vacuum created by our climate of growth and greed.

But they're cannibals! It is a charge still heard in inns and tackle shops and saloons throughout our trout country. *Eat baby trout like meat grinders!*

Big browns are guilty. But baby trout are not the only fish course on their menu. Dace and baby whitefish and shiners are easier to catch than juvenile trout, and they share the small insects in the trout's diet. Sculpins are brown-trout fare too, and the greedy sculpins gorge themselves on trout eggs and fry. Like mergansers and herons, big browns suppress less obvious fish-eating species like sculpins, and without them an even greater toll of baby trout would be lost, as recent studies have clearly demonstrated.

But meat eating is not a trait displayed only by brown trout. Other trout species are equally fond of small fish once they have grown to sufficient size, and the brook trout and its sister char are perhaps the most piscivorous species we have. Old-timers seldom saw brook trout of such size except perhaps in Maine, but anglers who have fished the Labrador know that there are few fish eaters as aggressive as *Salvelinus,* once it has grown large enough. The cannibal myth that surrounds the brown trout is only partly true. Browns are a relatively long-lived species, and demonstrate the cunning to grow large. The roots of their reputation for cannibalism are simple: more brown trout survive to reach meat-eating sizes.

There is little debate about the table quality of our native species. The brook trout and its sister char are a rare culinary treat. Neither rainbows nor browns can fully equal them. But steelhead poached in court bouillon at the Steamboat Inn on the Umpqua are superb. And anyone who has savored trout broiled with butter and sliced lemons at a chalkstream inn in Wiltshire, or lovingly prepared *truite au bleu* at some tiny country hotel in Provence, would laugh at the suggestion that brown trout fail to grace a proper table.

Modern taxonomy classifies the brown trout under the generic umbrella designated *Salmo trutta,* since ichthyologists currently believe that other discrete populations known from the British Isles to the Kirghiz are merely local subspecies. Older taxonomic keys separated riverine fish that did not migrate to salt water into the *Salmo fario* species, and the designation *Salmo trutta* was reserved for the sea-run strains that migrate into coastal and estuarine waters. Since both riverine and sea-run types evolved from a common marine ancestry, both were subsequently grouped together in the designation *Salmo trutta.*

However, taxonomy itself is seldom static, and its monographs are almost constantly changing. Our present use of *Salmo trutta* to describe the brown trout and its myriad subspecies will probably change again too.

Our taxonomic systems are still based entirely on morphology, the common physical traits involving scale counts and vertebra and pyloric caeca, as well as other structural benchmarks and fingerprints. But our system dates to the eighteenth century, and its past disciplines obviously lack our modern knowledge of genetic tissues and codes. Although the fish are structurally alike, the tissue samples of riverine and sea-run trout are utterly different. Their traits of riverine life or seaward migration, once widely believed the product of mere chance, are transmitted genetically. Modern genetics is a little like Pandora's box, and its future impact on existing taxonomy is still impossible to measure. But future changes will occur, and our present yardsticks defining species and subspecies seem likely to evolve too.

The morphology of *Salmo trutta* is unique. Horizontal scale counts at the lateral line average between 125 and 140, and a diagonal count between the lateral line and adipose fin will average from 13 to 16 scales. The dorsal and anal fins typically display between 10 to 12 rays, and the species has 30 to 60 pyloric caeca.

Like our native brook trout, *Salmo trutta* is a fall-spawning species. Bright males and females start gathering over spawning gravel when our rivers are low and clear. Their mating rites can occur between late September and February, depending on climate, altitude, and latitude.

Their redds vary considerably in shape, but will average sixty square inches. Unlike our native species, which seemingly prefer spawning in headwaters and tributaries, the brown trout will happily lay its eggs in the rivers themselves. Fish attempting to spawn in tail-water fisheries below dams will attempt to spawn at disparate sites, depending on the volume of discharge running, but such egg laying is seldom successful. Toleration of such varied spawning conditions is another factor in the singular hardiness of the Eurasian species.

Spawning behavior among brown trout is also similar to the egg laying of other species. Mating pairs typically select a smooth current-flow running five to fifteen inches per second over layers of clean, oxygen-saturated pea gravel. Cockfish guard the nesting sites while the females shape the redds, working and writhing against the bottom. Gasping and rolling until its redd is properly shaped, calibrating its depth and configuration with its lower fins, the female works the gravel until it is displaced in a saucer-shaped depression with a small mound of gravel tailing off downstream.

The female finally settles into the nest, thrusting and working until the male joins in its mating dance. During the actual egg laying, both fish writhe together until a cloudy mix of eggs and sperm settles into the gravel. Both parents rest momentarily. The male then takes a position to defend its mate and their nest, while the henfish slides just above its freshly laid ova. The female works its body against the bottom, gently displacing enough fine stones and pea gravel to cover the redd. Resting briefly again, the persistent henfish searches immediately upstream for the current speeds and aggregates that will sustain another cycle of egg laying.

Fecundity varies with both the size and condition of the henfish. Females will oviposit between two hundred and eight thousand eggs during their spawning rites, and a mating pair may build a series of redds. Spawning lasts about a week, until both fish lie spent and exhausted in a deep hole nearby. There is some spawning mortality in brown trout, and a higher percentage of cockfish is usually lost. Finally, the freshly spawned fish drift back to winter lower in the watershed. Their ordeal also involves the harsh percentages of winterkill. Both male and female kelts are easily identified the following spring and are dark and emaciated from both spawning and surviving the winter.

Some anglers are mistakenly worried about such kelts in the spring. *Some of them fish are pretty thin and sick* is a familiar observation each April. *Big heads and just like snakes—maybe we should kill them.*

But such fish are not really in poor condition. They are spawned-out kelts that are coming off the thinnest weeks of winter. Their lean bodies are not the negative symptom they might seem, but tangible evidence of egg laying and hardiness. Such trout have survived both spawning mortality and winterkill percentages, and their hardiness suggests that they are superb brood stock.

The period of incubation varies widely, both from river to river, and from season to season; weather and water temperature are among its subtle triggers. Average conditions find fertilized ova in about four weeks, and at approximately forty-two degrees, tiny alevins will wriggle up through the bottom gravel in eighty-odd days. The alevins are curious larvalike fish. Their nourishment is found in delicate yolk sacs still attached to their tiny, translucent bodies. When their yolks are expended, the delicate fry must start to forage for themselves. Such fry subsist on zooplankton and other minute food-chain organisms. After a few months, they have grown to fingerling size and turn to aquatic fly life.

Growth is relatively predictable. Males mature at nine to ten inches, and henfish typically reach fertility at eleven to twelve. After five years, most brown trout in habitat of average quality will measure between sixteen and twenty inches. Biologists believe this is optimal breeding age and size, and many fishing regulations are predicated on that benchmark. But such studies cannot fully apply to extremely fertile waters, like the Big Horn and Firehole and Henry's Fork, with atypical rates of winterkill and growth. Most spring creeks offer similar habitat. Brown trout in such fisheries can reach

sizes of twenty to twenty-eight inches while still within optimal spawning age, and cropping them with trophy-fish regulations at twenty-odd inches makes little sense.

Ichthyologists long believed that brown-trout growth
stopped after eight to ten years. Several specimens have
been recorded that lived between fifteen and twenty years,
but a ten-season fish is a patriarch. One large fish at the
Bellefonte Hatchery in Pennsylvania lived fifteen years,
grew three inches in its last four years, died at thirty-five
inches, and weighed twenty-seven pounds. The world record for *Salmo trutta* is still a thirty-nine-and-a-half-pound
fish caught in 1866 by William Muir at Loch Awe in western
Scotland.

Some American journals, perhaps motivated by their ad-
vertisers, have attempted to dismiss that record in favor of
trophy catches at Flaming Gorge. Its calculated unfrocking
was based upon the argument that it had been foul-hooked
and was tangled in its gut leader when finally landed. Few
Americans would understand that Scottish loch fishermen
harl with multiple-fly rigs, often with six to ten wet flies, and
landing a big trout would prove almost impossible without
some tangling. According to the ghillies at Dalmally, and the
boatmen of the Loch Awe Hotel, the Muir record fish was
hooked fair and became entangled during the fight. It should
be permitted to stand in spite of the short-lived fanfare surrounding Flaming Gorge, and there are several other record
fish almost as large as Muir's trophy from Europe and South
America.

Stomach-contents data recorded during the past forty-
five years, starting with the famous Needham studies published in 1938, suggest some interesting patterns in the
brown-trout diet. Paul Needham included those diet studies
in his book *Trout Streams,* and its tables displayed a strong
preference for mayflies in the brown-trout population in
small streams surrounding Cornell. Although mayfly forms
comprised almost 80 percent of brown-trout feeding in his
studies, Needham also discovered that 75 percent of those
Ephemeroptera had been ingested in nymphal form.

His figures also suggest that brown trout tend slightly

more toward adult insect forms, making them more suscepti-
ble to dry flies. Needham found that only 46 specimens had
taken five times as many adult insects as a parallel test group
of 250 brook trout. Although subsequent fieldwork suggests
that his data must be accepted with an understanding of the
small-stream habitat involved, his data remain intriguing
today:

Mayflies	1,907	79.3%
Caddisflies	230	9.5
Two-winged Flies	61	2.5
Earthworms	51	2.1
Slugs and Snails	30	1.3
Beetles	28	1.2
Ants, Bees, and Wasps	22	.7
Stoneflies	17	.7
Leafhoppers	17	.7
Crustaceans	16	.7
Salamanders and Baitfish	9	.3
Grasshoppers	8	.3
Other	10	.4
TOTALS	2,404	100.0%

The Needham data were gathered during a full season on
ledgerock streams of relatively small character. Their water
chemistry was only marginally fertile, like most eastern free-
stone streams. Freshets probably accounted for a dispropor-
tionate worm count. Forest habitat may account for the
percentages of slugs and snails, and meadow trout might
have ingested a considerably larger number of terrestrial
insects.

The specimen fish in the Needham studies were also relatively small, largely less than a pound in weight, and larger
browns would likely have taken a greater percentage of crayfish and stonefly nymphs and minnows.

Pesticides, urban growth, pollution, and increasing agriculture have radically changed our fisheries since the Needham studies. Timber cutting and overgrazing remain major
problems, and recent studies suggest that livestock opera-
tions rank among our most pervasive sources of erosion and

thermal pollution. Our citizenry is easily aroused by dams and nuclear plants and petroleum spills, but more subtle threats like livestock and acid precipitation are often more serious.

During several years of collecting aquatic specimens for *Matching the Hatch,* similar studies of the brown-trout diet were attempted. Fifty trout between seven and fifteen inches were collected and autopsied, and comparison with the Needham data is revealing:

Mayflies	1,861	71.8%
Caddisflies	365	15.2
Two-winged Flies	67	2.9
Beetles	61	2.6
Ants, Beetles, and Wasps	47	1.6
Leafhoppers	32	1.5
Stoneflies	23	.9
Slugs and Snails	20	.8
Crustaceans	19	.8
Grasshoppers	15	.7
Earthworms	11	.5
Salamanders and Baitfish	9	.4
Other	7	.3
TOTALS	2,537	100.0%

There are subtle but surprising differences between these data and the Needham figures collected almost twenty years earlier.

Mayflies are slightly less important. Caddis have increased to almost 6 percent in the stomach samples. The higher percentages of terrestrials, like ants and grasshoppers and beetles, is perhaps a result of fishing more meadow and farm-country water. Both nymphal and larval forms dominated these data, while the percentages of adult insects still suggest considerable surface feeding.

Another series of stomach autopsies was performed during the writing of *Nymphs,* which appeared eighteen years after the first publication of *Matching the Hatch.* These data indicate that some of the trends pinpointed since Needham have continued:

Mayflies	1,372	52.3%
Caddisflies	501	19.4
Two-winged Flies	183	7.1
Beetles	107	5.1
Leafhoppers	91	4.0
Ants, Bees, and Wasps	77	3.8
Stoneflies	69	2.8
Crustaceans	39	1.5
Grasshoppers	37	1.4
Earthworms	13	.4
Slugs and Snails	13	.4
Other	29	1.1
TOTALS	2,483	100.0%

These data include some startling changes over the past thirty-five years. Brown trout are apparently ingesting fewer mayflies and more caddis, and terrestrial insect species have increased subtly in importance too.

Mayflies have seemingly declined from almost 80 percent of the brown trout diet to slightly better than 50 percent. Caddis increased from slightly less than 10 percent to almost 20 percent. Terrestrial insects are apparently growing in importance. However, the figures suggesting an increasing role for the two-winged Diptera must be evaluated in terms of atypical hatches of *Bibio* flies during the test-year season. Equally atypical populations of inchworms inflated the miscellaneous category. It should perhaps be understood that our western rivers might have displayed strikingly different data, particularly involving big stonefly nymphs, since they have dense *Pteronarcys* and *Claasenia* populations. But it is obvious that our rivers are changing, largely because of degradation within their watersheds themselves, and the fish are continually forced to adapt.

The brown trout is perfectly suited to meet such challenges. The Pigeon River studies made in Michigan fifty-odd years ago demonstrate that it is difficult to catch, even in its hatchery strains. While 20 percent of stocked brown trout are caught in the same year of planting, almost 35 percent survive both predation and anglers. The studies suggest that 45

287

percent succumb between their stocking and the following spring, particularly through the steady attrition of winterkill. Such mortality is relatively low when compared with other trout species, and approximately 15 percent of hatchery brown trout are still alive in the following year.

Such data confirm the judgment of fish and game officials that *Salmo trutta* is a poor political choice for put-and-take management. It is simply not gullible enough for short-term harvesting. The species is primarily a long-term investment, because of its wariness and its ability to survive and spawn. Its life span also remains longer than hatchery strains in other species. It seems foolish to stock brown trout in marginal habitat, simply because it is capable of thriving at the threshold of the panfish temperatures our land use and rapacity have created. Brown trout are poorly suited to immediate catch-ratio gratification and should not be wasted on habitat that does not sustain spawning populations.

Salmo trutta has some singular qualities.

Some subspecies are quite famous. It is little surprise that numerous subspecies exist, given the extensive zoogeography of the brown trout. Its natural distribution reaches 4,500 miles from the Snaefjellsnes Peninsula of western Iceland to the Kirghiz watersheds that drain into Lake Balkhash and the Aral Sea. The original range of the brown trout dwarfs the range of our comparable species, except for the lake trout, or togue, which is found between Newfoundland and the Bering Sea. Only the ubiquitous Arctic char, with a distribution that is completely circumpolar, and the Arctic grayling, found eastward between northern Norway and Hudson's Bay, have a larger natural distribution than the brown trout of Eurasia.

Sea-run browns are found wherever the species exists naturally, except for desiccating watersheds draining into the relatively tepid Mediterranean. Yet riverine presence in such latitudes suggests that its waters once supported ancestral trout and salmon too. Riverine populations that do not migrate to salt water are found naturally throughout northern Europe, as well as Spain, France, Italy, Turkey, Morocco, Lebanon, Yugoslavia, Albania, and Greece.

The drainage basin of the Black Sea sustains both riverine and sea-run strains, which are found in Turkey, Bulgaria, Romania, and the Soviet Union. Russian taxonomists have also identified a subspecies called *Salmo trutta labrax*, which is a sea-run brown endemic to the Black Sea.

The Caspian Sea also hosts sea-run stocks. Its watersheds include the east-flowing drainages of the Caucasus, and the north-flowing rivers of the Elburz escarpment in northern Iran. Nonmigratory strains are also found throughout this region. Although the Caspian Sea is best known as the source of the finest beluga and sevruga caviar in the world, it also has a seemingly unique species called *Salmo caspius*. The fish is closely allied to both brown trout and Atlantic salmon in its taxonomy and has been harvested commercially to sizes reportedly exceeding a hundred pounds. Taxonomists remain at odds about its status. Some argue that it is merely an unusually large, piscivorous strain of brown trout, rather like our ancestral Pyramid Lake cutthroat in frontier times. Others argue that its fully mature weight suggests that *Salmo caspius* is a relict subspecies closely related to the Atlantic salmon. It seems unlikely that the debate matters, since a shrinking water level combined with commercial fisheries and power projects on the Terek and Kura rivers have decimated the population and threaten its survival.

Russian ichthyologists have identified a second anadromous subspecies, designated *Salmo trutta aralensis*, from the Aral Sea. Other brown-trout stocks are found in the alpine drainages that feed its waters, and the chill depths of remote Lake Balkhash. Taxonomists have also identified still another subspecies called *Salmo trutta ischchan* at Lake Sevan in Armenia. It seems likely that virtually all of the major Eurasian lakes within the range of brown-trout zoogeography boast discrete subspecies in the ancient silk-route world of Tashkent and Samarkand, at the threshold of Mongolia and Tibet.

Other unique strains probably exist in northern Russia too. Sizeable lakes like Onega are remarkable examples of lacustrine habitat. Brown trout share these drainages with the Atlantic salmon, and both species also share the watersheds of the Drina and Mazen and Pechora. The Pechora is a brawling, immense river that collects the snowmelt of tributaries draining the entire western face of the Ural Mountains. Its system marks the easterly limits of brown trout and salmon in northern Russia, but its future is clouded.

With the shrinking of the Caspian Sea, largely through deep wells and irrigation, Russian hydrologists and engineers have diverted huge volumes of water from the Pechora. The project carries water from the Urals, through a diversion canal from the Pechora into the Kama above Berezniki. The Kama discharges Pechora water southward into the Volga, the principal tributary of the Caspian Sea. The impact of borrowing water at such an immense scale—bitter lessons still half-learned from the dams and aqueducts sustaining the cities of California—cannot help but cripple the Pechora, its aquatic populations, and the ecology of an immense watershed. It is also reported that some of the most arduous excavation of the Pechora diversion canal was unwisely undertaken with nuclear devices.

There are brown trout in most of the Baltic drainages, including Denmark, Sweden, Finland, Latvia, Lithuania, Estonia, Poland, Germany, and the Soviet Union. Atlantic salmon also share some of these rivers, although their numbers have been steadily dwindling. Some of the largest sea-run browns in the world are still found in southern Sweden, in rivers like the Mörrum and Em, and even some of the rivers of Jutland in northern Denmark have sea-run populations.

Yugoslavia shelters several unique subspecies related to the brown trout, including the mottled *Salmo trutta marmoratus* of Montenegro, and *Salmo trutta letnica* still found in Lake Ohrid. Dalmatian rivers in the coastal mountains behind Dubrovnik have unique troutlike species designated *Salmothymus ohridanus* and *Salmothymus obtusirostris,* the rather strange soft-mouthed fish that some taxonomists believe are dwarflike echoes of ancestral salmon in the Adriatic Sea. Similar Yugoslav subspecies include *Salmothymus zetensis,* which is found in the rivers of Macedonia. Other Macedonian strains include *Salmo trutta taleri* and *Salmo trutta farioides,* and perhaps the quarry described by

290

Aelianus in the third century was one of these subspecies. *Salmo trutta dentex* and *Salmo trutta visovacensis* are still other subspecies of the Balkans.

There are other subspecies of brown trout throughout the Mediterranean basin. *Salmo trutta macrostigma* is isolated in the cedar-cloaked mountains of Lebanon, and *Salmo trutta pallaryi* is a relict subspecies from the Atlas Mountains of Morocco. The recently discovered *Platysalmo platycephalus* is another closely allied strain from southern Turkey. Other Turkish watersheds hold thriving populations of brown trout too, including the headwaters of the Tigris and Euphrates. Sometimes the natural distribution of species tells us something about geology and primordial climates, and these relict trout in Turkey and Iran are a perfect example. Since all trout have evolved from marine ancestors, their presence in the cold springheads of the Tigris and Euphrates demonstrated that the Arabian Sea and its Persian Gulf was once cold enough to sustain their ancestral stocks.

Since the introduction of *Salmo trutta* into the United States, the species has been successfully transplanted to every continent except Antarctica. Excellent exotic fisheries have subsequently developed in Tasmania, New Zealand, Australia, Zimbabwe, Uganda, Kenya, Tanzania, South Africa, Ceylon, Afghanistan, India, Pakistan, Kashmir, Bhutan, Argentina, Chile, and Tierra del Fuego. Some of these fisheries are among the finest in the world, although no trout of any species were originally found in the Southern Hemisphere.

Several strains of brown trout are indigenous to the British Isles, although contemporary taxonomy no longer classifies them as fully separate species. Some have a colorful place in fishing literature, like *Salmo trutta stomachichus,* the snail-eating Gillaroo trout from Ireland. Several large fjordlike lakes in western Scotland offer *Salmo trutta ferox,* which some ichthyologists believe is probably a sea-run fish that has remained in fresh water. Other common subspecies include *Salmo trutta eriox* and *Salmo trutta cambricus.* The most famous Scottish strain is perhaps *Salmo trutta levenensis,* the darkly spotted Loch Leven trout, widely transplanted across the Rocky Mountain region.

Like several allied subspecies from Iceland and the British Isles, the Loch Leven completely lacks the reddish-orange spots typical of the generic brown trout. Such unique spotting patterns are quickly lost when mixed with common *Salmo trutta* stocks, which has occurred in several American watersheds where both genetic types have been planted together.

When Loch Leven eggs were first shipped to the United States, fry were widely established in western drainages, and their progeny are still described as Loch Levens in colloquial terms. The Scottish strain was introduced into the Firehole in 1889, and plantings in other Yellowstone streams soon followed. The species persistently distributed itself throughout the Missouri watershed and is widely found today in Montana rivers that received no recorded plantings. Colorado and Wyoming drainages like the Gunnison and Roaring Fork and North Platte were stocked too, although their Loch Levens were subsequently mixed with other brown trout strains.

However, in habitat like the remarkable Lewis watershed in the Yellowstone, the Scottish subspecies has thrived in relative isolation. The Lewis rises in Shoshone and Lewis lakes, and extensive cascades at the outlet of Lewis Lake and in the lower river itself block easy migration. Neither lake supported fish when the Yellowstone was first explored and charted. Both lakes were stocked with lake trout and Loch Leven early in this century. The char are primarily reef spawners, offering little competition for the riverine gravel critical to the Scottish trout. Both lakes are fed by a series of small tributaries that seldom offer spawning volumes of flow each year, either in their lower riffles or in alluvial fans. The brown trout have several spawning sites in years having sustained autumn rainfall, but in most years the fish largely gather at the Shoshone Channel.

The entire channel is a warped hourglass drainage consisting of two pretty fountain-moss lagoons, its waist a narrow seismic fault in its cliffs of fractured lava. The lower lagoon is a still flowage lined with tules and lodgepole pines and deadfalls. Just above the lava narrows, the migrating trout gather in a smoothly flowing deep, lying in schools above its emerald weeds. They are waiting to move into the spawning shallows upstream, which are the principal source of trout fry for both alpine lakes. Shoshone holds some truly awesome brown trout in October, and, since there have been no subsequent fish plantings, its fish are still an undiluted strain of richly spotted Loch Levens.

Like other waters in the Yellowstone, the fishery is partly protected by special regulations. Its sport is restricted to artificial lures, and its bag limit is two fish daily. The trout are obviously thriving in both lakes under these rules, but their singular stock of Scottish browns is increasingly threatened in October, when the prime broodstocks of both lakes are gathering in Shoshone Channel.

The last time I fished it, George Kelly rowed us patiently across the lower lagoon. We discovered another party fishing just below the Hourglass Narrows, and we watched them catch and release several good fish as we worked past them. Kelly muttered angrily when we passed and finally reached the upper lagoon.

But they're letting fish go, I said.

Sure, Kelly agreed, *but they're fishing treble-hook hardware and they're still allowed to kill two fish—and those guys are culling through dozens until they get two really big ones! Apiece!*

Best bulls and cows in the herd!

That's right, Kelly said. *With the prime brood fish concentrated at Shoshone Channel in October, the lures-only regulations that work when they're scattered in the lakes are no longer workable—they're a serious threat, because a lot of those fish they're throwing back are dead meat!*

Although *Salmo trutta* was first introduced into eastern rivers, our finest brown trout fisheries now lie in our western mountains. The species thrives in a curious variety of American landscapes. Its desert habitat includes rivers like the Chama and Deschutes and Green. There are arid foothill waters like the Judith and Musselshell and Big Horn, and

293

famous drainages like the Madison and Yellowstone and Big Hole. And some of our best brown-trout fishing is found in the Missouri, between Three Forks and the outlaw badlands called the Missouri Breaks.

The species has displayed a remarkable tenacity. It thrives at ten thousand feet in the headwaters of the Arkansas, in the sagebrush flats of volcanic Idaho deserts, and in the strange geyser basins of the Yellowstone. Like the coyote, its hardiness and cunning help it survive in such curious places. Last season in Colorado, I spoke with a fisheries biologist who confirmed rumors of large brown trout in the seemingly tepid creeks and city drainage channels of metropolitan Denver.

It's hard to believe. He shook his head in grudging admiration. *But they're here!*

Few western plantings were the work of the western states themselves, and virtually all involved fry incubated at federal hatcheries. Several western states still refuse to propagate and stock brown trout. Extensive introductions of *Salmo trutta* largely took place during the Great Depression, and most of the fieldwork was done by the Civilian Conservation Corps. Such history is almost forgotten today, and Colorado is no exception. Until recent years, the state itself had never stocked brown trout, but it pumped its best waters full of hatchery rainbows. Truckloads and truckloads of fish were spilled into popular rivers like the South Platte at Deckers. Armies of Colorado fishermen and tourists followed their dripping tanks along the river, attacking the fish like wolves as soon as they were discharged from the hatchery trucks.

Twenty-five years ago, when I was involved in planning and building the Air Force Academy at Colorado Springs, I fished the South Platte often. Its fishing was excellent, and it was a welcome refuge from the daily pressures and scope of the project.

During the first weeks of the season, the fish we caught were the pale daintily striped rainbows from the hatchery trucks, but we steadily found more and more browns as the summer ripened and passed. Our catch was mostly brown trout in September, although *Salmo trutta* had not been planted in the South Platte for more than twenty years.

October held still more evidence that the species was thriving without help, and I remember hiking into the Deckers Canyon just before Halloween in 1957. It was a soft autumn morning that bloomed into a shirtsleeve afternoon, although a rippling gauze of clouds told us the weather was changing. We had the canyon to ourselves, and sporadic hatches of tiny *Baetis* flies emerged throughout the day. Except for a picnic basket and a bottle of Pouilly-Fuissé, we fished and took trout steadily, fishing patiently until the sky grew dark and threatening.

It was snowing before we reached the car. *You know?* Beno Walker puzzled happily. *We never saw a rainbow all day—what happens to all those hatchery fish they stock?*

They're already dead, Jim Wallace laughed.

Colorado hasn't planted a brown trout since the thirties. I shook my head. *But only the browns are left in October!*

Makes you wonder, Walker said.

[1983]

Book Three

EDGES
AND EDDIES

Edges and eddies are usually the most productive parts of any trout river, those places apart from the mainstream where larger trout lurk to snatch food from the current. And so it may be with the last part of this book.

We've already traveled this country and beyond with Schwiebert, exploring techniques and tactics for America's great waters. We've spent some productive time in matching the hatch, as well, as a means of sharpening our thinking and bringing more fish to net. It's time to stop and look quietly at the soul of angling, a spirit astream that Schwiebert describes as few other writers can. As the late Arnold Gingrich once wrote, Schwiebert can be "a near genius for evocative detail," of which this part offers several examples.

19

Spring

Spring has never come quickly enough to suit me. I've tried rushing things by fishing weighted nymphs deep in snowmelt and spate, and that's never very satisfying. H. T. Webster, the late cartoonist, once characterized the season through a young man's complaint: "Too hot for long underwear and too cold to go swimming." It's a time of restlessness in any angler's soul.

Schwiebert here shares his own evocative thoughts of spring, noting, too, the growing signs of fishing in the streamside plants. I used to be able to foretell the Hendrickson hatch when my neighbor started planting his field corn. The requisite soil temperature and the water temperatures that induce this hatch come at about the same time here in Vermont. This business of predicting ecological events by relating them to a climatic timetable, I recently found, has evolved into its own science, now called "phenology." Although present work in this field relates more to the seasonal activities of plants, it is equally applicable to your fishing, as you'll see in this essay.

It is awakening slowly each morning.

Its prelude begins softly, building gradually like the first lyric notes of a concerto. Its early signs are sometimes mixed, like the strange February storms that combine snow and sleet with startling claps of thunder.

Our weather has changed again.

It is snowing intermittently this morning, although we had no warning of the storm. Its scattering flakes gust fitfully on the wind. It is not sticking to the brickwork terrace.

Last night I got a telephone call from our fishing club. *The water looks pretty good,* the caller reported happily, *and we've been seeing a few dark little stoneflies.*

See any fish taking them?

Saw a few fish working just after lunch today, the caller said. *They were just below the bridge.*

It always starts there, I thought.

There are other clues in the late-winter woods. The trees can sense the changing seasons. Sugar maples are already alive with stirring sap, trickling slowly into polished buckets, long before there is any obvious trace of spring along the Battenkill.

Swelling buds come almost imperceptibly now, their faint punctuation mere tracings against the pale sky. The buds grow larger almost daily, until their tiny fruit is unmistakable in the rattling branches. Swamp maples along the Conetquot and Nissequogue have bright scarlet buds, their intense chroma strangely mixed with the other trees. Other buds follow in their swelling, touched with olive, ocher, and delicate green.

The winter gravel is teeming with life.

Its river-polished stones hide the fly hatches of the coming spring. Few anglers fully understand that a winter river holds more insect life than it shelters in late August.

The secrets of such riddles are simple enough. Its fly hatches are maturing quickly at the threshold of spring, its bottom currents alive with fully grown nymphs and pupal forms and larvae. Such embryonic flies are merely incubating eggs in late summer, tiny jewels hiding in their secret lies. Others are already freshly hatched nymphs and larvae, translucent and minuscule, scuttling from the light. Our best hatches are spent well before the summer dies.

There are trout ova in the winter gravel too.

The fat butter-colored brown trout have finished spawning, and their freshly spent kelts are wintering in deep holes, thin and waiting patiently for spring. Their fragile eggs have been sleeping among the stones in tiny colonies of life. The river has sustained them with its life-giving oxygen, until they are struggling to hatch from the pea gravel now, tiny alevins wriggling free. The bottoms swarm with these delicate yolk-sac fry. Alevins live like frightened sparrows, scattering from the light and scuttling among the winter-dark stones. The alevins are fearful of light until their yolk sacs are shriveled and empty. Hunger finally stirs them to forage among the pebbles and stones.

Hungry and still hiding, the tiny fish sense the urging of a faint trigger in their blood. Its fever is both metaphor and puzzle. Its stirring transforms their restless schools. Some brief tremor changes them, urging them to seek the sunlight, struggling up through the bottom rubble until they are swimming free in the current.

It is a curiously fleeting moment.

Seeking the light is filled with peril in their world, and some hapless fingerlings are certainly lost to carnivores like *Pteronarcys* nymphs, fat predators like immature dragonflies, and the greedy foraging of sculpins. The tiny fish seek the light for a fleeting time, are coaxed from hiding to forage in the river itself, and then its fierce illumination frightens them again.

How can they know? we wonder.

Late winter is a time for thoughts of spring, with snow still falling in the trees, and a time for fishing memories too. Our daydreams gather in the twilight, listening to the urgencies of a thawing wind.

Such daydreams include a helicopter chattering across the sheep stations outside Turangi, with the watery amphitheater of Taupo behind us now, watching our whirring shadow hopscotch across the rain forests. The volcano called Tongariro stands smoking. Another thickly grown hogback lies ahead, and the pilot flares slightly to clear its scrub, scattering flocks of bellbirds in our wake.

Rangeitiki! the pilot points ahead.

The river is low in February, winding tightly through its soft-walled pumice gorge. Pale autumn colors are starting in the cool nights. There are still pools connected by tinkling riffles, immense pools in the shadow of the cliffs, dark and swimming-pool green. It is possible to locate fish from the helicopter.

Other memories drift past and focus briefly.

Tierra del Fuego is alive with sea lions and silver sea-trout, cruising schools waxing fat on crustaceans and bait-fish. Its mountains are concealed in autumn storms. Hailstones rattle across the corrugated roofs at a sheep station so large that it runs a half-million Corriedales on its short-grass pampas. The river is bright with fish like freshly minted coins, and after billiards and cognac in the library, it is impossible to sleep with the ceaseless keening of the wind.

Patagonia lies a thousand miles north.

Its summer is still surrendering to its first wintry storms. Copper beeches are coloring the high country. Angry blizzards will sweep across the Andes, their winds filled with moisture from the Pacific, spilling fiercely down the lakes above San Carlos de Bariloche.

Such weather postpones our fishing, with its wild surf breaking on the steep beaches of Lago Traful. The *pampero* wind shrieks though the tall poplars that surround the big house, scattering their yellow leaves across its English gardens. The storm will pass, evolving into something like our warm October weather in the Yellowstone country. *You must not worry,* Mauricio de Lariviere tells his guests. *Our weather will improve and the salmon fishing will be wonderful tomorrow—but tonight we shall eat and laugh together and enjoy the wine!*

Argentine landlocks are stirring in late February, dropping back from the Andean lake into pools that are startlingly clear. The river is like crystal over its pale shallows. Pewter-colored salmon lie there restlessly in pools like Cipreses and Nellie Blood.

Other worlds fill our daydreams, but there are also thoughts of familiar rivers on these last, swiftly ebbing nights of winter.

Spring is only weeks away tonight.

It is probably time to build a beechwood fire and dress some flies. It is something I promise myself every winter, thinking ahead to the early hatches at Henryville, and seldom carry through. Our fly boxes are not exactly empty, but I will probably lose some sleep sitting at the fly vise before those April fishing trips.

The benchmarks of springtime are subtle, and each has its fishing secrets. Skilled fishermen can learn to use such clues on their favorite waters over the years.

Fishing and its cycle of fly hatches are tied to a lexicon of other echoes: pale shoots of skunk cabbages in the woodcock bottoms, the faint promise of forget-me-nots growing beside a steep river path along the Brule, the first May apples pushing through the withered leaves in a ravine above the Musconetcong, and white-flowered trilliums in the silver-barked popple along the Big Two-Hearted in Michigan.

Our gentle Brodheads is no exception.

There are usually winter stoneflies emerging with the first dog-tooth violets. Our first *Epeorus* hatches are measured by the delicately unfolding leaves of coltsfoot in the sheltered places, and there are late-morning hatches of smaller mayflies when the shadbush is flowering like wedding veils in the bigger trees. Dogwoods are blooming when the early *Ephemerella* flies are still hatching after lunch. Each season has its cycles, and each river has its unique fingerprints of climate.

Listen to the river! It is the wisdom of both poetry and science. *Listen and watch—it will tell you its secrets!*

[1983]

304

20

Thoughts in Coltsfoot Time

Our coltsfoot blossoms about two weeks before the streams warm sufficiently for good trout fishing, and their bright yellow heads are both cheerful harbinger and exquisite torture. It's a time of impatience. Sometimes groups of blossoms are found sticking up through a riffle in the sunlight, soon to be a gravel bar as the last of the snowmelt disappears and the river drops. Its leaves don't appear until a few weeks after the blossoms and are shaped exactly like the foot of a small horse. Old-timers here used the leaves as a medicinal tea.

It's a frustrating time of no fishing, which inevitably leads to thoughts of fishing. And so we find Schwiebert in this essay remembering, and we'll remember with him—sharing the subtle poetry of younger spring days in restless anticipation of rising trout.

It is still raining softly this morning, after several days of false spring that started the coltsfoot blooming in the sheltered places. Deer are browsing through the oaks and beeches behind the house, their coats still the somber color of winter leaves, although the snow is finally gone. Grouse are drumming in the overgrown orchard, and it is almost time for fishing.

Coltsfoot is a spare, dandelionlike flower, and as with many other wildflowers, history tells us that the coltsfoot is an alien species. It traveled across the Atlantic with our Colonial forefathers, since its tiny hoof-shaped leaves were dried and burned like incense to treat asthma and colds. Coltsfoot is found on the sheltered slopes and ravines that capture the late-winter sun, although only its bright blossoms are visible above the carpet of winter leaves this morning. Its flowers signal the weakening of winter, in spite of the bitter April weather, and in my library in these Appalachian foothills my thoughts are filled with boyhood summers in Michigan.

My first memories of fishing are there, in a simple cedar-shingle cottage among the hardwoods and pines, fifty yards above a tiny lake that shimmered in the August sun.

Lily pads filled its shallows, turning over lazily and drifting in the hot wind that smelled of orchards and cornfields farther south. Red-winged blackbirds called restlessly in the marsh. The lily pads were like the rowboats moored at the rotting dock, shifting and swinging in the wind until their stems stretched and pulled them back like anchor lines. The hot wind rose and stirred each morning, offering no relief from the late-summer heat.

The boats were poorly maintained, with peeling paint and rusting oarlocks and eyebolts. Their wrinkled seams desperately needed fresh caulking. Moss-colored water surrounded a half-drowned bailing can in the boat that went with the cottage. The other rowboat was completely filled with water. Its wainscot bottom rested on the mud in the planking shadows of the pier. Its middle seat sheltered a small colony of tadpoles.

The hot wind dropped and died. Locusts started their harshly strident cadenzas in the trees, and the little lake became a tepid mirror at midday, its still surface marred only by the restless hunting of its clear-winged dragonflies.

My mother was sleeping in the bedroom upstairs. Our

family had rented the cottage for the month, and my father planned to complete a textbook he was writing, but the fishing interrupted his daily schedule. The staccato of his typewriter on the screened porch filled our afternoon silences, and I dozed fitfully in the summer grass, thinking about the ice cream the farmer's wife made across the lake.

One morning when we went for eggs and milk, I watched the farmer's wife working with her tubs and cracked ice and salt in the springhouse. While she stopped to wipe her face, she let me wrestle with the crank of her ice-cream maker.

It was a summer of sweet corn and ripe watermelon and cherries, mixed with fishing for bluegills and yellow perch and bass. But it was also a summer of poverty and poor crops, when the wheat farmers were driven from their homesteads in the High Plains states, and the terrible dust storms soon followed. During those tragic years, my father and other college teachers were still employed. Small businessmen and major corporations and banks had failed, and many factories and mills stood ominously silent. Many families in southern Michigan had lost their orchards and house mortgages and farms, but that boyhood summer beside a lily-pad lake was strangely filled with riches.

It was perhaps the simple rhythms of our lives that sustained us through those Depression years, and the bass fishing was a critical part of family rituals that summer.

My father usually awakened just before daylight, while my mother still lay sleeping under the quilts, and climbed stealthily down the narrow stairs to the kitchen. Cooking smells of scrambled eggs and crumb-batter perch and sausages drifted through the cottage, and in spite of his efforts to let us sleep, there was always the grating scrape of the skillet on the wood-burning stove. Mixed with the muffled clatter of cups and plates, the rich aroma of coffee lingered in the cottage long after his breakfast was finished.

Sometimes the tiny lake was covered with fog, and I heard him collect the oars and fishing tackle from the porch. Sometimes he simply disappeared into its shroud, carrying his oars and tackle down toward the dock. It was delicious to lie there, partly awake under the patchwork quilting, listening to the familiar sounds and rituals of his embarkation. Planking creaked when he reached the dock, the lures in his tackle box rattled when he placed it in the boat, its padlock chain rattled across the eyebolts and pilings, and oarlock rhythms marked his passage through the lily pads.

His fishing was a liturgy that I was still too young to share that summer, although sometimes he took me along to sample its secrets, and on those mornings I waited restlessly through breakfast with delicious shivers of anticipation.

We caught nothing those mornings, but I clearly remember the spinning ivory handles of his reel, surrendering line as his lure arched out toward sheltering pockets in the tules and pickerelweed and lilies. Once there was a wild splash that engulfed his red-and-white plug, but the largemouth was not hooked, and when the summer ended it had been our only strike together. It was usually getting hot when we rowed back across the lake, and I sat happily in the stern, trailing my fingers in the water and listening to his strokes.

Textbook manuscript usually occupied the hours after lunch, and the rattle of his typewriter echoed across the lake. His work had progressed well that summer, except for the brief disaster on the screened porch when a sudden storm scattered his freshly corrected pages across the wet floor. Late in the afternoons, his interest in history waned and his preoccupations ebbed, and we knew that he was thinking about the evening's sport when he started to sort through his tackle.

It was time to clean and lubricate a prized Pflueger reel, its components lovingly collected in a saucer and sorted on the oilcloth-covered table. The weedless spoons and tiny spinner blades and wobble plates on his lures were meticulously polished. Pork frogs and fresh pork-rind strips were cut with his fishing knife on a cheese board, and he patiently sharpened the nickel-plated trebles too.

Supper was always early that summer, and when the shadows lengthened across the boat-pier shallows, it was finally time for fishing. My father gathered his equipment and loaded the boat, rowed out through the ragged lily-pad channel, and began casting along the weedy shoreline. His fishing

had its mixture of rhythms and rituals, and he seldom returned before nightfall. Sometimes it was completely dark
when we heard his rowing, and I usually met him at the dock,
waiting in the darkness while he secured its padlock. It was
always exciting when he reached down to lift a dripping
stringer of fish. There were usually two or three bass, and
once we returned proudly along the path to the cottage while
I held the flashlight on a six-pound largemouth.

It has remained a special summer in my mind, rich with
memories of swimming and bass fishing and sleeping on the
porch, with crickets and whippoorwills filling the night. It
was a bucolic summer when my parents were still young, and
mixed with such boyhood memories is a brief episode that
took place on a grocery trip to Baldwin.

Our route into town crossed a trout stream, and my
mother stopped the Oldsmobile just beyond the bridge when
a solitary fisherman caught my eye. The little river flowed
swiftly, tumbling past the trestlework of the bridge, and there
were mayflies dancing in the sunlight. Its riffles seemed restless over the pale bottom, where cedar sweepers and deadfalls intercepted its glittering currents. The counterpoint of
wind and river music filled the morning, its lyric images still
as sharply focused as yesterday after forty years.

The trout stream was utterly unlike the lukewarm shallows of the lake, tumbling clear and cold from springheads
in its cedar-swamp headwaters. Watercress thrived in the
seepage places below the bridge, and the passage of the river
only briefly touched the sunlight. Its ephemeral moments in
the sun were quickly lost again in its sheltering cedars and
willows. The bright currents seemed startlingly alive there,
collecting a rich palette of foliage and sunlight in its swiftly
changing prisms, until their lyric threnodies seemed to promise a world of half-understood puzzles.

The most pervasive memory of that summer remains the
solitary fisherman working patiently upstream, the swift
shallows tumbling between his legs, while his silk line
worked its lazy choreography in that August morning.

It was the genesis of a lifelong odyssey in search of trout
and salmon, a pilgrimage that started there in Michigan and

has since carried me to the remote corners of the world. There are many happy echoes of those travels, memories embracing rivers and river people and the richly colored fish themselves, and with a cold rain misting through the black-trunked trees, thoughts of fishing and butter-colored colts-foot in the sheltered places help pass this season of discontent.

[1976]

21

Summer

Our summer begins with haying in the meadows, the line between seasons marked as windrows of timothy, vetch, and clover. There are sultry days of sticky shirts and hay chaff down your back and cold beer and diving into the river off the village bridge. Summer can be a fickle time too, as Schwiebert points out in this essay, with days of windblown cold and rain.

Such was our summer past—so wet that first cuttings were a month late while the rivers ran bankfull into August. Hatching-insect activity continued in the high water, though, and the fishing was excellent, if different from summers past. Brown trout slashed at emerging caddis at the very edge of the alders rather than in midstream. Flooded backwaters held rising trout too, instead of the more usual horde of tadpoles. We could take fish wherever we could find relatively quiet water and listened with wry amusement to other anglers complaining at the bridges about how the high water had ruined the season.

It wears its subtle masks gracefully.

Over the past fifty years, its disguises have played across a theater of seasons, ceaselessly changing and filled with small surprises. Each summer has its own subtle character and moods.

Some years it arrives early. Spring is unpredictable and deceptive, mixing late blizzards with soft winds, circling north in front of the storms and smelling faintly of the Caribbean. Our fishing is often subject to fickle weather. The fly hatches trickle off in a false spring, sometimes before the fishing is legal. April squalls can atrophy the hatches too. Heat often arrives early in some years, with a midday sun that burns surprisingly on our faces, and works deep into the thawing earth.

The spring peepers have finally stopped their shrill vespers, and the summer night has other sounds. The trees are fully dressed now, their ripening buds swelling and unfolding, until their branches are interlocking labyrinths of leaves. The leaves can flutter in a sudden wind, showing their pale faces when they sense the smell of rain, and heat lightning flickers long after midnight.

Other summers prove quixotic and tardy.

Bitter rain chills the orchards, scattering the fruit-tree blossoms in the grass, and water glitters in the cornfields. The creeks are silty and swollen. Late blizzards still surprise us, particularly in our western mountains, shattering trees with their icy blight. Hatches are muted and sporadic. April mayflies are sometimes still emerging at the threshold of early summer, and their glistening spinners wait quietly to mate, elegantly patient under porch eaves and bridges.

The chill weather can persist stubbornly.

Such ripening mayflies molt in the sheltered places, splitting the brittle skin at their tiny shoulders, and stripping their shiny wings free. They work their slim bodies from the shuck patiently, until its skin hangs pale and tangled from their delicate tails.

Old urgencies stirring restlessly, they wait for warm evenings with little wind. The mating swarms are ephemeral and fragile too. But sometimes the warm evenings dissolve into

312

squalls. The mating mayflies are driven from the riffles, and they are forced to wait. Sometimes they atrophy and perish before they can lay their eggs. Such failures will echo into the following years.

Even in its full ripening, summer can have a quicksilver quality. It seldom dovetails completely with our winter daydreams. Expectations are as fleeting as mayflies.

Fitful summers are metaphors too.

Each becomes a scrapbook of happy echoes, starting with our memories of boyhood. There were grasshopper meadows in the dairy-farm pastures in northern Michigan, where the brook trout waited in their leafy tunnels, and sedges hopscotched at their egg laying on a sawmill pond. Our twilight rivers were alive with rising trout. Such memories are richly grown across the years, like the moss-covered ledges that shelter the half-glimpsed secrets of a favorite pool.

The cowboys on a family ranch in Colorado were wry about their summer weather. *We've only got two seasons out here in these mountains,* they explained jokingly. *There's high school bands and Coors and fireworks on the Fourth of July—and there's winter!*

With its snowmelt finally past, the first mayflies started coming in the headwaters of the Arkansas. Its alpine meadows were alive with lupine and paintbrush and balsamroot. Blue flax and coralroot and gentians are fingerprints of summer. The mountains were dark serrations against a cloudless sky before breakfast, but puffy scraps of cumulus would gather steadily through each morning, until fly hatches in the shadow of Mount Massive triggered sporadic rises of trout in the rain.

Other summers were spent fishing in other corners of the world. Our memories expand our horizons too, until our scrapbook of boyhood echoes is like the intricate patterns of a Pennsylvania quilt or the delicate window traceries of Vezelay or Chartres.

Salmon memories include the almost-frightening George, its wild torrents draining a labyrinth of boulders and stunted forests and pale lichens, in the empty heart of the

313

Labrador. Salmon fishing is a mixture of patience and failure and hope. There were mornings at Ashford Castle and Ballynahinch, with its castle beats and casting weirs, and summer squalls building in the Irish mountains beyond the Derryclare Butts.

Stags drifted through the trees at Braemar, ghosting restlessly with their summer hinds, antlers still hung with tatters of velvet. The herds drifted in soft green fields along the storied Braes of Mar. Across the iron bridge from the gatekeeper's house is a sprawling shooting lodge belonging to the Duke of Fife. Queen Victoria spent a summer there in 1848 and loved the valley so much that Prince Albert started to acquire the highland acreages that would later evolve into Balmoral.

The old shooting manor where she stayed is called Mar Lodge. *'Tis a fine old house,* our ghillie explained beside the famous pool called Queen's Favorite. *Most salmon fishermen think 'tis only a famous salmon-fly dressing, but 'tis a fine old house too!*

There were also mornings so quiet at Laerdalsøyri, in its steep mountain-walled valley above Oslo, that I could hear the river almost hissing its swift course toward the Sognefjord. The horse carts moved along the narrow street toward the ferry slips below the village. Laerdal mornings were filled with a lyric spilling of waterfalls in the steep escarpment above the hotel.

Other rivers tumble swiftly in the mind.

Alta drains the Arctic heart of Lapland, in a glacier-scarred highland like the barrens that surround the Labrador, and we fished it from graceful Karasjok longboats. Målangsfössen is a single pool, its fierce currents circling a frightening caldron the size of a football stadium. Its boatmen take turns back-rowing against its flow, their anglers fishing patiently through the long summer nights, while the others warm themselves at cookfires on the rocky beach.

The Flåm is a gentle poem in its wildflower meadows. It holds fish in less than three miles of water, where the ferryboats come into a quiet harbor under its pretty Victorian hotel. The Gaula has a high waterfall just above tidewater, and a big fishing house with the silhouettes of giant salmon carved into its sitting-porch floor. There were pools we shared on the Driva with a British tea planter from Ceylon, and another summer we shared the lower pools with Roger Gailliard and the storied Charles Ritz. His casting was still poetry itself in those years.

The Årøy Steeplechase is a wild reach of water, and its currents once sustained salmon that averaged thirty-three pounds, powerful fish with armor polished in the sea. *My river is filled with tigers,* Nicholas Dennisoff shook his head when I once brought a big sea-trout to the fishing house above the Årøy. *My river is filled with tigers—and you waste our time with field mice!*

Summer memories circle in quiet eddies.

Sculptured snowfields are still melting in the high Sawtooths and Absarokas, their shapes echoing strange beasts that survive in fossils and bogs, blocking the gravel passes between half-forgotten towns like Tincup and Humbug Creek and Telluride.

Yellow-head blackbirds are calling in the cattails along Silver Creek at Picabo, with the twilight still soft on the Timmerman Hills. The gathering dark comes swiftly on the Henry's Fork, with its afterglow still surprisingly bright on the Tetons, and the mating of its sandhill cranes sounds like children beating on pots and pans. Their mating liturgies fill the paintbrush bottoms along the river, shrill footnotes of half-forgotten seas.

The noisy long-legged cranes are echoes of a planet still awash in their life-giving salinity. *Listen to them out there in the dark!* I stopped fishing and shivered. *Listen to the cranes!* Their choreography is older than time itself, its harsh clamor struggling to be heard across the centuries, like the tiny seashells in a mountain pass.

[1983]

315

22

Salmon or
Steelhead?

It's easy to make conversation within some groups of fly fishermen. All you need to say is that Atlantic salmon are superior to steelhead or vice versa, and the argument will go on all night without your having to say another word. One key is Schwiebert's comment in this essay to the effect that there are very few people who have caught enough of both sorts of fish to make any adequate judgment. Schwiebert is himself one of those few. Lee Wulff is another. Both men have compared salmon and steelhead in print, and both have wisely declined to declare one superior to the other.

I've caught northwestern steelhead and also those in some Great Lakes tributaries. I've caught salmon in the Northeast and in Europe. Some trips have been better than others. Some fish have fought harder than others. But there has been no generalization possible, and I think I'll quite happily continue fishing for both.

It started at Slopbucket Lake in Alaska, with a film of ice on the water and thick frost on the planes. It was still bitter cold at breakfast. The pilot made a series of circling trips in the skiff to clear the lake, and it took an hour with hemp ropes and hot buckets of water to melt the ice from the Cessna.

The pilot had wakened me before daylight. *It's clear from Yakutat to Nome,* he said, *and the wind has stopped—let's try for Kodiak today.*

We crossed the Aleutian Range at Gibraltar Lake and followed the broken coast toward Cape Douglas. Ebony cliffs and skerries and lava beaches passed under our floats. Rivers spilled over cliffs into the sea. The volcano offshore was smoking fitfully, and pale green lakes under the glaciers at Cape Douglas were filled with icebergs. Beyond the cape, there was a solitary bear walking a black beach piled high with salt-bleached logs. The deadfalls were littered with orange buoys and glass floats lost by Japanese netters.

We stopped to fish at Uganik, finding a shoal of dark coho at its inlet and a few small steelhead below the lake. The poplars were bright yellow, and we sat on the floats eating lunch in a surprisingly hot October sun.

Later we passed the big canneries at Larsen Bay, crossing the steep bear-grass hills to Karluk. The tides were wrong for landing, in the mountain-rimmed lagoon famous for its coho fishing. We flew upriver between low hills crisscrossed with a scrimshaw of bear trails, into a world that looked surprisingly like California wine country.

We circled the big pool at Karluk Lake, over an immense shoal of spawning coho. Small schools of rainbows and char held below them, stealing eggs. Other big fish were holding where the lake currents gather and slide into the river, and we landed at the salmon-census cabin, laughing at its mixed *sgraffiti* of bear comments. The party quickly attacked the big bulb-nosed coho, hauling in a series of scarlet olive-backed fish with straining rods, shouting and laughing. The smaller fish lying in the shallows were more intriguing, and I quickly hooked and lost two fresh coho. The pilot shouted that we were running out of time to reach Iliamna when a silvery fish porpoised, sixty feet out.

I dropped a Black Comet well above the fish, reaching a mend upstream as it settled, and quickly mended the line again. The strike stopped the fly with a curious half-sucking pull, and a savage wrench exploded downstream into three wild cartwheels that pulled free.

What in hell was that? the pilot shouted across the river.

Steelhead! I yelled back weakly.

What else! he laughed.

Such wild fish are the steelhead of myth and legend, the great fish that beat an angler before he can gather his wits and follow. It is such fish that inspired writers like Zane Grey and Clark Van Fleet and Roderick Haig-Brown. Steelhead are not alone. Atlantic salmon have their charisma too, and a rich theology that has evolved since Walton called them the King of Fishes in 1653.

Explosive fish are the wild steelhead and salmon that stalk our memories and dreams. We forget the winter steelhead that stop a fly in the sinking-line belly of the pool as sluggishly as a big catfish and struggle lethargically onto the beach. Writers ignore the steelhead almost black with spawning that stops a fly drifting with a three-shot dropper in a cedar-sweeper jam and fights like an exhausted heavyweight, leaning against his opponent and hooking sullen punches into his shoulders and elbows. Each fish is unique. No salmon fisherman thinks about the salmon hooked late in the run, its silvery armor gone tea-colored and mottled, its clumsy jumps like a Japanese wrestler attempting a pirouette. We forget the fish hooked on a small river in Iceland, stubbornly refusing to leave its tiny pool under the sheltering banks, with no room to display its speed and strength. It is always the explosive fish we remember, thrust from the river like a mythic sword, like a ballerina tightroping a performance precisely between grace and sanity.

Steelhead and salmon.

Their worlds are too varied for simple yardsticks. The fish are similar in character, but in many ways they are completely different too. Arguments about their merits are noisy—and utterly incomplete. Such disputes are too deeply rooted in regional pride and storytelling to permit anything like a truce.

Certitude is typical of anglers who have not fished both species, or have not fished both species widely. Myth permits

318

arguments that evolve farther and farther from truth. Wide experience with both species throughout their distribution should tell us that certitudes about their behavior are both doubtful and silly. Life should tell us that certitudes are better left to the Vatican.

Several years ago I fished the Grimsá with a steelhead fisherman from California. It was late in the season, with only a few bright fish still coming, and there had been a drought throughout Iceland. The river was low and few of its pools were fishing.

They're overrated, he told me firmly after beaching his third salmon. *Tie one tail-to-tail with a steelhead, and he'd tow it around the river.*

You've never caught a fresh-run salmon.

Pantywaists, the angler insisted. *Our steelhead would wipe their eyes!*

Maybe, I said quietly, *but ask yourself how much is the river and how much is the fish—and how long they've both been out of the salt.*

Another old friend has often shared salmon beats with me and has recently been fishing in British Columbia, working a small river over September steelhead. His Grimsá fishing has always focused on the bright salmon coming early from the fjord, and his verdict on steelhead was almost lukewarm.

Steelhead take well and jump a lot, he said sadly, *but they just don't fight like salmon.*

And the debate continues hotly. Steelhead addicts who have never fished Atlantic salmon think they are overblown, effete fish that echo a world of Norfolk shooting jackets and flies as intricate as Victorian scrollwork eaves. Salmon fishermen still think of steelhead in terms of frostbitten fingers and winter gravel-bar fires and books written about drifting spoons and cherry bobbers and roe wrapped in scraps of pantyhose.

Steelheaders like to think their fish are symbols of the Pacific frontier, of the hardy trappers and sourdough prospectors and lumberjacks who tamed it. Salmon fishermen

319

like to think their fish are echoes of chivalry, cast for them in tweed hacking coats and soft hats woven in the Hebrides, and remember that salmon were called the most stately fish in fresh water when the storied *Boke of St. Albans* was published in 1496.

Both myths are parochial and true.

Some salmon fishermen have paid sufficient dues on steelhead, probably more than the steelheaders who have fished salmon. Yet too many salmon fishermen think of steelhead as roe-eating roughnecks, and too many steelheaders think about salmon the way Texas oilriggers think about Harvard and Yale.

Both viewpoints are silly and a little sad. Such city-mouse and country-mouse quarrels still plague us, and not just in our fishing. Steelhead and salmon are simply too varied for easy pigeonholing, and there are surprising differences within each species itself. Summer steelhead and their winter-run cousins have completely different life cycles, and the primary techniques of fishing them are different. The North Umpqua summer fish are not like their winter cousins on other Oregon rivers like the Newhalem and Clackamas. Farther north, summer steelhead on the Stillaguamish have little in common with fish ascending the Kalama and Skagit after Christmas. California fish still enter rivers between Big Sur and Oregon and offer fine winter sport. The Deschutes is still a great summer-run fishery, spilling north toward the Columbia through its sprawling desert canyons. Its character is shared by other rivers, like the Clearwater and Salmon in Idaho. Each river has its discrete populations. Winter-run steelhead are usually taken deep, with flies drifted along the bottom on high-density lines and shooting heads. Summer fish are caught with such methods too, but when conditions are right, they also succumb to floating-line methods. Such character makes them highly prized, but because a summer steelhead has a much longer juvenile life in its parent river, its winter-run relatives suffer less predation before reaching the sea and are more plentiful.

Steelhead are still found between Los Angeles and the Gulf of Alaska. Biologists tell us that no true pelagic steelhead

are found in our Bering Sea drainages, although nonmigratory rainbows are indigenous to its watersheds as far north
as the Kisaralik and Aniak in the Kuskokwim drainage. Afognak and Kodiak also have steelhead runs. Others enter a
series of small coastal rivers in the Shelikof Strait, between
Kamishak Bay and the mountainous fjords east of Ugashik
and Mother Goose Lake.

These Shelikof fish start coming in late summer and fall,
and their behavior varies with the weather. Sometimes they
act like winter fish, coming only to flies worked slow and
deep, but I have also caught them with floating lines and
small wet flies in the small rivers across from Kodiak.

Steelhead tactics must vary throughout their native
range, but our transplanted steelhead populations in the
Great Lakes are still more different.

The transplanted winter fish found throughout the Great
Lakes are not typical of their ancestry. Perhaps displacing
them into unfamiliar habitats—from western Lake Superior
to Lake Memphremagog in Vermont—has changed their old
behavior. Forty years ago, cracker-barrel experts had surrendered these fish (Pacific Coast fishermen still believed such
myths about their steelhead too) to bait-fishing colleagues,
seldom attempting to try flies. It was a few Michigan fishermen who worked out the shot-dropper technique on rivers
like the Muskegon and Little Manistee. It uses a triangle
swivel with a shot dropper and a tippet, which gets the fly on
the bottom quickly in tangles of deadfalls and sweepers.
Other transplanted steelhead fisheries have long existed in
the Finger Lakes of western New York, the Esopus in the
Catskills, and the Willoughby in northern Vermont. Tributaries throughout the Great Lakes in both Canada and the
United States hold steelhead today, and the Michigan shot
dropper is found on both sides of the border.

Pacific anglers have scolded their colleagues on the
Brule and Pere Marquette for fishing a shot dropper, not
understanding that the lines of drift on these heartland rivers
are brief, and there is seldom much room to cast. Other
Pacific critics have scolded them for fishing steelhead that are
dark and ripening to spawn (conveniently forgetting that

Kispiox and Babine fish are often quite dark when they are caught), although some Michigan fish are often bronze and already dark when they first enter their rivers. Such zealotry tells us that Walton was wrong; angling is neither contemplative nor soothing, judging from the pickle-minded disputes it triggers.

Wild steelhead fisheries offer discrete genetic stocks that vary widely in their behavior and fishing tactics, and Atlantic salmon are not completely alike either.

Several years ago, our riverkeeper in Iceland found that a party of doctors intended to fish only dry flies during the week they had booked, as they had for many years together on the Jupiter in Canada. The doctors were stubbornly filled with the certitudes of science, insisting that a species should respond the same way throughout its natural distribution. Since the rivers in Iceland have mainly tiny aquatic Diptera to sustain their fish, mixed with a few small caddisflies and aquatic moths, there is little to trigger a rise. Such salmon behavior is relatively common in Canada, which has more plentiful fly life.

You've got to talk with them, the riverkeeper insisted in desperation. *They won't catch anything with dry flies—maybe dragging a Bomber, but not with regular dries!*

I'll try, I promised unhappily.

Although others took salmon regularly, the doctors fished dry flies for six days without moving a fish, and caught only two their last morning fishing a small wet pattern. It was an expensive failure.

But six years later, a series of atypical factors combined to trigger some dry-fly sport on that same fishery. The spring ice-out had purged the bottom of a long flat that seldom holds fish until late summer. It was strangely holding fish in early July. These circumstances combined with an infestation of red-legged *Bibio* flies, small terrestrial insects that pupate in the moist stream margins. They are seldom important except in rare years of peak population cycles. The flies emerged for about ten days. The levels of flow were perfect to hold fish in the pool called Grafahylur, and there was little wind that week, which is unusual too. The *Bibio* flies came struggling down the lines of drift, and the fish sampled them consistently. There *was* some dry-fly fishing that week, enough to convince several anglers that the salmon in Iceland *would* take dry flies readily. But their luck was more complex than they knew, with pieces of a puzzle falling accidentally into place like the tumblers in a bank vault, and it is unlikely that the same conditions will occur again.

Canadian salmon will take dry flies consistently, and summer steelhead will take them too, when conditions are right. Salmon in Europe and Iceland are seldom caught with dry flies on a drag-free float. Dan Callaghan fished dry flies exclusively on steelhead one winter on the Umpqua and took fish when the Oregon weather was right.

Winter steelhead will take dries, Callaghan concluded drily, *but don't hold your breath.*

Atlantic salmon are highly unpredictable, but there are some relatively consistent patterns in their behavior. The United Kingdom (excepting minor runs in rivers draining the chalkdowns of Hampshire and Wiltshire) lacks the water fertility and latitude to sustain heavy runs of salmon. Norwegian rivers drain such extensive snowfields and glaciers, unlike other Atlantic salmon fisheries, that their problems of water chemistry and temperature and fishing tactics are unique. Ireland has dredged its salmon rivers and has crippled several with hydro projects. Its rivers drain both limestone bedrock, with its rich alkaline fertility, and peatbogs so acid and ale-dark they strangle aquatic life.

Canada has a varied palette of salmon fisheries: Newfoundland and the Labrador are primarily old Precambrian geologies, relatively infertile and yet sustaining fish in their remote drainages. Subarctic latitudes and lakes are part of the secret. Labrador rivers seem almost like Scottish and Norwegian fisheries, except that their fish respond more greedily to dry flies. Anticosti rivers and the Miramichi watersheds are optimal dry-fly fisheries that fish best in late summer and early fall, but anglers familiar with such sport are ill-prepared to deal with the tactical puzzles of Norway or Iceland. Big Canadian rivers like the Restigouche and Grand Cascapedia and Moise offer still different riddles, with big freight-canoe pools much like those of the Alta and Vossa in Norway. Sinking lines and bigger flies are among their secrets, particularly early in the summer.

Iceland lies astride the North Atlantic Rift, with its volcanoes and geysers and hot springs, and is completely different. Its rivers are relatively short, interrupted where lava flows and earthquakes create impassable waterfalls. Its fish are relatively fresh-run (I have caught salmon with sea lice in their highest pools) and respond unusually well to tube- and prawn-flies obviously suggestive of food, as well as surprisingly small patterns (size 12 and 14 doubles) fished on floating lines.

Across the world of their full zoogeography, Atlantic salmon are a chess game of happy riddles.

The basic wet-fly techniques of Atlantic salmon fishing are virtually the same for steelhead, with the entire spectrum of floating and sinking-tip and full-sinking lines.

Such tactics involve a conventional wet-fly presentation quartering downstream. The casting angle is about forty-five degrees across swift currents, becoming less acute as current speeds drop, until casts are made almost directly across a glassy flow. The fly is simply allowed to swing back across on a fixed length of line. Wars can be started over simply letting the fly swing without rod-tip action, or teasing the fly with a subtle tip-rhythm throughout its swing. With enough current to swim the fly through its entire quarter-circle, it is allowed to swing until it hangs directly downstream and is retrieved in a teasing series of six-inch pulls before lifting into another cast.

The wading angler takes a step and repeats the same casting angle and fly swing. Canoe-drop fishing on a big Canadian river involves letting the fishermen down two to three feet on the anchor line. Norwegian fishermen use river-worthy prams and Lapp longboats, with boatmen back-rowing against the current to let the fly swing through precisely below each previous cast. These principles are basic in fishing both steelhead and salmon, covering water with a patient series of precise, concentric swings.

Fly speed is everything.

Steelheaders usually mend and mend throughout the swing to work the fly deep and kill its swing. Salmon fishermen tease the fly through and even retrieve when it reaches quiet water downstream to extend fly speed. (This has also worked for me on summer-run steelhead.) But continual mending and not mending pinpoints an intriguing difference often found between steelhead and salmon: steelhead usually like flies worked deep and mended into their lines of drift, while salmon like a teasing fly speed and will readily leave their lines of drift.

Dan Callaghan is among the skilled steelheaders who fish the North Umpqua, perhaps the most famous steelhead fishery in the world. Callaghan helped me take my first Umpqua steelhead years ago and later joined me in Europe for his first attempt at salmon. Our entire party was taking fish consistently, but Callaghan went fishless for two days.

Come with me and watch, he suggested over dinner. *Tell me what I'm doing wrong.*

Callaghan fished while I watched from a low cliff. His casts were flawless, but he mended line immediately and kept mending throughout the entire drift in the Umpqua style. Twice I saw salmon start to follow his fly swing only to drift back when he mended his swing.

What's wrong? he called.

You moved two fish that stopped when you mended line, I yelled back. *You mended them off the fly.*

What should I try?

Rest the pool a few minutes, I suggested, *and fish it through again without mending.*

Callaghan promptly hooked his first salmon, and it made the point clearly. Steelhead are usually worried by fly speed, while salmon are attracted to its teasing swing. But Callaghan taught *me* a lesson that week too. It was darkly overcast, the barometer had nearly collapsed, but it was not raining. The fish were unusually dour. Dan took a salmon behind me, and I laughed.

Okay, I yelled. *What were you doing?*

Callaghan had been daydreaming, and had reverted to

mending steadily in the Umpqua style. His flies were working deeper than mine with less fly speed, and it worked. I started through again with a series of wrist-rolling mends and moved a fish. Two casts later it was hooked. It taught me something about salmon fishing with a foul barometer.

Steelheaders have recently adapted the full spectrum of floating-line salmon techniques to their summer-run fish. Anglers have been experimenting with conventional dry flies, skittering patterns, the skimming tactics of the riffling hitch, waking flies, salmon Buck Bugs and Bombers, and the British greased-line technique. The greased-line method involves a small wet fly cast across a smooth current and fished through its teasing swing with a series of mends. It was first developed at Cairnton in Scotland, where Arthur H. E. Wood held a beat of long, smooth-flowing pools on the lower Dee. Several seasons back, I was privileged to fish his water for several days, including famous pools such as Grey Mare and Malt Steep. Their silken currents were perfect for his greased-line theories on salmon, and an inventive generation of summer-run steelheaders has transplanted them to the Deschutes and Grande Ronde and Clearwater.

The Wood greased-line method takes its name from a time of braided silk lines that were dressed with red-stag fat to float properly. Simple wet-fly tactics are more effective after coming partly through the fly swing, with the fly sunk to its optimal depth and speed before starting back toward the surface. Steelheaders who mend steadily with a floating line call their technique greased-line fishing, and it is a useful variation on Wood, but their mending serves a purpose that pinpoints the major difference between steelhead and Atlantic salmon.

Steelheaders mend steadily to reduce fly swing and fly speed, but Wood's purpose was to achieve and extend the length of a teasing fly-speed swing. Once his cast had settled into its precise salmon-teasing speed, his mends were intended to keep the fly swimming at its proper speed much longer through its quartering circle. More simply put, steelhead mends reduce fly speed and the salmon mends sustain it. The difference is everything, and it delineates the character of both species. Sometimes they are alike, and sometimes they are poles apart.

This summer I returned to Norway, where I had fished extensively twenty years ago, to fish salmon on the Gaula. Earlier I had explored other rivers, but I had never fished the Gaula near Trondheim, which has been producing fish even when its sister rivers offer lukewarm sport. Swedish friends insisted that it was a serious sin of omission.

Our week had low water when I arrived, and torrential rains left the Gaula high and discolored on our last afternoon, but I managed better than a salmon each day. The last morning I drew Sverrehølen, a sprawling pool between steep rapids where salmon like to stop. Its shallow throat spilled against big cobblestones and alders, sliding into the deepening belly of the pool. The thick alders ended about halfway down, where a goatherder's cottage stands under a single tree. Depending on the river levels, Sverrehølen can surrender a fish anywhere in its three hundred yards. It had already given me two salmon that week, including a bright henfish better than twenty-five pounds.

The ghillie sat patiently on the rocky beach while I started at the throat of the pool. There was nothing in the places where I had moved fish earlier that week. I fished through the holding lie at the bottom of the alders, where my neighbor James Gray had taken a fine salmon that week, but no fish showed. The Gaula was high and strong that morning. It took deep wading until my fly boxes were nearly awash, and throwing the entire line to reach the fish in the gathering tail shallows below the goatherder's hut.

The big Sheep pattern was working through its swing, when the smooth currents bulged and a giant boil rolled up behind the fly. It was still coming, almost into the slack water downstream, and I started a smooth retrieve to extend its speed. There was a strong pull and the salmon was hooked. It had stalked the fly throughout its entire swing.

The fish moved sullenly upstream, with immense dignity and strength, angrily shaking its head. The ghillie was grinning and I thought we were in control.

Suddenly the fish exploded downstream and left the

pool. I stumbled from the shallows. We were running down the long cobblestone bar with a nearly empty reel. My backing was almost gone. The salmon stopped, holding easily in the strong rapids, and I had just recovered the backing when it exploded again. It emptied the reel and stopped again, and I reeled wildly.

He's getting tired, the ghillie said.

The fish drifted back stubbornly into a channel against our bank. *He doesn't seem to know it yet,* I replied, trying to pressure the salmon from downstream. *What will we do if we can't stop him this time?*

We were wading back toward the fish across wide, rocky shallows. The salmon was holding in the deep currents along the bank, and it was thirty yards upstream to a crossing point we could wade. We had followed the fish almost a mile. It still shook its head harshly. Another reel-emptying run would reach the wild chutes downstream, with huge boulders blocking our route and cliffs on the opposite bank. The channel between our position and the bank looked deep.

I don't like it. The fish still felt strong and impossible to turn. *He's still awfully strong—I think we should decide how to follow him again.*

We'll hold him, the ghillie insisted. *He's tired.*

I don't like it, I said.

We worked gingerly upstream to cross above the fish and reach the far bank safely. We had still not seen the salmon when it turned slowly, gathering strength and speed in that deep channel. The reel was frighteningly shrill. It was too late to circle above the salmon now, and we followed grudgingly, trying to hold it. Twice I burned my fingers on the backing, and the fish had almost reached the rapids.

We're going to get soaked, I laughed.

The ghillie took my old Leica. We each grabbed the other's collar and started across the channel, well over the plimsoll line and gunwales completely awash. It was surprisingly deep, but we hopscotched through, dancing to find brief toeholds on the boulders and floundering. It was chin-deep and deeper, but our arms were still locked when we found good bottom and clambered gratefully ashore.

He's still going, I sighed.

The fish was well into the rapids, and it was hopeless, steeplechasing down the boulders in pursuit. The reel was empty and we were soaked. We looked at each other, still dripping like otters, and laughed helplessly. The fly had finally pulled out. The line was fouled in the rocks, and only my hat and camera were still dry.

Steelhead or salmon?

You tell me.

[1987]

23

Fall

A fisherman's fall is a time of bittersweet choices. In spring I can choose a particular pool to fish knowing that the next riffle or another river will be just as good tomorrow. In the fall just about everything happens at once and then disappears with November.

I'll fish the Battenkill for rising brown trout on these Indian summer days, and then make a hurried trip south for striped bass in the surf. I'll remember spectacular displays of frosted grasses along Montana's Big Horn River and wish I was there again, or perhaps farther west peering into a riffle for the silver-gray shape of a steelhead. And by mid-November I'll probably give up on October. As Schwiebert so correctly intimates in this essay, the only trouble with fall is that there's so little of it.

It has been hot these past weeks.

Spring came late, with the dogwoods and orchards behind schedule, and friends report in their letters that the early summer was unusually cool all across the country. There were fine hatches on many rivers. The salmonfly hatches were particularly heavy too, but a fierce winter had left such snowfields in the high country that many famous rivers ran milky until midsummer. The fish never saw the flies.

It has been a strange year.

The August heat quickly made us forget how cool the early summer had been. It shimmered in the trees, like the ice-wagon heat of our boyhood summers, a choking heat that filled the senses like the angry crucible of some Ohio hayloft under its corrugated roof, or the searing heat of Kansas grain elevators with a harvest coming in.

But the oppressive heat has finally broken. Early storms have swelled across the northern Rockies, building and spilling south across the prairies of Manitoba and Saskatchewan. The late-summer squalls quickly cleared the sailboats and sunbathers from the Great Lakes, and it has already snowed heavily in the wild mountains of Montana and northern Idaho.

Driving out toward the country post office, I discovered an immense flock of swallows resting on the telephone wires. Starlings were foraging in the cornfields beyond, and the morning felt surprisingly cool. The soft summery haze is gone from the first Appalachian ridges behind Princeton, and their tree-filled hills are crisp and blue.

The weather will change again. It will still be hot in the coming weeks, hot enough to shimmer out across the stubble fields, reducing the brooks to tepid trickles in the stones, until the trees in the distance float again in summer illusions of haze and mirage.

Summer can surrender grudgingly too.

But its heat seems more bearable, because we can sense something imperceptible in the wind, in the sharp morning light in the trees, in these restless gatherings of birds.

The coming fall is still only a faint mixture of preludes and premonitions. Its signs are unmistakable to anyone who still feels a circling of seasons in the blood. There is a chill in the wind, emptying scrollwork porches from Kennebunkport to Mackinac. The squirrels have lost their August lethargy and are busily working through the woods behind the house. Sunday morning there was a chainsaw humming like a shrill steel-jawed locust on the neighbor's ridge, and the cordwood piles are growing outside clapboard farmhouses in Vermont.

Border checkpoints are busy with families coming back from Quebec and Nova Scotia and Ontario, and lines of tractor rigs stand waiting farther west, hauling Kansas combines back from the wheat-field seas that fill the prairie provinces of western Canada. The salmon-boat quotas are also filled, and their crews are ashore in Alaskan ports like Sitka and Dillingham and Kodiak, with fat summer paychecks in their pockets.

Other signs lie outside the house. The swale fields are filled with mustard and wild carrots and pyeweed. It was warm and still yesterday, with a few cobwebs drifting delicately in the afternoon. But the most certain symptom came this morning, walking in a neighbor's overgrown orchard, when I flushed a fat woodcock.

Most fishermen who started out forty-odd seasons ago, in trout country that closed its season at Labor Day, still think of autumn as a time to put away their tackle.

But fall is a priceless season for fishing.

The August tides are alive with salmon ascending the rivers from the Tobique to the River of Whales, and fresh steelhead are running in the Rogue and Umpqua and Deschutes in Oregon. The late-summer runs are still holding in the lower Deschutes, although a fisherman must risk its mixture of rapids and desert heat and rattlesnakes, and I remember a fine three-fish twilight at Water Tower with the light warm on the pictograph cliffs upstream. Our season of heavy snowmelt has helped both salmon and steelhead to ascend the labyrinth of dams that chokes the Columbia drainages, and the bellwether fish have already reached the Salmon and Grande Ronde and Clearwater.

Steelhead are a harbinger of autumn, and September is a happy fulcrum between seasons. The summer doldrums are finally broken, and eastern fishermen flock back into the Berkshires and Catskills, to famous rivers like the Housatonic and Kinderhook and Beaverkill. September nights cool the geyser spillages in the Yellowstone country too, bringing the tepid Gibbon and Firehole to life again, and start the elk and buffalo drifting down from their high summer ranges. There are still blizzards of tiny *Tricorythodes* spinners in the mornings, on chalkstreams in Idaho like Silver Creek and its incomparable Henry's Fork, and dense twilight spinnerfalls of *Pseudocloëon* flies.

You've got to come back out here, Bill Mason wrote from Sun Valley. *You won't believe the fly hatches!*

September finds still more steelhead running from the Pacific, lithe ghosts flashing like polished Sheffield, searching restlessly upstream in rivers from San Francisco into the mountains of British Columbia, where they find spawning riffles on the Sustut and Kispiox and Babine.

September is my favorite season in Alaska too. Its immense runs of salmon are ebbing then, runs that turn entire riverbottoms silver and scarlet, filled bank-to-bank with restlessly milling fish. Big rainbows follow them upstream from lakes like Naknek and Kukaklek and Iliamna to steal *caviar rouge* from drainages in the Tikchik mountains to the smoking volcanoes of the Katmai.

You won't believe your eyes! Sonny Peterson promised the first time we took off from Naknek in his floatplane Cessna. *You'll see schools of big rainbows stealing eggs—rainbows so big you can spot them from the plane!*

Peterson was telling the truth. The Katmai rivers were alive with fish, churning schools of spawning sockeyes, scarlet fish mixed with pewter-colored rainbows pirating their ova. It was an exciting world, and we flew and fished it happily from the tidal moraines at Ugashik to Talarik, which winds sluggishly toward Lake Iliamna. There were shirt-sleeve lunches on gravelbars along the American, and there were nights that left a delicate skim of ice across the shallows, until it took an hour to strip the frost from the wings and floats at Slopbucket Lake.

October is sometimes better still. Late sockeyes hold the trophy-size rainbows in the shallow Katmai headwaters, but salmon fishing in eastern Canada has been winding down. The Michigan coho and silvery olive chinooks are still running, lying in dark flotillas in the Muskegon and Pere Marquette, and the steelhead are gathering in the marshy estuaries at Ludington and Manistee. The cottonwoods and aspens are bright with color in the northern Rockies, and the fall storms have started the browns migrating to spawn, in rivers like the Green and Yellowstone and Big Hole. Trophy hunters are seeking giant hookbills in the dark winter-chilled riffles of the Missouri and in the desert bottoms where the Green winds toward Flaming Gorge. Sometimes we have these October rivers to ourselves, in the delicious solitude that is missing along our rivers through the summer months, and a shot echoing from the ridges reminds us that our fishing is almost finished.

October is almost a perfect season in itself. Thinking about its bright mornings and soft afternoons, savoring those images with anticipation, I remember an old ruffed grouse hunter I knew in Wisconsin years ago. *Sure wouldn't go to hell to shoot partridges,* the old hunter shook his head and smiled. *But I'd fool around the edge until I fell in!*

October is a little like that.

[1983]

24

The Ghosts of Treasure Cay

The archaic spelling of complete *in this book's title refers directly to Walton's description in 1653 of* The Compleat Angler, *meaning one who is well rounded. The characterization certainly applies to Schwiebert, who is anything but archaic and whose angling exploits are most happily diverse. This bonefishing essay is one example from an author better known for his trout and salmon fishing. As you'll see, he is as adept at turning a phrase along a bonefish flat as he is along our favorite trout streams.*

You'll note in this essay his pointing out to his guide that the barracuda they catch are likely to be poisonous, which his guide dismisses. If you have the opportunity or inclination to eat 'cuda, don't! Schwiebert is quite correct in his warning, although Bahamians often seem able to eat these fish with impunity.

It was still and cool just after daylight, and I walked the perfect chalk-colored beach at Treasure Cay, enjoying the remarkable clarity and richness of its lagoon. Schools of

335

silvery little jacks and snappers and needlefish scattered when I approached. Stilts and oystercatchers were foraging in the sand, where the tide had left its fingerprints of shells and sand dollars and starfish. Beyond the pine-covered point, a solitary frigate bird explored the shallows of the reef. The *Miami Herald* had reported a fresh snowfall in Manhattan, with sanitation workers joining the street crews in clearing its drifts. The soft wind stirred, riffling the still surface of the bay, and moved restlessly in the pines and palmettos.

The faint wind smelled freshly of the sea, mixed with a perfume of scarlet hibiscus and flamboyant. Red-legged thrushes and yellowthroats were hunting breakfast in the hotel gardens, and a pair of bright-green hummingbirds were quarreling among the flowering vines. The sun still lingered below the horizon, but in the distance beyond Green Turtle Cay there was a single sailboat and the sun had tinted a few scraps of clouds into pink flamingos.

Should be a fine morning for bonefish, I thought.

The yacht mooring lies across a narrow part of the island, using the sheltered bay for its access. Big pleasure boats rocked lazily in the piling wash, along with a flotilla of fine sailboats and a pair of costly powerboats outfitted for billfishing. The brightwork on their decks and flying bridges and outriggers gleamed in the early sun, and I walked to meet the Preacher.

The old man was leaning back in his cane-seat chair, dozing under the white frangipani that hangs over the tackleshop porch. *Mornin'!* he grinned toothlessly. *Mornin', copm!*

Preacher was not a large man, although everything about his face and character and body seemed to spell size. His stomach and his good humor seemed to spill over in their free generosity. His voice was surprisingly lyrical and soft, almost a singsong whisper as the old man worked his boat pole and searched the tidal flats for bonefish. There was a wild half-rumbling quality to his laughter, which always ended in a choking, high-pitched giggle. The other guides often joked about his fierce temper. Several teeth were missing, and several others had gold fillings that flashed in the bright sunlight on the Bahamas bonefish flats. His hands and

leathery ears and happy grin were huge, like the chest and stomach that bulged in his faded shirt. His dungarees were cutoffs amputated just at his knees, beltless and rolled over under his spreading girth. His calves were hard and knobby, and his big pigeon-toed feet splayed across the planking.
Sorry I'm late! I lowered my gear to the boat.
Dass awright, copm! the Preacher shook his head. *Dem bonefish is spose to wait—and dem fish is waitin' awright!*
Should we fish the creeks? I asked.
Dass right, copm! he agreed.

The Bahamas were discovered on a soft October night in 1492, when a seaman on the *Pinta* named Rodrigo de Triana first sighted a silvery beach in the moonlight. Like many thinkers before that time, his expedition commander Christopher Columbus had become convinced that our world was spherical. But unlike the more competent astronomers of his century, who calculated its circumference with remarkable accuracy, Columbus thought it was slightly less than 20 percent of its actual size. His error helped Columbus to enlist the support of King Ferdinand and Queen Isabella for his three-ship expedition. Columbus planned to reach the fabled wealth of the Orient, sailing westward rather than traveling the arduous trade routes across Asia Minor, or attempting to circle the entire continent of Africa.

Rodrigo de Triana had actually sighted San Salvador, merely one of many outlying islands in the Bahamas, although Columbus and his company still believed they had reached the threshold of the Orient. Their ships wandered these subtropical seas, looking for the half-legendary cities of jewels and precious metals and jade built in the centuries after Kublai Khan, and finding only more Caribbean islands. Columbus added Rum Cay and Long Island to his ship's charts before sailing back toward Cuba, partially aware that he had stumbled across the peripheral landfalls of the New World.

Juan Ponce de Leon followed Columbus into the Bahamas in 1513, exploring Rum Cay, Mayaguana, Samana Cay, San Salvador, and Elbow Cay. Although their expedition had sought the capture of slaves at Bimini, Ponce de Leon and his party failed to locate that island, and passed northward to strike the coast of Florida.

Ponce de Leon was completely unaware that he had landed on the American continent, believing that Florida was merely another island larger than the others he had explored above Puerto Rico. His route back to its colonial harbor at San Juan, and the sheltered anchorage under the mammoth walls of its Morro fortifications, carried Ponce de Leon past the shallow reefs of the Bahamas Banks. His meticulous ship's logs described these shallow seas, and maritime history has proved the shallow Bahama passages remarkably perilous.

Perhaps the first cartographic references to the Bahamas appear in a chart prepared by Juan de Costa in 1500. His remarkably accurate map included Exuma, Rum Cay, Long Island, Caicos, Crooked Island, San Salvador, and Great Abaco and its beautiful Treasure Cay.

Vague references to these islands are also found in the charts prepared by Pieter Martyr in 1511, and twelve of them are precisely drawn in the famous Turin folio maps prepared a dozen years later. The hazardous coral reefs and limestone outcroppings in these subtropical Bahama passages were more quickly known to the Spanish mariners who sailed these waters than to the cartographers in the institutes of Italy and Portugal and Spain.

Throughout the sixteenth century, navigators returning to Portugal and Spain from ports in the Caribbean were terrified of the storms and shallows in the Bahamas. Seventeen ships from a single Spanish fleet foundered among the outlying islands and were lost in a wild storm off Abaco in 1595.

Britain claimed the Bahamas in 1629, when Charles I granted proprietary rights to both these subtropical islands and the relatively unmapped territories in the Carolinas. However, the king was captured and executed before his royal grants became established, although the proprietary rights were renewed with the restoration of the throne. The earlier French attempts to colonize the Bahamas had proved abortive, and little remains of their tenure on Abaco.

Like the Colonial settlers in Massachusetts, the first British settlers in the Bahamas were Puritans in search of religious freedom. William Sayle was their leader in Bermuda, and after several disputes in that colony, Sayle returned to England seeking help in 1647. His stories of persecution in Bermuda bore fruit. Sayle reached the Bahamas with a party of seventy settlers the following year. Sixty more Puritan immigrants arrived in 1649, along with food and clothing and other supplies donated in the Massachusetts colony. It was a hard existence in those first years, hunting whales and cutting braziletto scrub for dye wood, and these Puritans in the Bahamas had almost decided to give up when a treasure ship was salvaged off Abaco in 1657.

When Britain completed its first census in the Bahamas fourteen years later, almost eleven hundred people were recorded. Perhaps half of that population were slaves, and that mixture forms the principal ethnic structure of the Bahamas in our time. The American Revolution triggered a wave of refugees who had remained loyal to King George III, and these fresh immigrants trebled the population in the Bahamas in the five years that followed the surrender of Cornwallis at Yorktown in 1781. These colonial refugees from the American territories totaled almost eight thousand, including a fresh influx of slaves, and brought plantation life and cotton to the Bahamas.

Treasure Cay was a part of these changes in the late eighteenth century. Its charming little hotel is sited on a slender beach-pine peninsula in the Abacos, where hundreds of colonial refugees settled on Man-of-War Cay in the winter of 1782. There is a fine candy-striped lighthouse rising one hundred feet above the harbor at Hope Town, which is located on Elbow Cay.

Marsh Harbor is a settlement of several hundred people on Great Abaco, and like Treasure Cay farther north on the island, it has regular air service from both Miami and Nassau. Abaco had few inhabitants in the early years of the Puritan settlements on New Providence and Eleuthera, and its existing population is largely rooted in the migrations of the Loyalist refugees and their slaves, who fled the mainland after Yorktown. The highly skilled carpenters and ship-wrights on Man-of-War Cay, as well as the lobster fishermen and guides, are all descended from these immigrations in 1782.

The Preacher started his outboard, maneuvered his skiff skill-fully through the sailboat moorings, and we skimmed out the channel at full throttle toward the tidal creeks. Coming around the rocky point, we startled a somber heron and several egrets from the shallows, our wake spreading deep into the mangroves. There was a large bow wave ahead of our boat where we flushed a sand shark from a muddy backwa-ter, and we watched it undulate slowly into deeper water.

Dat shark be bad lazy, copm! the Preacher grinned.

The old man cut his outboard and drifted toward a lime-stone outcropping in the brackish flat, lifting his pole rhyth-mically to handle the boat. The limestone was scoured and undercut over centuries of September storms, and a good fish flashed in its shadows. Picking up my fly line and accelerat-ing its speed with an urgent left-hand haul, I dropped a pink bucktail shrimp over the swirl. It disappeared in a slashing strike.

Sass a dommed 'cuda! the old man cursed. *'Cuda, copm!*

The silvery barracuda made a strong run across the shal-low flat and threshed wildly. *Preacher,* I said, *you're right!*

Dommed ole 'cuda! he grumbled.

The slender fish fought bravely for its size, making a half dozen runs that reached into my backing. It was surprisingly strong, but its razor teeth somehow failed to sever my tippet, and I finally forced it back toward the gunwale of our boat. The Preacher struck skillfully with his gaff and wrestled the struggling barracuda aboard. His brass priest mercifully dis-patched the fish, but it smashed a gill-cover and blood splat-tered across the lapstrake hull. The barracuda shuddered as its eyes glazed and dimmed.

Get dat bastard 'fore he gets me! the Preacher said.

Makes pretty good sense! I agreed. *Barracuda can cut you pretty good if you're not careful with them!*

Dat 'cuda done bleed everyplace! the old man growled.

Better clean that off, I suggested.

Copm! The old man shook his head. *We swab down dat gurry 'fore it go bad sticky and smell sour!*

You eat barracuda at Treasure Cay? I asked.

The Preacher carefully wiped the duckboards and hull, and washed the bilge with several fruit cans of seawater. *Some folk dey tells dem 'cudas bad poison.* He grinned and his teeth flashed in the sun. *Some folk tells de spots is de poison too!*

Some places, I nodded, *the barracudas are poison!*

Dass right enough, copm! the Preacher agreed. *But our Abaco folk dey eats dem 'cudas regular—spots and stripes too!*

They must be okay. I laughed.

We searched all morning for bonefish, finding only two small schools that scattered like quail, long before we could cover them with a fly. We caught several more barracuda, and lost several flies to the teeth of others we hooked. Back in the mangrove shallows, we took a few snappers that darted out from the roots.

Finally the wind came up behind the island, cool and smelling of the Gulf Stream, and when the tide began gathering imperceptibly in the creek we decided to quit. The Preacher started rowing back toward the yacht channel while I took down my tackle and stowed my other gear in the duffle. There were laughing gulls beyond the tidal flats, and in the freshwater lagoon beyond the point we watched a kestrel hunting its breakfast in the shallows.

Copm? the other guides called laughingly when we cut the motor and coasted toward the dock. *Had some luck?*

Not much, I said ruefully. *Caught some barracuda.*

Copm! they laughed. *Everymon cotch 'cuda!*

The Preacher grinned toothlessly and fussed with the mooring lines. *Dass awright!* his eyes twinkled with suppressed laughter. *Copm gonna cotch a boatful ob bonefish tomorra!*

Where can we find a boatful of bonefish? I asked.

Copm, he said quietly, *behind dis here cay we got de biggest bonefish flats in dese here parts—call dat place de Marls!*

341

Lots of bonefish on that side? I asked.

Copm! the others agreed. *Marls got plenty bonefish.*

Okay! I said. *Meet you after breakfast!* The Preacher was waiting behind the boathouse when I walked down through the palm trees, and I helped him load a cooler of fruit and sandwiches and beer into his vintage Plymouth. It was a strange palette of color, its original lacquer scoured over years of traveling the coral-dust track of Abaco. The windshield was badly shattered, its glass terribly pitted with blowing sand, and it was virtually impossible to drive into a setting sun. The fabric was badly stained, and rusting springs protruded through the seats. The Preacher crawled across the front seat, because the driver's door was loosely wired shut with a coathanger.

Copm! the Preacher grinned. *We got a good mornin'!*

Chalk-colored dust billowed out behind the Plymouth when we left the pavement beyond the hotel, and the old man careened along the back roads of the island, fishtailing through axle-deep places in the sand. We surprised a small herd of wild pigs that was rooting along the twin-rut trace, and they bolted into the palmettos.

Copm, we sprise dem wild pigs! The Preacher flashed his gold-filled teeth. *We cotch dem wild pigs pretty good!*

You have lots of wild pigs on Abaco? I asked.

Copm, he grinned, *we got plenty pigs!*

The trace wound through the palmettos toward an overgrown inlet among the mangroves. Half concealed in marsh grass, the weathered pier provided a mooring for two small boats. Rainwater glistened under the duckboards, and the Preacher spent several minutes with a bailing can while I transferred our gear from the Plymouth.

Copm, we ready! he said finally.

The small freshwater creek was overgrown and mysterious. The labyrinths of mangrove roots rose from the dark water, mahogany colored and encrusted with tiny mussels. Bitterns and cattle egrets and terns watched our passage toward the estuary. The Preacher dipped his paddle into the still, tea-colored creek, stroking deep and slow until he raised the dripping blade while we drifted toward the sea.

Baitfish darted ahead of our boat. Baby jacks and mangrove snappers bolted into the shadows, and swamp cuckoos were trilling in the brush. The tiny creek finally widened into its marshy estuary, where a huge flock of spoonbills roosted in a thicket.

So this is the Marls, I thought.

The tidal estuary spread into an immense chalk-soft flat reaching to the horizon except for a few mangrove shoals and tidal bars. The Marls stretch along the entire western shore of Abaco, spreading hundreds of miles along its completely undeveloped coastline. These huge flats lie seventy-five miles across the channel to Grand Bahama and its famous bonefish club at Deep Water Cay.

Both islands are prime spawning and feeding grounds for some of the largest bonefish in the Caribbean. Fish of six to twelve pounds are relatively common there, and even bigger fly-caught bonefish are taken each season. Sometimes these trophy fish cruise in small schools, but the really large fish always forage alone, solitary shadows that drift like ghosts over the pale bottom.

Copm! the Preacher said. *Marls got plenty bone!*

We hooked a good fish almost immediately, but its swift flight quickly stitched my fly line through the mangrove roots, breaking the tippet. Several small bonefish came restlessly across the flats, tailing and stirring up blossoms of muddy water. My pink shrimp imitation dripped ahead of the school, and I let it settle while they approached, starting a slow-stripping retrieve. We held our breath when a pewter-colored shadow darted forward and seized the fly.

Bonefish! I said happily.

The Preacher giggled with excitement and planted his push pole in the marl to steady the skiff. The fish was small, perhaps two or three pounds, but its reel music was sweet when it burned a hundred yards of backing from my old Hardy. Pumping and reeling steadily, we worked the fish back toward the waiting net. When it finally saw us silhouetted against the sky, it bolted again, and I raised my arms high to hold the line free of the water. It was a circling run almost as fast as the first, and the backing audibly sliced the surface.

Bone! the Preacher sang softly. *You old bone!*

Finally the old man netted the fish, unhooked the pink shrimp fly, and released it with a giggle. The Preacher clearly loved his bonefish and their crystalline feeding shallows. Several times I found him daydreaming, watching an osprey stalking baitfish in the mangroves, or the interlocking circles of a frigate bird.

Bone, you ole bone! His singsong was deep and scarcely audible. *Where you hidin' youself dis mornin', you ole bone?*

These liturgies and incantations were mixed with the sucking rhythms of his boat pole in the bottom marl.

Bone! he repeated. *You old bone!*

We explored the shallows along a small mangrove-covered island, and I watched a pair of stripe-headed tanagers quarreling over a possible nesting site. Stilts and skimmers were feeding in its gentle wash, and a solitary godwit competed for food with a flock of sandpipers on the tiny beach. The boat was drifting when the Preacher suddenly whistled a warning and pointed.

Bone! the old man whispered. *Big bone!*

Two large shadows ghosted through the pale-bottom shallows to starboard, and I stripped line while they came within range. *Dass some big bonefish!* the Preacher added. *Dem bone comin', copm!*

They're big! I thought excitedly.

My fly line worked back and forth quickly, accelerating until it had the velocity for a left-hand stroke, and I dropped the pink shrimp far ahead of their foraging. Both shadows turned suddenly and disappeared when I delivered the cast.

Damn! I muttered to myself. *You spooked them!*

The Preacher stood on his toes, shielding his eyes from the sun while he searched the flats. *Copm!* he whistled through his teeth. *Copm, dem bone ain't spooked—dey comin' back, copm!*

You're right! I exhaled.

The fly rolled out with the working line and settled in front of the fish. Swirls and brief boils of discolored water betrayed their passage beyond the boat, and for several heart-stopping seconds I lost them in the light, but I started my retrieve.

There was no warning flash or rolling take in the surface. The reel started screaming shrilly before I knew a fish was hooked, and its run stripped my backing until it threatened to reach the bare spindle. With two hundred yards of backing gone, I strained to hold the rod as high as possible, hoping to keep the running line free of the bottom. Twice it raked through the marl or caught briefly on a small mangrove shoot, but the nylon tippet miraculously survived. The fish was still hooked and circling fast. Several times I patiently worked to recover backing, only to lose it when the bonefish spotted us, and stripped out line in a run that made the Saint Aidan sing.

Bonefish music! I thought.

Finally the big bonefish circled the boat, still too strong for the waiting net, and the Preacher giggled boyishly when he ducked under the straining fly line. The old man laughed and slapped his thigh when the fish circled back and forced him to duck again. The struggle was almost finished, and he readied his boat net. Its linen meshes blossomed like a parachute in the tidal wash, and the old man stood waiting like a fat grinning heron.

The fish shook itself weakly now and bored away from the net, but its explosive strength was gone. Its run was less than twenty-five yards and I turned it easily. The fight was over, and the old man scooped it into his long-handled net with a surprisingly quick stroke. We stood like a pair of schoolboys, admiring its slender olive-mottled length in the meshes.

Copm, dass a big bone! the Preacher said. *Big bone!*

You're right, I said. *What will he go?*

Copm, we got big bone on dese marls, the old man replied. *Dat bone go maybe twelve pound—dass my guess, copm!*

Good fish, Preacher! We shook hands. *Thank you!*

Copm, dass my pleasure! he said.

Filled with excitement over the twelve-pound bonefish, we decided to stop fishing and started back. It was still too shallow for the outboard, and the old man worked his boat pole across the flats, humming to himself with the rhythms of his sixty-five years. It was getting hot, and the sun beat straight down into the turquoise shallows. Spoonbills were still roosting in the mangroves, and we almost passed over a small stingray. It bolted off in a churning flood of dirty water, its rubbery wings undulating powerfully along the bottom. Our passage across the marl shallows was lyrical and slow, its pace measured in the lazy boat-pole cadences of the Preacher.

We had almost reached the swimming pool–green depths of the channel when I turned to ask the old man something, but he was lost in memories, listening to the secret music in his mind.

Ole bone? he sang softly. *Where you hidin' dis time, bone?*

[1978]

25

The Fly Book

Of the various forms of antique fishing tackle, artificial flies seem the most ephemeral. I spent a number of years rummaging through American and European angling artifacts as the director of a fishing museum and often encountered flies that were of a purported age and value, but that were often ragged and motheaten beyond recognition.

Sometimes, though, there were surprises, such as an ancient fly book that carried an Edinburgh address. Here were pre-Victorian salmon flies in excellent condition and with documentation that dated them to 1835. There were clusters of North Country trout flies too, that were small and superbly imitative and carefully tied on small handmade hooks. Fly books can indeed hold treasure and sometimes much more, as Schwiebert points out so well in this essay.

It is late summer in Princeton, and walking down through the campus toward the railroad station, we can sense the coming fall. Fishing is almost finished on the Beaverkill and the gentle Brodheads for another year. Sycamores are turning yellow on the streets where the old Princeton families built their mansions a half century ago, near the big houses of Grover Cleveland and Woodrow Wilson.

There are only a few weeks before the football crowds will gather on the playing fields beyond the station, their split-willow baskets filled with cheese and cold chicken and wine in the rich tradition of Scott Fitzgerald.

It is the season of change, with a faint perfume of burning leaves drifting on the wind, mixed with a cackle of pheasants from the cornfields. There are a few shooting friends who ride my commuter train, and there are scraps of talk about shotguns and bird dogs. It is difficult to hide our disappointment in the morning papers, because we are deskbound in the first days of woodcock hunting.

But this particular morning was not without its compensations for a fisherman. The train finally appeared through the autumn haze, its cyclops eye staring toward Pennsylvania Station. Its regular passengers came aboard, and the daily bridge games and sports-page dialogues started. Once the train had left the station, a commuter whom I had met a few times at cocktail parties walked back to my seat.

Understand you fish salmon, he said.

That's right. I folded my paper and smiled. *Probably more than I can afford.*

Salmon fishing's getting expensive? he asked.

That's right, I said.

Well, the commuter explained, *my uncle used to fish salmon and he left me his old fly book—don't fish myself, and I wondered if you'd take a look at his collection.*

Where did your uncle fish? I asked.

Don't really know. The man shook his head absently. *Quebec and New Brunswick, and maybe a little in Europe.*

Let's take a look, I said finally.

The commuter returned to his seat and rummaged through a thick pile of memorandums in his attaché case. *Here's the fly book,* he said. *Thought you could tell me something about them.*

We'll see, I smiled.

348

The fly book was surprisingly thick, a vintage Hardy still found only in the beautiful catalogues that followed the First World War. Its leather glowed with the patina of many summers, its thick felt pages surprisingly fat and secured with a thin strap and small, leather-covered buckle. There were several hundred flies, all carefully sorted and aligned.

They're beautiful, I thought.

Some of the heavily dressed traditionals were quite old, with loop eyes of fine cable and silkworm gut. There were several big strip-wings from the Dee in Scotland, including two thickly dubbed Ackroyds and a single Jock O'Dee, dressed on huge 8/0 irons. The same felt held a half-dozen beautifully slim dressings from the Spey farther north, using 3/0 and 4/0 hooks, with darkly mottled wings of brown mallard and trailing hackles of palmer-tied heron. Although I have never fished the Spey in late winter, somber Scottish patterns like the Grey Heron and Lady Caroline and Green King were familiar enough.

It was possible to imagine the old man in some past season, working these big winter irons in the swelling snow-melt at Grantown-on-Spey or switch casting patiently down the rocky pools between Invercauld and Balmoral.

Perhaps he fished Punt and Wash-House and Brig o'Dee! I studied the flies thoughtfully, lost in my memories of salmon rivers. *Perhaps he took a fish at Queen's Favorite!*

There were many classic fly patterns too, richly conceived flies like the Durham Ranger and the Thunder and Lightning and Jock Scott. Green Highlanders and Silver Greys also held places of honor. Bright-feathered flies like the Childers and Dusty Miller and Black Ranger were mixed with darker dressings like Sir Richard and Black Doctor and Black Dose. There were a few silvery flies, several Night Hawks and Lady Amhersts mixed among a rich palette of exotic patterns, like the Benchill and Candlestick Maker and Gordon.

These treasures were old and authentic dressings with married wings of florican, swan, and bustard, with touches of blue chatterer, macaw, toucan, and jungle cock. Golden

349

pheasant veiled bodies of slightly tarnished silver and fading, bright-colored silks. There were tiny tips of tinsel, and ribbings that combined flat tinsels edged with a delicate strand of oval silver wire, and these gleaming embellishments had faintly oxidized with the passing years. Such patterns were tied in the storied tradition of old masters like George Kelson and T. E. Pryce-Tannatt.

Can't tell where he fished, I thought. *Perhaps he was after springers on the Tweed or the Wye, although he might have fished the Restigouche or the Cascapedia.*

The felt leaf that followed held similar traditional flies, mixed with several big Waddingtons veiled with delicate herls of heron, in standard dressings, adaptations of the Thunder and Lightning, Black Doctor, and Jock Scott. Several tube flies in simplified dressings of the Blue Charm, Thunder and Lightning, and Garry Dog were hooked there. These tubes had delicate, nickel-plated trebles pushed inside their hollow cores. With these modern patterns were a dozen huge Scottish flies, mostly gargantuan variations of the Torrish and a pair of gaudy Helmsdale Doctors.

These Waddingtons and tubes look like the workmanship at Dickson's in Edinburgh, I mumbled half aloud, drawing a startled look from a stockbroker in the adjacent seat. *But those big Torrish irons are the work of Megan Boyd!*

Megan Boyd is the premier fly dresser of salmon patterns in the United Kingdom, her feather-littered cottage located along the Brora in Sutherlandshire. She was recently awarded the British Empire Medal, when the royal honors list from Buckingham Palace cited her singular magic with fur, feathers, and steel, and called attention to her unique contributions to foreign exchange through a small but thriving worldwide trade in salmon flies. Her versions of the Torrish, which is called the Scalscraggie by fishermen in the Strath of Kildonan, are immensely popular during the late-winter spates that drain Sutherland and Caithness.

Look at that! I admired a huge Torrish.

Its bright hackles gleamed in the sunlight that filtered in through the grimy windows, and its silvery body was veiled in tiny feathers of the rare Indian crow. The train shuddered

350

and braked clumsily into the station at New Brunswick, while I studied its richly mixed feathers.

The opposite felt was covered with big hairwings dressed on 1/0 to 3/0 hooks. There were several sparsely winged Orange Blossoms, the hairwing variation of the Dusty Miller that first evolved in Quebec, mixed with a dozen heavily dressed Abbeys, their bodies shaped from a dark, wine-colored crewel. The collection of hairwing patterns included a full compliment of Black and Silver and Rusty Rats, with a brace of big green-bodied Cossebooms providing their counterpoint of bold color.

These flies smell like the Restigouche! I thought excitedly. *But they liked the Abbey on the Alta too!*

Admiral William Read loved to fish similar patterns on the Alta twenty-five years ago and favored its upper beats above Jøraholmen. His giant, fifty-nine-pound cockfish was killed there with a 5/0 Abbey on the Steinfossnakken, the sprawling pool that lies under sheltering escarpments at the wild Gabofoss waterfall. His trophy salmon was lovingly traced on the wainscoting at Sautso, in the sitting room of the old fishing house built for the Duke of Roxburghe.

Turning the felt leaf slowly, I discovered several gaudy patterns dressed with startlingly bright feathers. These large flies were mixed with smaller dressings, although most were shaped on gleaming 4/0 and 5/0 irons. *These flies look like the work of Olav Olsen,* I thought. *Perhaps the old man fished with him at Hunderi, and walked the casting platforms there when the glacier-melt was coming on the Laerdal.*

The smaller flies included a few somber versions that looked like the workmanship of Erling Sand, who comes from a family of Norwegian flymakers farther south in Engerdal. His flies are fully dressed in the typical Norwegian style, but his feathers are prepared in a more subtle mixture of chroma. Several of these flies were tied on graceful low-water hooks. There is good late-summer fishing on several rivers in the Sognefjord country, like the Aurland and Naerøy and the pastoral little Flåm, but the best of these summer salmon fisheries is unquestionably the swift-flowing Laerdal.

Maybe these Dusty Miller irons were bought for the Årøy! I thought happily. *And he probably fished the pools at Tønjum in low water.*

Beyond the soiled windows of the train, the jungle of storage tanks and refinery towers and piping systems reached toward Staten Island, but my thoughts were several thousand miles farther east in the steep-walled valley at Laerdalsøyri, where herring gulls fill the mornings with their cries above its ferry slips.

The old man must have loved the casting platforms above Moldebu. I remembered their gentle planking structure and the current tumbling through their pilings. *And perhaps he enjoyed a twilight supper on the scrollwork porch at the Lindström.*

There were almost six dozen exquisite low waters, with sparse throat hackles and a slender feather-wing style. Such flies had their roots in the philosophy of Arthur H. E. Wood, who developed a unique method of fishing salmon on the lower Dee in Scotland. The classic Wood low-water patterns were all there. Most of these flies were delicate Blue Charms, mixed with a few Silver Blues and March Browns. The others were a colorful assortment of other dressings like the Jeannie, Jockie and Logie, plus a few slender Lady Carolines tied on exquisite Wilson low-water hooks.

It seemed possible that the old man had actually fished them on the lower Dee, where Wood had perfected his theories on the shallow pools a few miles above Banchory. His water is still beautiful, and I fished it with a mixture of wonder and reverence a few seasons ago. There were also a dozen sparsely tied hairwings mixed with these low-water standards, their bodies scarcely thicker than the hooks their silk concealed, and their slim style unmistakably the work of John Smith, a famous Scottish flymaker at Ballater.

He must have fished there! I stared down at the brackish channels below a refinery trestle, where a gull sat watching the oil-covered water. *Wonder how he liked Canary and Malt Steep?*

The train gathered speed slowly again, sliding out under the trusswork structure of the Newark station, and the sunlight reflected dully on the dark current that eddied through the bridge pilings.

The fly book concealed some familiar artifacts, as well as dressings from the fly shops of Europe, and I fingered happily through a collection of Miramichi patterns. Several looked like the craftsmanship of Ira Gruber and Wallace Doak, and included dressings like the Oriole. There were the flies that John Atherton loved also, and painted for his lovely book *The Fly and the Fish*, beautiful patterns like the Squirreltail and Minktail. The pair of delicate little Blackvilles seemed to suggest that they had been born at the fly-dressing bench of Bert Miner. Frayed nylon that remained in a brittle half hitch behind the head of a solitary Green Butt seemed to indicate that its owner had fished the widow hitch in Newfoundland.

Jack Russell's old camp on the Miramichi is possible. I studied the frayed silk wrappings and dull tinsel. *But the old man might have hitched on the Serpentine or the River of Ponds, and maybe with Lee Wulff.*

Still other patterns were clustered together in the felt, and these flies were puzzling, although I discovered that they included a small assortment of pale Crosfields and Blue Sapphires and somber black-winged Sweeps. These were old favorites of mine.

Iceland! I thought. *He fished there too!*

These patterns are immensely popular among knowledgeable men who regularly fish the rivers of Iceland. The fishing logs on its subarctic rivers from the Laxá in Pingeyjarsýsla, to the tumbling waterfalls of Straumfjardará under the Snaefjellsnes volcano, are ample testimony to their effectiveness. The single purplish-hackled Blue Vulture confirmed my conviction that the old man had traveled to Iceland, since its unusual guinea-fowl dressing had its origins on the little rivers outside Reykjavík.

It seemed certain that the old man had fished the lingering twilights there, perhaps the gathering ledge shallows in the wildflower meadows of the Laxá at Húsavik. Perhaps he worked his greased-line tactics at the Holakvorn and Peat on the lower Vatnsdalsá, where storied salmon fishermen like Charles Ritz and John Ashley-Cooper and Roderick Haig-

Brown have plied their craft. It was also possible that he fished Stekkur on the Nordurá, and Dyrafljot on the pastoral little Langá. *Maybe he even fished the Grimsá, I whispered, and learned to love old favorites like Strengir and Skardshylur and Laxabakki, like I have.*

Other patterns were still puzzling in spite of familiar dressings like the Peter Ross and Watson's Fancy. Mixed with these Scottish flies were several darker dressings aligned in the felt, flies like the Black Pennell and Bibio and Sooty Olive. But it was the frayed Connemara Black that tipped the scales, and I wondered when the old man had traveled to Irish rivers like the Blackwater and Ballynahinch.

Bibio and Watson's Fancy are seatrout flies, I thought. Perhaps he fished at Cashla or Lough Currane.

It was pleasant to speculate about the old man in his twilight years, journeying through the lovely countryside of Ireland, and I remembered the time I spent at Ashford Castle, with the swans in the gardens that reach down toward Lough Corrib. Such memories drift like a fishing boat on Lough Mask during its mayfly season, and I thought that the fly book had also journeyed with its owner through Limerick to explore the famous seatrout lakes along the Ring of Kerry.

Its owner probably enjoyed fine suppers in the high-ceilinged dining room at Ballynahinch, lingering over a subtle Pauillac before taking coffee in the castle library. It even seemed possible that the old man had walked upstream through the trees to fish from the masonry casting platforms above Ballynahinch, worked the pondlike holding water that Paul Hyde Bonner loved in the moors downstream, and enjoyed the swiftly spilling currents at Derryclare Butts.

It's beautiful there, I thought, remembering the painting of Lough Inagh over the mantelpiece at Ballynahinch. He must have loved it.

Six final flies were baffling. Five were relatively dark dressings with gold bodies and a thorax dubbing of olive seal fur. Claret hackles were faced with speckled guinea. The fully dressed wings were intricately married, mixing golden pheasant with a multicolored veil of swan, all sheathed in teal and brown mallard. The topping was a shining layer of golden-pheasant crest, and the wing was completed with jungle cock and blue chatterer. Paired horns of bright macaw were gracefully arched above the curving feathers that formed the wings.

What are these? I puzzled.

The last dressing was silver-bodied and equally unfamiliar. It had a delicate butt of scarlet crewel, its throat hackles a pale green and faced with speckled guinea. The wing was shaped over a pair of large jungle-cock feathers sheathed with golden-pheasant tippets. There were accents of multicolored swan dyed a delicate blue. The entire wing was partly veiled in barred mallard from the flanks of a mature drake, and completed with jungle cock and kingfisher. There were horns of blue macaw and a topping of pheasant crest, its delicate golden fibers exquisitely curving to sheathe the wing feathers.

Finally I remembered where I had seen such patterns, thinking about the half-dozen flies from the feather-littered shop of Belarmino Martinez in the collection of William Ropner in Yorkshire. His dressings are created in Pravia, where the swift Nalon joins the Narcea in their tumbling descent from the forests of Cantábrica in northern Spain. My head was quickly filled with thoughts of the Navia and Eo, where the late General Francisco Franco often fished with his dark-haired granddaughter, and of the ruined Roman bridge that vaults gracefully over the Deva-Cares.

It was possible to imagine the old fisherman there, enjoying a tureen of richly mixed seafoods and rice in some riverbank *hostería* with a bottle of simple Spanish wine. Perhaps that dark Rioja would last through his supper to the platter of Asturian cheeses and coffee, and later he might finish with a brandy glass of Fundador.

Such Spanish villages along that northern seacoast are a peaceful refuge in this cacophonic century. There would not be many salmon in a week's fishing, perhaps no fish taken anywhere along the entire river, but it would not matter. Spain is the only place in the salmon angler's world where camellias and orange blossoms are blooming when its coin-bright fish are coming from the salt.

That's what these flies are. I was thinking about the Spanish salmon flies in my own collection. *They're the Martinez patterns!*

When our train crossed the brackish marshes below Hackensack and plunged into the Stygian depths of the railroad tunnel under the Hudson, these pleasant reveries were shattered. The train roared through the darkness, its rumbling multiplied to such earsplitting crescendos that all thoughts and conversations were completely erased.

We finally escaped the tunnel, clattering in through the intricate network of switches and spiderweb wires, until the train shuddered and slowed itself jerkily into Pennsylvania Station. It was time to join the milling crowds that fill its labyrinth of stairs and escalators and corridors. Reluctantly I closed the leather fly book and secured its strap and returned it on the platform.

They're beautiful flies, I said.

We started toward the stairs through clouds of steam. *Are they worth anything?* my friend asked eagerly. *Should we try to sell them or should we just keep them?*

They're a whole fly fisher's life, I protested.

So we should keep them. He nodded thoughtfully. *You mean you could figure out where he fished just from his flies?*

Something like that, I said.

That's pretty exciting! The man slipped the fly book into his raincoat. *Anything else you can tell me?*

Nothing, I said. *Except that I wish I'd known him.*

[1977]

356

26

Winter

With any luck there will be grouse for Christmas dinner or perhaps a wild turkey from the mountain behind the house. We have late hunting seasons for these birds in Vermont, which extend after snow has forced me off the river. And even if I have no luck myself, I'll be able to get the feathers from my neighbor's birds.

Those feathers cover my fly-tying bench in winter. Hackles from the wild grouse become the legs on my wet flies and nymphs. Turkey feathers transform into Muddler Minnows and stonefly nymphs. I can dream of spring in the tying, when I'll catch trout on these flies below the ridges where the feathers themselves originated. There is some poetry in this circle, I like to think, and winter is the daydreaming time when such circles are completed.

It is almost winter, according to the calendar in the kitchen, but looking out into the trees behind the house there is little need of clocks and calendars.

The morning has a brooding quality.

357

Its winds are no longer crisp and bracing, like the winds of October, and the branches are bare and rattling. The gusts are growing sullen and raw. We have already seen a little spitting snow. The tall, straight-trunked ash behind the house has been leafless for days, and last night, under a chill moon ringed with a delicate halo of crystals, the other trees were stripped bare too. Before daylight I was awakened by the wind, and I stood in the darkened house, watching.

The dark trees seemed transformed, seething and twisting in the wind. The branches clashed and rattled in the night. Gusts sighed down the wooded ridge behind the house, stirring showers of brittle leaves, while the big trees writhed and groaned.

It's here, I thought. *The trees always know.*

The restless fisherman travels many seasons through his books and his sport. My private clocks tell me that winter is coming when I have finished reading (although I am not a turkey hunter) familiar books like *The Tenth Legion* and Havilah Babcock's perennial favorite *My Health Is Better in November.* Roderick Haig-Brown helps to lift my moods beyond these winter-stripped woods. There is a signed copy of *Fisherman's Winter* beside the bed, and its pages are filled with images and happy echoes of fishing in our opposite hemisphere. It is not necessary to have traveled to the rivers of Chile and southern Argentina to love the stories in *Fisherman's Winter.* Haig-Brown fished them several years before my first trip to the Argentine, about the time I first met him in New York. Reading him again today, more than thirty-odd years after that first trip through Patagonia, it is possible to relive those wild rivers and enjoy the startling beauty of another world.

Some fishermen are so caught up in the act of fishing itself that they read only about tackle and tactics, or books about the rivers they fish regularly. *It's really a little sad,* Haig-Brown observed during a long talk-filled dinner at Campbell River. *They missed the point when they were struggling with* Hamlet *and* The Mayor of Casterbridge *and Yeats. Books are like passports to other times and places that we will never actually see—and fishing's a better excuse than most for getting two springs and two falls each year.*

It is almost winter in our eastern mountains, but I have already had three autumns this season. The first occurred on a minor spate river in Argyllshire, a little river rising beyond Kingshouse Bridge in the empty Moors of Rannoch. Its currents had dwindled to a trickle through the summer, its salmon waiting restlessly in the sea loch off its mouth, waiting for the summer's drought to break.

Storms attacked the western coasts of Scotland in late summer, just when I arrived at Prestwick, and I took a room in a charming little Tudor hotel at Troon. The weather improved slightly, although fierce storms still lashed across the Hebrides and the mountains behind Oban and Ballachulish. The little river was suddenly swollen with water, its currents rising with the spilling of highland cataracts and burns. Ragged clouds hung in the mountains and steep-walled glens. Both snow and rain filled the mountains, and when the weather broke again and steadily improved, the mountains were purple with heather and the river was alive with salmon.

Our little party had twenty-one salmon in six days. *It's really fishing quite well,* Lawrence Banks observed wryly. *We've had lots of fishless days together when you've come over to fish before—I'm not sure we're really in Scotland!*

Alaska offered a second autumn this year, its alders and beargrass bottoms and popple already changing color when we crossed in the floatplane from Naknek. The chill wind had stripped a confetti of yellowing leaves into the winding channels of the American, where the nesting swans were preparing their young to migrate south. The grizzlies along the Brooks were fat after weeks of gorging on salmon. The salmon were already gone from their pea-gravel spawning grounds on the Gibraltar and Battle, and their big rainbows had drifted back into the lakes. Talarik held scores of big trout, silvery rainbows freshly run from Lake Iliamna, but its still lagoons were already sheathed in delicate shrouds of ice each morning.

There were still days too, with little wind forecast from Cordoba to the Bering Straits, and we used them to fly the glaciers and volcanoes beyond the Valley of Ten Thousand Smokes. The region surrendered several trophy rainbows this season, fish between thirty and forty inches, but most were released. It was clearly autumn in the Katmai country, although ice crystals forming in the guides and frozen reels were wintry omens, and the desiccating skeletons of dead sockeyes littered the river shallows and bars.

Twice our little camp at Kulik was covered with fresh snow at breakfast, and the shuffling tracks of huge grizzlies reminded us who owned the nights. *Paws the size of skillets.* Bob Buckmaster laughed nervously when we saw the claw marks. *Those tracks weren't made by parka squirrels!*

Autumn was still waiting at home.

We shot a few woodcock, and hunted pheasants in the corn stubble and swale fields in the stone-barn counties along the Delaware. Sometimes we hear a shrill clamor of geese and hurry outside to glimpse a wavering phalanx crossing the pale morning sky. Yellow sycamores line the quiet streets where the old Princeton families built their mansions. The football crowds still come on the weekends, bringing their tailgate celebrations of *pâté* and chicken and champagne, in the tradition of Scott Fitzgerald.

But there are winter daydreams, too.

It is late spring in Argentina and Chile, and fresh snow still glitters on the volcanoes between them. Chilean winters are rainy, like the winters of Oregon and northern California. Argentine winters are colder, with snow in the foothills and brush-country *pampas,* and their bitter winds chill a desert country like Nevada.

Although their trout-filled rivers are only a mountain range apart, the Andes are such a formidable barrier that the climates of Argentina and Chile are utterly different.

Argentine rivers are still torrents of snowmelt in December and are sometimes still high and barely fishable until after the New Year. Their spring fishing is usually best at several *bocas,* particularly at Pichi Traful and Correntoso, in flowages that drain or enter big Andean lakes. Big trout and landlocked salmon migrate toward these flowages in the spring to intercept the smeltlike *pejerrey,* and the translucent little *puyen* baitfish, which are spawning before Christmas.

But the best Argentine fishing comes much later, when the summer doldrums of February have passed, and the cool nights start the *mimbres* and copper beeches and poplars turning, until their leaves are bright with April color.

The Chilean spring is more gentle, arriving softly in the fertile wine country below the capital, until the junglelike rain forests farther south are scarlet with fire trees and butter-yellow *pelu*. Both browns and rainbows are gorging on spawning baitfish. Big rainbows drift back slowly from their egg laying, having gathered in the small bamboo-thicket tributaries, and are waxing fat on both minnows and *pancora* crayfish. The fishing is excellent while there is rain enough to maintain sufficient volumes of flow, but with the coming of summer weather after Christmas, the big fish often drop back into the Chilean lakes. It is a beautiful countryside with steep Chinese-looking volcanic hills in the Calcurrupe valley, and I fish its rivers often in my mind.

But some winter daydreams are only daydreams.

There was no time to join friends this season at Georgetown, in the prime bonefish weeks before Thanksgiving, and I am still regretting the decision to stay home. The wind is scuttling leaves across the brickwork terrace, but my thoughts are on the white-bottomed flats of Exuma and a charming seaside inn called Peace and Plenty.

It was a fine daydream postponed until another year, perhaps worth savoring through the winter, but another happy daydream is already forming. Cold weather can drive the fish off the big flats at Islamorada, but if the early winter remains mild in the Florida Keys, there is always the chance of a Christmas tarpon.

[1983]

361

27

Beauty

*Beyond the paradox of beauty's invitation to degrada-
tion is a growing number of fishermen who have
chosen to intervene. The loveliest and most productive gorge in a river may well be the best site for a
dam. Or the simple beauty of a river may draw so
many recreational users that the quality of the recreational experience itself is diminished. Schwiebert
himself became deeply involved, at the invitation of
Jack Hemingway, in a countrywide campaign to protect Silver Creek in Idaho. Over the past thirty years
the collective voices of other conservationist anglers
have been increasingly effective in addressing such
problems. But not effective enough.*

*A few of the problems that Schwiebert clearly
describes in this essay have been resolved—for the
time being. The Hill Farm along Vermont's Battenkill
has been saved from intensive development thanks to
the hard work of Bill Herrick and other members of
the Battenkill Conservancy, for example. But farming
along the river is less economical these days, and
there are other open sections of bottomland that will
eventually be proposed for development, threatening*

362

the wonderful pastoral qualities of this famous river.
A dam site remains as such, whether the dam is
built or not. The proposals will be recurring, as will
be the battles. Beauty in these terms is much deeper
than the simple currents of a river or its fish, and its
jeopardy seems perpetual.

Beauty is quite fragile.

Its gentle world is shrinking quickly in our time. Obvious beauty still survives in wild places, but it is rare in the places we have made and in the malignant cityscapes and honky-tonk highways we are still making. Ugly growth is choking our countryside with trailer parks and used-car lots and truckstops. Empty factories stand along railways and river-fronts, their shattered windows staring eyelessly across abandoned switchyards and dirty backwaters. Finding a new surveyor's stake in a favorite cornfield or woodcock covert, its bright plastic ribbon fluttering in the wind, is a symptom so heart-stopping that it seems like a gloomy report from a pathologist.

Several years ago, hunting woodcock with an old friend in the Catskills, we found a fuchsia strip of plastic hanging from a freshly sharpened lath.

God, my friend said quietly, *I hate progress!*

History has eroded the theology of progress in most countries except ours, particularly in this troublesome century. Wisdom should tell us that our century has witnessed little progress, but has seen an avalanche of change.

Our woodcock covert is buried in asphalt today, its tiny creek imprisoned in underground pipe, and its site covered with cars. It is happening everywhere. Even wilderness is not safe. Abandoned canneries scar the coasts of Alaska in giant jigsaw puzzles of bleached timbers and pilings. The villages there are often shockingly ugly, almost like elephants' grave-yards, where rotting boats and bulldozers and other derelict machinery have crawled away to die.

You really think, another friend observed sadly in Alaska last September, *we actually see the trash and derelict boats and trucks when we talk about living in God's country?*

Wild rivers are still beautiful, among the last beautiful

artifacts we have. Yet their beauty is shrinking. Forgetting their fish, rivers are worth protecting for themselves alone. But wild rivers are plagued with a strange irony. Our most fertile rivers and their most beautiful places are always the first sites chosen for highways and clear-cutting and dams.

The list is always surprising.

Several famous rivers are still in jeopardy, from Maine to the Pacific. Such struggles will perhaps always be with us, and stopping such projects is still our purpose. Fighting off a reservoir or development or pump storage project is never really finished. During a recent drought, the Corps of Engineers again suggested building the Tocks Island Dam, pointing out that its storage capacity was still needed. The engineers have clearly forgotten that millions and millions of chickens are grown along the upper Delaware. Their fecal wastes contribute to its fertility, but would collect steadily behind Tocks Island until they ultimately posed a threat to public health. Such health risks played a major role in blocking the project, but Tocks Island is still not dead, and some people have seemingly forgotten that it would have slowly become a giant cesspool.

When we win, Frank Moore told me years ago on his storied Umpqua, *it's only an armistice—when they win it's all over.*

Our neighbors on the Bow tell me their river is threatened, too. Water storage for agriculture is the purpose, and the dam would impound its winding cottonwood channels back to the doorstep of Calgary. The thirsty prairie towns want to impound the Crowsnest too. The Broadback and its sister rivers, harboring the finest genetic stocks of brook trout in existence, have already been virtually destroyed by a gargantuan power network of dams and diversion systems and turbines in the Hudson Bay drainages of Quebec.

The Henry's Fork in eastern Idaho is threatened by the power industry too. Its managers are apparently oblivious to the unique ecology of the Henry's Fork, perhaps the finest public trout fishery in the United States. Proposals for a series of hydropower sites have been filed.

Shouldn't surprise you, a well-known Idaho guide wrote

me. *People around here want to rebuild the Teton Dam—made so much money on the federal damage claims they bought his-and-hers Corvettes.*

Greedy rural counties farther south have insisted on storing so much water in recent winters that huge fish kills have occurred below Last Chance, but there was little public outcry until the minimal flows from Island Park also killed a flotilla of trumpeter swans.

The Two Forks project has surfaced again on the South Platte above Denver. It proposes to drown the beautiful walk-in canyon at Deckers, where thousands and thousands of urban anglers have enjoyed their sport over the years. There are already six dams on the river system upstream. Two Forks will not increase total water storage for Denver and the Colorado ranchers farther east. It will merely provide more storage capacity for water borrowed from the Colorado watershed on the western slope, sending it east from Breckinridge. Some hydrologists and planners believe that Two Forks should be replaced with a small reservoir on the tributary already used to borrow water from the Blue, and with several minor impoundments in the mountains north of Denver, much closer to the agricultural communities that need them. Such smaller dams would supply the water required and still save the South Platte fishery.

Biologists tell us the river displays the best trout-per-acre population anywhere in Colorado, in a beautiful ponderosa canyon an hour from downtown Denver. No comparable urban fishery exists along the entire Front Range of the Rockies between Santa Fe and Calgary, although there are still other workable reservoir sites.

The power boys politicians have several options, Ed Exum told me on the South Platte in April, *but they always want the only girl in town.*

Western rivers are not the only fisheries in trouble. The Penobscot is our best remaining fishery for Atlantic salmon, having been restored by a mixture of federal funding and local husbandry. Its West Branch sustains perhaps the finest landlocked salmon population on any river in Maine, yet it has also been through a siege of proposed dams. The Great

365

Northern Paper Company has grudgingly abandoned its dam project on the West Branch. Corporate planners ironically defended their project in terms of competition with Canadian mills that already enjoyed cheaper energy costs, power generated by those same penstocks and turbines that are decimating the wonderful Broadback and its sister rivers in northern Quebec.

Sunderland is a tiny village in Vermont, the place where the storied Ethan Allen and his family once lived along the Battenkill. There is a dairy farm at Sunderland controlling two miles of that famous river, and it was sold this year to a developer who proposes a sixty-family condominium project for the Hill Farm. Its pastoral beauty is a lyric Pleissner watercolor come to life, the soft beauty of paintings like *Lye Brook Pool* and *Benedict's Crossing*. Yet that lyric beauty is clearly at risk.

The Umpqua also has its scars.

Several miles below Steamboat, where its emerald currents slide into a mysterious S-shaped bend, feathery scraps of fog drift through the tall conifers. The river is narrow and incredibly deep, eddying among house-size boulders, filling a dark volcanic fissure. Giant cliffs rise vertically, darkly streaked with a mixture of seepages and October rain. Their façades are a rich palette of ochers and bright greens and mustard clinging to their rhyolite and obsidian, almost like a canvas by Rauschenberg or de Kooning.

The mustard yellow of the lichens is quite startlingly out of place above the eerie depths of the pool. Scarlet leaves identify a tiny maple struggling to root itself in a fissure. Fiddleheads and bunchgrass are bright orange after the first hard frosts.

But something else is even more startling. Where a daring surveyor hung from his ropes and soft-iron pins and steel rings, there is a brightly painted number. Its brushwork was controlled by a transit party sighting its instruments from across the river, and it was the engineer's benchmark for a dam. The number itself is shocking, like an obscenity scrawled across the Sistine ceiling.

Such men were utterly tone-deaf to the beauty of the

366

Umpqua and its cliffs, or they could not have defaced them so easily. The dam was never started, but its benchmark is still there. Such ugly *sgraffiti* echo the dark price we have often paid for our Faustian dreams of prosperity and growth.

Drowning the Umpqua and its cathedral of giant conifers is unthinkable, yet a timber company recently clear-cut an entire hillside along the river. Beauty is increasingly important to both sanity and survival, and it may prove the most endangered thing of all.

[1984]

28

The Alchemy of Bamboo

By virtue of being early, I had Cairns Pool on the Beaverkill all to myself—unusual even for a morning in August. Trout rose gently in the ledge shadows, and I was able to take several in the main current on a tiny Red Quill dry. Within an hour, other anglers started to show up. One such—inexperienced, or so I judged by his casting—waded into the current tongue above me and started covering water I'd already fished.

The bigger fish here always seem to rise across the pool at the very edge of the rocks, and I leaned harder on the rod to drop the little fly seventy feet away in a boulder-edged slick. There was a small dimple, and I finally landed and released an eighteen-inch brown trout made all the sweeter for an audience.

The rod was bamboo, one made for me by Jim Schaaf in California on Lyle Dickerson's old equipment with a delicate tip and powerful butt section to allow fishing even a light line at considerable distance. As I started to wipe down the rod before putting it in the car, the other angler walked over.

"You cast very well," he said. "What kind of rod is that anyway?"
I handed him the rod sections. "Why, it's bamboo!" he exclaimed in disbelief. I spent a few moments assuring him that in this age of graphite and synthetic-fiber fly rods classic bamboo rods were by no means out of place. They have a poetry all their own, and I think no one has conveyed that feeling better than Schwiebert in this particular essay.

It is a late February afternoon, and a fine dust of snow lies on the carpet of leaves behind the house. The pale-trunked beeches still hold their amber-colored leaves, but our oaks are stripped bare long before Christmas. The glacier boulders are starkly outlined through the woods. The slender ash and dogwood trees stand dark against the pale February light, and the bleak wind stirs faintly in their branches. Leaves scuttle across the moss-stained brickwork. It is a time for speculation about the coming spring, and for lazily remembering our rivers past.

Every fisherman feels strong emotional ties to his tackle. Some anglers understand how their equipment can transport them backward through time, and in late winter I sometimes fill the library with several split-cane friends. Each is carefully extracted from its case, assembled and flexed lovingly and taken down again, while the beechwood coals shift and settle in the grate.

The first really fine rod that I ever saw was an eight-foot Payne owned by a physician in Chicago. It had been built by Edward Payne, one of the apprentices in the original Leonard shop in Bangor, and had been refitted by James Payne many years later. Their names were nothing to an eight-year-old who was still more interested in merely catching fish than in the subtle rituals of fishing, yet the craftsmanship and beauty of the rod were obvious—although I found it strange that the doctor loved his four-ounce Payne so much that he seldom fished with it.

It was many years before I fully understood such things, but lying in the lamplight, that gleaming Payne obviously had the overtones of some liturgical relic. The rod possessed beauty and an almost votive elegance. It was my first exposure to the curious alchemy of split bamboo.

The Payne was kept in a saddle-leather case. Its heavy stitching was frayed and pale against the tube and cap. There was a leather carrying strap that fastened the cap with a small leather-covered buckle. The case was scuffed and worn, smelling faintly like a fine saddle or a polished pair of English riding boots, but its patina was only a prelude to other sensory riches it held.

The faintly musty odor of the original poplin bag came first, mixed with the rich perfume of tung-oil varnish. The delicate silk wrappings were a pale brown that almost matched the color of the cane itself, and were embellished with ornamental wraps of primrose. It was a three-piece Payne with an exquisitely slow action. The ferrules were beautiful, each female socket sealed with a perfectly fitted German silver plug. The guides were English tungsten steel. The elegant grip was shaped of handcut specie cork, remarkably free of checks and markings. It was the classic Payne grip, slightly flared to conceal a reel cap inside the cork. The reel-seat filler was a rich Spanish cedar, and its fittings gleamed like fine jewelry. The locking threads were exquisitely machined, and although the butt cap and locking hood were only aluminum, their weight and elegant knurling and polish seemed more like fine sterling—as beautiful as silver pieces in a showcase at Tiffany's.

Such qualities are typical of the finest split-cane rods, and in my library this afternoon there is an example that is unique. The rod is a magnificent early Leonard, certainly the oldest Leonard that can accurately be dated. It belongs to the California rodmaker Gary Howells, and it has an intriguing history in itself.

The old Leonard was built in 1873, only two years after Hiram Leonard established his little shop on the Penobscot. Its fixed reel fitting is inscribed from its maker to H. H. Howells, with the date engraved below. The doweled ferrules are prototypes of the Leonard patent ferrule of 1874, their tubing rolled and soldered from sheets of German silver and reinforced at the throat with a simple welt. Ring-and-keeper guides were used. Fittings of German silver form the grip check, sliding ring, and fixed reel band. The butt cap is also shaped from German silver into a crowned ornamental cup, its throat embellished with machined rings. The grip itself is fashioned of solid wood, the six strips of cane laminated over a shaped core, with alternating strips of tapered Port Orford cedar. It is like a fine violin in its perfect equilibrium of utility and aesthetic pleasure and craftsmanship.

The rod was apparently made in payment for legal work in obtaining the Leonard ferrule patents of 1874, since H. H. Howells was a young fly-fishing lawyer in Bangor. It later traveled west with H. H. Howells to the Wyoming territory where the young attorney practiced law in frontier towns like Rock Springs and Cheyenne. Howells journeyed farther at the close of the century, settled and raised his family, and ultimately became a distinguished judge in San Francisco. The rod is still fishable more than a century later, its action poetic and impossible to describe, like a well-seasoned Petrus or Château Margaux.

It traveled across the frontier with my grandfather, Gary Howells told me last spring in the Yellowstone country. *What stories it could tell!*

Sixteen years ago, on the threshold of my first trip to Patagonia, another classic rod arrived at Princeton. Its return address revealed that the sender was Martha Marie Young, the fishing widow of Michigan rodbuilder Paul Young. The package was puzzling, since I could not remember ordering another installment in my growing collection of Young rods, and I unwrapped it with curiosity.

It contained a unique Young Parabolic 17 with three tips, one bringing its length to eight-and-a-half feet, and two extending the rod to almost nine feet. The short tip was intended for distance work, and the others were special tapers designed for nymphs and dry-fly tactics. The butt is extra slow, unusually flat in its taper from the grip to its stripping guide, and it demands a patient casting stroke. With its different tips, this remarkable rod could fish dry flies or nymphs on 5X leaders, or deliver a WF-8-S line more than a hundred feet with ease.

371

Most customers considered this early prototype of the famous Parabolic 17 too radical in its calibrations and casting stroke, but Paul Young loved its demanding character, and grudgingly modified his subsequent Parabolic 17 tapers to satisfy his audience. The original has a unique character, with a willful spirit of its own, and it was some time before I successfully adjusted my casting rhythms to fulfill its obvious potential.

"Paul always wanted to fish Patagonia," Martha Young wrote in the letter that accompanied the rod. "He'd be happy to have you fish it for him down there."

The rod has since taken salmon in Iceland and the Labrador, and has done yeoman duty on heavy western rivers like the Madison and the Yellowstone, but nothing can surpass the memories of that first trip to the Argentine in 1959. It took a six-pound rainbow the first evening on the Pichi Traful, fishing a big Variant on its dry-fly tip, but failed to defeat a much bigger rainbow at the famous Boca Chimehuin.

The Boca fish took almost angrily, with a steady pull that grudgingly refused to surrender line, and moved sullenly upstream into the angry surf that crashed across the outlet ledges of the lake. Suddenly it jumped in the heaviest currents, catching the sun as it cartwheeled downstream past the gravelly beach. It looked like ten or twelve pounds, and my arms were shaking as I scrambled to follow its run. The rainbow jumped again and again, forcing the fight into the swift-running currents below the Boca itself. The line sliced audibly through the water and the reel shrieked above the shrill wind.

The rainbow exploded into another series of wild acrobatics, and when I forced it back, the fly came sickeningly free. It seemed like a tragedy, since that was the biggest trout I had ever hooked in those days, but the bittersweet feelings did not last.

Two weeks later, the Parabolic 17 performed beautifully in Tierra del Fuego, using its special distance tip to combat the strong winds that prevail below the Straits of Magellan. It was there on the Dos Palos water that it took a brace of magnificent seatrout, weighing eight and twelve pounds, and

I cannot take this beautiful rod from its case without remembering its baptism in southern Argentina.

When *Life* magazine sent me to Norway the following summer, my collection of fly rods seemed hopelessly unsuited to throwing a 5/0 double at the salmon of the Alta and Målangsfossen and Årøy. My letter to Martha Young triggered the arrival of another rod from her late husband's collection. It was a muscular Parabolic 19 this time, one that Paul Young had built for himself to fish tarpon. It took a full WF-11-S line and was designed to punch out long casts on the windy flats at Islamorada and Homasassa Springs. It seemed perfect for hundred-foot casts with a 5/0 Dusty Miller on the Jøraholmen water at Alta, or the fishing platforms of the Årøy Steeplechase.

It was a full nine-and-a-half feet, built from the dark flame-tempered cane that Young favored. The rod was powerful and a little tiring to use until a caster sensed its peculiar rhythms. Its stroke did not really begin until fifty or sixty feet of line were working, and a brief session on the casting pond at Henryville taught me that the wine-bottle calisthenics that Charles Ritz prescribed in his *Fly Fisher's Life* were needed to strengthen my wrist and casting arm. Later I found that considerable refinement of my double-haul technique was also necessary to extract the full potential of the Parabolic 19, with its exacting stroke and muscular tapers. It was also fitted with a reverse-locking seat that permitted a two-inch extension butt, a feature I ultimately learned to appreciate when a heavy fish forced a fight into the wild Battagorski rapids on the Alta.

But whenever I remove this Young Parabolic 19 from its case, it is not only the Alta I remember, although it was the rod I was fishing at Sautso the night I took three fish over thirty-nine pounds after losing a cockfish over sixty-five. That monster survived a fight that lasted almost two hours, and traversed several rapids in a wild two-mile odyssey that ended at the Sirpinakken hut.

That night's fishing is recorded in the anthology called *A River for Christmas,* but strangely it is another night in Norway that I remember better when I handle the Parabolic

19. My wild moment of truth occurred a summer earlier on the Vossa, several hundred miles farther south in the steep-walled mountains of Hordaland.

Nils Bolstad was waiting on its Langhølen beat, and we pushed out into its smooth currents. The pool is four hundred yards from its tumbling throat to its spreading tail shallows. Salmon can hold throughout its length.

Fishing light was already waning as we started working the pool, and after a half-hour I changed flies, selecting a Dusty Miller with a bright silver body to catch the light in the gathering darkness. The fly dropped along a ledge, where the big river eddied over unseen boulders. The line bellied deep across the current, and I felt the fly start to swim.

Suddenly it stopped swimming, and the line tightened with a weight that spelled salmon. When I tightened back firmly into the fish, nothing happened. There was only its ponderous sense of power while the fish simply ignored the straining Parabolic. Bolstad worked the boat below the salmon and I stripped out line, trying to force the fish off balance with pressure from downstream.

There were two brief runs, measured more in their sullen strength than their distance or swift acceleration. Finally the boat grated on the stones and I waded ashore. *I'm tired,* I thought, surprised at my aching muscles.

The great fish seemed spent. It still wallowed powerfully in the huge counterclockwise currents off the rocky beach. Several times we tried to coax the salmon within gaffing distance, and each time it stubbornly fought back into that nightmare of merry-go-round whirlpools. Bolstad waited silently with the gaff.

He's finally beaten! I thought.

The salmon rolled weakly in the surface, and the eddying currents carried it toward the beach. Bolstad stared hard into the dark water as I forced the fish, reached like a cautious heron with the gaff, and struck hard. There was an enormous splash that showered us both. Bolstad shouted in surprise and almost went down in the river, wrestling the huge salmon ashore. Its size seemed awesome in the growing darkness as the ghillie delivered the *coup de grâce,* and the great fish shuddered.

374

Twenty-two kilos, Bolstad guessed as the fifty-pound scale gently touched bottom.

Fifty-one pounds! I thought happily.

Memories like that are priceless, and I never expect to take a larger salmon in my lifetime. Perhaps there is even more pleasure in the observation that it was a privilege to take such a remarkable fish on a rod from the collection of Paul Young—or the corollary that his split-cane craftsmanship still has echoes of immortality.

During these past months, that feeling existed strongly through several long afternoons at the Anglers' Club of New York. My purpose was to examine the rare fly rods in the club's collection and make a series of measured drawings of its most important artifacts. Those were quiet hours spent above Fraunces Tavern, studying the nineteenth-century memorabilia, with the street traffic strangely muted.

The fire gradually guttered out in the grate below the forty-pound Cascapedia salmon and the fly box of Theodore Gordon on the millwork mantelpiece. Each rod was examined in its turn, and each worked its unique magic, evoking speculation about the past. There was a fine greenheart built by Ebenezer Green, and a pair of pale lemonwood rods from the planing blocks of Thaddeus Norris in Philadelphia. The prize artifact was perhaps the elegant six-strip bamboo built by Solon Phillippe after the Civil War, although there was also an exceptional hardwood rod with a graceful handle wrapped in black-lacquered cord from the workshop of William Mitchell.

There was also a princely presentation rod built for John Lee Pratt, one of the founding officers of Standard Oil, its delicate split-cane sections in a polished butternut case lined with faded velvet. The rod was a Wilkinson, and its obvious artistry was the work of Eustis Edwards, Fred Thomas, and Edward Payne. These men had been principal apprentices in the Leonard shops from their Bangor days, and they formed a brief partnership after leaving Leonard at the close of the nineteenth century. This particular rod had peculiarly rococo embellishments of actual gold on its ferrules and reel fittings. The gold-plated guides were embellished with gold thread, and the reel seat was polished gold-bearing quartz.

The rod was kept in a glass-covered vitrine, and I had always viewed it with awe until I discovered that this cabinet also housed a Leonard that had once belonged to George Michel Lucien LaBranche, and the graceful Payne that Theodore Gordon had acquired by bartering thirty-nine dozen of his exquisitely dressed Catskill flies.

But the ultimate treasure was perhaps the solitary Leonard wrapped in a musty cloth sack, standing in the glass-door cabinet above the staircase. It was not a particularly pretty Leonard, its cork grip surprisingly clumsy to anyone familiar with the classic Leonard designs of the past half century. Its tag identified the rod as the property of Otto von Kienbusch, the famous art collector and antiquarian who had been a stalwart member of the Anglers' Club since before the First World War. The tag whetted my curiosity and when I opened the faded poplin, my heart almost stopped.

It belonged to Skues! I thought. *Skues!*

It was the model that Hewitt had first demonstrated in London with tournament caster Edward Bate Mills, at the Crystal Palace Exposition in 1904. George Edward Mackenzie Skues had already acquired a heavier ten-foot Leonard the year before, through his American fishing companion, Walter Durfee Coggeshall. Skues was steadily gaining fame as the father of nymph tactics—and had suffered notoriety for his debates with Frederick Halford and his dry-fly disciples. Edward Bate Mills was a partner of William Mills & Sons, long the principal agents for Leonard equipment, and Skues had eagerly studied his catalogues. The following winter, Skues completed some particularly successful legal work in London, and a grateful client offered him the finest rod that British sterling could purchase. His fishing friends were shocked when Skues selected another Leonard, and in his *Nymph Fishing for Chalk Stream Trout* Skues writes that its poetry and precise character played a major role in his chalk-stream studies.

It is tragic that these irreplaceable artifacts of American angling history were either destroyed or badly damaged in a meaningless bombing that killed four people, and mindlessly scarred both the Anglers' Club of New York and Fraunces Tavern in 1975.

This past summer at Sun Valley it was a rare privilege to study a vintage Hardy that once belonged to Ernest Hemingway. It was the classic John James Hardy, fitted with an elegant reverse-locking reel seat and gleaming back filler. The locking hood was richly engraved with the Royal Coat of Arms that went with Hardy's designation by the Court of Saint James's. Concealed inside the reel seat was a turf blade unique to British chalkstream rods, and Hemingway had purchased it in London with the royalties that followed his *Farewell to Arms*. It was a remarkably fine Hardy, with the elegant fittings and delicate ornamental wrappings typical of British workmanship after the First World War.*

Papa liked the country vintages, Jack Hemingway laughed as he poured two glasses of Corbieres. *It's a perfect wine for inspecting his Hardy—you might enjoy both!*

Why? Puck Hemingway teased with a merciless grin. *You see one fish pole and you've seen them all!*

Not quite, I said.

The fireplace was growing almost cold, and I carefully put away a favorite Leonard to carry some fresh logs from the cordwood stacked under a sheltering eave. The coals quickly ignited the fresh logs with a brief coaxing, the fire flared eagerly toward the flue, and several favorite rod cases still remained.

One held a favorite Orvis Battenkill, the delicate eight-foot taper that weighs four ounces and takes a six-weight line. Although it is primarily intended for trout fishing, its first baptism took place on the salmon rivers of Iceland.

That baptism was actually an accident, since it occurred when an angler from Zurich suddenly became ill, and I was offered the last hour of his beat on the Nordurá. It was early summer, and the swift little river was filled with fish bright from its fjord at Borgarnes. The pool I had luckily drawn was

---

*The rod is now in the collection of my old friend Adrian Dufflocq, who is the most accomplished fisherman in Chile.

the Stekkur, where the river works smoothly against a steep cliff of lava, its currents swelling above the chutes downstream. Asgeir Ingolfsson is perhaps the finest salmon fisherman in Iceland, and Ingolfsson was excited about fishing the Stekkur.

It's a great pool, Ingolfsson explained. *Some people even like it better than the Laxfoss.*

We've only got an hour, I said.

When the Stekkur is right, he countered quietly, *we don't need the whole morning.*

We walked down past a summer fishing house, with the pool still lying in its morning shadows. The current was smooth and swimming-pool green against the ledges, and while Ingolfsson carefully explained its holding-lies, a salmon porpoised in the tail shallows. Arctic terns were quarreling shrilly above our heads, and I slipped carefully into the shallows.

It feels right, I thought excitedly.

Those feelings were quickly confirmed when my fly swing stopped on the second cast. It was a six-pound henfish that jumped twice before I coaxed it away from the primary holding-lie against the ledges. I tailed it quickly in the shallows. Less than five minutes passed before the bright flash of a salmon showed deep in the current, and I was into a second six-pound fish. It cartwheeled wildly downstream, and I was certain it had alarmed the other fish against the upper ledge. Finally it surrendered, and when the little Blue Vulture was carefully reknotted to the tippet, I patiently started fishing through again.

Apparently the salmon had frightened the others, because I worked through the pool without another taking fish, although a salmon rolled tentatively behind the fly swing. There was a grilse that came as a bonus, lying away from the usual taking lies, and I landed it quickly.

Try the fish that rolled, Ingolfsson suggested. *Those fish along the ledge have forgotten you now.*

Only five minutes, I warned myself.

The salmon that had followed my fly swing was still there, and still in a curious mood. It rolled twice as the little Blue Vulture teased past its lie. With only two minutes left before the midday curfew, I changed to a small Black Fitch-tail and it worked. The salmon took with a lazy porpoise roll and jumped wildly, its splash exploding in the bright sunlight. It was a strong fish, better than fifteen pounds, and it bulldogged upstream against a bellying line. Suddenly the line fouled on a boulder at midstream. The throbbing tension told me the salmon was still hooked, and there was nothing left except to wade out and free it.

Your hour is already over! Ingolfsson laughed.

The river was swift and strong, and icy trickles worked over my waders and down my legs. Finally I could reach beyond the boulder with the little Orvis, and the fouled line throbbed briefly and worked free. There was still another halfhearted run in the fish, but I forced it toward the shallows and tailed it.

That was something! Ingolfsson helped carry the salmon back along the path. *I've got to get one of those rods!*

That was some hour we picked! I added.

It was an unforgettable baptism for the little Battenkill, but a week later I was fishing the Grimsá with John Hilson, and it took a memorable thirty-pound salmon at Laxfos-shylur that still holds the fly record for the river.

Such memories led me to a relatively new treasure in my collection, and it has served me so well that I uncased it gladly. It is a nine-and-a-half-foot rod that takes a seven-weight line, its design a remarkable mixture of qualities. Its maker is Samuel Carlson in Connecticut, a fine craftsman who owns the rodmaking patents and equipment of William and Eugene Edwards. The rod is a three-piece design of four-strip construction, using the four-strip calibrations of William Edwards and the reel-seat fittings of his brother Eugene. Each of the brothers made rods under his own imprint in the eastern Connecticut village of Canterbury. They were the sons of Eustis Edwards, one of the original Leonard apprentices in the old Bangor shop.

The casting stroke of this Carlson quadrate is lazily poetic, yet it will handle both an entire WF-7-S line and fish relatively light tippets with its delicate tip calibrations. The quadrate has traveled with me to Scotland, fishing the Invercauld beats from the Brig O'Dee to the Wash-House Pool opposite Balmoral Castle, and on the classic Cairnton water fished by the late Arthur H. E. Wood at Banchory. It has also served me well this past summer on the Stillaguamish, fishing early summer steelhead with Ralph Wahl and Wes Drain. Its performance at Blue Slough and Skier's led me to carry it west again in October, fishing the Umpqua with Jack Hemingway, Dan Callaghan, and Frank Moore at Steamboat. It took a fine tail-walking steelhead at Wright Creek Pool, but I can also remember hours of casting without luck, when I went fishless in the cold rain at Kitchen. But the most exciting fish came on the Grimsá, where I hooked a twenty-three-pound cockfish with a riffling hitch, and had to follow along the lava-cliff battlements when it left the pool over a twelve-foot waterfall.

There is another rod in my collection that I already fish with happy thoughts, a poetic Howells of seven-and-a-half feet and a delicate three ounces, designed to fish a DT-4-F line. It had its baptism at Hewitt's Flat on the Brodheads, handling 7X tippets perfectly during an April hatch of *Paraleptophlebia* flies. It has also fished the Au Sable, on a pilgrimage back to such boyhood rivers in Michigan, and it later worked well on the Firehole at Biscuit Basin in August.

But its most pervasive memory involves a morning in early June, fishing the Longparish beats with Dermot Wilson on the Test. It was a surprisingly cold day, with intermittent periods of misting rain. Longparish is a charming village of thatched-roof houses, its beats divided at a mill that bridges the river. The keeper's hut is a hexagonal tower with a steep roof of thatch, its leaded-glass windows looking down into the pool under the mill itself. During lunch we spotted a five-pound fish nymphing quietly along a bed of undulating weeds. We fished up from the lower water after lunch, finding the trout concentrating on nymphs in the smooth-flowing channels between the ranunculus. Dermot Wilson followed along the path, pointing out good fish and holding places, and I was as surprised as anyone when the big fish we had spotted from the mill tower took my nymph.

Cooperative fish! Wilson applauded. *Well played!*

The exquisite Howells reminds me that a fine bamboo rod has the magic to evoke the future, as well as echoes of rivers past. There is a second Howells in my collection now, unfished and smelling freshly of its flawless tung-oil varnish. Its tapers are designed specifically for the cobweb-fine tippets under .007 inches and a DT-3-F British silk line. It is difficult for me to wait until the early-summer hatches on the Firehole and the Henry's Fork, where the fish are both large and wonderfully tippet-shy.

Thoughts of those Henry's Fork rainbows working steadily to thousands of tiny *Ephemerella* olives turn to another rod that I have never fished, although it is hardly new. It is a remarkably delicate three-piece Thomas weighing only three ounces, measuring a full eight feet, and perfectly mated to a three-weight Kingfisher silk. Its weight and ³⁄₆₄ths tip calibrations make it perfect for light-tackle work, and the number stamped into its butt cap makes it the thirtieth Thomas Special of its design. That should date its birth to the beginning of the century, and should humble the cracker-barrel opinions that attribute the origins of ultrafine fishing solely to our generation.

The Thomas Special was a Christmas present from the family, and it is only six weeks until dogtooth violets offer their faint prelude to springtime in the Appalachians—when that venerable Thomas can work its alchemy on the Brodheads, with regattas of tiny *Baetis* flies hatching under its mossy April ledges.

[1976]

Appendix

MATCHING THE *TRICORYTHODES* AND *PSEUDOCLOËON* MAYFLIES

The following are the author's descriptions of the ten species of *Tricorythodes* and the nineteen species of *Pseudocloëon* mayflies found in American trout streams, together with their imitations. The lengths cited for the bodies are from the head to the end of the abdomen. Wing lengths refer to the length of a single wing. Also given is the zoogeographic distribution of each species with the following abbreviations: *NE* (northeast), *SE* (southeast), *SC* (south-central), *NC* (north-central), *W* (west), *SW* (southwest), and *NW* (northwest).

Tricorythodes

SPECIES	REGION	NYMPH COLOR	NYMPH LENGTH (mm)	NYMPH HOOK SIZE
albilineatus	SE	Dark brown	5.5	20
allectus	SE	Dark brown	5.0	22
atratus	NC	Olive brown	5.5	20
explicatus	SE	Olive brown	7.0	16
fallax	NC, NW	Dark brown	6.5	18
fictus	NC, C	Rusty brown	6.5	18
minutus	W, NW	Chocolate	4.5	24
peridius	NC, W	Pale brown	5.0	22
stygiatus	SE, NE, C	Brown	5.5	20
texanus	SC, SW	Olive	4.5	24

Tricorythodes

SPECIES	WING LENGTH (mm)	BODY LENGTH (mm)	SUBIMAGO WING COLOR	SUBIMAGO BODY COLOR
albilineatus	5.5	5.0	Gray	Dark brown
allectus	5.0	4.5	Gray	Brown
atratus	5.5	5.0	Gray	Yellowish brown
explicatus	6.5	6.0	Gray	Rusty brown
fallax	6.0	5.5	Gray	Rusty brown
fictus	6.0	5.5	Gray	Rusty brown
minutus	4.5	4.0	Gray	Dark brown
peridius	5.0	4.5	Gray	Amber
stygiatus	5.5	5.0	Gray	Blackish brown
texanus	4.5	4.0	Gray	Dark olive

Tricorythodes

SPECIES	DUN HOOK SIZE	IMAGO WING COLOR	IMAGO BODY COLOR	SPINNER HOOK SIZE
albilineatus	22	White	Dark brown	22
allectus	24	White	Pale brown	24
atratus	22	White	Amber	22
explicatus	18	White	Chocolate	18
fallax	20	White	Rusty brown	20
fictus	20	White	Rusty brown	20
minutus	26	White	Blackish brown	26
peridius	24	White	Yellowish	24
stygiatus	22	White	Blackish brown	22
texanus	26	White	Yellowish olive	26

Pseudocloëon

SPECIES	REGION	NYMPH COLOR	NYMPH LENGTH (mm)	NYMPH HOOK SIZE
alachua	SE	Yellowish	5.5	20
anoka	C	Pale olive	5.5	20
bimaculatum	SE	Olive	5.5	20
carolina	NE, SE	Dark olive brown	5.0	22
chlorops	NE	Dark brown	5.0	22
cingulatum	NE	Brown	5.0	22
dubium	NE, SE	Rusty brown	5.5	20
edmundsi	W	Bright olive	4.5	24
elliotti	C	Dark olive	5.0	22
etowah	SE	Olive	5.0	22
futile	NW	Yellowish	4.0	26
ida	C	Olive	5.5	20
myrsum	C	Brown	5.5	20
parvulum	C	Pale olive	4.0	26
punctiventris	C	Pale brown	5.5	20
rubrolaterale	NW	Rusty brown	5.0	22
turbidum	SW	Dark brown	5.0	22
veteris	C	Dark olive	6.0	18
virile	NE	Brown	6.0	18

Pseudocloëon

SPECIES	WING LENGTH (mm)	BODY LENGTH (mm)	SUBIMAGO WING COLOR	SUBIMAGO BODY COLOR
alachua	5.5	5.0	Gray	Olive
anoka	5.5	5.0	White	Olive
bimaculatum	5.5	5.0	Gray	Olive
carolina	5.0	4.5	Gray	Dark olive brown
chlorops	5.0	4.5	Gray	Brown
cingulatum	5.0	4.5	Gray	Sepia
dubium	5.5	5.0	Gray	Brown
edmundsi	4.5	4.0	White	Green
elliotti	5.0	4.5	Gray	Dark olive
etowah	5.0	4.5	Gray	Olive
futile	4.0	3.5	White	Olive
ida	5.5	5.0	Gray	Olive
myrsum	5.5	5.0	Gray	Brown
parvulum	4.0	3.5	White	Olive
punctiventris	5.5	5.0	White	Olive brown
rubrolaterale	5.0	4.5	Gray	Rusty brown
turbidum	5.0	4.5	Gray	Olive
veteris	6.0	5.5	Gray	Olive
virile	6.0	5.5	Gray	Brown

384

Pseudocloëon

SPECIES	DUN HOOK SIZE	IMAGO WING COLOR	IMAGO BODY COLOR	SPINNER HOOK SIZE
alachua	22	White	Brown	22
anoka	22	White	Amber	22
bimaculatum	22	White	Amber	22
carolina	24	White	Brown	24
chlorops	24	White	Brown	24
cingulatum	24	White	Amber	24
dubium	22	White	Brown	22
edmundsi	26	White	Green	26
elliotti	24	White	Brown	24
etowah	24	White	Amber	24
futile	28	White	Yellow	28
ida	22	White	Amber	22
myrsum	22	White	Brown	22
parvulum	28	White	Amber	28
punctiventris	22	White	Brown	22
rubrolaterale	24	White	Yellow	24
turbidum	24	White	Brown	24
veteris	20	White	Brown	20
virile	20	White	Brown	20

Index

Abacos Islands, 338–46
Abbett, Bob, 19
Abbey fly, 351
Ackroyd fly, 88, 349
Acroneuria hatches, 224
Adams spentwing fly, 77, 126, 128, 229, 276
Adventures in Fishing (Grey), 145
Aelianus, 273
Afognak Island (Alaska), 321
Alaska, 363–64
    see also specific locations
Albert, Prince, 314
Alkalinity of water, 123–28, 224, 244, 246, 274
Allen, Ethan, 366
Allen, Zeke, 144, 149, 153
Alta River (Norway), 314, 324, 351, 373
Amateur Rodmaking (Frazer), 35
American Angler's Book (Norris), 18, 25, 26
American Trout Stream Insects (Rhead), 17
American Trout Streams (Ingraham), 27, 35

Analomink River (Pennsylvania), 23–24
Anderegg, Gene, 126
Anderson, Don, 150
Angler's and Sportsman's Guide (Rice and Held), 35
Anglers' Club of New York, 18, 27, 35, 37, 38–39
    fly rods of, 375–77
    founders of, 33–34
Angler's Entomology, An (Harris), 163
Angler's Roost, 12
Aniak River (Alaska), 321
Anitcosti Island (Canada), 323
Antrim Lodge, 21
Ants, 54, 114, 121, 128, 196, 205
Any Luck? (Connett)
Apple-green tree worms, 205
Arbona, Fred, 161
Arctic char, 288
Arctic grayling, 288
Argentina, 303, 358, 360–61, 371–73
Arkansas River (Colorado), 231–33, 294, 313

Åroy River (Norway), 315, 352, 373
Arte of Angling, The, 50
Art of Tying the Wet Fly, The (Leisenring), 39
Ashford Castle, 314, 354
Ashley, William Henry, 109
Ashley-Cooper, John, 353
Ashokan Reservoir, 11
Atherton, John, 14, 19, 179, 353
Atlantic salmon, 260–66, 289, 313–15, 359
  on dry flies, 322–24
  fly rods for, 373–75, 377–80
  greased-line method for, 326–27
  in Maine, 365–66
  patterns of behavior, 323
  steelhead versus, 316–29
  on wet flies, 324–27
Aurland River (Norway), 351
Au Sable River (Michigan), 84, 185, 192, 196–99, 206, 215–16, 380
Ausable River (New York), 186, 204
Averill, Walter, 215–16

Babcock, Havilah, 358
Babine River (British Columbia), 322, 333
Babine Special fly, 88
Baetis fly, 196, 250
Baetis hatches, 115, 120, 121, 128, 171, 274, 295, 381
  Pseudocloëon confused with, 194–98
  species of, 198
Bahamas, 335–46
  bonefish in, 335–37, 341–46
  history of, 337–40
Baldvinsson, Steingrimur, 264, 265
Baldwin, Edward, 27
Baldwin River (Michigan), 69
Ballater River (Scotland), 352
Ballynahinch River (Ireland), 314, 354
Bamboo fly-rods, 26, 34, 44, 368–81
Banks, Lawrence, 359
Barnes, Pat, 129

Barometric pressure, 325–26
Barr, Manning, 40
Barracuda, 335, 340–41
Bass, 10, 307–309
Bataviakill River (New York), 8, 10
Battenkill Conservancy, 362
Battenkill River (Vermont–New York), 103, 179, 185, 192, 193, 207, 301, 330
  Hill Farm property and, 362–63, 366
Battle River (Alaska), 359
Beaverkill River (New York), 4, 7, 15, 23, 32, 50, 129, 185, 198, 205, 206, 271, 279, 332, 368
  described, 17, 19–21
Beaverkill Trout Club, 19
Bechler River (Idaho), 107
Beetle larvae imitation, 99, 100
Beetles, 128, 196, 205
  on the Henry's Fork of the Snake, 114, 115
  on the Letort, 55–56, 60–61
Bellefonte Hatchery, 284
Benchill fly, 349
Benn, John, 144
Bergman, Ray, 14, 17, 124, 150–51, 231, 235
  described, 40
Berners, Dame Juliana, 50, 161
Besse, Art, 98–102
Bethune, George Washington, 7, 25
Bibio fly, 354
Bibio hatches, 287, 322–23
Big Bend Club, 13
Big Hole River (Montana), 219, 223, 224, 225, 334
Big Horn River (Montana), 192, 193, 221, 279, 283, 293, 330
Big South Branch (Michigan), 70
Big Spring (Pennsylvania), 274
Big Two-Hearted River (Michigan), 304
Big Wood River (Idaho), 245–46
Biology of Mayflies (Needham), 180–81, 196, 197
Bird, Cal, 150
Bivisible flies, 43
Black, Cappy, 144

Black and Silver fly, 351
Black Comet fly, 317
Black Doctor fly, 349, 350
Black Dose fly, 349
Black Fitchtail fly, 88, 379
Black Forest streams (Germany), 270
Black Gordon fly, 150
Black hellgrammites, 221
Black Pennell fly, 354
Black Ranger fly, 349
Blacktail Spring Creek (Wyoming), 192
Blackville fly, 353
Blackwater River (Ireland), 354
Blades, Bill, 66
Blue Charm fly, 88, 263, 350, 352
Blue Crane Spring Creek (Wyoming), 192
Blue Quill fly, 122, 128
Blue Sapphire fly, 353
Blue Vulture fly, 353, 378
Blue-winged Adams fly, 225
Blue-winged Olive flies, 9, 128, 194–95
Blue-winged Olive hatches, 16, 77, 122, 165, 193–95, 205
    see also Pseudocloëon mayflies
Boardman River (Michigan), 185, 206
Boca Chimehuin (Argentina), 372
Boies, Edward, 33
Boke of St. Albans, 320
Bolstad, Nils, 374
Bolter, the, 239–40
Bonefish, 335–37, 341–46, 361
Bonner, Paul Hyde, 354
Book of Trout Flies, A (Jennings), 8, 39, 207, 209
Borgeson, Dave, 85–94
Bow River (Canada), 364
Boyd, Megan, 350
Boynton, C. B., 32
Brachycercus mayflies, 181, 182, 183
Bradley, William, 18
Bradner, Enos, 152
Brass Hat fly, 88
Bridger, Jim, 121, 125

Bright Salmon and Brown Trout (Lamb), 41
British Empire Medal, 350
Broadback River (Quebec), 364, 366
Brobst, Hiram, 43
Brodhead, Captain Daniel, 23–24
Brodheads Creek (Pennsylvania), 22–47, 50, 129, 210, 304
    fly rods for, 380, 381
    hatches on, 42–43, 46, 47, 274–75
    hurricane of 1955 and, 42–43, 46
    introduced trout and, 32–33, 271–75
Brodheads Forest and Stream, 39, 40
Brooklyn Flyfishers, 19, 27, 46
    founders of, 32, 33
Brooks, Don, 39
Brooks River (Alaska), 359
Brook trout, 179, 274
    in the Brodheads, 27–32
    described, 278–79, 280
    destruction of habitat of, 267, 270, 279–80, 364
    grasshoppers and, 229, 238
    in the Neversink, 14
Brown, Page, 40
Brown Drake hatches, 275
Brown-hackled sedge fly, 166
Brown trout:
    in the Au Sable, 216
    bamboo rods for, 368–69
    in the Brodheads, 32–33, 38, 41–42, 43, 271–75
    in the Cane, 214
    in Chile, 361
    European, 32–33, 267–71
    in the Firehole, 120–30
    grasshoppers and, 228, 230, 232–40
    Hendrickson hatches and, 204, 210, 211
    introduced, see Introduced brown trout
    in the Letort, 50–64
    in the Namekagon, 97–102
    in the Neversink, 15
    in the Pegnitz, 254–55

in the Pere Marquette, 73, 78,
79–80, 83–84
reservoirs and, 11, 15
in the Saugeen, 258–59
in the Schoharie, 9, 10
Brown-winged bucktail fly,
220–21
Brule, Étienne, 74
Brule River (Wisconsin), 100,
186, 304, 321
Brush, William, 84
Bryan, Bob, 262
Bryan, Charles, 27, 32, 33, 46
Buchan, John, ix
Buckmaster, Bob, 360
Bucktail flies, 16, 340, 343, 344
Buffalo Bill, 36
Buffalo River (Idaho), 106
Buffalo Springs (Ozarks), 244
Bullwinkle, J. E., 32
Burks, B. D., 181, 183
Burnett, Ralph, 32
Burnham, Fred, 144, 145–46,
150

Caddisfly hatches, 225, 226, 275,
311
on the Firehold, 124, 126
on Henry's Fork of the Snake,
114–15
on the Maigue, 169–71, 175–76
on the Pere Marquette, 68–69,
73
stomach contents of browns
and, 285–87
Caenidae family of mayflies,
180–82
Caenis hatch, 180–81, 183
Cahill fly, 71, 205
Callaghan, Dan, 111
on the Madison, 217–18
on the North Umpqua, 136–40,
149, 155–56, 323, 325, 380
Callibaetis hatches, 114, 115
Callicoon River (New York), 6, 7
Camogue River (Ireland), 167
Camp, Raymond, 8
Camp, Samuel, 18
Campbell, Charles, 18
Canada, *see specific rivers*
Candlestick Maker fly, 349

Cane River (North Carolina),
213–14
Cane River Camp, 213
Canoe-drop fishing, 324
Caperer hatch, 175–76
Capnia hatches, 274
Carlson, Samuel, 379
Carlson fly rods, 379–80
Carmichael, Bob, 255–57, 260
Carpenter, Morris, 29
Carson, Sumner, 144
Cascapedia River (New
Brunswick), 350
Caspian Sea (Soviet Union), 289,
290
Castalia Club Creek (Ohio), 245
Casting:
for Atlantic salmon, 324–27
for rainbow trout, 116
with a Young Parabolic 19 fly
rod, 373
Catch-and-release fishing, 277
Catskill Creek (New York), 6
Catskill Mountains trout
streams, 4–21, 23, 26, 32,
49–50
reservoirs and, 7
sources of, 6–7
Catskill School of fly dressing, 4,
10, 13, 14, 17, 18
Cave, Edward, 33, 35
Cedar Run (Pennsylvania), 233
Chalkstreams:
in Britain, 50, 51–52, 120, 244,
271
fly rods for, 376–77
in Iceland, 264
in Idaho, 109, 333
in Wisconsin, 98–102
Chama River (New Mexico), 221,
293
Chandler, William, 14
Char, 280, 288, 292, 317
Childers fly, 349
Chile, 358, 360, 361
Chinook salmon, 94–95, 149,
333–34
Chironomus midges, 54
Christian, Herman, 14
Cinnamon sedge fly, 164, 166
Cinnamon sedge hatch, 170, 175

Civilian Conservation Corps, 294
Claasenia hatches, 216–17, 225, 226, 287
Clackamas River (Oregon), 320
Clark, Dick, 39
Clearwater River (Idaho), 320, 326, 332
Cleveland, Grover, 25, 30, 31
Coachman fly, 77
Coffee Pot Club, 110
Coggeshall, Walter Durfee, 376
Coho salmon, 317, 333–34
Cold Spring Harbor hatchery, 268–71
Coleman, John, 144
Coleman, R. M., 32
Colgan, Mary, 162–63
Colorado River (Colorado), 222, 223, 365
Colter, John, 109, 121
Coltsfoot, 305–306
Columbus, Christopher, 337
Combs, Trey, 145
Compleat Angler, The (Bethune), 25
Compleat Angler, The (Walton), 335
Complete Book of Fly Casting (Knight), 39
Conetquot River (Long Island), 271, 301
Connemara Black fly, 354
Connett, Eugene, 29, 38
Conover, Scott, 18
Coolidge, Calvin, 36, 47
Corey, Ralph, 84
Corey calftail fly, 77
Corps of Engineers, U.S. Army, 364
Corrib Lake (Ireland), 163
Cosseboom fly, 351
Cowles Communication, ix
Cramer, Vic, 84
Cramer nymph, 84
Crater Lake (Oregon), 142–43, 244
Crooked Creek (Oregon), 244
Crosfield fly, 353
Cross, Reuben, 7, 17
Crowsnest River (Canada), 364
Cummings, Ward, 150

Cummings fly, 139, 150
Current Springs (Ozarks), 244
Cutthroat trout, 71, 289
  in Jackson Hole, 255–58, 274

Darbee, Elsie, xi, 4
Darbee, Harry, xi, 4, 16, 18–19
Dark Donnelly Variant fly, 128
Dark Hendrickson fly, 128
De Bergh, Clare, 164–65, 174
De Costa, Juan, 338
Dee River (Scotland), 262, 326, 349, 352
De Lariviere, Mauricio, 303
Delaware River (New York–Pennsylvania), 15, 24, 192, 364
Delaware River, East Branch of (New York), 6, 185
  described, 15–17
Delaware Water Gap, 24
Dennisoff, Nicholas, 315
De Rasloff, Harold, 33
Deren, Jim, 12
Deschutes River (Oregon), 142, 143, 221, 224, 225, 226, 244, 279, 293, 320, 326, 332
De Triana, Rodrigo, 337
Dette, Mary, 4
Dette, Walt, 4, 18
Dette, Winnie, 4
Dickerson, Lyle, 84, 368
Doak, Wallace, 353
Dolan, Richard, 167–68
Donnelley, Roy, 150
Donnelly Variant fly, 257
Downsville Dam (New York), 16
Down the Rogue (Grey), 148
Drain, Wes, 152, 380
Driva River (Norway), 315
Dry Brook (New York), 6, 7
Dry flies, *see specific flies*
Dry Fly and Fast Water (La Branche), 14, 35
Dry-fly method, 34
  Fox-Marinaro and, 54–58
  Halford-Marryat and, 54, 56–57
  Norris and, 26
Du Bois, Allen, 40
Duffing, Harry, 68

Dunraven, Lord, 170, 174
Dunraven Arms, 167, 177
Dunraven Castle, 168–69
Durkam Ranger fly, 349
Dusty Miller fly, 349, 351, 373, 374
Dutchman's Hole (New York), 179–80

East Kill River (New York), 8
Edmunds, George, 181, 184, 197
Edwards, Eugene, 379
Edwards, Eustis, 375, 379
Edwards, William, 379
Eel River (California), 142, 144, 150
Engerbretson, Dave, 103
England, *see specific rivers*
Epeorus hatches, 100, 274, 304
Ephemera hatches, 114, 115, 116, 128, 205
  brown trout and, 275
  in Ireland, 166, 169–77
Ephemerella hatches, 77, 113, 114, 115, 128, 195, 199, 200, 206–11, 215, 304, 381
  brown trout and, 274–75
  described, 208
  nymphs, 208–209, 210
  species of, 207, 209
  spinner stage, 209–10
Esopus Creek (New York), 7, 8, 321
  described, 11–13, 15–16
Esquire, 44, 48
Exum, Ed, 365

Fairy Creek (Yellowstone Park), 126
Fall, 330–34
Fall Favorite fly, 88
Falling Springs Run (Pennsylvania), 186, 192
Fall River (California), 186, 192, 244
Fall River (Idaho), 107
Farewell to Arms, A (Hemingway), 377
Fathers of American fly fishing, 35
Female Beaverkill fly, 209

Ferndon's Pool (New York), 206
Field & Stream, 12, 18, 34, 35
Field Book of Fresh Water Angling (Knight), 39
Fife, Duke of, 314
Finger Lakes (New York), 321
Firehole River (Yellowstone Park), 119–30, 245, 277, 283, 292, 333
  described, 123–28
  fly patterns for, 128
  fly rods for, 380, 381
  geysers in, 120, 130
  hatches on, 120–28, 201–203
  management regulations on, 128–30
  water temperature of, 120–28
Fish and Fishing (Forester), 25
Fisherman's Curses, 180
Fisherman's Luck (Van Dyke), 31
Fisherman's Winter (Haig-Brown), 358
Fishing Creek (Pennsylvania), 205
Fishless Days (Hackle), 32
Fish Spring Creek (Wyoming), 192
Fitzgerald, C. H., 32
Fitzgerald, Scott, 348, 360
Fitzgibbon, Edward, 26
Fjelstad, Kristjan, 266
Flaming 'Gorge (   ), 284
Flåm River (Norway), 314, 351
Flat Rock Club, 110
Flat Spring Creek (Wyoming), 192
Flick, Art, xi, 4–5, 8, 10, 18, 207
Flies, *see specific flies*
Floating-line techniques, 326
Fly and the Fish, The (Atherton), 14, 179, 353
Fly book, 347–56
Fly-dressing, 347–56, 357
  for brown trout, 277
  for grasshoppers, 230–31, 234–36
  for Hendrickson flies, 205, 207
  for Henry's Fork of the Snake, 116–18
  impressionism versus reality, 212–13

Fly-dressing *(continued)*
  for Irish waters, 163–77
  for *Isonychia* flies, 259
  for the Letort, 55–58
  for minute flies, 180, 191–92
  for the North Umpqua, 139–40,
    150
  for the Pere Marquette, 71, 77,
    84, 88
  for steelhead, 88
  for stoneflies, 214
  for Wisconsin chalkstreams,
    99
Fly Fisherman, ix, 178
Fly-Fisher's Entomology
  (Ronalds), 54, 56
Fly Fisher's Life (Ritz), 373
Fly-fishing-only waters:
  on the Beaverkill, 21
  on the Firehole, 129–30
  on Henry's Fork of the Snake,
    107–108
  on the Namekagon, 96
  on the North Umpqua, 145
  on the Pere Marquette, 88
  on the Silver Creek, 249–50
  in Yellowstone Park, 293
Fly Fishing Strategy (Richards
  and Swisher), 85
Flying ants, 53–54
Fly rods, 26, 34, 44, 368–81
Fly Rods and Fly Tackle (Wells),
  27
Folkert general store, 11–12
Foote, John Taintor, 18, 33, 44
  described, 34
Forest & Stream, 82
Forester, Frank, 25
Forest Service, U.S., 106
  on the North Umpqua, 135,
    149, 151–52, 154
Foster, Roger, 165–77
Fox, Charles, 43, 44, 48, 51, 186,
  233
  grasshoppers and, 235–40
  terrestrial imitations of, 54–55
Franco, Francisco, 355
Fraunces Tavern, 375–77
Frazer, Perry, 33, 35
Frontenac, Comte de, 74
Fur, Feathers and Steel (Cross), 17

Gailliard, Roger, 315
Game Fish of the North
  (Roosevelt), 25
Garnett's & Keegan's tackle shop,
  163–65, 176
Garry Dog fly, 350
Gaula River (Norway), 315,
  327–29
George River (Labrador),
  261–64, 313–14
Gibbon River (Yellowstone
  Park), 127, 245, 333
Gibraltar River (Alaska), 359
Gibson, Rainbow, 144
Gilbert, W. L., 269
Gilboa Reservoir (New York),
  10, 16
Gill, Emlyn, 18
Gillaroo trout, 291
Gingrich, Arnold, xi, 43, 48, 299
  described, 43–44
Gold Darter fly, 179
Golden Demon fly, 150
Gold-ribbed Hare's Ear fly, 128
Gordon, Clarence, 149–53
Gordon, Theodore, 7, 13, 17–18,
  26, 35, 40, 50, 375, 376
Gordon Quill fly, 13, 349
Gordon Quill hatches, 15, 18, 205
Gould, Jay, 7
Grand Cascapedia River
  (Canada), 260, 323
Grande Ronde River (Oregon),
  326, 332
Grant, George, 212, 217
Grant, Ulysses, 5, 121
Grant-style nymphs, 212–14, 217,
  218
Grasshopper flies, 230–31,
  234–36, 250
Grasshoppers, 53–54, 60, 62, 114,
  115, 122, 128, 228–40
  grasshopper wind, 231–34,
    237–38
Gray, James, 327
Gray Fox flies, 205
Gray Fox hatches, 46
Grayling, 253–54, 288
Gray-winged Olive fly, 116–17
Greased-line fishing, 262, 326–27,
  353

Great Lakes, 81–83, 321
Great Northern Paper Company,
  365–66
Green, Ebenezer, 375
Green, Seth, 245, 279
Green Butt fly, 88, 140, 353
Green Drake hatches, 14, 205
Green Highlander fly, 349
Green King fly, 349
Green River (Wyoming), 191,
  279, 293, 334
Grey, Zane, 144–48, 154, 318
Grey Heron fly, 349
Grimsa River (Iceland), 265–66,
  319, 354, 379, 380
Grimwood, Victor, 37–38
Grindstone Lake (Wisconsin), 98
Groody, Louise, 38
Grouse and Green fly, 128
Grove Creek (Idaho), 245, 246
Gruber, Ira, 353
Gun Dog (Wolters), 44
Gunnison River (Colorado),
  219–25, 233–34, 292

Haase farm, 30, 39, 40
Hackettstown Hatchery, 271
Hackle, Sparse Grey, 18, 32, 40,
  41
Haig-Brown, Roderick, 265, 318,
  353–54, 358
Hairwing fly, 352
Halford, Frederick, 17, 50, 53,
  376
  dry-fly theory and, 54, 56–57
Hall, R. J., 184
Halliday, Len, 84
Handbook of Angling
  (Fitzgibbon), 26
Hanes, Borden, 213–14
Hanes, Millie, 213
Hanlon, John, 163
Hardy fly book, 349
Hardy fly rods, 377
Hardy reels, 93, 118, 343
Harger, Don, 150
Harriman, Jack, 38
Harriman Ranch, 105, 107, 108,
  111, 114, 116, 189
Harris, J. R., 163–65, 169
Harrison, Benjamin, 30

Harrison, Carter, 110
Harrop, Rene, 103, 109, 114,
  116–18, 204
Hatcheries, *see specific hatchery*
Hatchery trout, 51, 245, 267–71
  brook, 279
  brown, 267–71
  in the Firehole, 119, 129
  in the Letort, 59
  in the Pere Marquette, 81
  rainbow, 277–78, 294–95
  in the Silver Creek, 248
  in the Snake, 258
Hatches, 16, 20
  on the Brodheads, 42–43, 46,
    47, 274–75
  brown trout and, 274–77
  favorite, 205–206
  on the Firehole, 120–28
  of Hendrickson flies, 204–11
  on the Henry's Fork of the
    Snake, 105, 107, 111–18
  in Ireland, 164–77
  on the Letort, 53–58
  masking, 111–13, 227, 275–76
  matching, 161, 255, 256,
    275–77, 383–89
  microhabitat and, 115–16
  of minute insects, 121–22,
    178–92
  multiple, 111
  on the Namekagon, 100–101
  in the Pegnitz, 254
  on the Pere Marquette, 68–73,
    77–79, 83
  of *Pseudocloëon*, 193–203
  salmonfly, 219–27
  on the Schoharie, 8–10
  springtime, 301–302
  stonefly, 212–18
  summertime, 311–13
  of *Tricorythodes*, 179–92
  see also specific insects
Hat Creek (California), 244
Hayden, Colonel Frank, 150
Headrick, Frank, 152
Hearthstone Hotel, 18
Hebgen Lake (Yellowstone
  Park), 127
Held, Reuben, 33, 35
Heller Branch (Pennsylvania), 28

Hellgrammites, 128
Helmsdale Doctor fly, 350
Hemingway, Ernest, 44, 249,
    270, 377
Hemingway, Jack, 108–109, 111,
    116, 200–201, 377
  Nature Conservancy and, 242,
    249, 362
  on the North Umpqua, 132–34,
    149, 154–55, 380
Hemingway, Puck, 155, 377
Hendrickson, Albert Everett, 18,
    206
Hendrickson fly, 14, 18, 19, 128
  fly dressing for, 205, 207
Hendrickson hatches, 10, 15,
    204–11, 300
  described, 208
  nymphs, 208–209, 210
  spinner stage, 209–10
Henry, Colonel Andrew, 109
Henry, Arthur, 24
Henry, Eugene, 41
Henry, James, 25, 30
Henry, Luther, 25, 47
Henry, Russell, 41
Henry's Fork of the Snake River
    (Idaho), 103–18, 192, 217,
    221, 224, 245, 274, 283,
    333
  described, 106–109
  fertility of, 110–11, 186
  fly rods for, 381
  hatches on, 105, 107, 111–18,
    189, 200, 225
  microhabitat of, 115–16
  plans to dam, 364–65
Henry's Lake (Idaho), 104, 106,
    109, 110
Henryville Flyfishers, 45–46
Henryville House, 22–47, 272
Henryville Special fly, 43
Herman to His Grandchildren
    (Rethoret), 40
Hesperoperla hatches, 224–25,
    226
Hewitt, Edward Ringwood, 7,
    13–14, 18, 29, 33, 45, 47, 50,
    52, 62, 64, 260, 376
  described, 34–35
Hexagenia fly, 80, 83, 84

Hexagenia hatches, 68–69, 70,
    78–79, 83, 206, 220
"Hidden Hatch, The," 178
Hidy, Vernon, 39
Hill Farm, 362–63, 366
Hilson, John, 379
Hoback River (Wyoming), 258
Holland, Ray, 18
Hooks, 128
  for minute flies, 180, 185
Hoover, Herbert, 144
Hot Creek (California), 245
Hotel Rapids, 39, 40
Housatonic River
    (Connecticut–Massachusetts),
    332
Houseman, Maurice, 83
Howard, F. S., 32
Howard, Herb, 17
Howells, Gary, 370, 371
Howells, H. H., 370, 371
Howells, Joe, 154
Howells fly rod, 380–81
How to Take Trout on Wet Flies
    and Nymphs (Sens), 12
How to Tell Fish from Fishermen
    (Zern), 39
Hudson River (New York), 5–6
Humpy fly, 276
Hunt, Richard Carley, 40, 41, 47
Hurst, Peter, 258, 259
Hutchens, Jim, 144
Hybridization, 249, 278
Hydropsyche hatches, 275

Iceland, see specific rivers
I Go A-Fishing (Prime), 29
Iliamna, Lake (Alaska), 333, 359
Indians, 23–24
Induced-rise method, 175–76
Ingolfsson, Asgeir, 378–79
Ingraham, Henry, 27–28, 33, 35
Inks, David, 242, 250–51
"In Praise of Trout—and Also
    Me," 12
"In the Tail of the Flat," 38
Introduced brown trout, 267–95
  alevins, 283, 302
  in the Brodheads, 32–33, 271,
    272, 274–75
  as cannibals, 280

controversy over, 272–73, 277–80
described, 278, 281
fighting ability of, 278–79
fly patterns and, 273, 276–77
habitat destruction and, 267, 270, 279–80, 285–86
hatches and, 274–75
kelts, 283, 302 ·
life cycle of, 281–84, 302
life span of, 284
origin of, 267–71
riverine versus sea-run, 281, 288–92
as selective feeders, 271–77
size of, 272, 283, 284
spawning of, 281–83, 302, 334
stomach contents data, 284–87
subspecies of, 281, 288–92
survival rates of, 287–88
in western rivers, 292–95
winterkills of, 283, 288
zoogeography of, 269, 288–92
Invercauld River (Scotland), 379–80
Ireland, 162–77
Iron Blue Dun fly, 128, 165, 171, 172, 176, 254
Iron blue mayfly hatch, 169, 170, 176, 177
Iron River, East Fork of (Wisconsin), 98–102
Isaacs, Toggery Bill, 144
Island Park Reservoir (Idaho), 106, 108, 110, 225, 365
Isonychia hatches, 12, 100–101, 205, 258–59
Ivan's Lodge, 71

Jacklin, Bob, 228
Jackson Hole (Wyoming), 192
cutthroat trout in, 255–58, 274
Japanese beetles, 60, 63
Jassid flies, 56, 128, 237
Jeannie fly, 352
Jefferson, Joseph, 25, 31
Jenkins, Guy, 18, 40
Jenkins, Henry, 40
Jennings, Preston, 8, 17, 39, 40, 161, 207, 209

Jockie fly, 352
Jock O'Dee fly, 349
Jock Scott fly, 349, 350
Joe's Hopper fly, 235
Joliet, Louis, 74–76
Judith River (Montana), 293
Junction Pool (New York), 17
Jupiter River (Canada), 322–23
Just Fishing (Bergman), 40

Kade, Art, 230
Kade pattern grasshoppers, 230–31, 234–35
Kahn, Robert, 40
Kalama River (Washington), 320
Kalama Special fly, 88
Karluk Lake (Alaska), 316–18
Katmai, Mount (Alaska), 333, 360
Kattermann, George, 43
Kattermann fly, 43
Kelly, George, 293
Kelson, George, 350
Kennedy, Mike, 152
Kern rainbow trout, 81
Kettle River (Pennsylvania), 186
Kilrain, Jake, 30
Kinderhook River (New York), 332
Kisaralik River (Alaska), 321
Kispiox River (British Columbia), 322, 333
Klamath River (Oregon), 142
Klune, Frank, 234
Knight, Anson, 13
Knight, John Alden, 17, 18, 39
Knotted midge fly, 164–65
Knudsen, Al, 152
Kodiak Island (Alaska), 321
Koller, Larry, 14, 15
Kreider, Claude, 141–42
Kukaklek Lake (Alaska), 333
Kuskokwim River (Alaska), 321

LaBranche, George Michel Lucien, 7, 14, 18, 33, 47, 50, 64, 260, 376
described, 35
Lady Amherst fly, 349
Lady Beaverkill fly, 78
Lady Caroline fly, 349, 352

Laerdal River (Norway), 260, 351

La Farge, John, 33

Lake trout, 288, 292

Lamar River (Wyoming), 192

Lamb, Dana, 8, 29, 40, 41

Lamison, Jason, 32

Lamoille River (New England), 185

Langá River (Iceland), 354

Langtry, Lily, 30

Largemouth bass, 307–309

Lassen National Park (California), 244

Lawrence, Robert, 33

Laxá River (Iceland), 264–65, 353

Leaders:
  on the Firehole, 122
  for grasshopper flies, 237
  for rainbow trout, 116

Lead-winged Olive hatches, 101, 111–15, 275

Leafhoppers, 54, 55, 56, 121, 205

Legends, 49–50

Leisenring, James, 39

Lemire, Harry, 152

Leonard, Hiram, 370, 379

Leonard, Justin, 181, 185

Leonard fly-rods, 34, 369–71, 375–77

Leptoceridae caddisfly, 225

Letort Hopper fly, 228, 235–36

Letort Spring Run (Pennsylvania), 44, 48–64, 274
  fish stocking on, 59
  grasshoppers and, 235, 239–40
  hatches on, 53–58
  as limestone river, 51–52
  pollution of, 62–63
  regulations along, 51
  riseforms on, 59–62

Levison, Chancellor, 28, 32, 33, 43
  described, 26–27, 37

Lewis Lake (Yellowstone Park), 292

Lewis River (Yellowstone Park), 194–95, 196, 198, 292

Life, 11, 373

Light Cahill fly, 14, 100, 128

Light Hendrickson fly, 128

Lighthouse Tavern, 30

Lilly, Bud, 129, 195

Limestone streams, 205, 244–45
  in Germany, 252–55
  grasshoppers and, 235–40
  in Ireland, 167
  in Pennsylvania, 50–64, 185, 235–40
  in Wisconsin, 98–102

Little Firehold River (Yellowstone Park), 123–24

Little Lehigh River (Pennsylvania), 186

Little Manistee River (Michigan), 321

Little Rivers (Van Dyke), 31

Little South Branch (Michigan), 69, 70–74, 94

Loch Awe (Scotland), 284

Loch Leven Hatchery, 271, 292, 293

Lockwood, Ken, 43, 45

Lockwood Gorge fly-fishing water, 45

Logie fly, 352

Longest hatch, 178–92

Long Island streams (New York), 271

Lough Inagh (Ireland), 354

Loving Creek (Idaho), 245

Lower Mesa Falls (Idaho), 108

Loyalsock River (Pennsylvania), 186

McClane, Al, 12

McCloud rainbow trout, 81, 249

MacDonald, Alexander, 109

McDonald, John, 13

MacGregor, Russell, 29

McLeod, Ken, 152

Madison River (Yellowstone Park), 127, 224, 225, 228, 294, 372
  stonefly hatches on, 216–18, 221, 226

Magic Hours (Connett), 38

Maigue River (Ireland), 165–77

Maitland, Sir Ramsey Gibson, 271

Malangsfossen River (Norway), 373

Mammoth Springs (Ozarks), 244
Manistee River (Michigan), 84,
    89, 185, 206, 229, 321
March Brown fly, 352
March Brown hatches, 46
Marinaro, Vince, 48, 51, 62, 178
    terrestrial imitations of, 54–57
Marlin, 146
Mar Lodge, 314
Marls, the (Bahamas), 341–46
Marquette, Jacques, 74–76
Marshall, H. B., 32
Martinez, Belarmino, 355–56
Martyr, Pieter, 338
Masking-hatch principle, 111–13,
    227, 275–76
Mason, Bill, 333
Mason, George, 84
Matane River (Canada), 260
Matapedia River (Canada), 260,
    261
Matching the Hatch
    (Schwiebert), x, 8, 98, 101,
    161, 286
Mather, Fred, 268–72
Mausser, Karl, 152
Mayflies, 207–208, 229, 274
    April, 312–13
    on the Brodheads, 46
    egg-laying behavior of, 115
    on the Firehole, 122, 128
    on the Henry's Fork of the
        Snake, 105, 111–18
    in Ireland, 163–77
    on the Letort, 55–58, 60
    minute, 179–203
    nocturnal, 68–69, 184
    on the Pere Marquette, 68–69,
        77–79
    on the Schoharie, 8–9
    on the Spring Creek, 247,
        250
    stomach contents of brown
        and, 284–87
    two-winged, 193–203
    weather and, 116
    wings on, 57–58
    see also specific mayflies
Mayflies of Illinois (Burks), 181,
    183
*Mayflies of Michigan Trout
    Streams* (Leonard), 181, 185

*Mayflies of North and Central
    America, The* (Edmunds),
    181, 184, 197
Mazama, Mount, 142
Memphremagog, Lake
    (Vermont), 321
Menendez-Behety, Fernando, 259
Merwin, John, ix–xi
Metolius River (Oregon), 192,
    244
Michigan, Lake, 82
Michigan Hopper fly, 229–31,
    235
Middle Branch (Michigan), 69,
    70
Midges, 54
Midtown Turf, Yachting and
    Polo Association, 44
Miller, Dusty, 352
Mills, Edward Bate, 376
Mills, Steve, 43, 44–45
Miner, Bert, 353
Minktail fly, 262, 353
Miramichi pattern flies, 353
Miramichi River (Canada), 260,
    261, 323, 353
Missouri River (Montana), 216,
    292, 294, 334
Mitchell, Captain Laurie, 144
Mitchell, William, 375
Mixed palette, 162–77
Modern Angler (Knight), 32
Modern Dry-Fly Code, A
    (Marinaro), 48, 51, 54, 60
Mohawk River (New York), 6
Moisie River (Canada), 260, 323
Monell, Colonel Ambrose, 260
Mongaup River (New York), 6, 7
Montana Nymph fly, 128
Moore, Don, 258, 259
Moore, Frank, 144, 152–55, 364,
    380
Moseley, Martin, 53
Mott, Major Lawrence, 144, 149,
    153
Muddler Minnow fly, 128, 235,
    276, 357
Muir, William, 284
Musconetcong River (New
    Jersey), 186, 205, 271, 304
Muskegon River (Michigan), 89,
    192, 321, 334

Muskellunge, 97, 98, 102
Muskrat Nymph fly, 128
Musselshell River (Montana),
    293
My Health Is Better in November
    (Babcock), 358
Mývatn Lake (Iceland), 264

Naeroy River (Norway), 351
Naknek Lake (Alaska), 333
Nalon River (Spain), 355
Namekagon River (Wisconsin),
    96–102, 186
Narcea River (Spain), 355
Nash, Philip, 29, 40
Nature Conservancy, 241–42,
    249–50
Needham, James, 180–81, 196,
    197
Needham, Paul, 284–86
Nelson Ranch, 195
Neversink Reservoir, 13
Neversink River (New York), 7,
    50, 207
    described, 13–15
Neumann, Arthur, 199
Newhalem River (Oregon), 320
New York Board of Water
    Supply, 11
New York Herald-Tribune, The,
    44
New York Times, The, 8, 44
Nez Percé Creek (Yellowstone
    Park), 127
Night fishing, 78–80, 83
Night Hawk fly, 349
Nissequogue River (Long
    Island), 207, 271, 301
Noble, Ralph, 66, 95
Noble's Lodge, 71
Nolphe, Simmy, 85, 87, 89
Nordurá River (Iceland), 164,
    354, 377–79
Norris, Thaddeus, 18, 25–26, 35,
    47, 375
North Atlantic Rift, 324
North Country flies, 347
North Fork Club, 110
North Platte River
    (Colorado–Wyoming), 292
North Umpqua Lodge, 149

North Umpqua River (Oregon),
    131–57, 320, 323, 325, 332
    beauty of, 366–67
    fly dressings for, 139–40, 150
    mystique of, 141–42
Northville Hatchery, 271
Norton, Jeff, 16–17
Norway, *see specific rivers*
Notes and Letters of Theodore
    Gordon, The (McDonald), 13
Not Far from the River (Lamb),
    8
Noyes, Fred, 144
Nymph Fishing for Chalk Stream
    Trout (Skues), 376
Nymphs, 9, 16, 115, 173, 258–59,
    275
    see also specific species
Nymphs (Schwiebert), xi, 286–87

Oakley, Annie, 36, 37
Oatman, Lew, 179
O'Byrne, Vic, 149
Oecetis hatches, 225, 226–27, 275
Ojo Caliente spring (Yellowstone
    Park), 121, 126, 128
Old Faithful geyser, 123
Olive Spinner fly, 199
Olsen, Olav, 351
On Becoming a Fly Fisherman
    (MacDonald), 109
O'Neill, Paul, 12
"On the Heller Branch," 27–28
On Trout Streams and Salmon
    Rivers (Lamb), 41
Orange Blossom fly, 88, 351
Orange Cahill hatches, 16
Orange Charm fly, 88
Oriole fly, 353
Orvis Battenkill fly rod, 377–79
Otter River (New England), 185
Ovington, Ray, 12, 43
Owls, 66–67, 95
Oxford, William, 32
Oxygen, 224, 243–44

Pacific salmon, 81, 85, 149
    spawning of, 94–95
Pale-bodied mayfly hatches,
    112–13, 15
Pale-bodied spinner fly, 251

Pale Cahill hatches, 46
Pale Evening Dun hatches, 274–75
Pale Morning Dun hatches, 275
Pale Sulphur hatches, 205
Pale Watery Dun fly, 128
Palmer, Ernest, 32
Paraleptophlebia hatches, 120, 128, 205, 254, 380
Parkside Club, 35, 38, 39, 40
Parmachene Belle fly, 273, 277
Partridge and Brown fly, 128
Partridge and Olive fly, 128, 171
Paulinskill River (New Jersey), 186
Payne, Edward, 369, 375, 376
Payne, James, 369
Payne fly rods, 369–70, 375–76
Peace and Plenty Inn, 361
Pechora River (Soviet Union), 289, 290
Pegnitz River (Germany), 252–55
Penns Creek (Pennsylvania), 240
Penobscot River (Maine), 365–66
Pepacton Reservoir (New York), 15
Pere Marquette "PM" River (Michigan), 65–95, 271, 277, 321, 334
 big trout in, 78–84
 branches of, 69–74
 fishermen on, 84–85
 hatches on, 68–73, 77–79, 83, 185, 206
 history of, 74–76
 Pacific salmon in, 94–95
 shot-dropper technique on, 89–91
 steelhead in, 85–94
Pere Marquette Rod & Gun Club, 84, 85, 93
Peter Ross fly, 354
Peterson, Sonny, 333
Petrie, Lou, 17
Phasganophora nymphs, 217
Philips, Don, 199–200
Phillippe, Samuel, 26
Phillippe, Solon, 375
Pichi Traful (Argentina), 372
Pigeon River (Michigan), 287
Pinchot, Gifford, 28–29, 36, 47

Pine River (Pennsylvania), 186
Pink bucktail shrimp fly, 340, 343, 344
Platysalmo platycephalus, 291
Pleissner, Ogden, 19
Plumley, Ladd, 18
Pocono Mountains trout streams, 22–47, 49–50
Pocono Shot (Foote), 34
Polar-bear bucktail fly, 80
Polywing flies, 117–18
Ponce de Leon, Juan, 337–38
Potamanthus hatches, 18
Practical Fly Fishing (Wetzel), 40
Pratt, John Lee, 375
Pray, Jim, 144, 150
Preacher, 336–37, 340–46
Prime, William Cowper, 29
Pryce-Tannatt, T. E., 350
Pseudocloëon mayflies, 114–17, 193–203, 250–51, 333, 383, 387–89
 Baetis confused with, 194–98
 on the Firehole, 201–203
 rises to, 194–95
 species of, 196–98, 387–89
 spinner falls of, 198–200, 250–51
Pteronarcella hatches:
 described, 223
 life cycle of, 223
 species of, 222–23
Pteronarcys hatches, 114, 128, 216–17, 219, 226, 287
 described, 223
 life cycle of, 223
 nymphs, 221–22, 302
 species of, 222–23
Pulman, G.P.R., 26
Puyans, Andre, 104–109, 114, 116, 118, 276–77
 on Silver Creek, 242, 250–51
Pyramid Lake cutthroats, 289

Quackenbush, L. Q., 18
Queen, Gerry, 71
Queen Bess fly, 88
Queen's Favorite Pool (Scotland), 314, 349

Rainbow Riffle (Yellowstone Park), 127, 128
Rainbow trout, 11, 15, 62, 63, 214, 280, 317, 359, 361
  in Argentina, 372
  in the Esopus, 12–13
  fighting ability of, 278
  in the Firehole, 120–25, 277
  grasshoppers and, 234
  from hatcheries, 277–78, 294–95
  in the Henry's Fork of the Snake, 103–18, 274, 381
  in the Pere Marquette, 78, 80–94
  salmonfly hatches and, 220–21
  in the Silver Creek, 242, 247–51
  tackle for, 116–18
  Tricorythodes flies and, 189
  see also Steelhead
Randolph, John, 43, 44
Random Casts (Connett), 38
Raritan River (New Jersey), 186, 207
Read, Admiral William, 351
Recueil des Voyages (Thevenot), 76
Red Ibis fly, 273, 277
Red Quill fly, 128, 207, 210, 368
Reed, Nathaniel Pryor, 213
Reeder, George, 29
Restigouche River (Canada), 260, 323, 350, 351
Rethoret, Analomink Charlie, 30, 40
Reuben Held, 33
Rhead, Louis, 17
Rice, Edward, 27, 33, 35
Rice, James, 32
Richards, Carl, 85, 88, 161, 204
Riffling hitch, 263, 264, 380
Rifle River (Michigan), 185
Ringneck-feathered beetle, 55–56
Ring of Kerry (Ireland), 354
Rio Grande (Tierra del Fuego), 259–60
Rising River (California), 244, 274
Rising Trout (Fox), 51
Ritz, Charles, 315, 353, 373

River for Christmas, A, 373
River of humility, 103–18
River of Ponds (Newfoundland), 353
River of Whales (Quebec), 332
Riverside Geyser (Yellowstone Park), 123
Roaring Fork River (Colorado), 292
Robbins, Richard, 21
Rock Creek (Colorado), 231–33
Rogowski, Ted, 43
Rogue River (Oregon), 142, 143, 144, 145, 148, 332
Rolled nylon stocking emerger patterns, 204
Ronalds, Alfred, 53, 54, 169
Rondout Creek (New York), 7
Roosevelt, Robert Barnwell, 25, 41
Roosevelt, Theodore, 29, 36, 41, 47
Ropner, William, 355
Rosborough, Polly, 154
Ross, Henryville Charlie, 36–37, 47
Rouselle, Albert, 33
Roxburghe, Duke of, 351
Royal Wulff fly, 276
Russell, Jack, 353
Rusty Rat fly, 351

Salmo caspius, 289
Salmon, 332–34, 355
  Argentine, 303, 360–61
  Atlantic, *see* Atlantic salmon
  Pacific, 81, 85, 94–95, 149
  steelhead versus, 316–29
Salmonfly hatches, 114, 219–27, 275, 330–31
  microclimate and, 224
  peak, 225–26
  rainbow trout and, 220–21
  rivers for, 223–26
  species of, 221–23
Salmon in Low Water (Hunt), 40
Salmon River (Idaho), 320, 332
Salmothymus species, 290
Salmo trutta, see Introduced brown trout
Salt Fork River (Wyoming), 258

Index

Sand, Erling, 351
Sand shark, 340
Saugeen River (Ontario), 258–59
Sayle, William, 339
Sayre, J. J., 32
Scalscraggie fly, 350
Schaaf, Jim, 368
Schaldach, William, 18
Schoharie Creek (New York), 5, 6, 192, 207
  described, 7–11
Schuylkill Fishing Company, 22
Scotland, *see specific rivers*
Scott, Scotty, 40
Scott, Stinson, 43
Sculpins, 280, 302
Seatrout, 259–60, 372–73
Secrets of the Salmon (Hewitt), 34
Sedges, 114–15, 225, 226
  in Ireland, 163–77
  on the Spring Creek, 247, 250
Selective Trout (Richards and Swisher), 85
Sens, Ed, 12
Sens nymph patterns, 12
Sentinel Creek (Yellowstone Park), 126
Sericostoma hatch, 175
Serpentine River, 353
Shadflies, 240
Sheelin Lake (Ireland), 163
Sheep fly, 327
Shelikof Strait (Alaska), 321
Sheridan, General Philip, 31
Shot-dropper technique, 89–91, 321
Shoshone Channel (Yellowstone Park), 292–93
Shushan Postmaster fly, 179
Silver Blue fly, 352
Silver Creek (Idaho), 186, 192, 200–201, 241–51, 333
  described, 242–43, 245–46
  fertility of, 246–47
  Nature Conservancy and, 241–42, 249–50, 362
  wildlife surrounding, 247–48
Silver Darter fly, 179
Silver Grey fly, 349
Silverhorn fly, 164

Silverhorn hatch, 175
Silvius, Lloyd, 144
Siphlonurus mayfly hatches, 115
Sir Richard fly, 349
Skagit River (Washington), 320
Skues, George Edward Mackenzie, 376
Skunk fly, 88, 139–40, 150
Skykomish Sunrise fly, 88
Slate-colored *Baetis* hatch, 171
Slate-colored silverthorn hatch, 175
Slate-winged Olive hatches, 114, 115, 275
Slaymaker, Samuel, 43
Slopbucket Lake (Alaska), 316–17, 333
Smallmouth bass, 15, 97
Smedley, Harold, 84
Smith, Art, 43, 44
Smith, James, 33
Smith, John, 352
Smith, Lodie, 32, 33, 46
Smith, Milton, 33
Smith, Sibley, 39
Smutting fish, 54
Snake River (Idaho), 129, 132, 191, 244, 258
  see also Henry's Fork of the Snake River
Snedecor, Abraham, 32
Snedecor, J. L., 32
Snows of Kilimanjaro, The (Hemingway), 270
Sooty Olive fly, 354
Soule, Henry, 144
South Platte River (Colorado), 294–95, 365
South Raritan River (New Jersey), 45
South Side fishing club, 271
South Umpqua River (Oregon), 142, 143
Speckled trout, *see* Brook trout
Spentwing flies, 105, 163
Spey River (Scotland), 349
Spinner falls, 276
  on the Henry's Fork of the Snake, 105, 107, 114, 115, 116

Spinner falls *(continued)*
of *Pseudocloëon*, 198–200, 250–51
of *Tricorythodes*, 180, 184–91
Sports Illustrated, 39
Spring, 300–304
Spring Creek (Montana), 245
Spring Creek (New York), 245
Spring Creeks, 241–51
birth of, 244–46
hydrothermal, 245
see also specific waterways
Spruce Cabin Inn, 30, 35, 40
Squirreltail fly, 353
Stamp, Henry, 110
Stauffer, Chip, 39
Stauffer, John, 39
Steamboat Inn, 132, 135–37, 149, 152–54, 280
Steel, Walter, 40
Steelhead, 280, 332, 334, 380
hybrid, 249, 278
in the North Umpqua, 131–57
in the Pere Marquette, 80–94
salmon versus, 316–29
shot-dropper technique for, 321
summer- versus winter-run, 320–21
Steelhead (Kreider), 141–42
Steelhead Fly Fishing and Flies (Combs), 145–46
Steelhead to a Fly (Van Fleet), 143
Steenrod, Roy, 14, 17–18
Steenrod flies, 206
Stenonema hatches, 205
Stepath, Charles, 33
Stevenson, Charles, 150
Stevenson fly, 150
Stillaguamish River (Washington), 142, 320, 380
Stocker Creek (Idaho), 245
Stocking fish, *see* Hatchery trout
Stonefly flies, 212, 216, 357
Stonefly hatches, 10, 114, 128, 212–18, 274, 275
nymphs, 215
salmonflies, 219–27
on western rivers, 216–18
Stony Clove stream (New York), 11

Strangest trout stream on earth, 119–30
Straumfjardará River (Iceland), 353
Streamside Guide to Naturals and Their Imitations (Flick), 8, 207
Sturgeon River (Michigan), 192
Sullivan, John L., 30
Summer, 311–15
Sun Valley Ranch, 249
Superior, Lake, 321
Sustut River (British Columbia), 333
Sweep fly, 353
Swisher, Doug, 85, 161, 181, 204

Tackle:
on the Firehole, 122–23
for grasshopper flies, 237–38
for minute flies, 186, 187
for rainbows, 116–18
for steelheads, 88–89
Taeniopteryx hatches, 274
Takahashi, George, 146–48
Tales of Fresh-Water Fishing (Grey), 145, 147–48
Tales of Southern Rivers (Grey), 145
Tales of Swordfish and Tuna (Grey), 145
Tales of Tahitian Waters (Grey), 145
Tales of the Angler's El Dorado (Grey), 145
Tales of Virgin Seas (Grey), 145
Telling on the Trout (Hewitt), 34, 52
Terrestrial hatches:
on the Firehole, 121, 128
on the Letort, 53–58
Test River (England), 50, 52, 54, 380
Teton Dam, 365
Teton River (Idaho), 107–108
This Wonderful World of Trout (Fox), 44
Thomas, Fred, 375
Thomas Special fly rod, 381
Thompson, Leslie, 8, 109
Thompson, William, 39
Thorax-fly theory, 56–58

Index

Thor fly, 88, 150
Thunder and Lightning fly, 349, 350
Tierra del Fuego, 303, 372-73
Tippets:
    for cutthroat trout, 257-58
    on the Firehole, 122
    for grasshopper flies, 237, 238
    for minute flies, 186, 187
    for rainbow trout, 116
Tobique River (New Brunswick), 332
Tobyhanna River (Pennsylvania), 29
Tocks Island Dam, 364
Togue, 288
To Hell with Fishing (Zern), 39
Tomah-Jo fly, 273
Torrish fly, 350
Traver, Jay, 181
Treasure Cay (Bahamas), 335-46
Treasury of Angling (Koller), 14
Treatyse of Fysshynge wyth an Angle, 169
Trichoptera hatches, 43, 114
Tricorythodes mayflies, 105, 114, 115, 179-92, 199, 200, 333
    classification controversy over, 180-81
    described, 181
    fly dressing for, 180, 191-92
    hooks for, 180, 185
    life history of, 182-92
    nymphs of, 182-83, 186-88
    species of, 183-85, 383-86
Trimmer, Ross, 51, 56, 62, 185, 236, 239-40
Trout:
    in big water, 16-17
    table quality of, 280
    see also specific species
Trout (Bergman), 14, 40, 124, 150-51, 231
Trout (Schwiebert), xi
Trout and Salmon Fisherman for Seventy-Five Years, A (Hewitt), 13-14, 34, 50
Trout Flies (Wetzel), 40
Trout Streams (Needham), 284-86
Trout-without-a-Mouth, 58, 62
Trude, Alfred, 110

Tunkhannock River (Pennsylvania), 29
Tuscarora Club, 7
Tweed River (Scotland), 350
Twelve Apostles, 39
Two Forks project, 365
Tying American Trout Lures (Cross), 17
Umpqua River (Oregon), 332, 366-67, 380
    see also North Umpqua River
Umpqua Special fly, 88, 150
Unfamiliar streams, 252-66
Upper Ausable River (New York), 186
Upsalquitch River (Canada), 260
Vade-Mecum of Fly-Fishing for Trout (Norris), 26
Valley of Ten Thousand Smokes (Alaska), 359-60
Van Dyke, Henry, 29, 30-31, 33
Van Fleet, Clark, 143, 150, 318
Van Loan, Jim and Sharon, 153
Van Luven fly, 88
Van Zandt, Josh, 144
Variant fly, 372
Varnsdalsa River (Iceland), 353
Victoria, Queen, 314
Von Behr, Baron Friedrich, 268, 270
Von Kienbusch, Otto, 29, 376
Vossa River (Norway), 324, 374-75
Waddington fly, 350
Wahl, Ralph, 152, 380
Walker, Beno, 295
Walker, James, 32
Walking Purchase, 23-24
Wallace, Jim, 295
Walleye, 15
Walton, Izaak, 322, 335
Ward's DeBruce Club, 18
Warm Springs (Oregon), 244
Washougal River (Oregon), 142
Water snakes, 69
Water temperature:
    brook trout and, 270, 271
    in the Firehole, 120-28

INDEX

Water temperature (continued)
in the Letort, 53
Tricorythodes flies and, 188
Watson's Fancy fly, 354
Webster, H. T., 300
Wedding Gift (Foote), 34
Weir, Alden, 33, 35–36, 39
Wells, Henry Parkhurst, 27
Wells, Sam, 144
Welshman's Button fly, 163
Werra, 267–68
West Kill River (New York), 8
West Kill Tavern, 8, 10–11
Wetzel, Charles, 39–40
Whitcraft fly, 128
Whitefish, 256, 258, 275
White River (Arkansas), 22
Widdicomb, Ralph, 84
Widdicomb badger spentwing
fly, 84
Wilkinson fly rod, 375
William Mills & Son, 44, 376
Williamson River (Oregon), 143,
192, 244
Willoughby River (Vermont),
321
Willowemoc River (New York),
4, 6–7, 16, 50, 271
described, 17–19
Willowflies, 223, 225
Wilson, Dermot, 380
Wilson low-water hooks, 352
Windsor, Curtin, 40
Winnie, Art, 84
Winter, 357–61
Wisconsin Department of
Natural Resources, 96, 97
Wise, John, 28–29
Wise River (Montana), 224
Wolf Lake (Michigan), 185

Wolters, Richard, 43, 44
Wood, Arthur H. E., 262, 326,
352, 380
Woodcock Spider fly, 171
Woodland Valley stream (New
York), 11
Wood River (Oregon), 143
Woodruff, John, 18
Woodsmoke and Watercress
(Lamb), 8
*World of Wood, Field and
Stream, The* (Randolph), 44
Wright, Phil, 279
Wright Creek (Oregon), 138–40
Wulff, Joan, 4
Wulff, Lee, 4, 179, 316, 353
Wyandanche fishing club, 271
Wye (England–Wales), 350
Yellow Comet fly, 88
Yellowstone River (Montana),
129, 191, 194, 221, 224, 226,
294, 334, 372
Yellowstone Park (Wyoming),
217–18, 224, 226, 244, 245,
333
introduced brown trout in,
277, 292–94
see also Firehole River
Young, Martha Marie, 371, 372
Young, Paul, 66, 84, 371, 372,
373, 375
Young Midge fly rod, 44
Young Parabolic 17 fly rod,
371–73
Young Parabolic 19 fly rod,
373–75
Zern, Ed, 39
Ziff-Davis, ix